FAIRY TAIL

フェアリーテイル

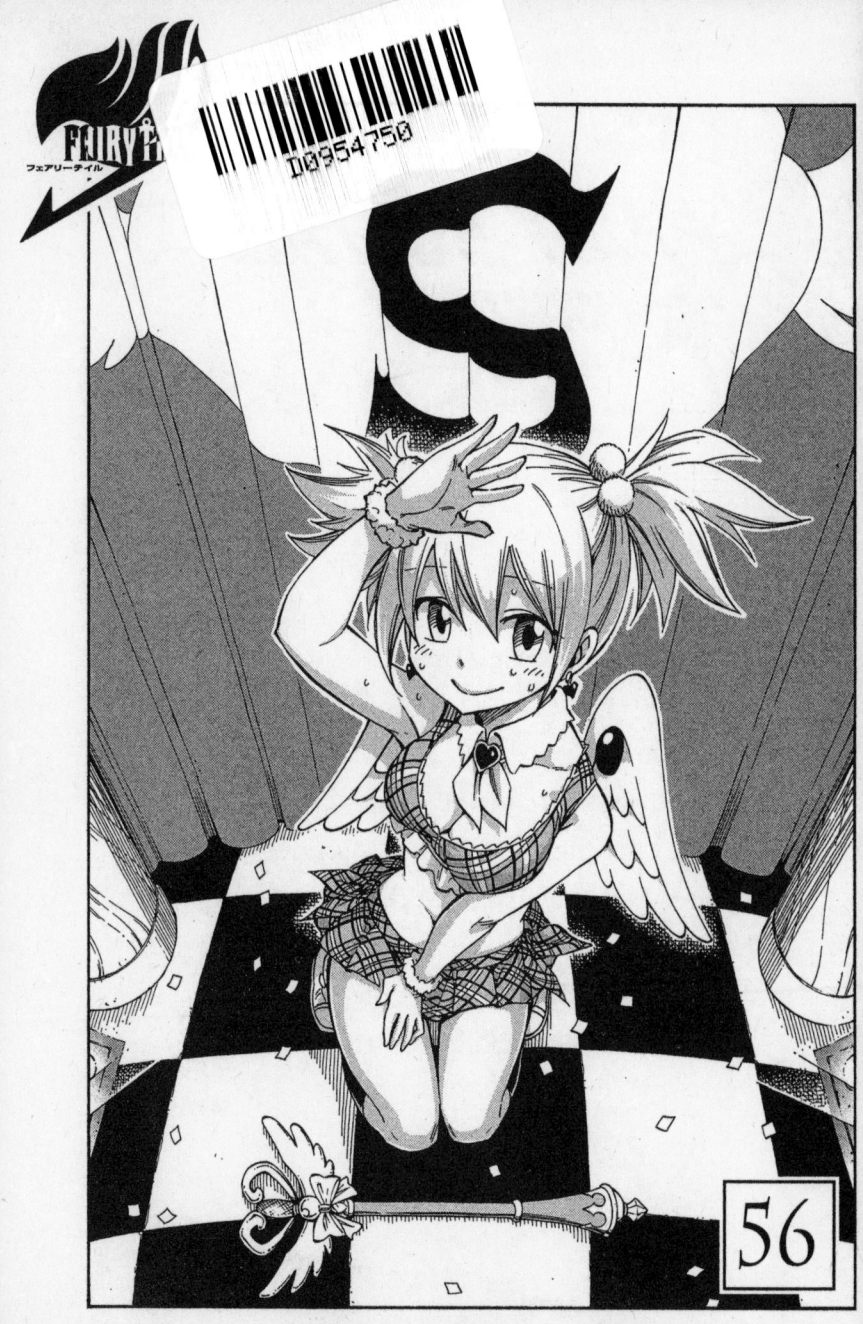

56

HIRO MASHIMA

FAIRY 56 TAIL
CONTENTS

Bloodman
Rogue
VS
Minerva
Sting
Yukino
Mirajane
Gajeel
Elfman
Levy
Lisanna
NORTH
Warrod
Wolfheim
Hyberion
August
Jacob
Jura
MAGNOLIA
WEST
Acnologia
EAST
Zeref
Makarov
Mavis
Invel
Natsu
Lucy
Laxus
HARGEON
VS
Wall
Wendy
Sherria
Lyon
Erza
VS
SOUTH
DiMaria
Gray
Juvia
Kagura

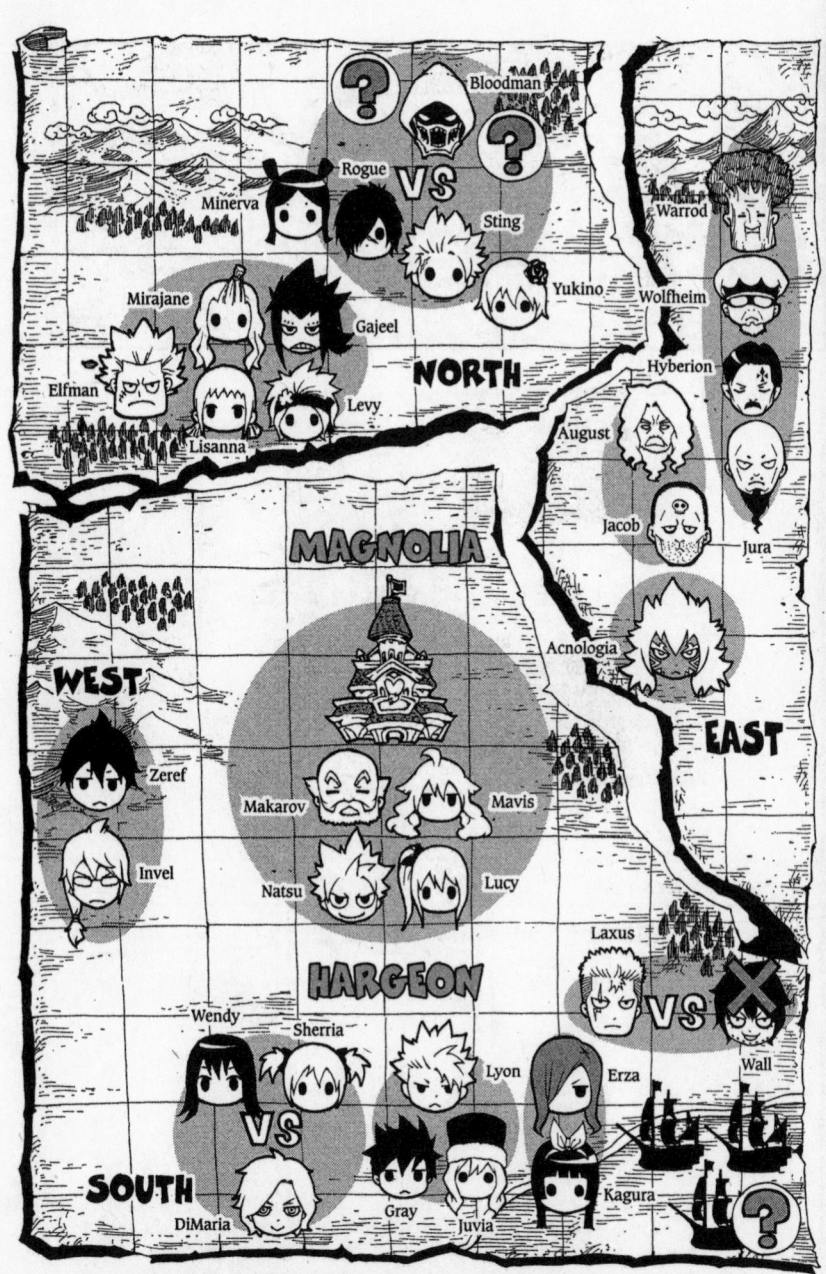

Chapter 474: During Hushed Times

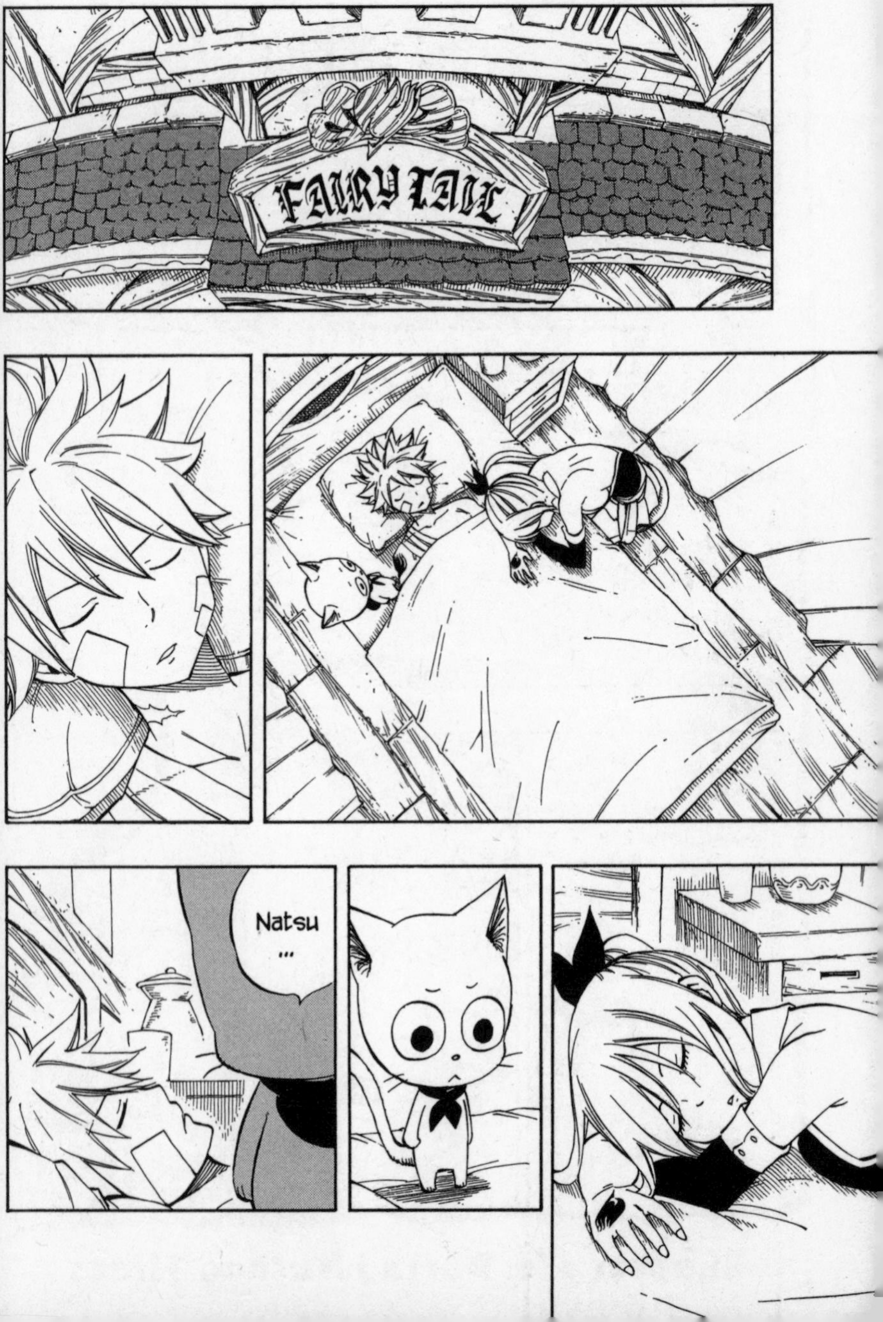
FAIRY TAIL
Natsu
...

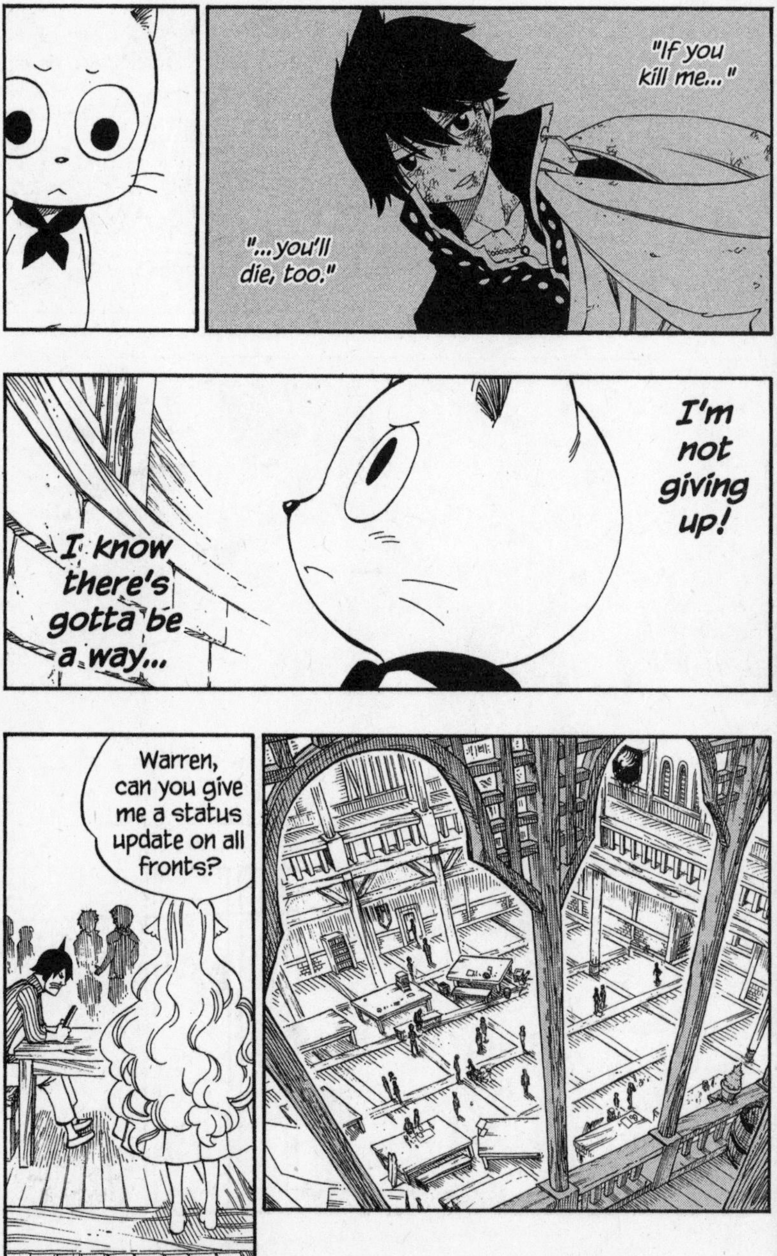
"If you kill me..."
"...you'll die, too."
I'm not giving up!
I know there's gotta be a way...
Warren, can you give me a status update on all fronts?

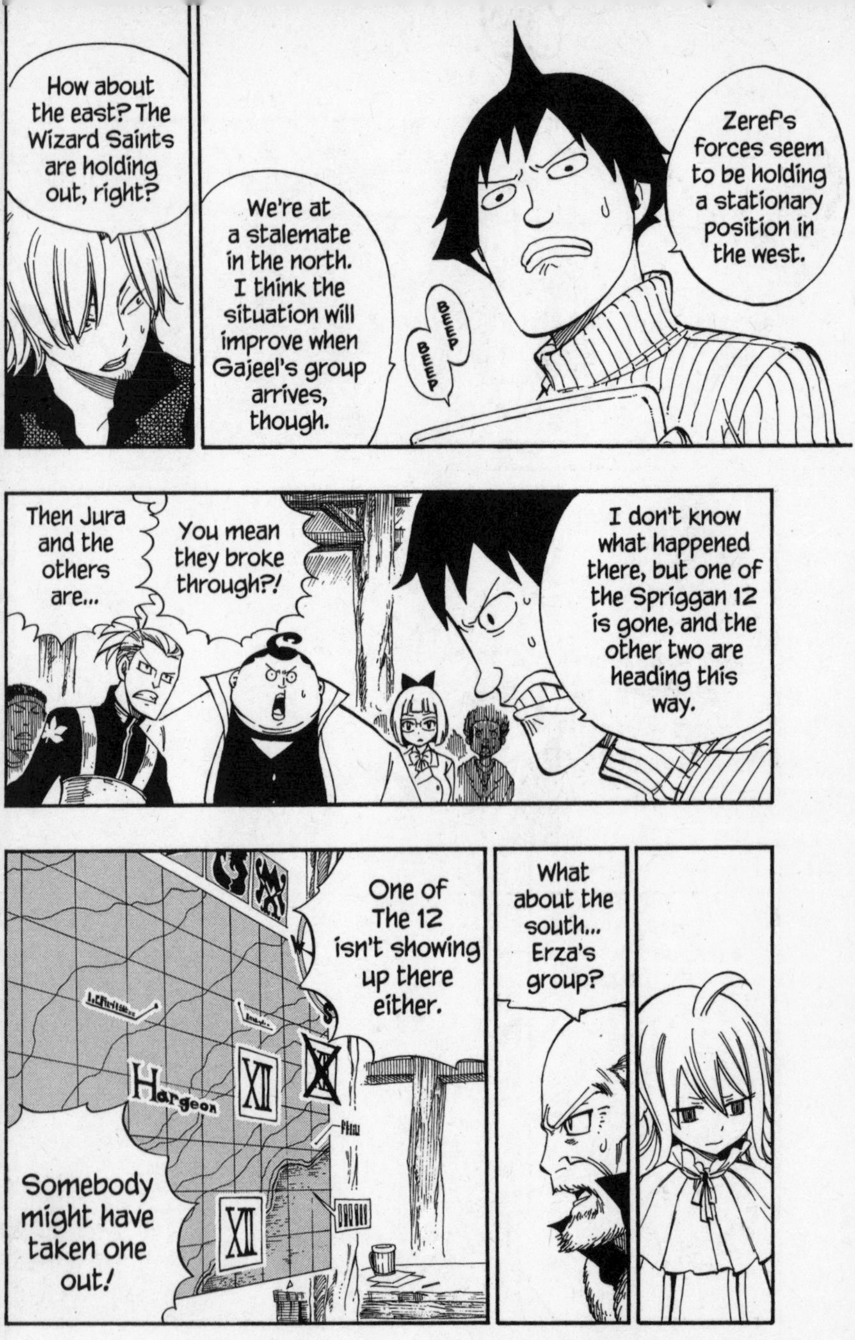
Zeref's forces seem to be holding a stationary position in the west.
BEEP BEEP
We're at a stalemate in the north. I think the situation will improve when Gajeel's group arrives, though.
How about the east? The Wizard Saints are holding out, right?
I don't know what happened there, but one of the Spriggan 12 is gone, and the other two are heading this way.
You mean they broke through?!
Then Jura and the others are...
What about the south... Erza's group?
One of The 12 isn't showing up there either.
Hargeon
XII
XII
Somebody might have taken one out!

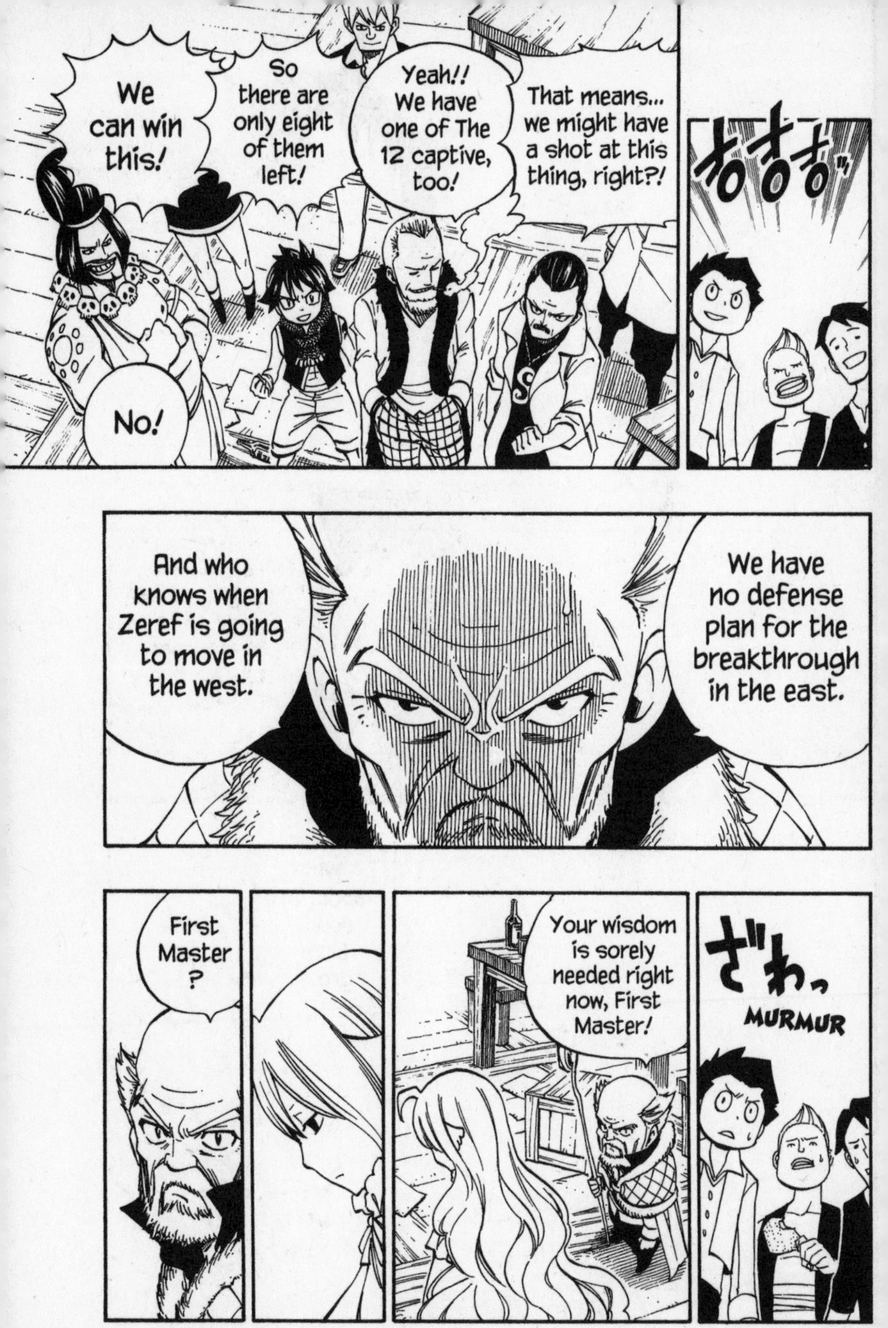

おおお
That means... we might have a shot at this thing, right?!
Yeah!! We have one of The 12 captive, too!
So there are only eight of them left!
We can win this!
No!
We have no defense plan for the breakthrough in the east.
And who knows when Zeref is going to move in the west.
ざわっ
MURMUR
Your wisdom is sorely needed right now, First Master!
First Master ?

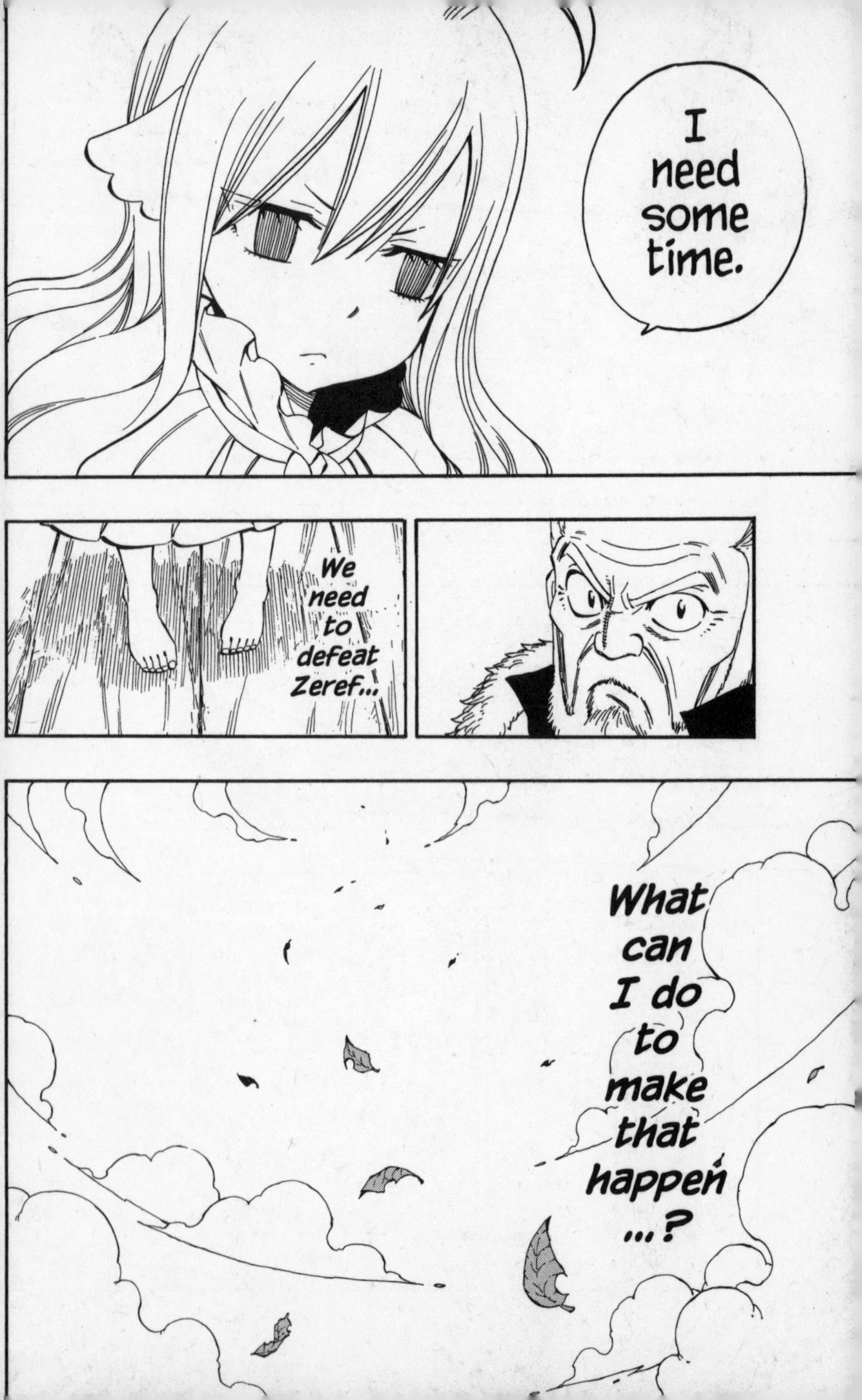
I need some time.
We need to defeat Zeref...
What can I do to make that happen...?

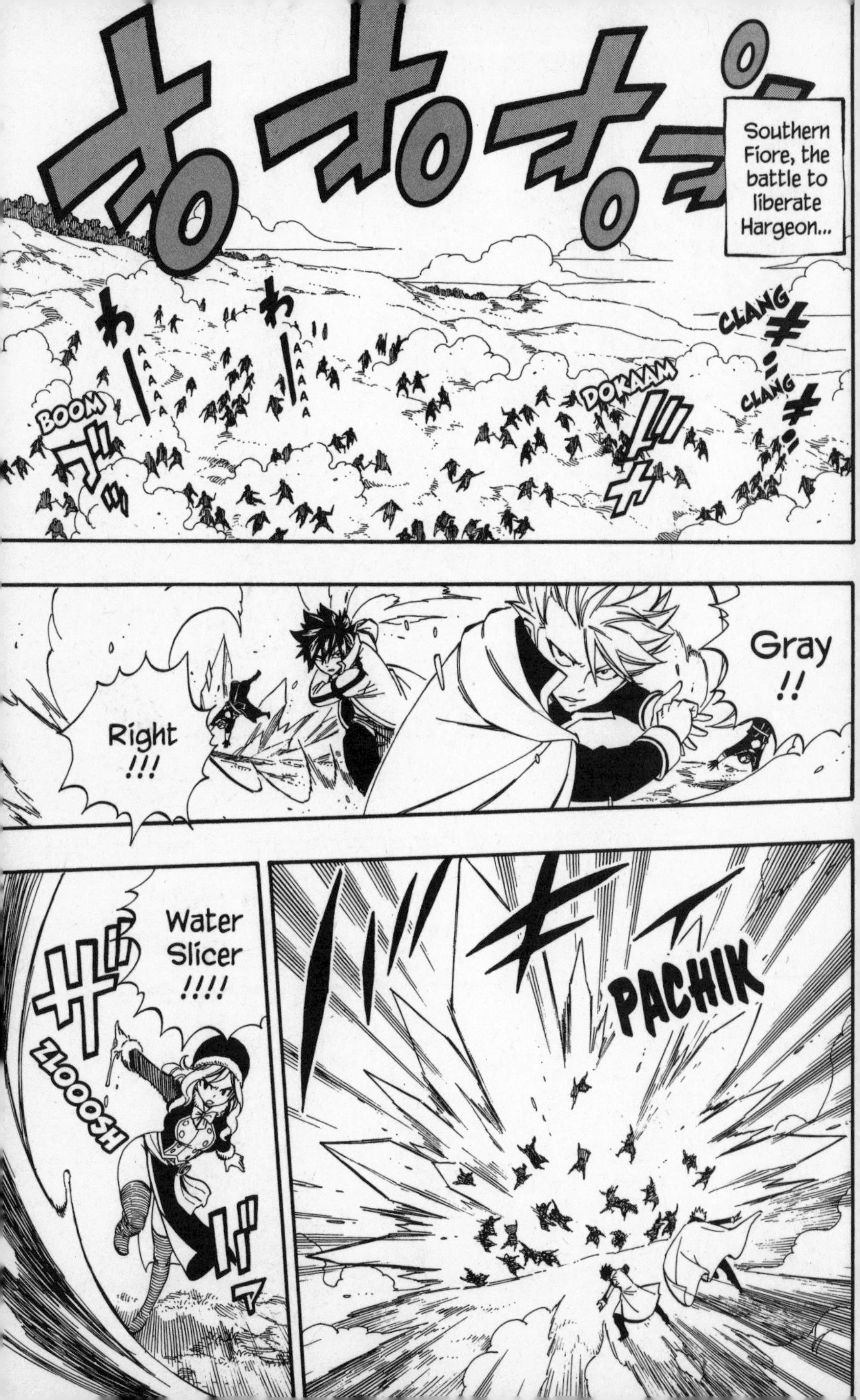
Southern Fiore, the battle to liberate Hargeon...
CLANG
CLANG
DOKAAM
BOOM
Gray !!
Right !!!
PACHIK
Water Slicer !!!!
ZLOOSH

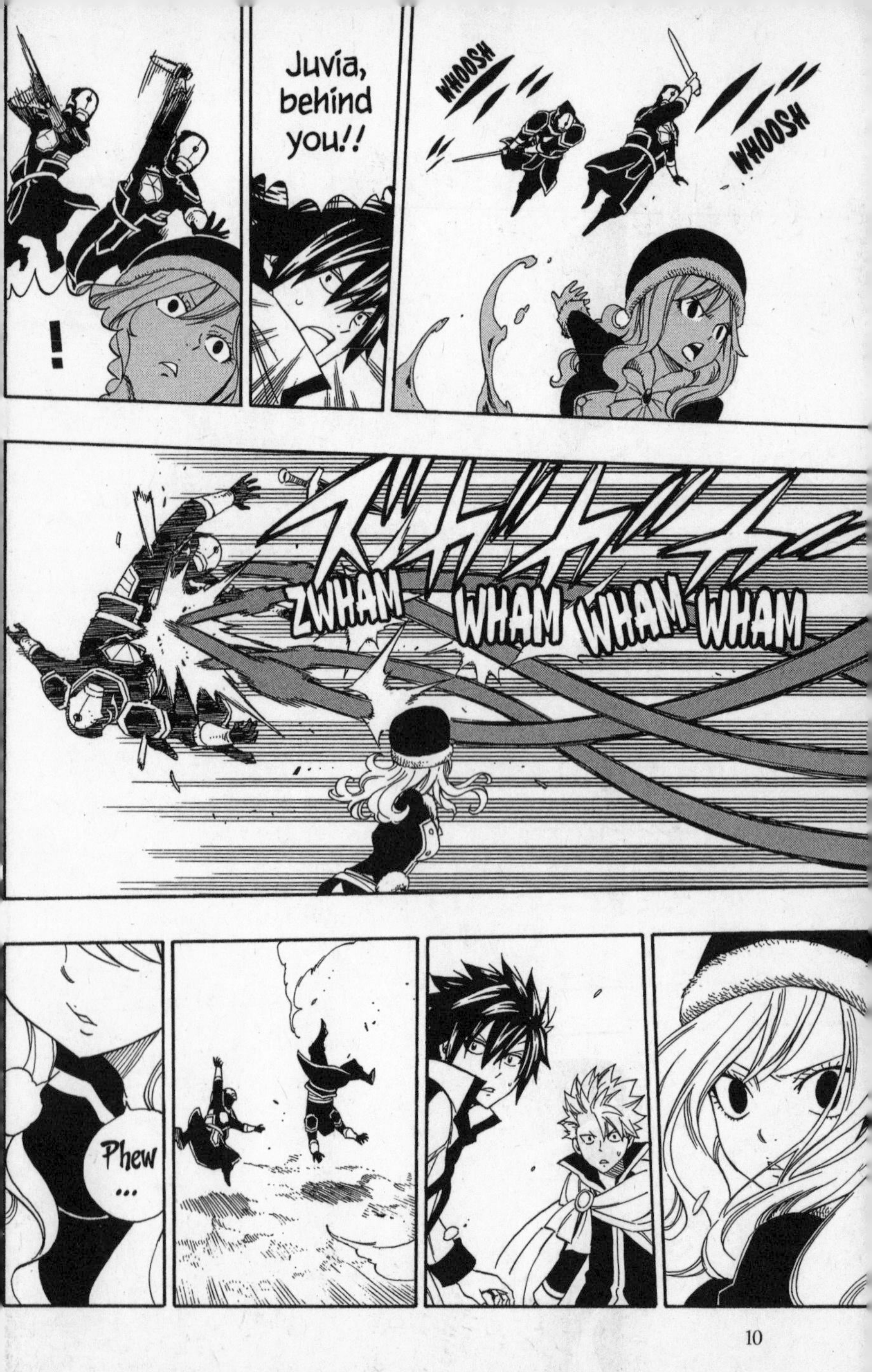
WHOOSH
WHOOSH
Juvia, behind you!!
!
ZWHAM
WHAM WHAM WHAM
Phew ...

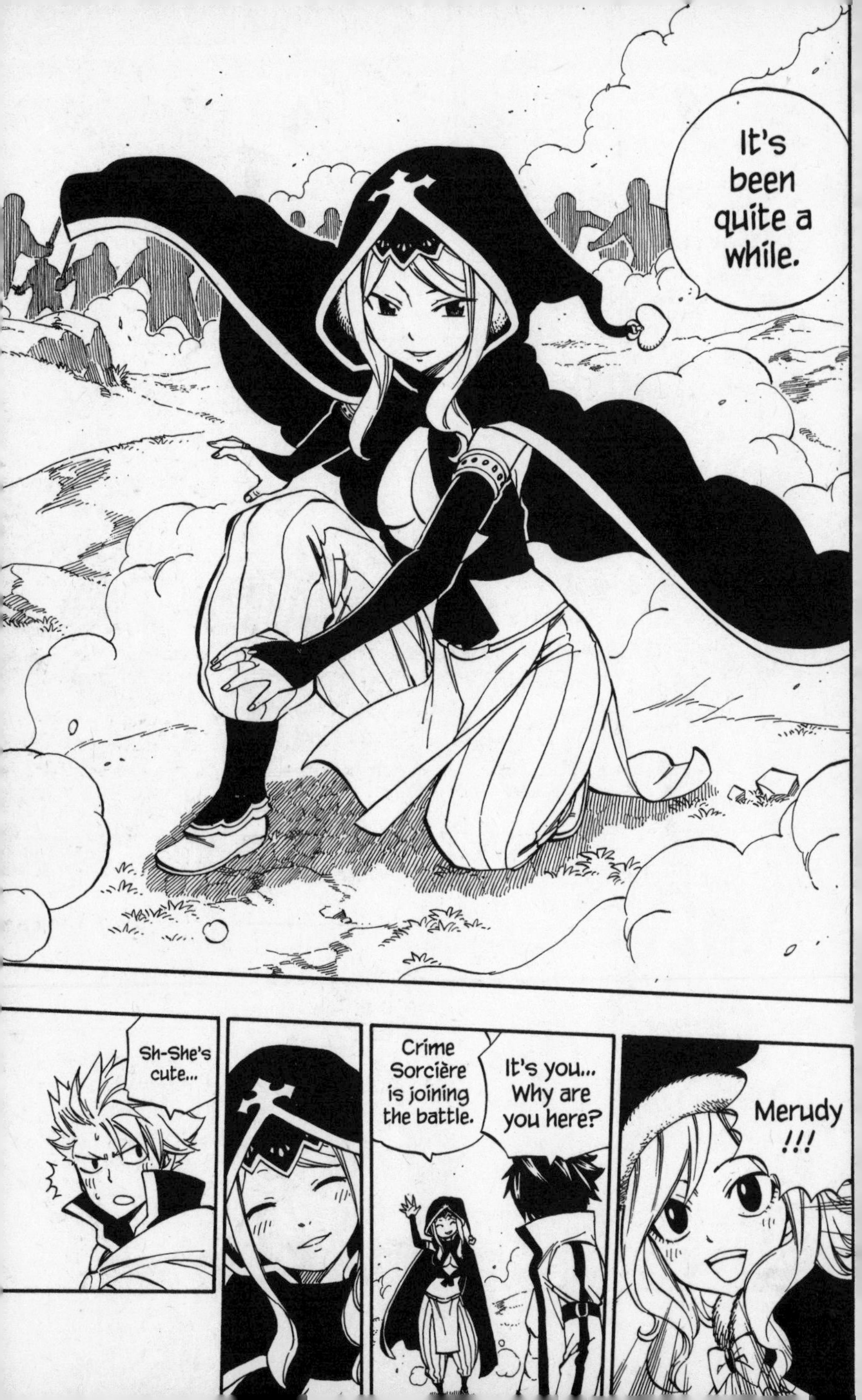
It's been quite a while.
Merudy!!!
It's you... Why are you here?
Crime Sorcière is joining the battle.
Sh-She's cute...

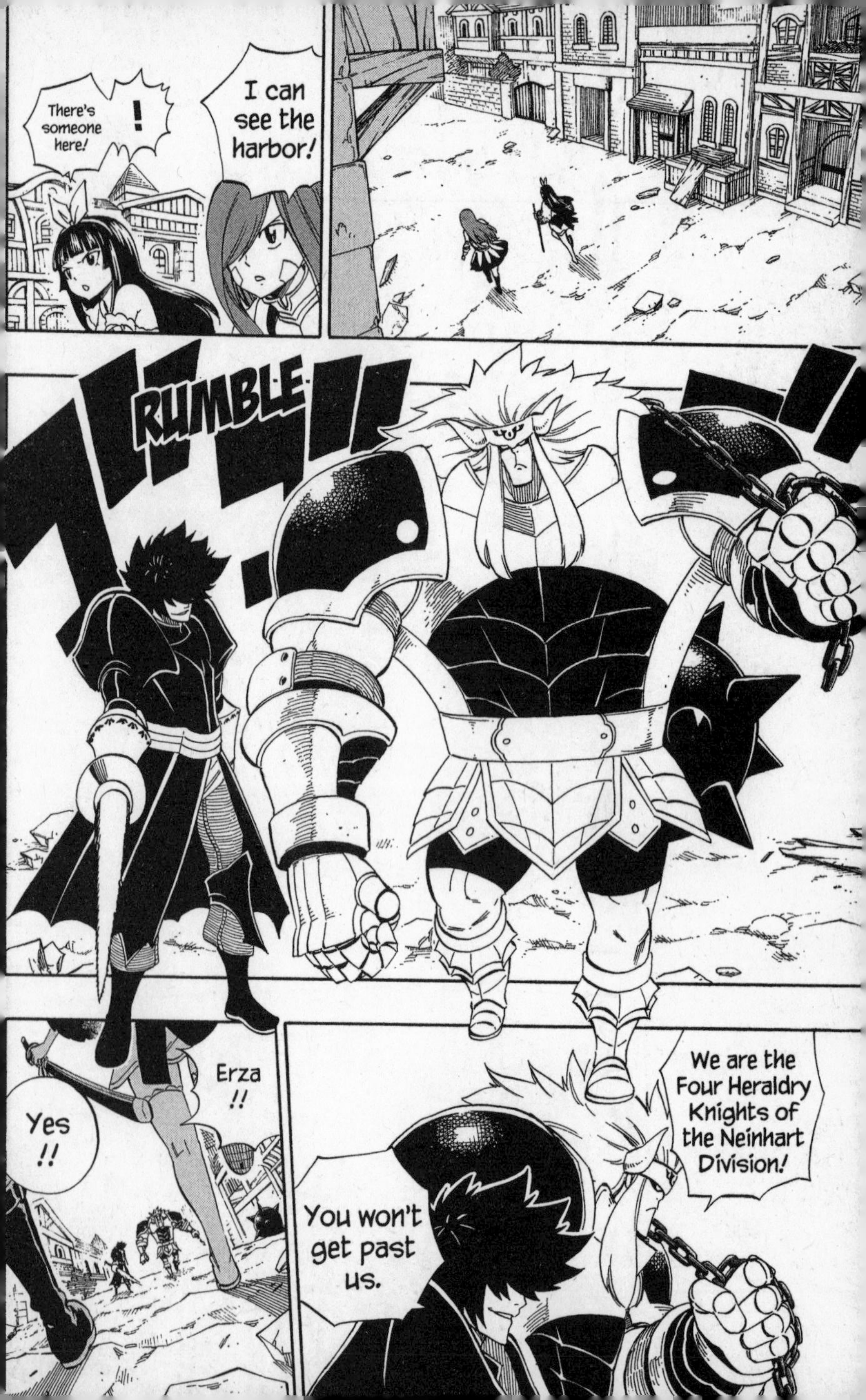
I can see the harbor!
!
There's someone here!
RUMBLE
We are the Four Heraldry Knights of the Neinhart Division!
You won't get past us.
Erza !!
Yes !!

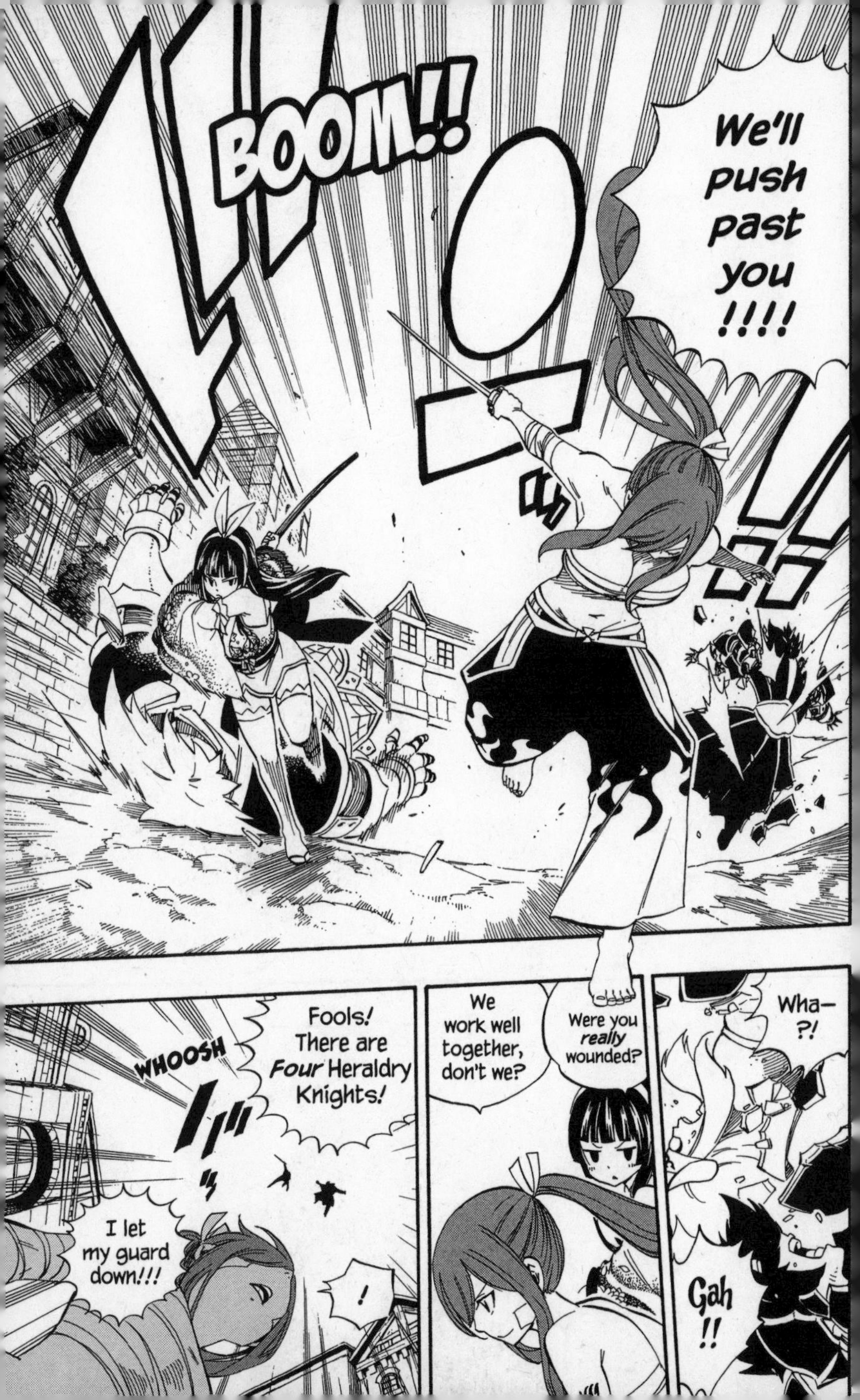
We'll push past you!!!!
BOOM!!
Wha-?!
Gah!!
Were you *really* wounded?
We work well together, don't we?
Fools! There are *Four* Heraldry Knights!
WHOOSH
!
I let my guard down!!!

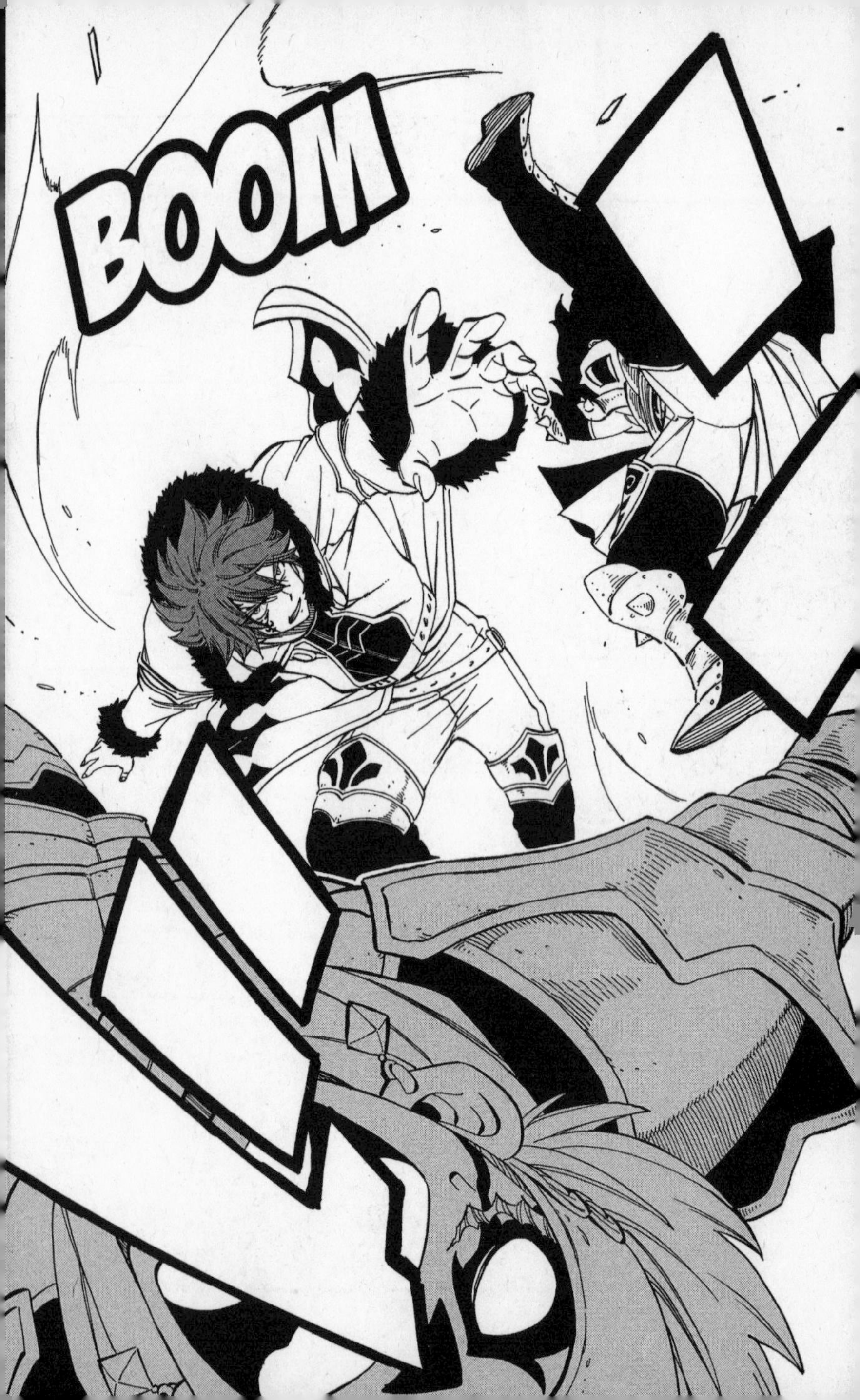
BOOM

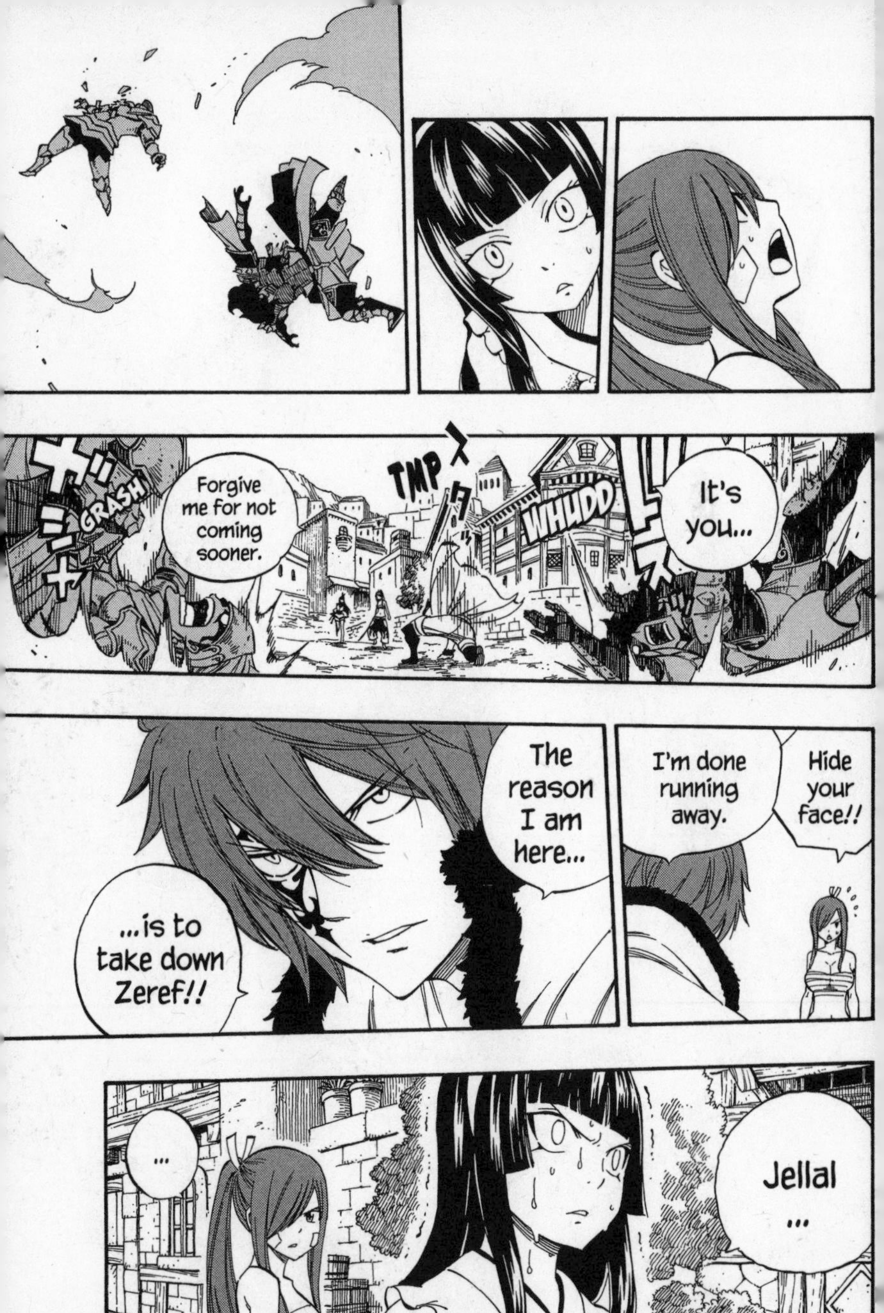
It's you...
WHUDD
TMP
Forgive me for not coming sooner.
CRASH
Hide your face!!
I'm done running away.
The reason I am here...
...is to take down Zeref!!
Jellal ...
...

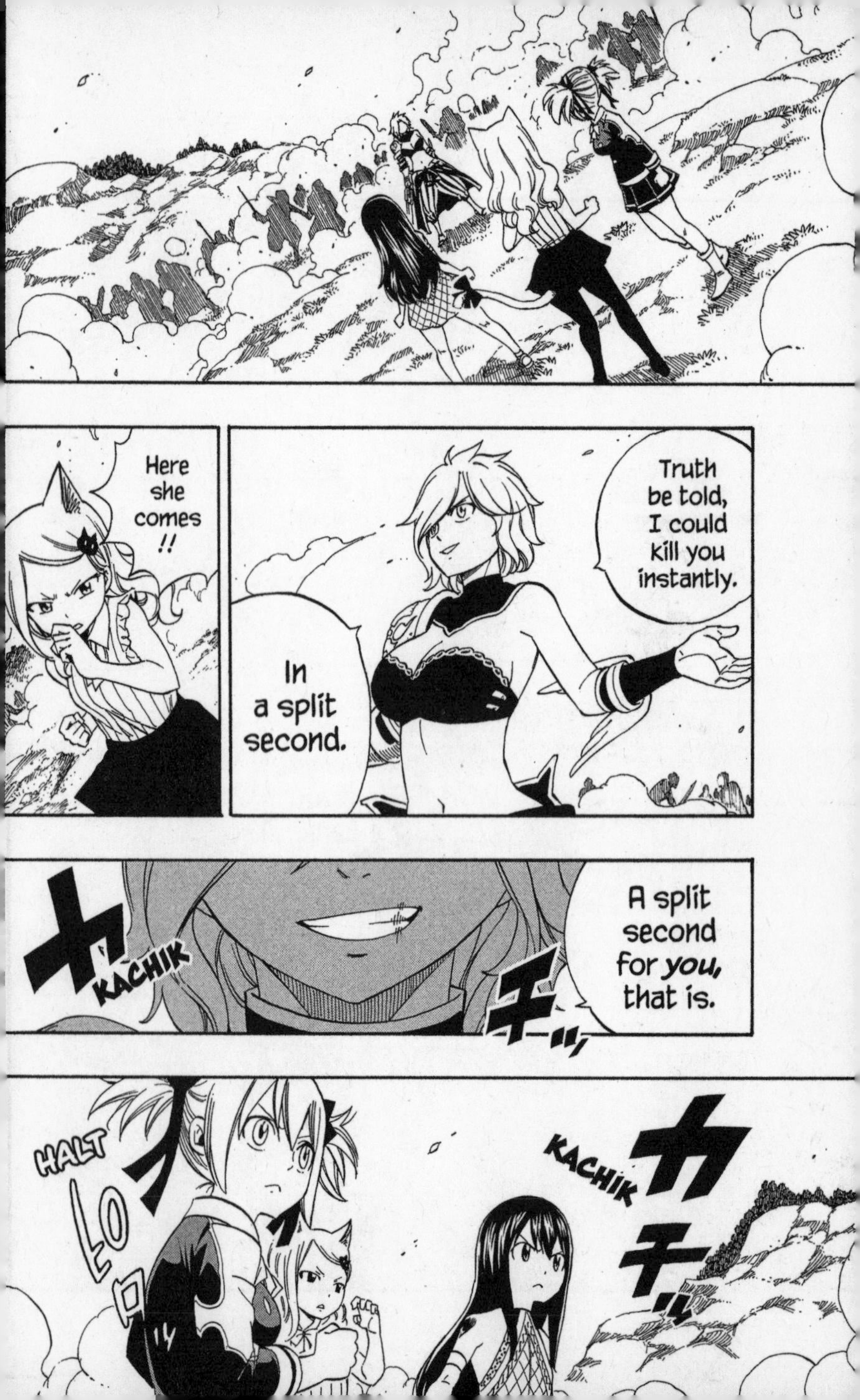
Truth be told, I could kill you instantly.
In a split second.
Here she comes!!
A split second for you, that is.
KACHIK
KACHIK
HALT

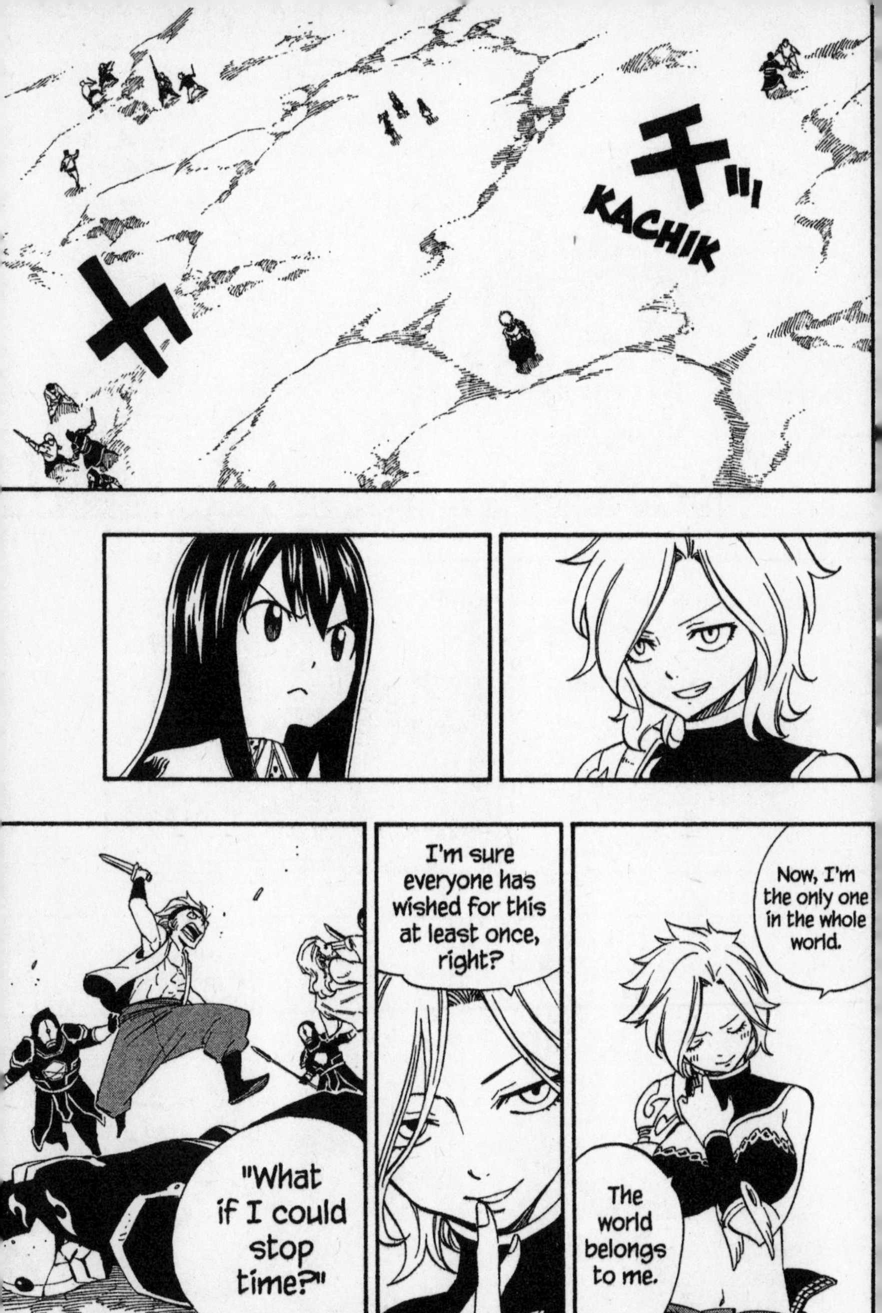
KACHIK
Now, I'm the only one in the whole world.
The world belongs to me.
I'm sure everyone has wished for this at least once, right?
"What if I could stop time?"

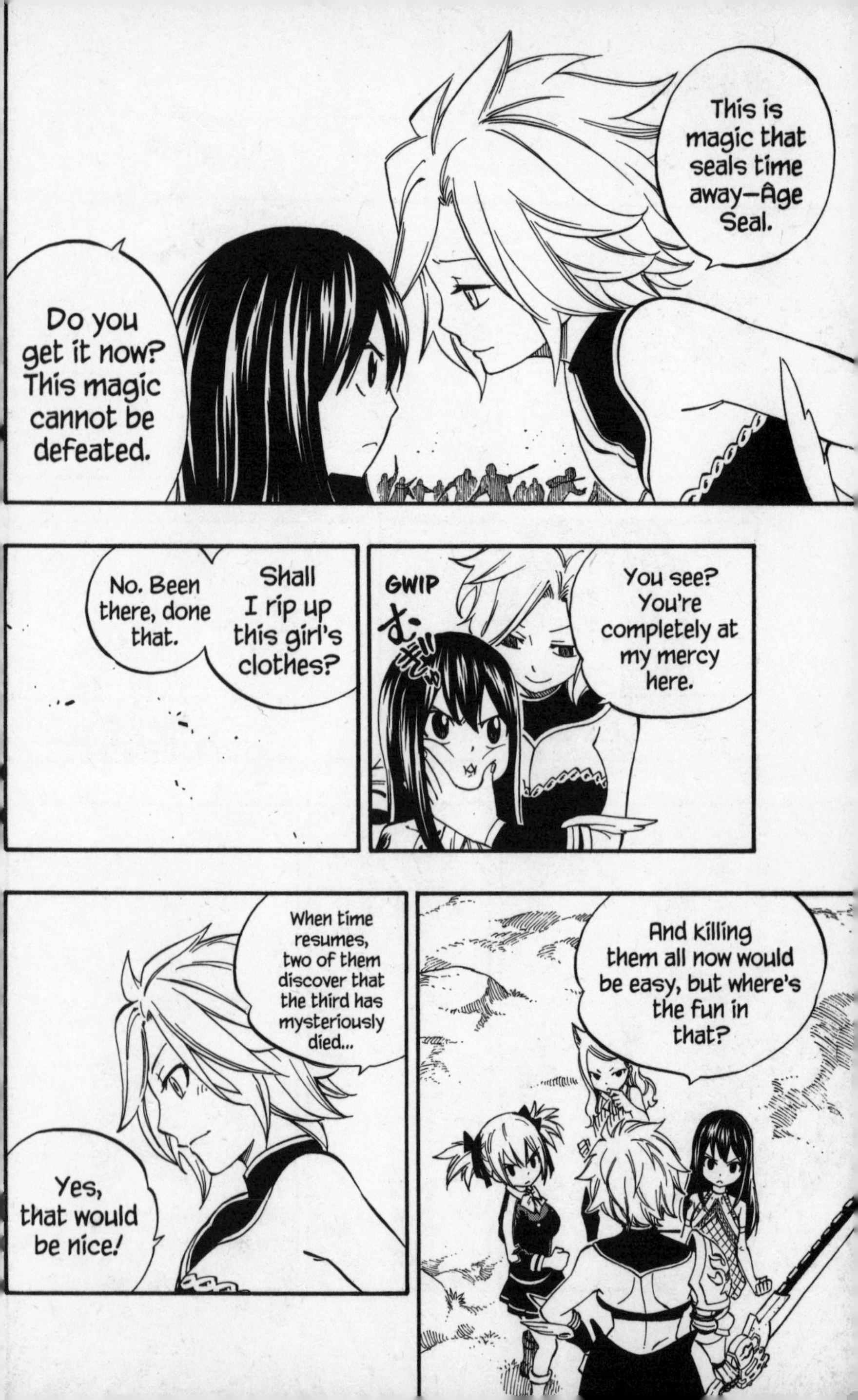
This is magic that seals time away—Âge Seal.
Do you get it now? This magic cannot be defeated.
GWIP
You see? You're completely at my mercy here.
Shall I rip up this girl's clothes?
No. Been there, done that.
And killing them all now would be easy, but where's the fun in that?
When time resumes, two of them discover that the third has mysteriously died...
Yes, that would be nice!

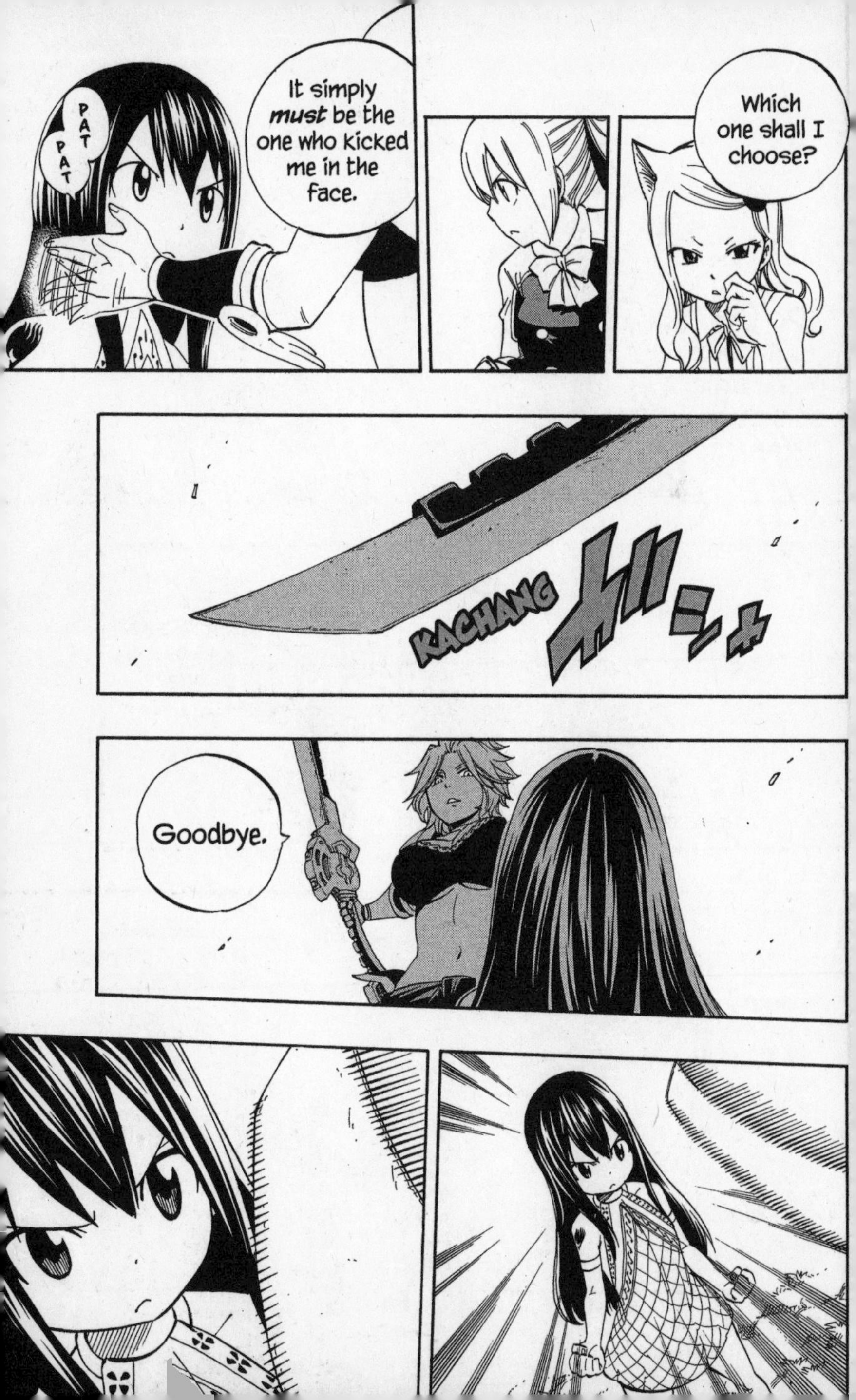
Which one shall I choose?
It simply *must* be the one who kicked me in the face.
PAT PAT
KACHANG
Goodbye.

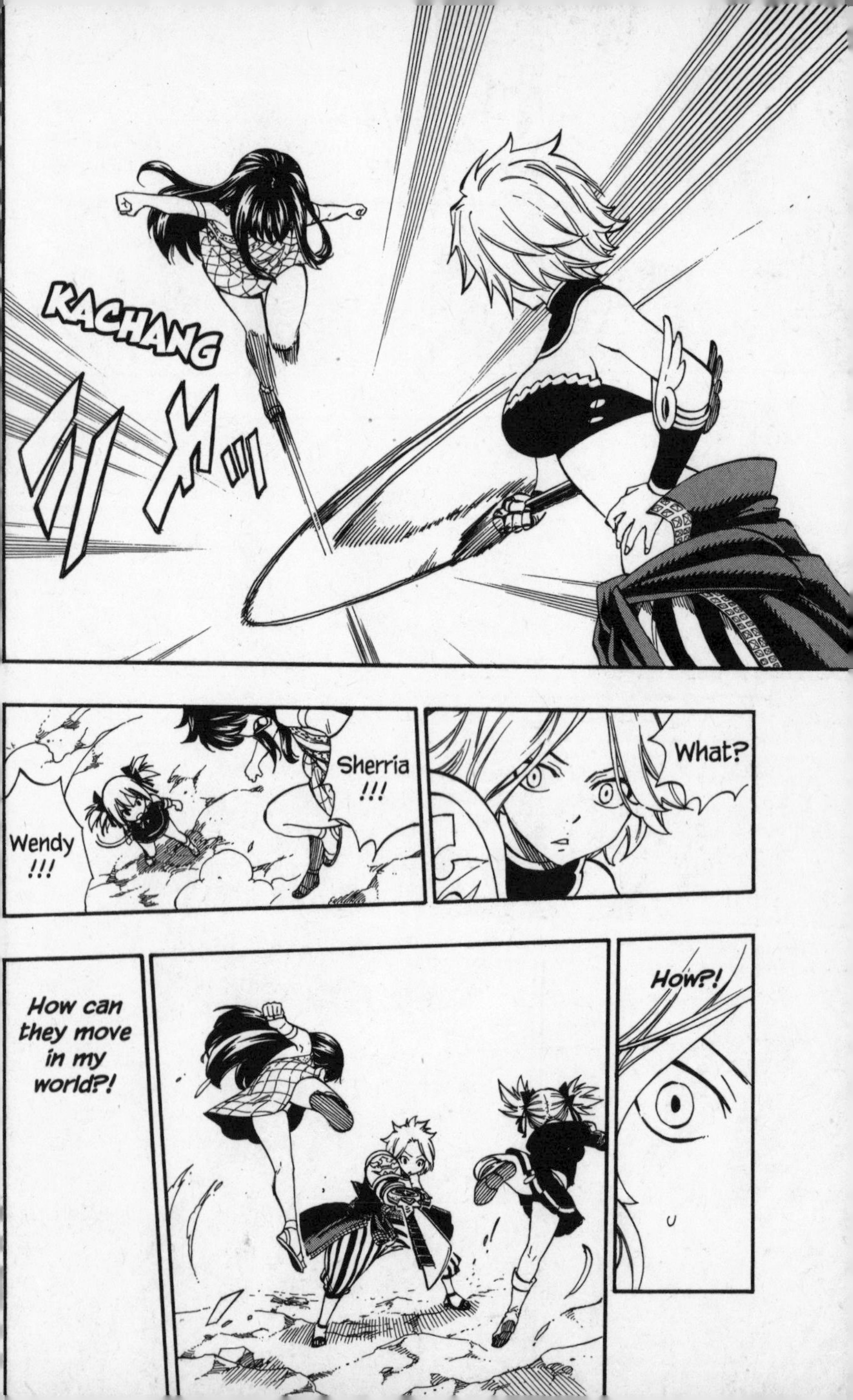
KACHANG
What?
Sherria !!!
Wendy !!!
How?!
How can they move in my world?!

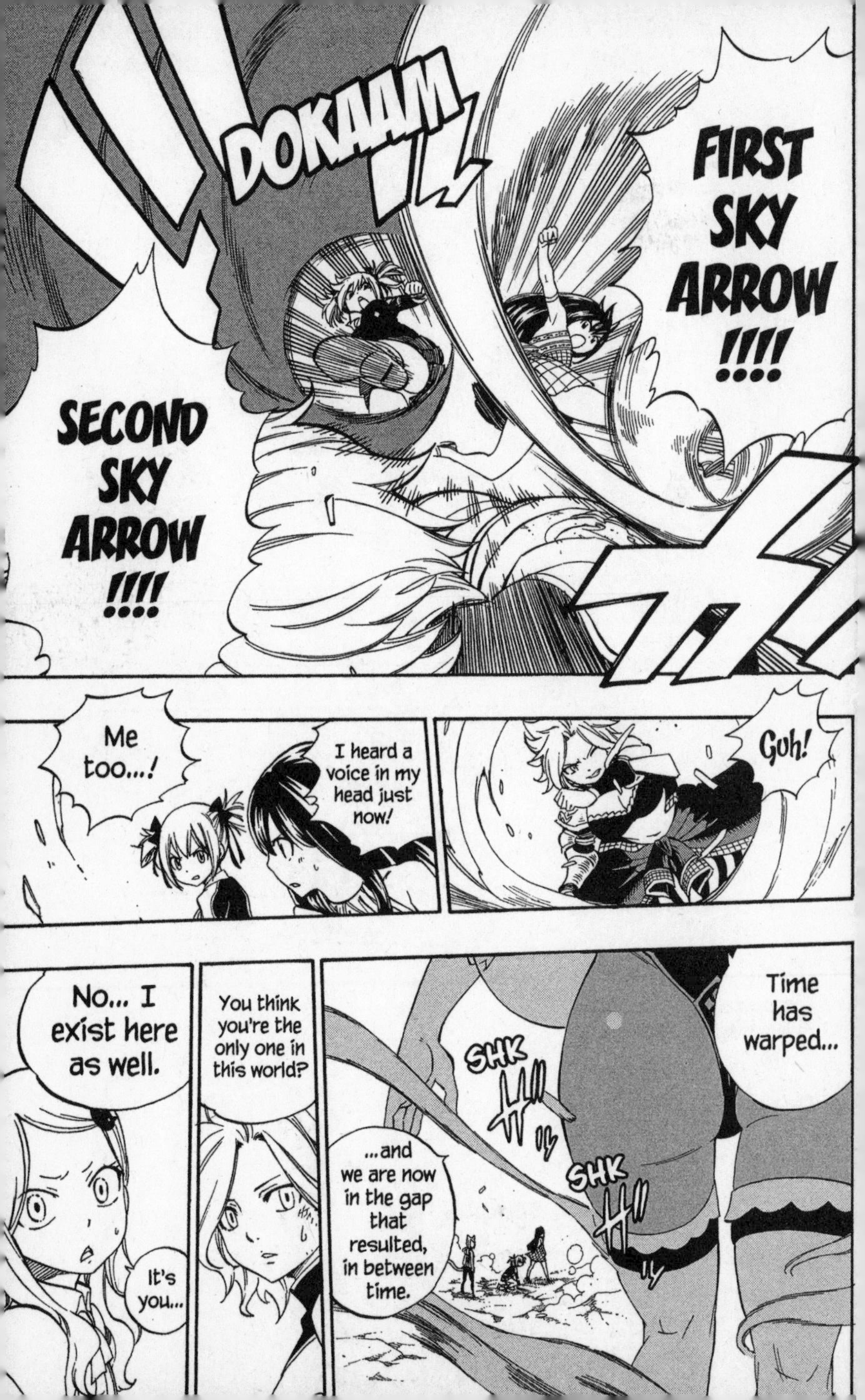
FIRST SKY ARROW!!!!
DOKAAM
SECOND SKY ARROW!!!!
Guh!
I heard a voice in my head just now!
Me too...!
Time has warped...
SHK
SHK
...and we are now in the gap that resulted, in between time.
You think you're the only one in this world?
It's you...
No... I exist here as well.

This is the prison of time.
And Crime Sorcière will bring the hammer down on you for your crimes!!

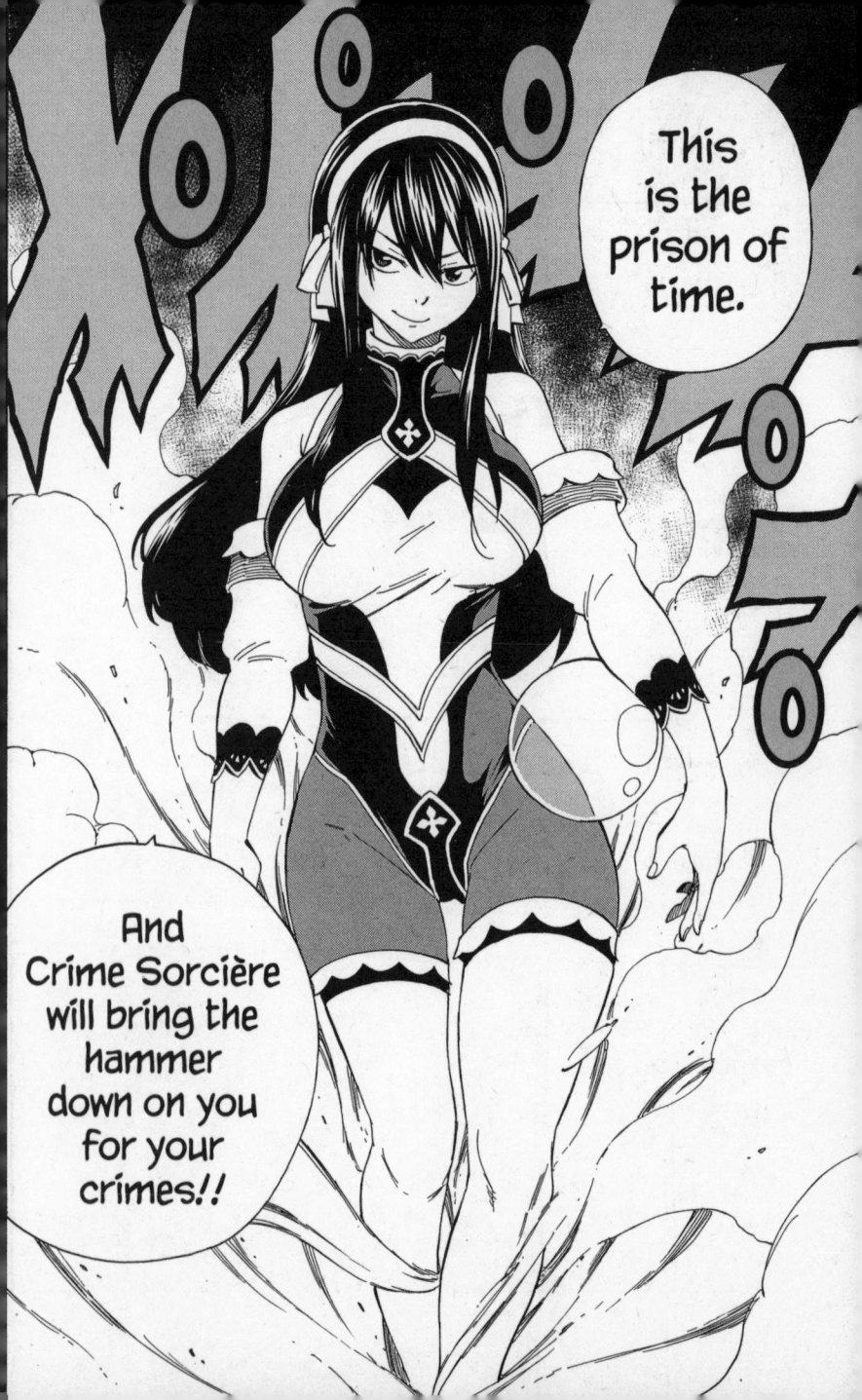

FAIRY TAIL
フェアリーテイル

Chapter 475: DiMaria Chronos Yesta

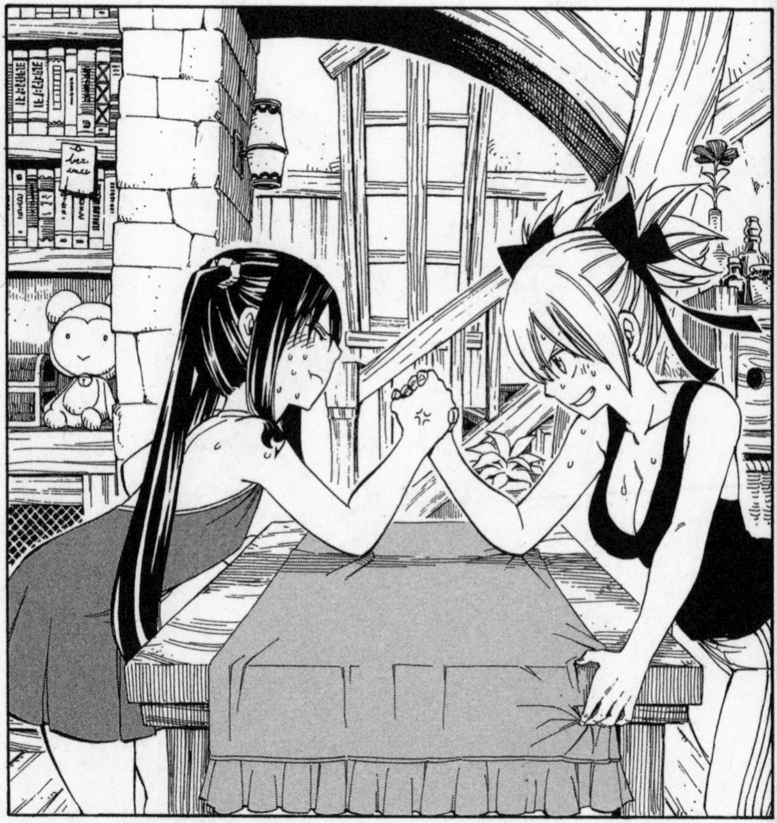

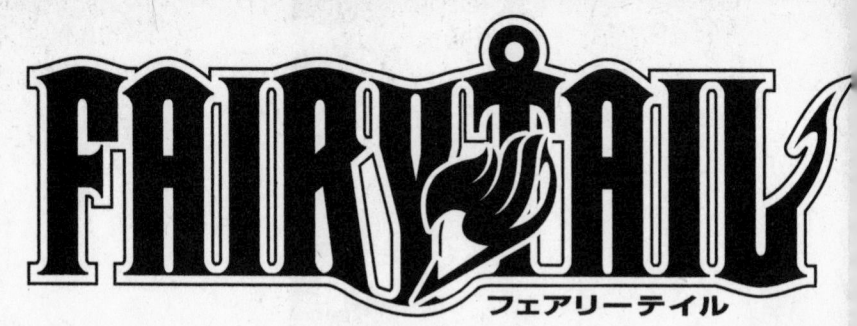

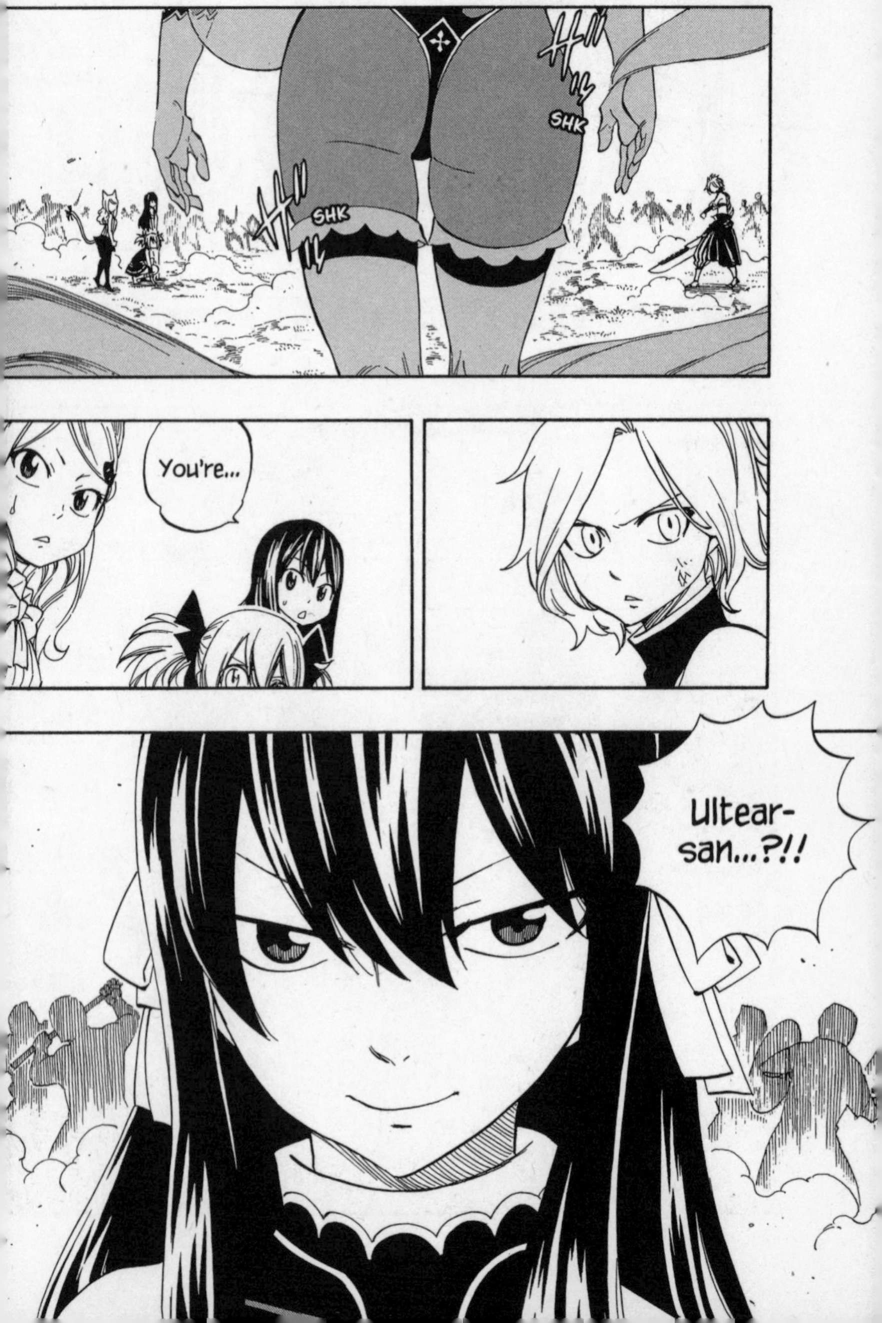
SHK
SHK
You're...
Ultear-
san...?!!

Time?

It was *you* who made time move again?

No. Time is still stopped.

I live in the spaces between time.

In other words, I can only exist within stopped time.

So when you used your magic to stop it...

SHK

...I, who cannot exist in natural time...

...found myself here.

SHIKK

25

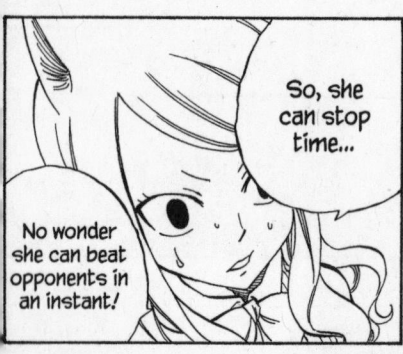

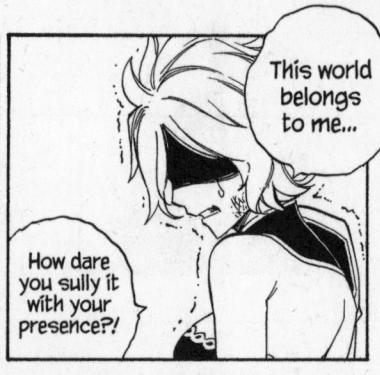

This world belongs to me...
How dare you sully it with your presence?!
So, she can stop time...
No wonder she can beat opponents in an instant!
So I was frozen in place when she attacked me before?!
ZWAT
Ultear-san, what does this mean ?!
She has time-stopping magic.
It seems that I can exist in this form while time is stopped.
And with my power, I was able to give you the ability to move here as well.

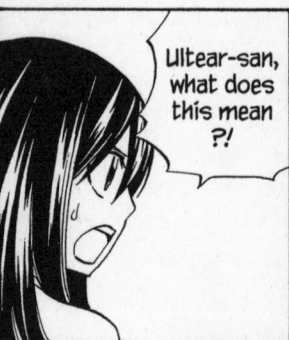

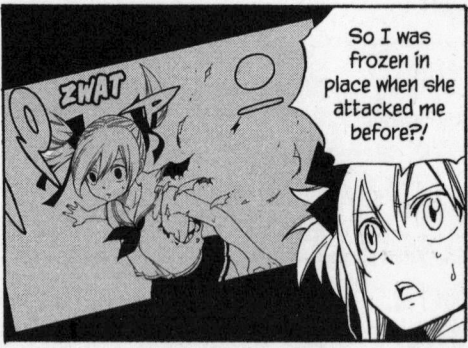

Didn't you... vanish right after the Grand Magic Games...?

It isn't so bad living between time.

Ultear-san!!!

...So I can't help you battle.

I'm only an echo of myself...

CRICK

Get out!!!!

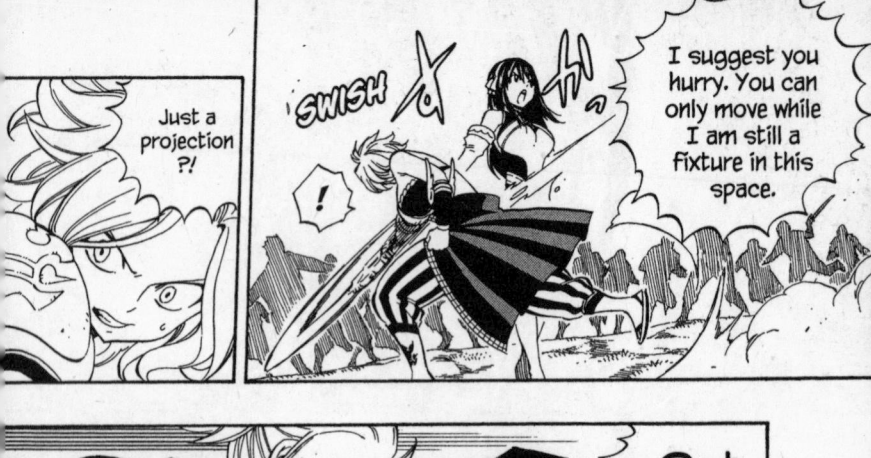

I suggest you hurry. You can only move while I am still a fixture in this space.
SWISH
!
Just a projection ?!
Got it!!!!
ZOOM
And thank you !!!
This is *my* world!
ZWAT
ZWAT
No one else is allowed in here!
ZWAT
ZWAT

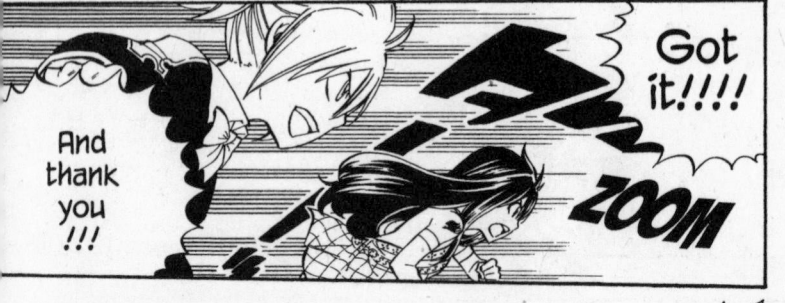

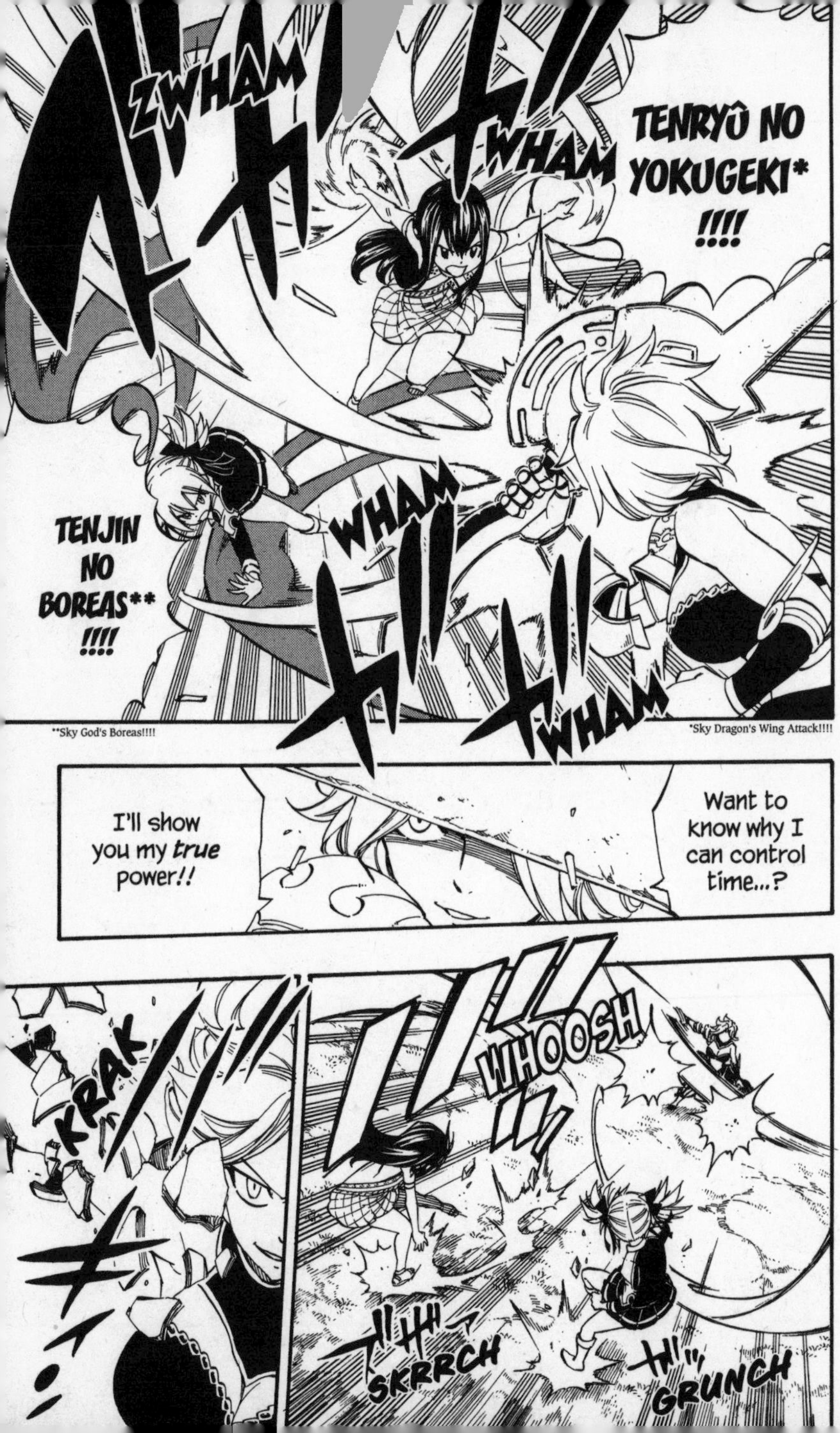
TENRYÛ NO YOKUGEKI* !!!!
WHAM
WHAM
WHAM
WHAM
TENJIN NO BOREAS** !!!!
Want to know why I can control time...?
I'll show you my *true* power!!
WHOOSH
GRUNCH
SKRRCH
KRAK
*Sky Dragon's Wing Attack!!!!
**Sky God's Boreas!!!!

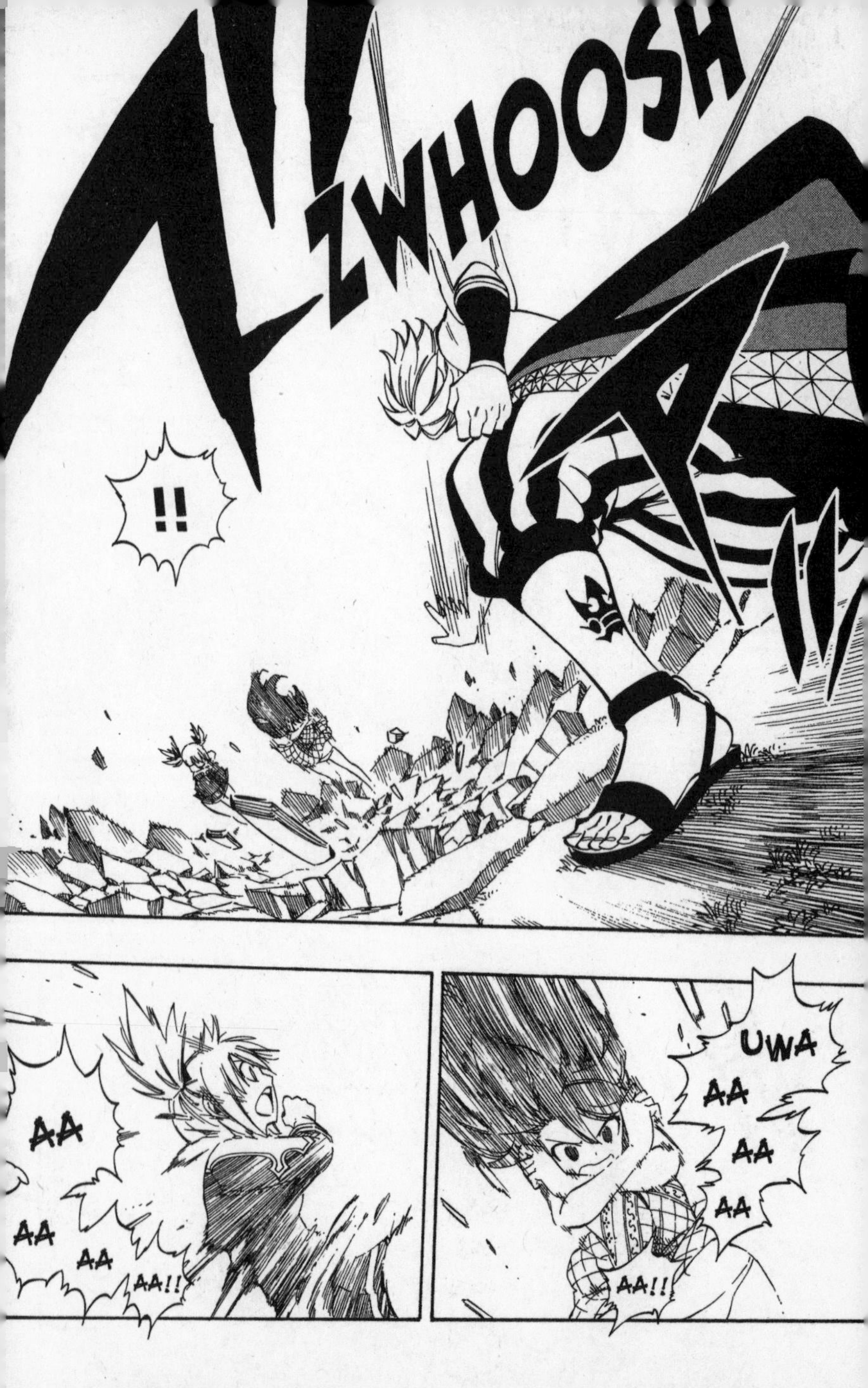
ZWHOOSH
!!
UWA AA AA AA AA!!
AA AA AA AA!!

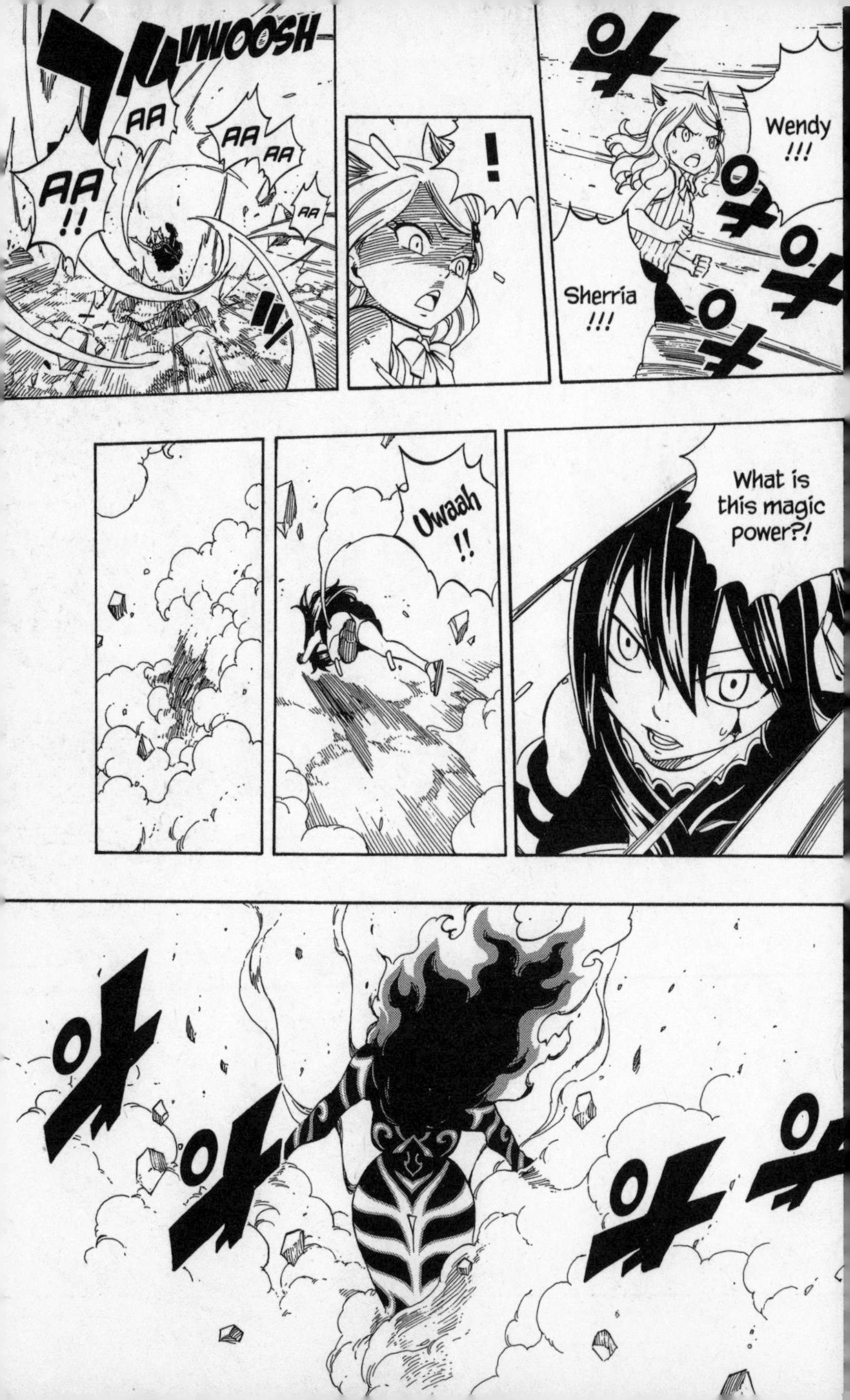

Wendy
!!!
Sherria
!!!
!
VWOOSH
AA
AA
AA
AA
!!
AA
What is
this magic
power?!
Uwaah
!!

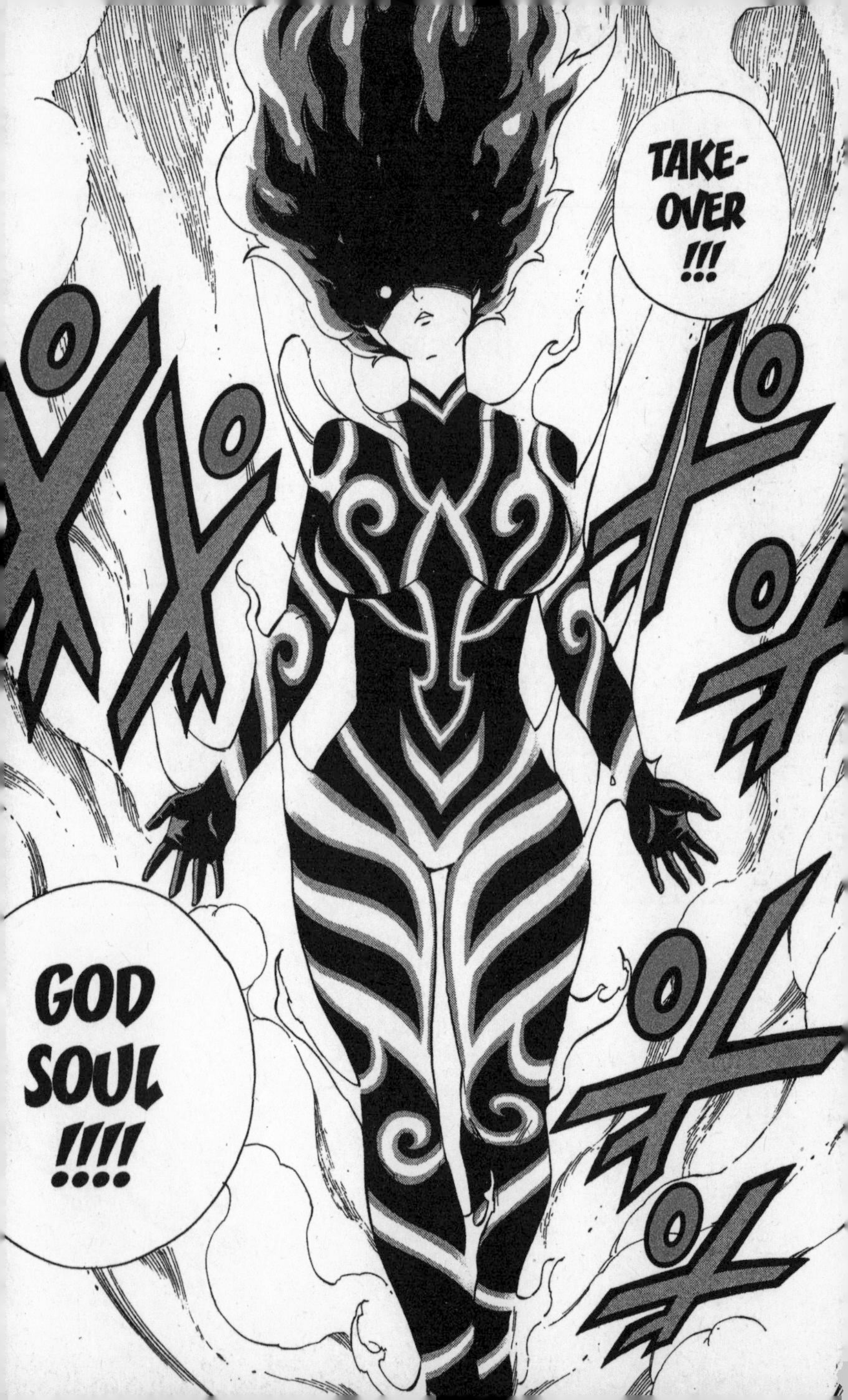
TAKE-OVER !!!
GOD SOUL !!!!

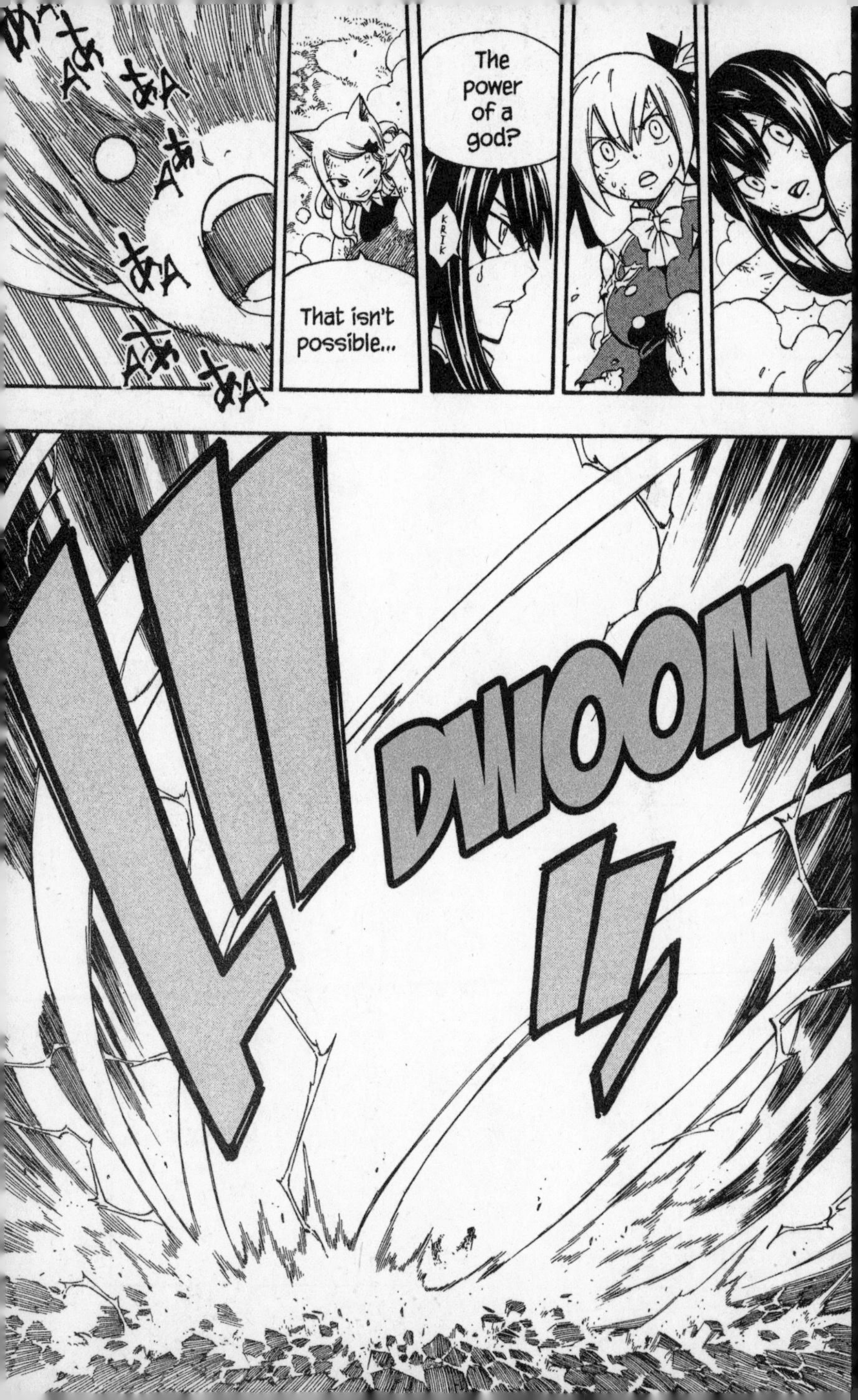
The power of a god?
KRIK
That isn't possible...
DWOOM

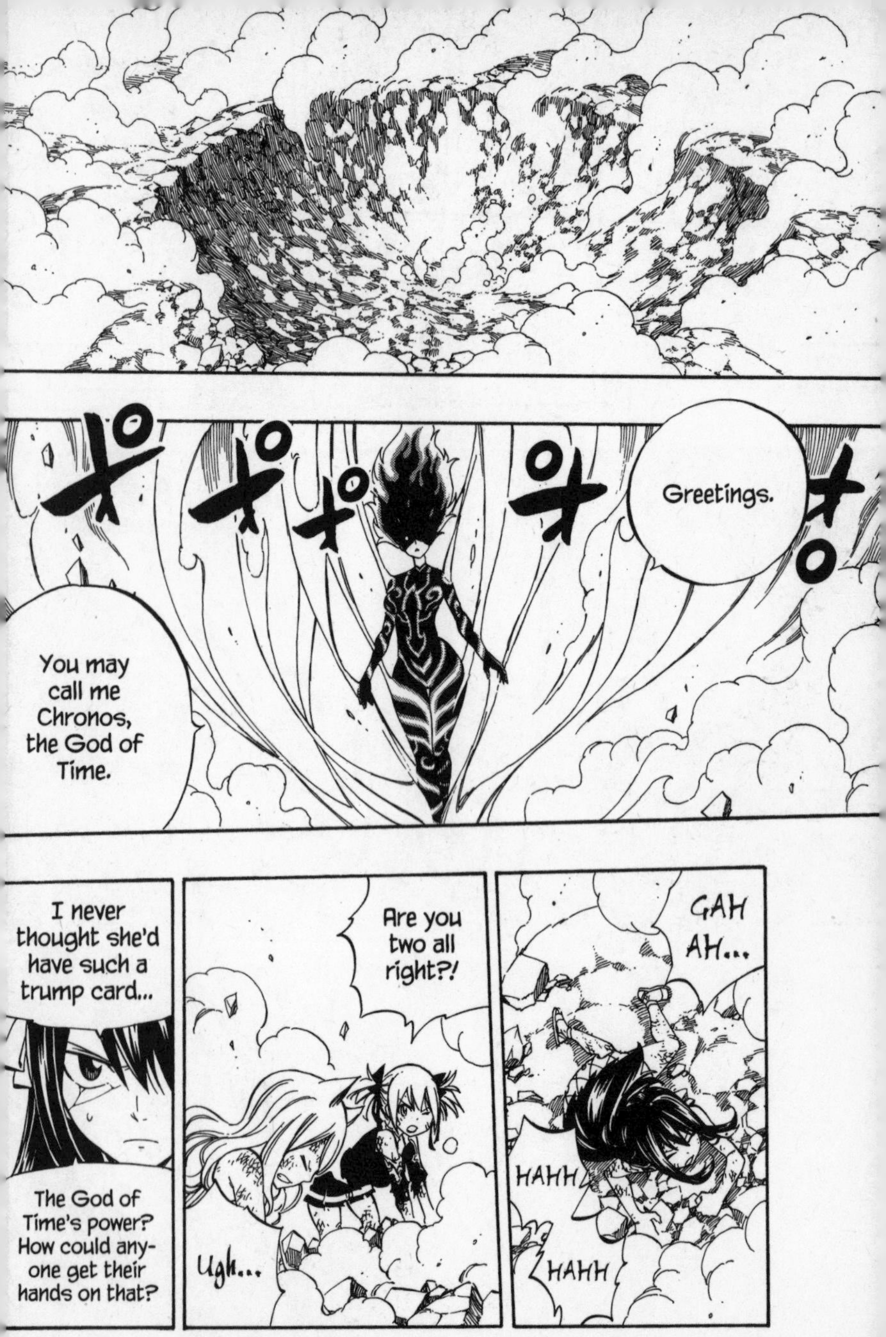
Greetings.
You may call me Chronos, the God of Time.
GAH AH...
HAHH
HAHH
Are you two all right?!
Ugh...
I never thought she'd have such a trump card...
The God of Time's power? How could anyone get their hands on that?

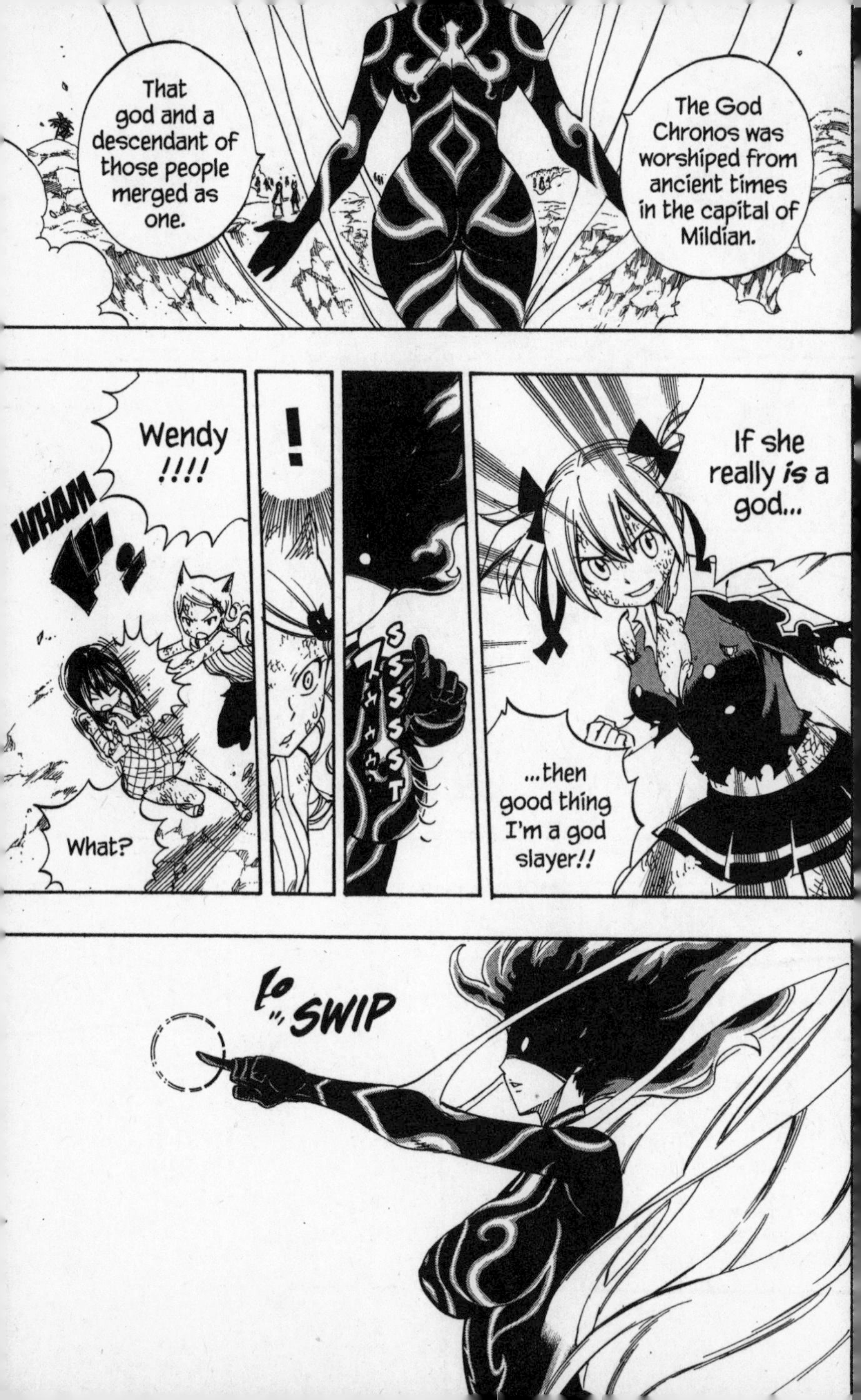
The God Chronos was worshiped from ancient times in the capital of Mildian.
That god and a descendant of those people merged as one.
If she really *is* a god...
...then good thing I'm a god slayer!!
SSSST
!
Wendy !!!!
WHAM
What?
SWIP

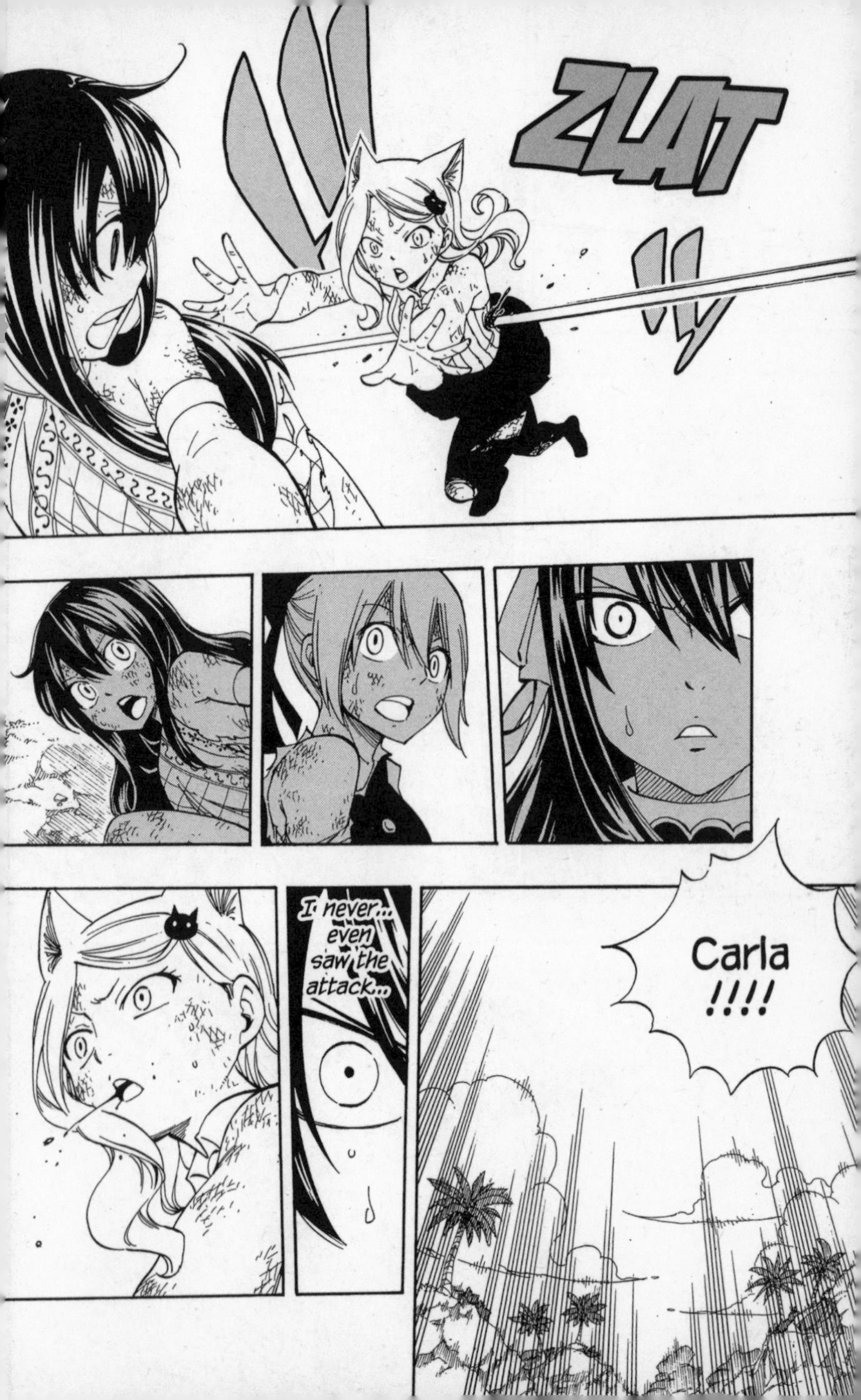
ZLAT
Carla !!!!
I never... even saw the attack...

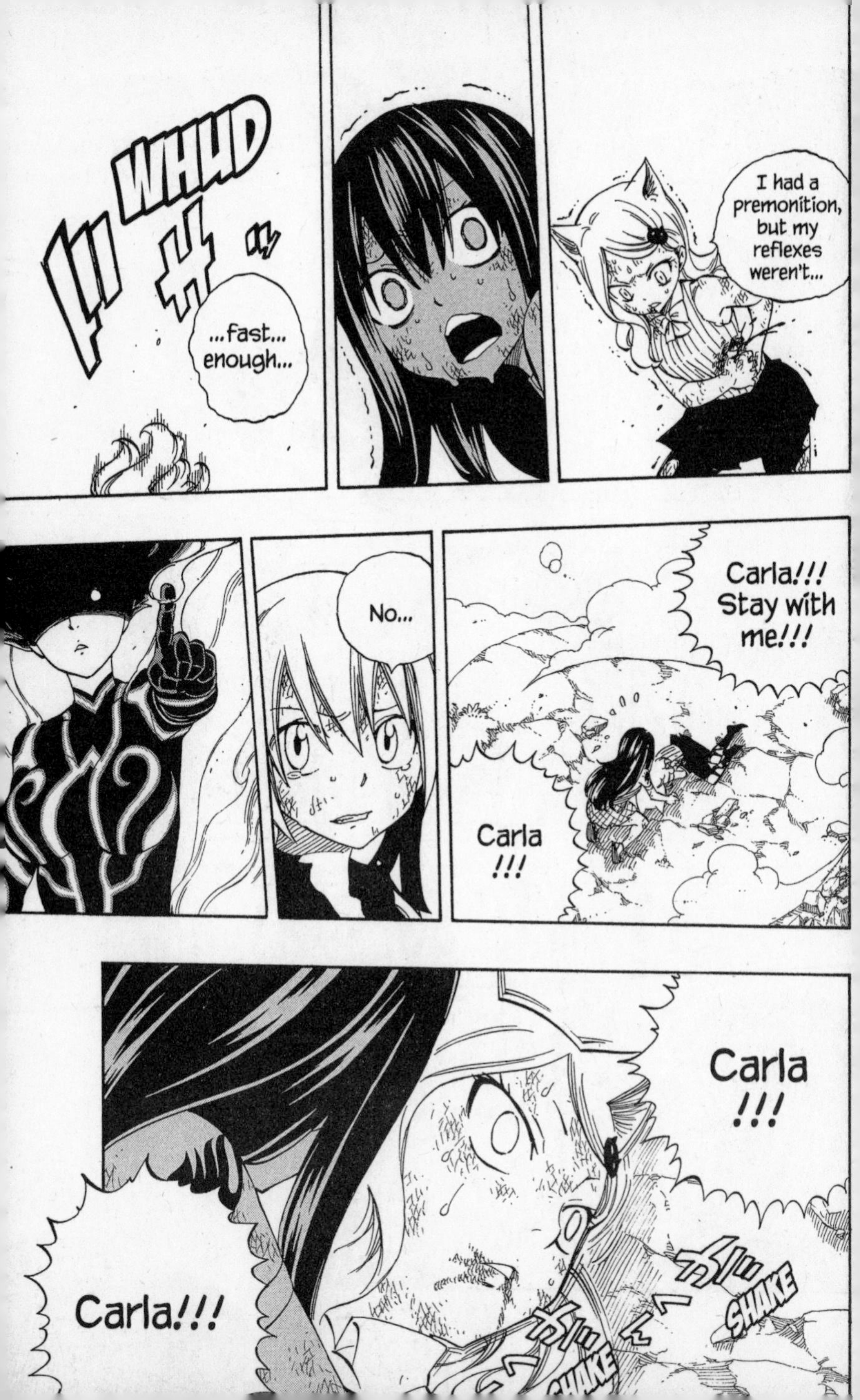
I had a premonition, but my reflexes weren't...
...fast... enough...
WHUD
Carla!!! Stay with me!!!
Carla!!!
No...
Carla!!!
SHAKE
SHAKE
Carla!!!

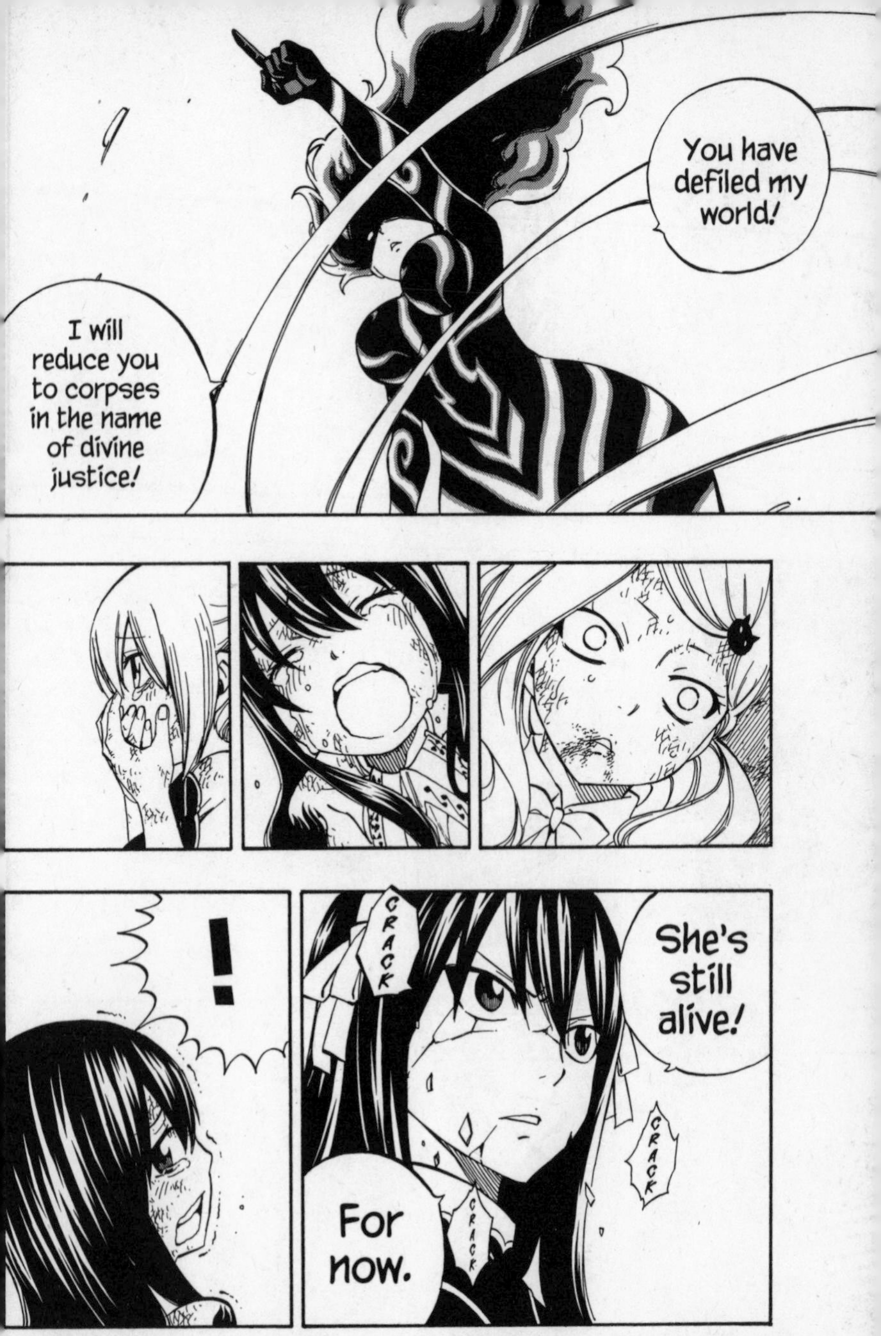
You have defiled my world!
I will reduce you to corpses in the name of divine justice!
CRACK
She's still alive!
CRACK
CRACK
For now.
!

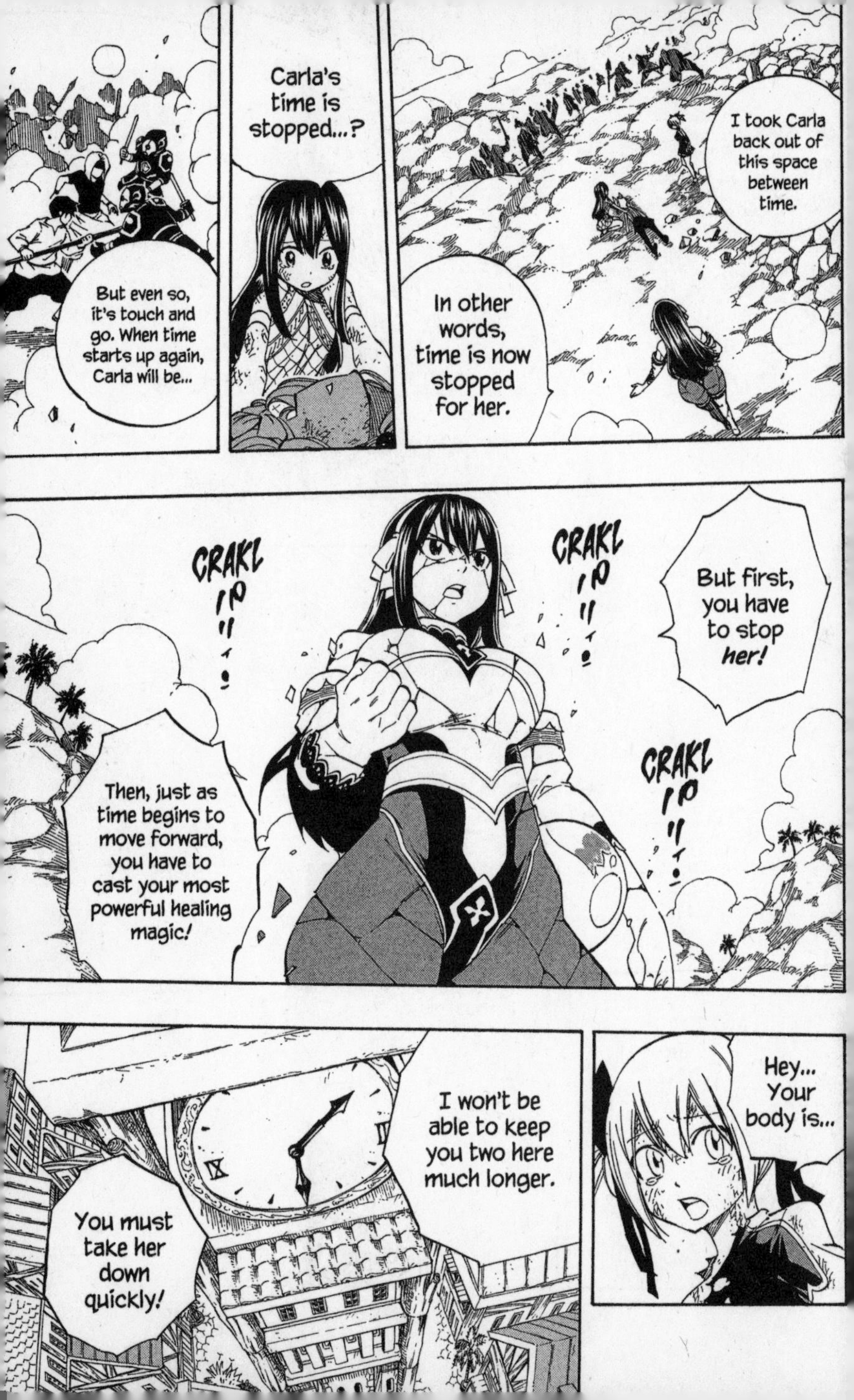
I took Carla back out of this space between time.
In other words, time is now stopped for her.
Carla's time is stopped...?
But even so, it's touch and go. When time starts up again, Carla will be...
But first, you have to stop her!
CRAKL
CRAKL
CRAKL
Then, just as time begins to move forward, you have to cast your most powerful healing magic!
Hey... Your body is...
I won't be able to keep you two here much longer.
You must take her down quickly!

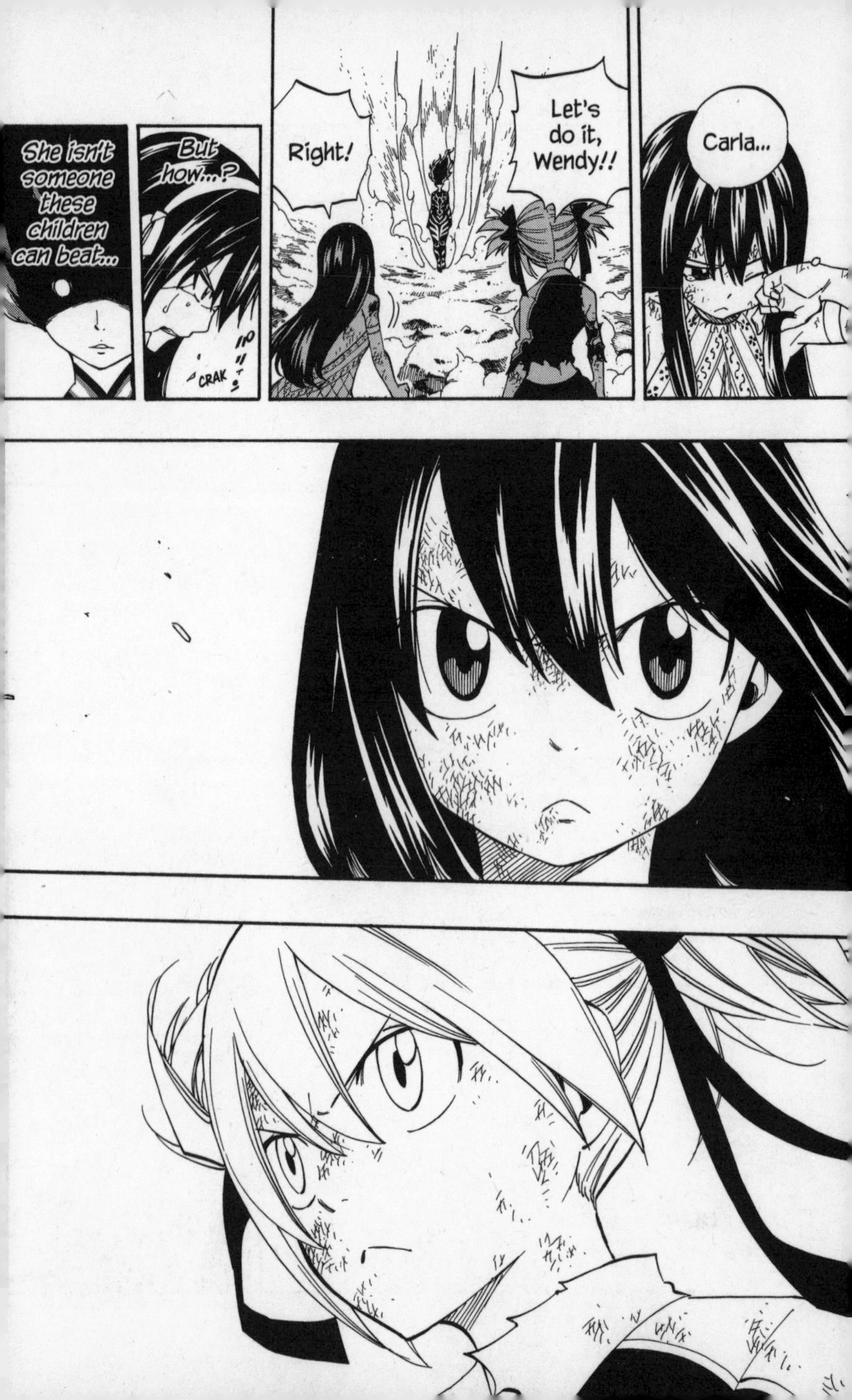
Carla...
Let's do it, Wendy!!
Right!
But how...?
CRAK
She isn't someone these children can beat...

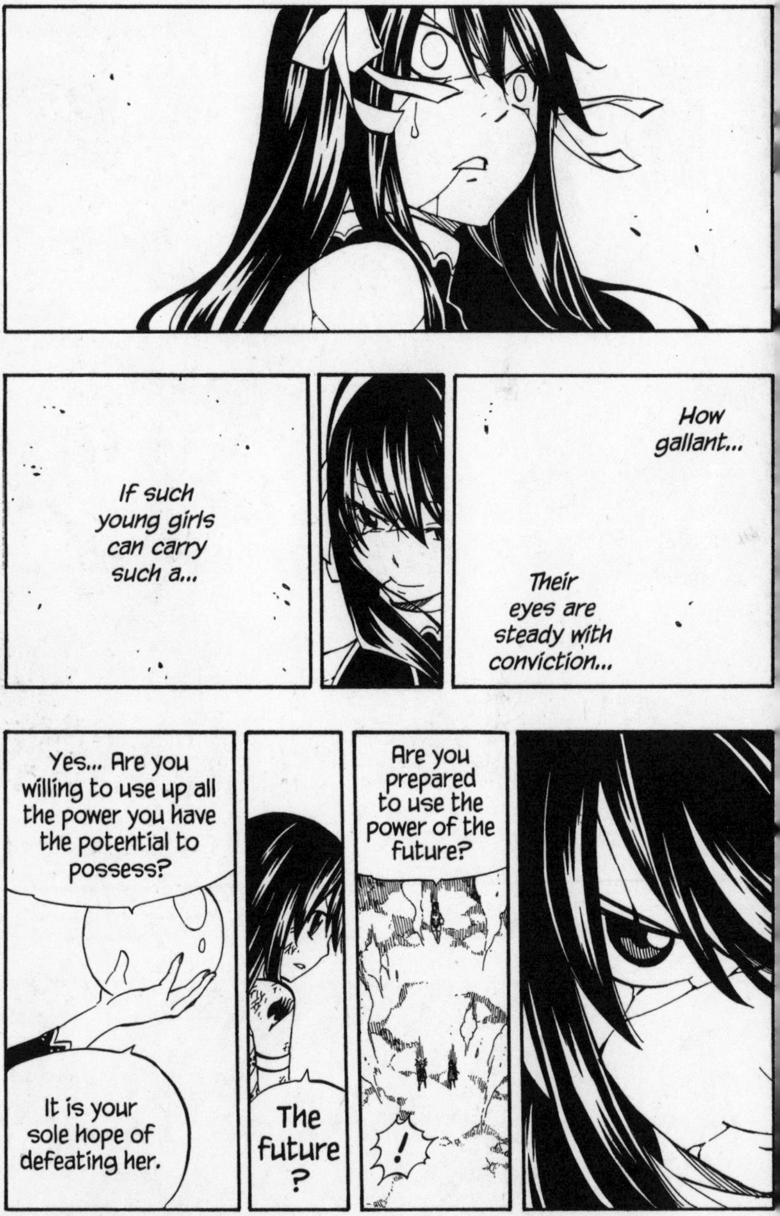
How gallant...
Their eyes are steady with conviction...
If such young girls can carry such a...
Are you prepared to use the power of the future?
!
The future?
Yes... Are you willing to use up all the power you have the potential to possess?
It is your sole hope of defeating her.

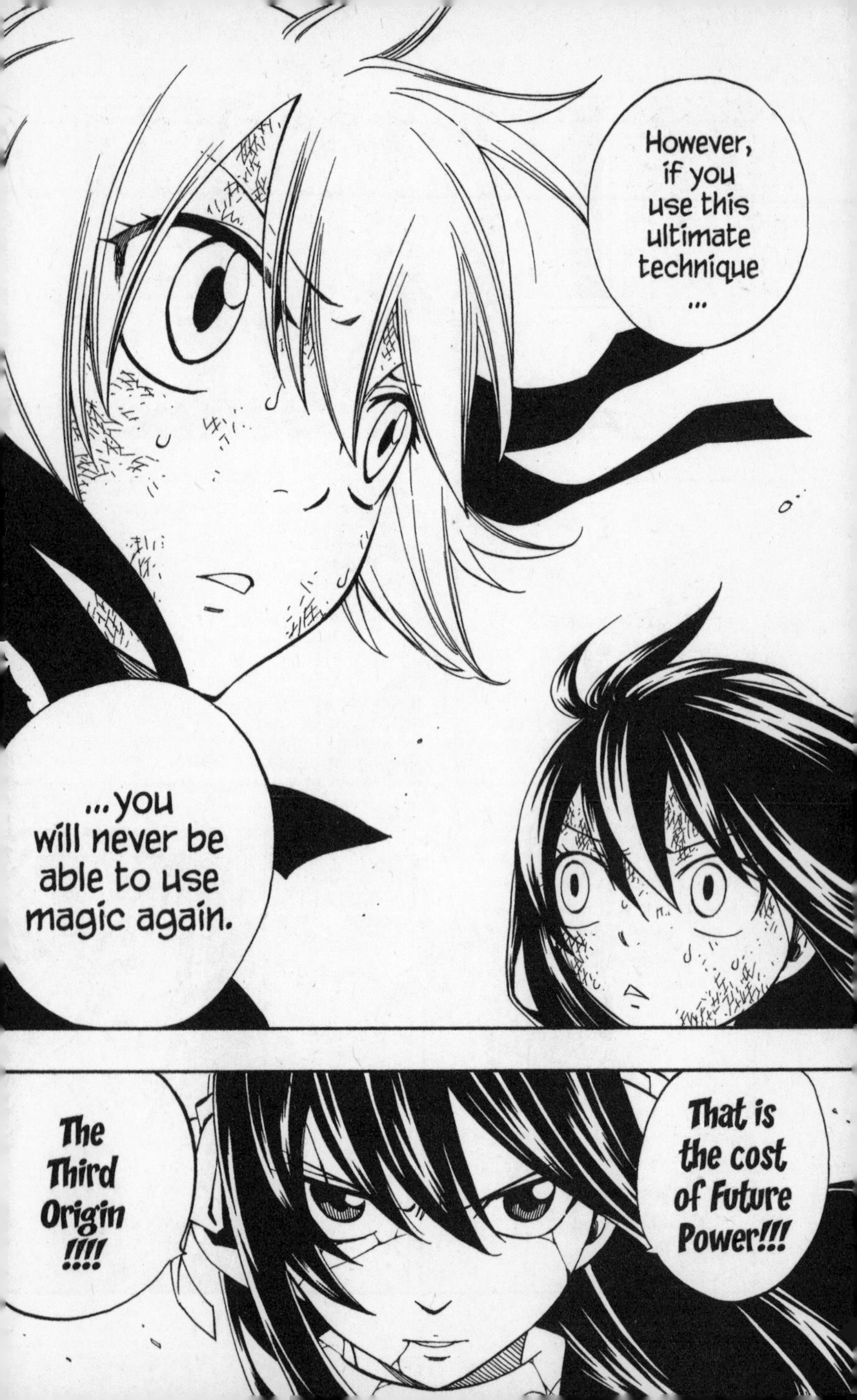
However, if you use this ultimate technique ...
...you will never be able to use magic again.
That is the cost of Future Power!!!
The Third Origin!!!!

FAIRY TAIL
フェアリーテイル

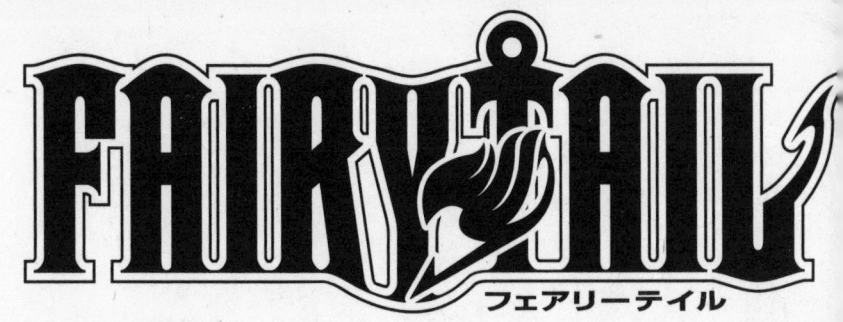

Chapter 476: Farewell, Magical Girl

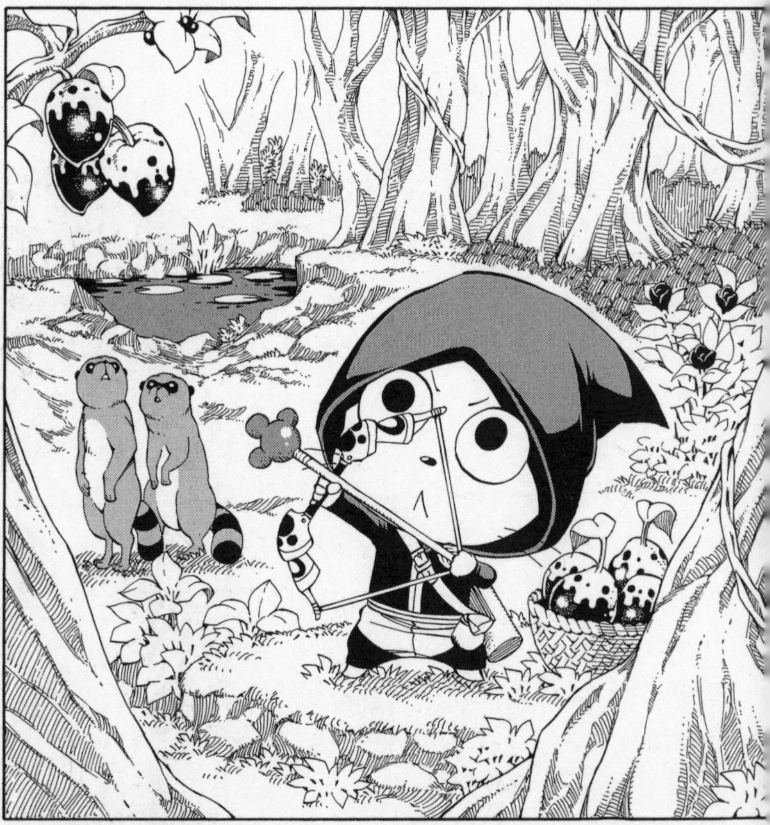

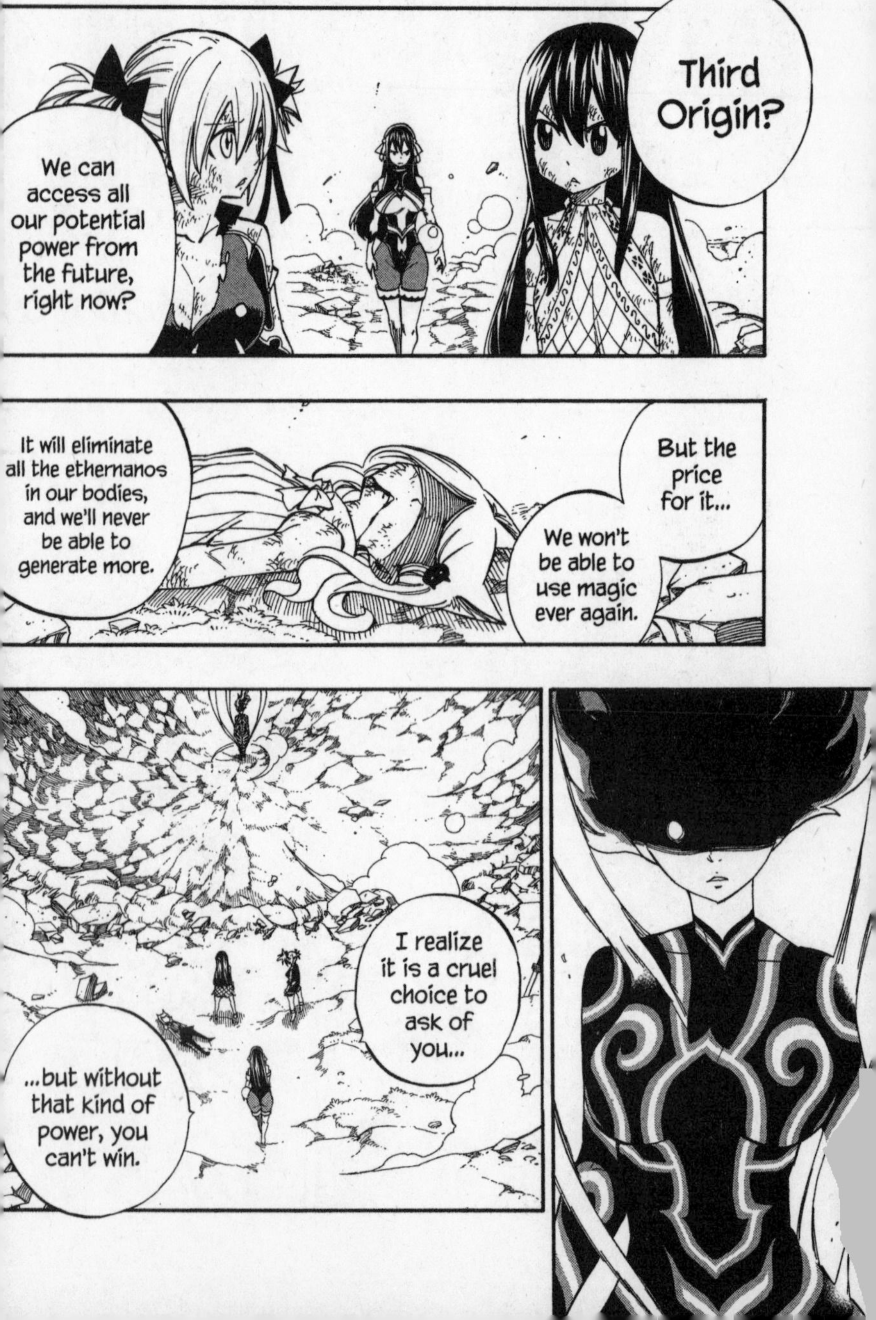
Third Origin?
We can access all our potential power from the future, right now?
But the price for it...
It will eliminate all the ethernanos in our bodies, and we'll never be able to generate more.
We won't be able to use magic ever again.
I realize it is a cruel choice to ask of you...
...but without that kind of power, you can't win.

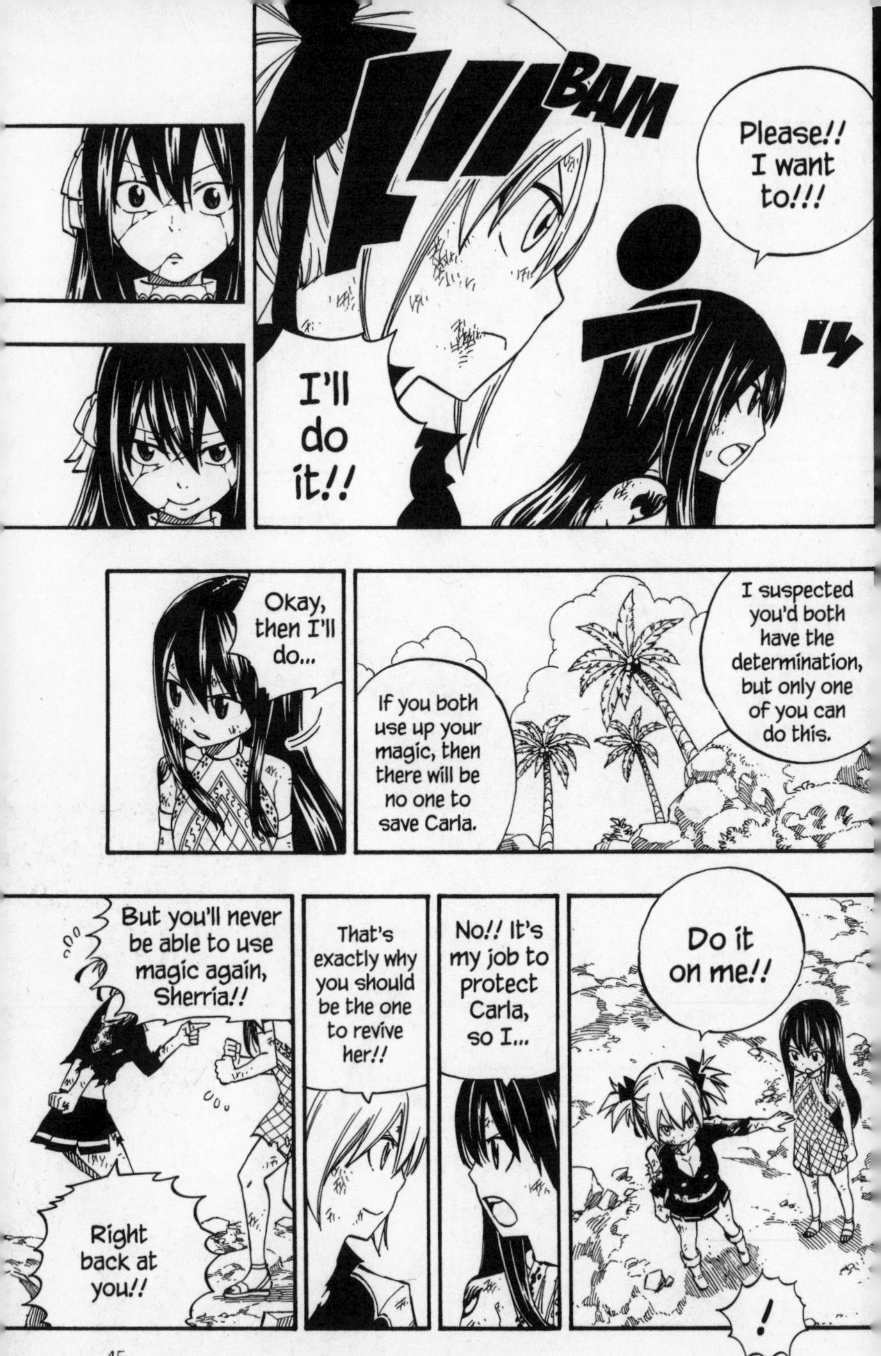
BAM
Please!! I want to!!!
I'll do it!!
I suspected you'd both have the determination, but only one of you can do this.
If you both use up your magic, then there will be no one to save Carla.
Okay, then I'll do...
Do it on me!!
!
No!! It's my job to protect Carla, so I...
That's exactly why you should be the one to revive her!!
But you'll never be able to use magic again, Sherria!!
Right back at you!!

I came here to save you, Sherria!!!!
If I can't protect you, I'll never forgive myself!!!!!
Ultear-san, if you please!!!!
...
Are you truly prepared to do this?
If this will save Sherria and Carla, then I'm...
Wendy, no!!!!
VYUUUM
For what reason do you quarrel amongst yourselves?
WHUMP
She's coming at us!!!! Please hurry!!
Ah!
Here it comes, Wendy!!!!

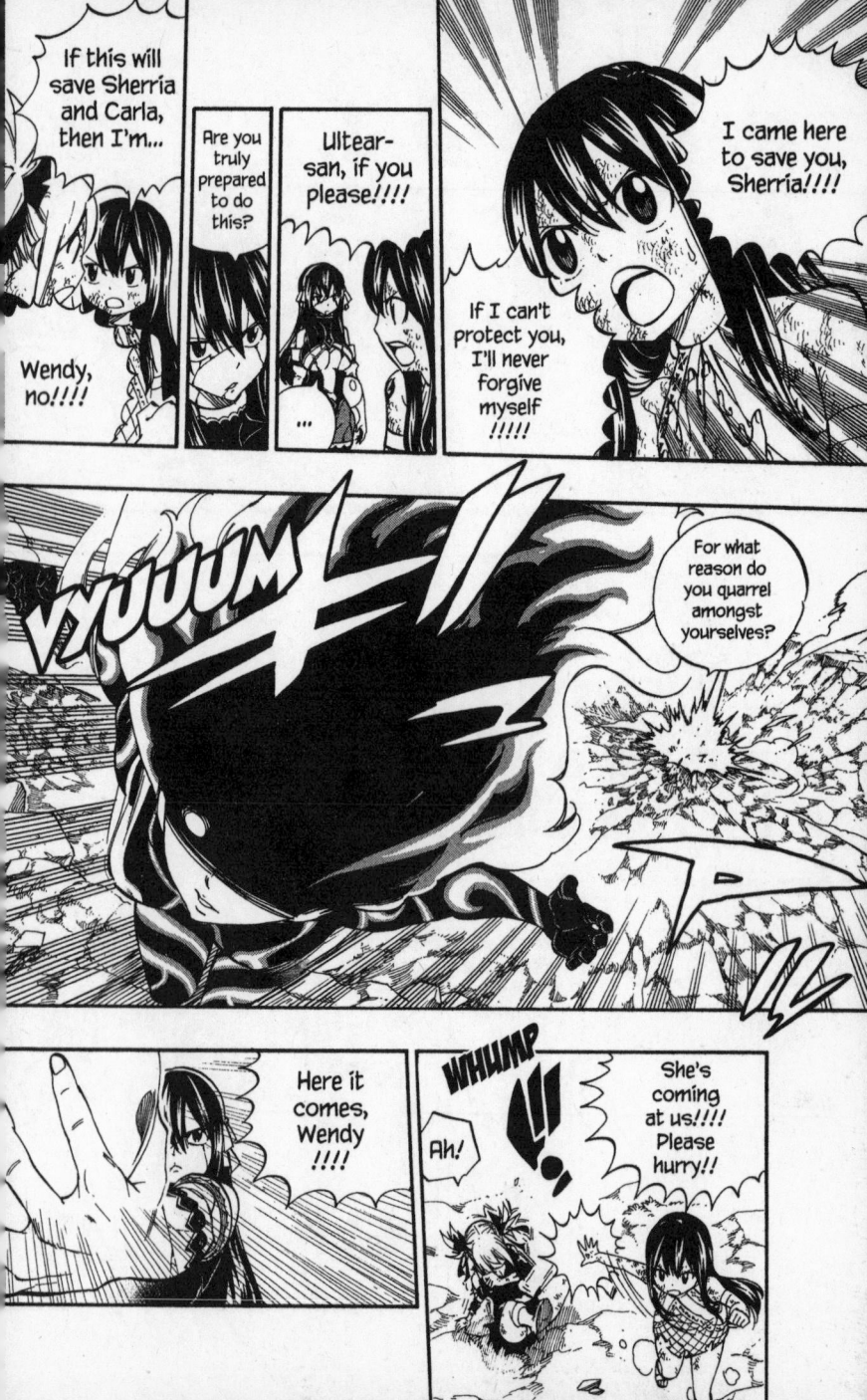

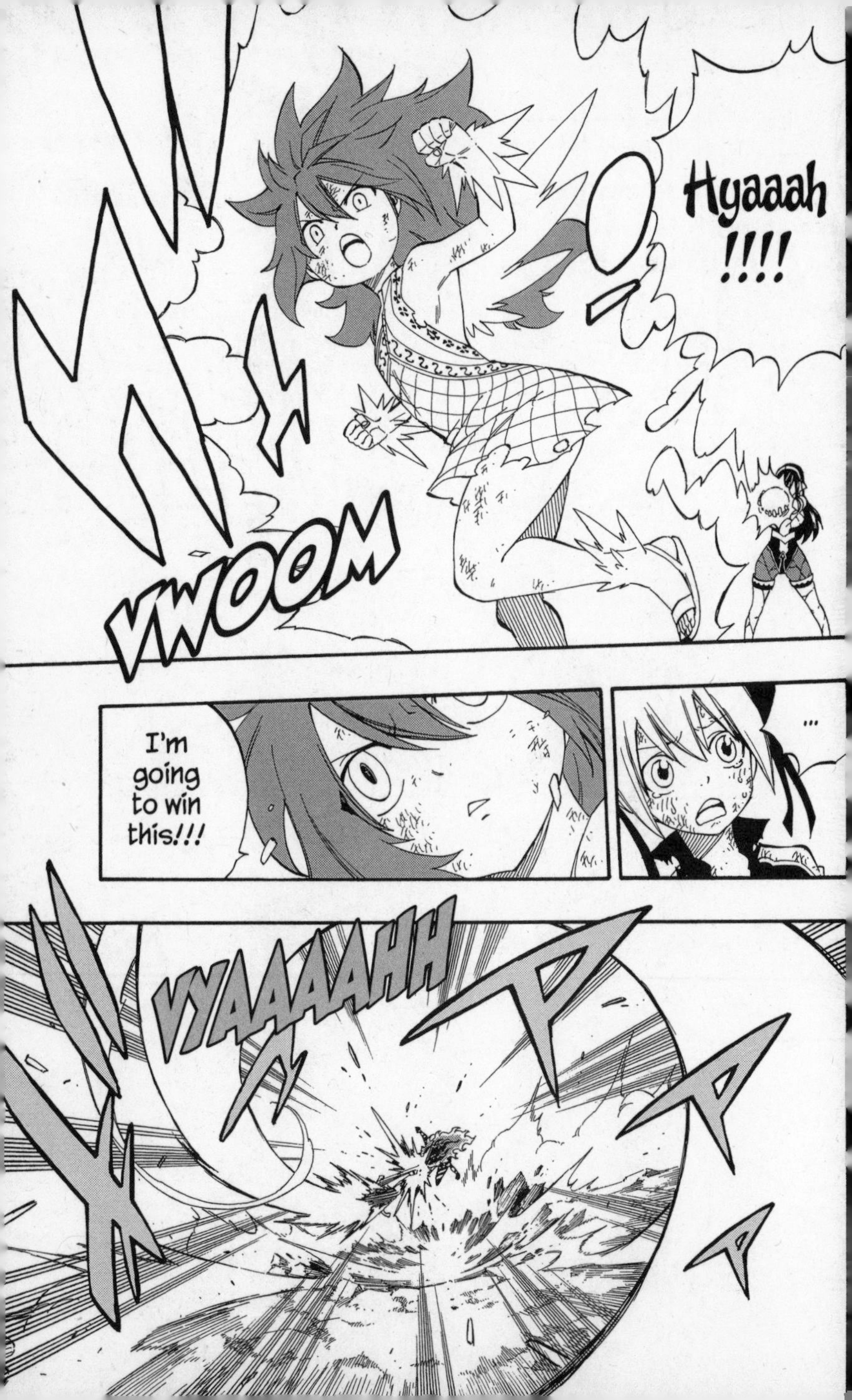
Hyaaah !!!!
VWOOM
...
I'm going to win this!!!
VYAAAAHH

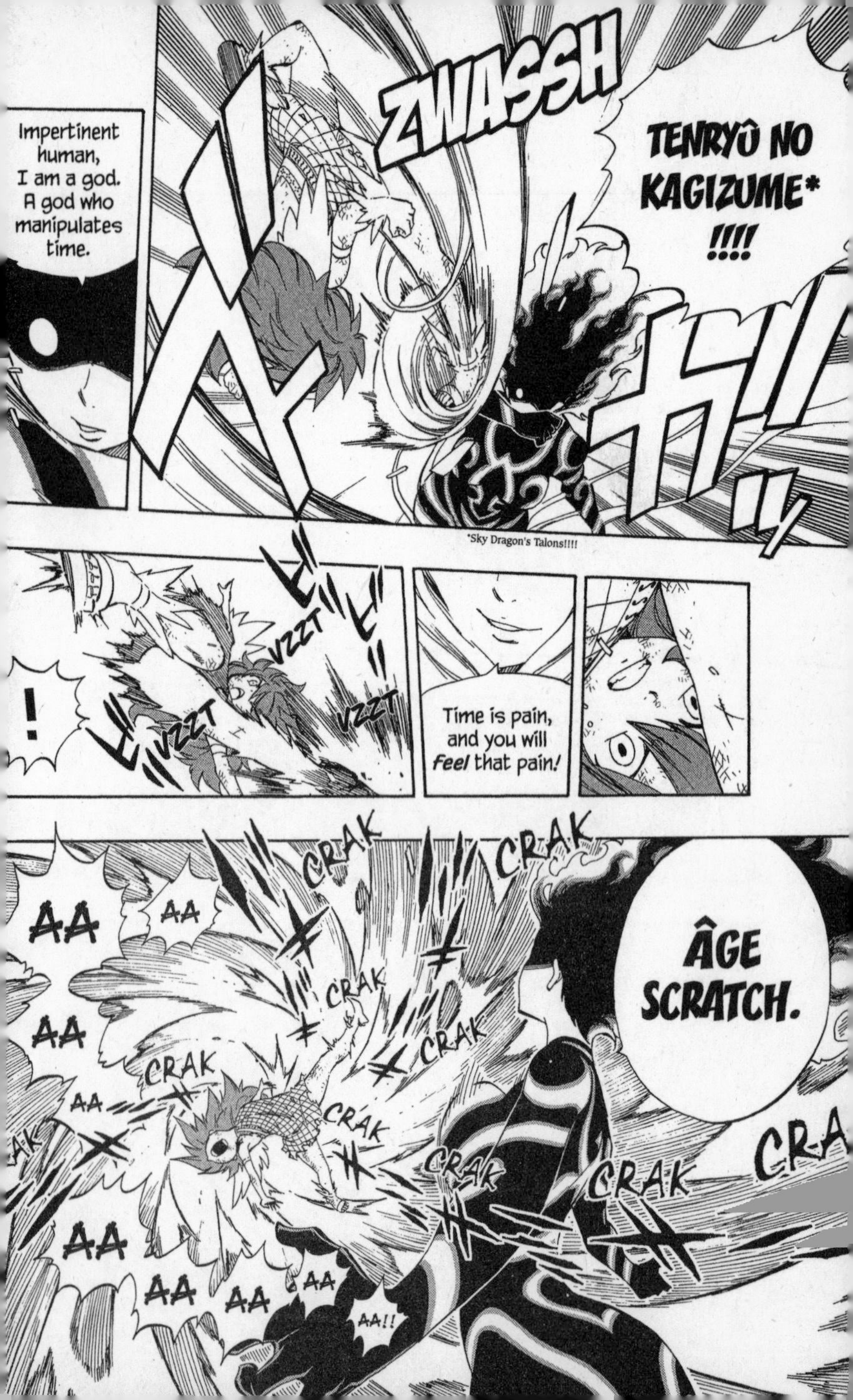
TENRYÛ NO KAGIZUME* !!!!
ZWASSH
Impertinent human, I am a god. A god who manipulates time.
Time is pain, and you will *feel* that pain!
VZZT
VZZT
VZZT
!
ÂGE SCRATCH.
CRAK
CRAK
CRAK
CRAK
CRAK
CRAK
CRAK
CRAK
CRA
AA
AA
AA
AA
AA
AA
AA
AA!!

*Sky Dragon's Talons!!!!

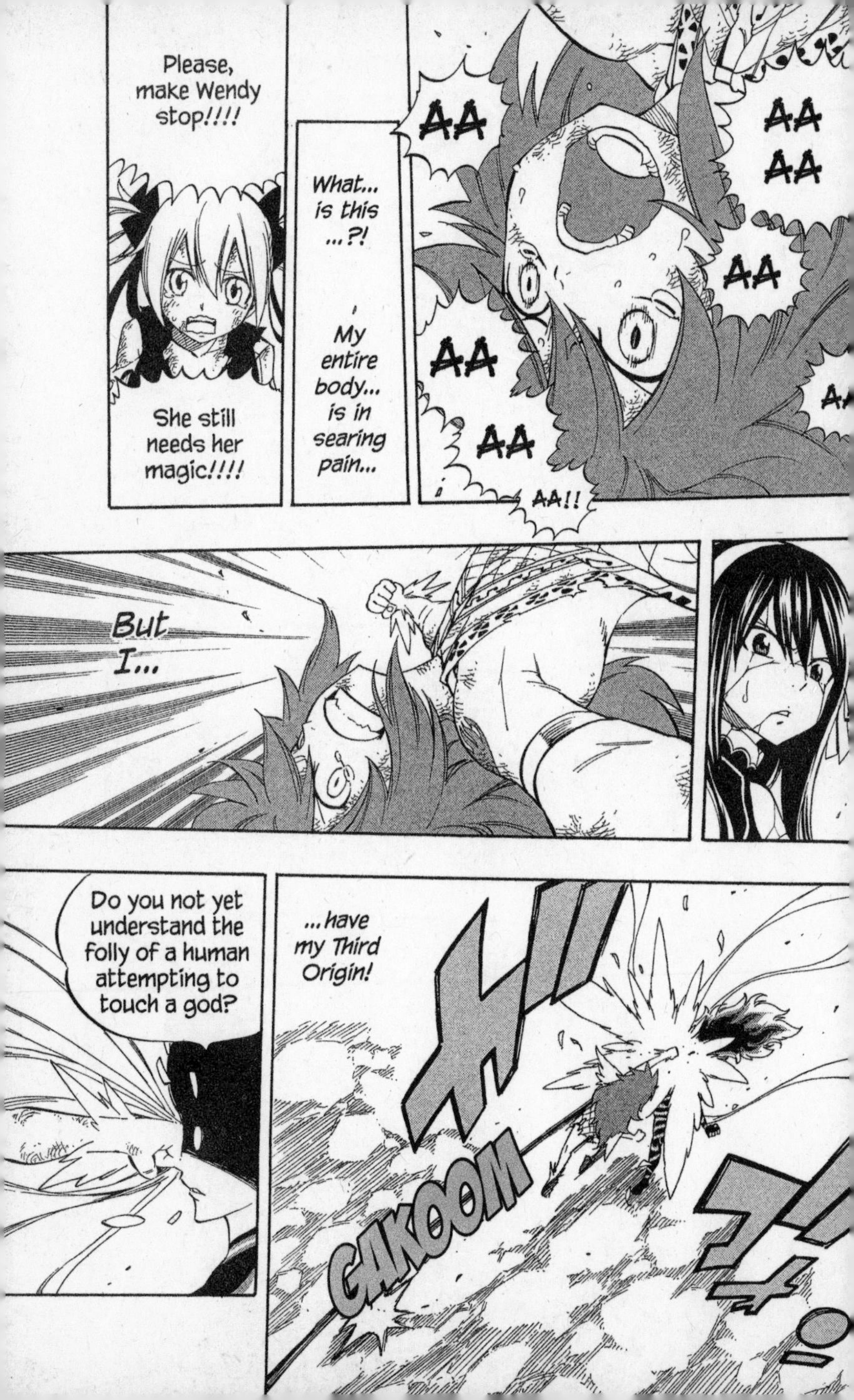

AA
AA
AA
AA
AA
AA
AA!!
What... is this ...?!
My entire body... is in searing pain...
Please, make Wendy stop!!!!
She still needs her magic!!!!
But I...
...have my Third Origin!
GAKOOM
Do you not yet understand the folly of a human attempting to touch a god?

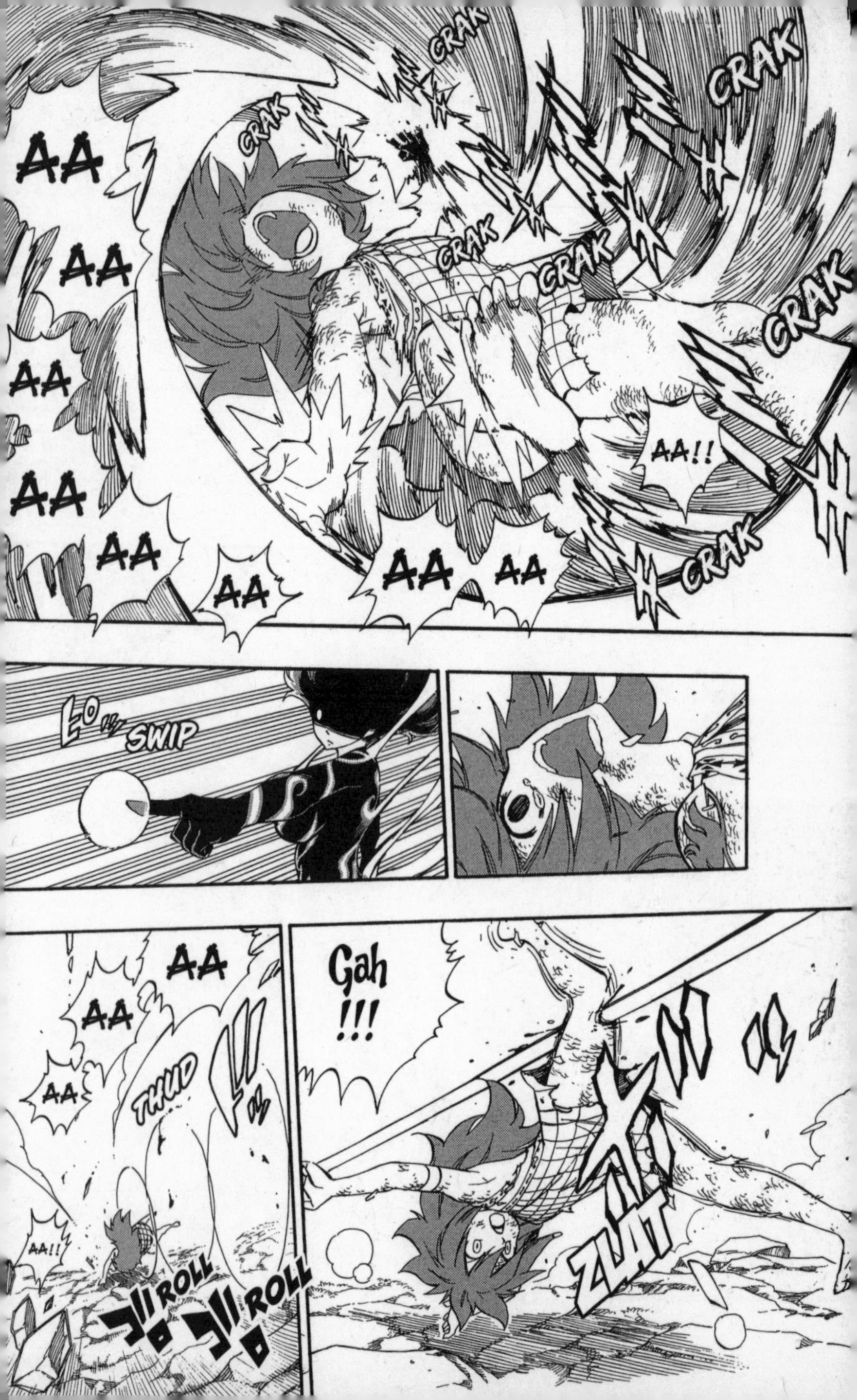
CRAK
CRAK
CRAK
CRAK
CRAK
CRAK
CRAK
AA!!
AA
AA
AA
AA
AA
AA
AA
AA
AA
SWIP
Gah !!!
ZWAT
AA
AA
AA
THUD
AA!!
ROLL
ROLL

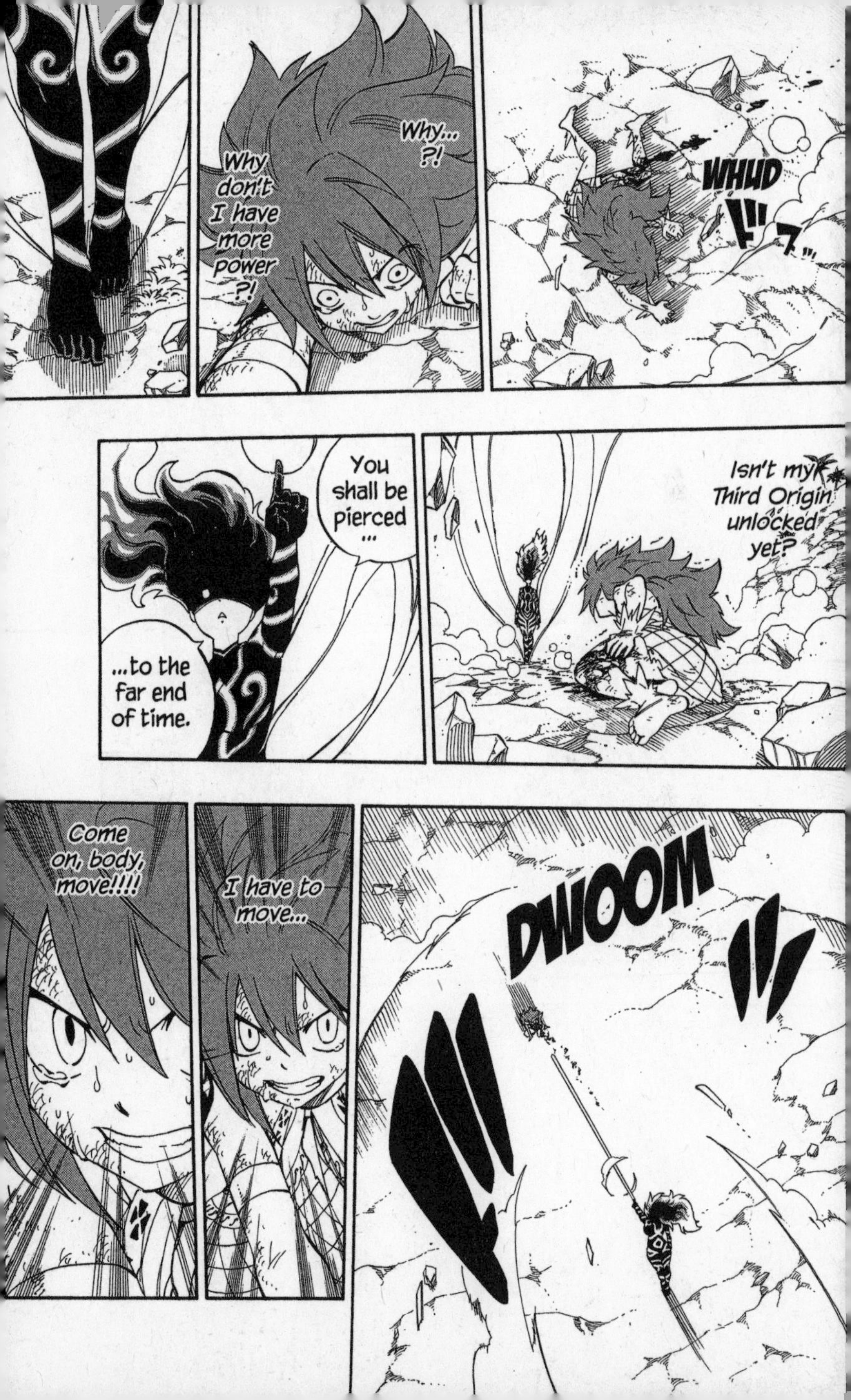
WHUD
ドッ
Why... ?!
Why don't I have more power ?!
Isn't my Third Origin unlocked yet?
You shall be pierced ...
...to the far end of time.
DWOOM
I have to move...
Come on, body, move!!!!

GACHIIING
I made it...
...in... time...
Sherria ?
!
You can leave the rest to me, Wendy.
Don't worry. I'll win this!!!

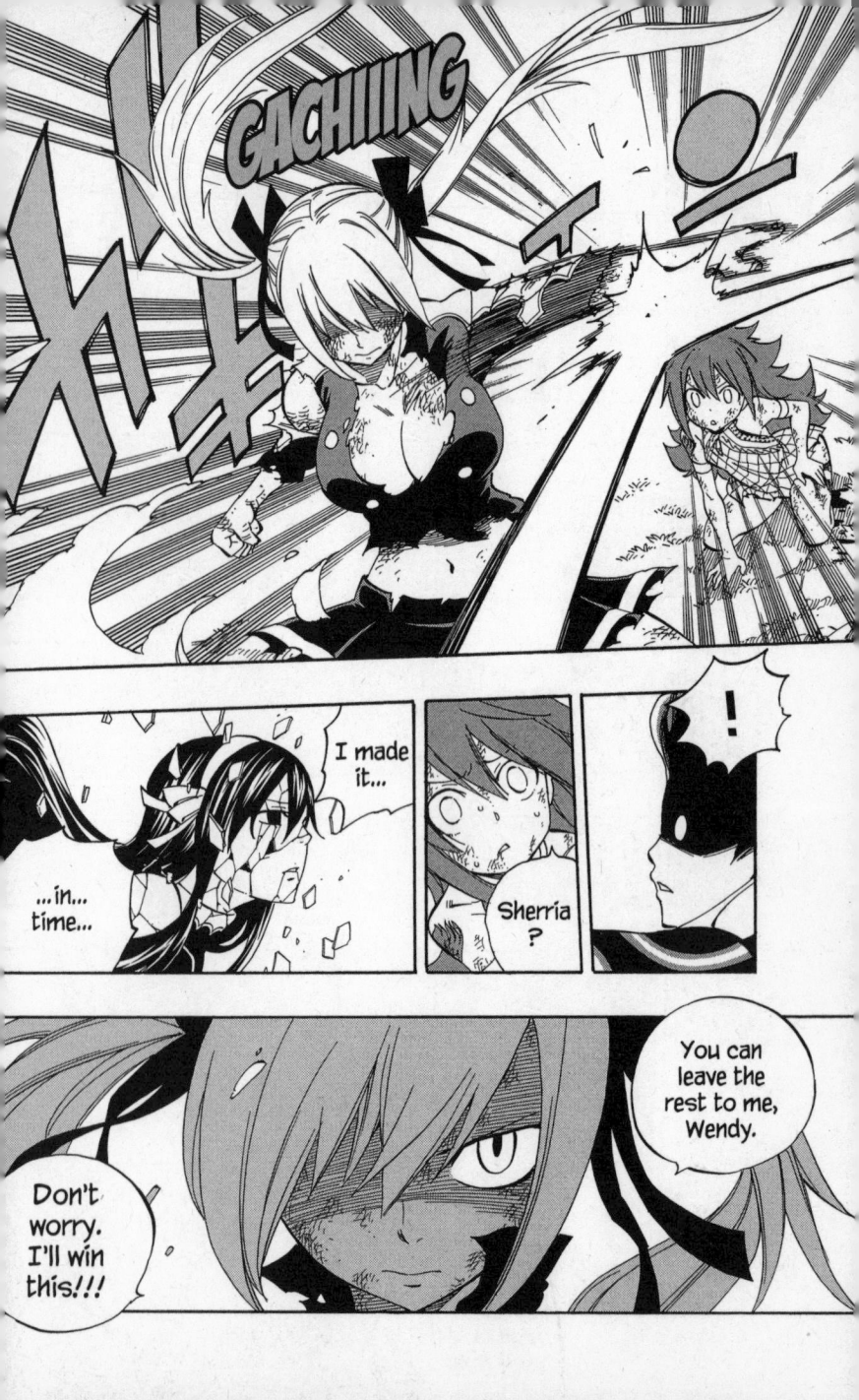

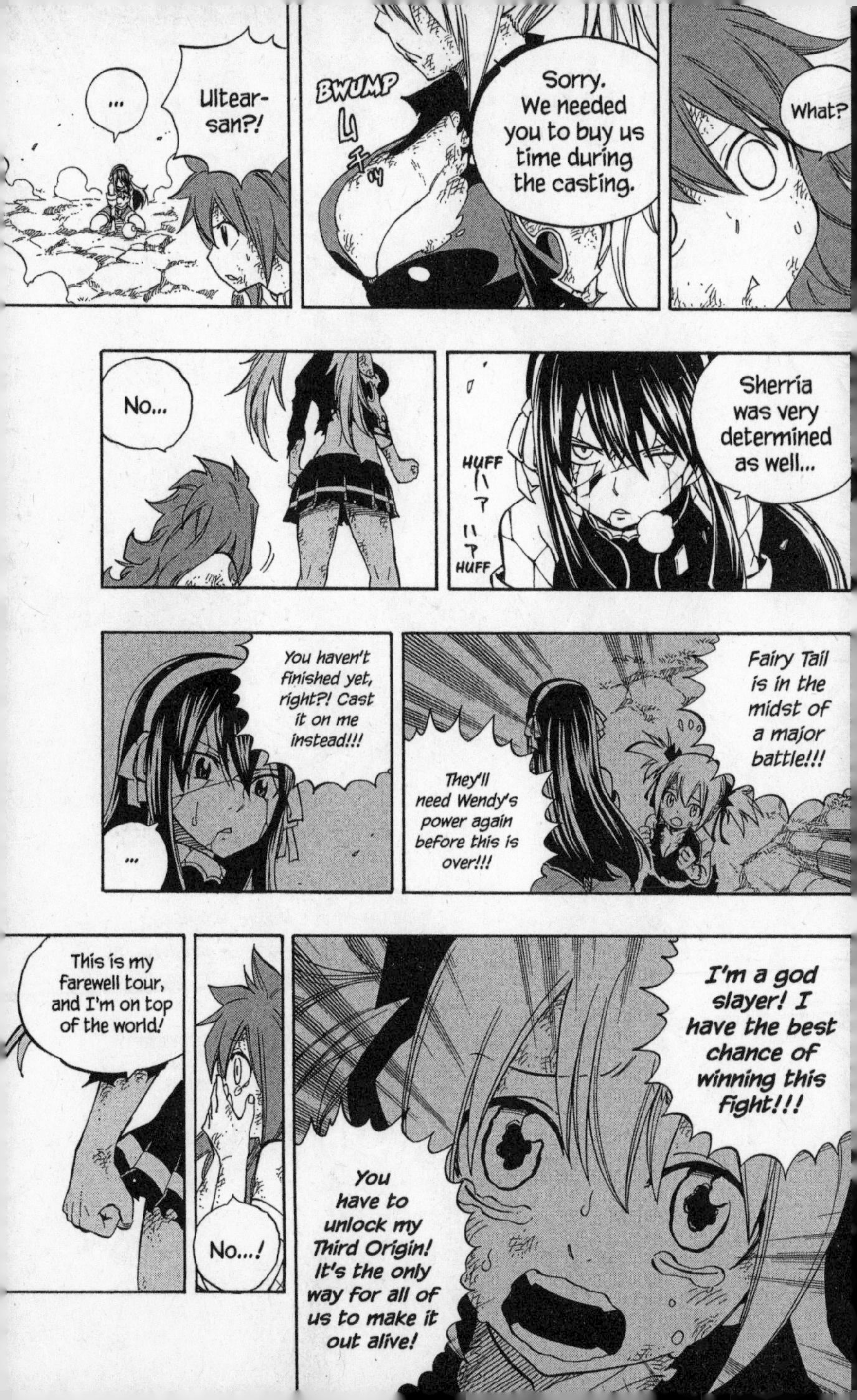
What?
BWUMP
Sorry. We needed you to buy us time during the casting.
Ultear-san?!
...
Sherria was very determined as well...
HUFF
HUFF
No...
Fairy Tail is in the midst of a major battle!!!
They'll need Wendy's power again before this is over!!!
You haven't finished yet, right?! Cast it on me instead!!!
...
I'm a god slayer! I have the best chance of winning this fight!!!
You have to unlock my Third Origin! It's the only way for all of us to make it out alive!
No...!
This is my farewell tour, and I'm on top of the world!

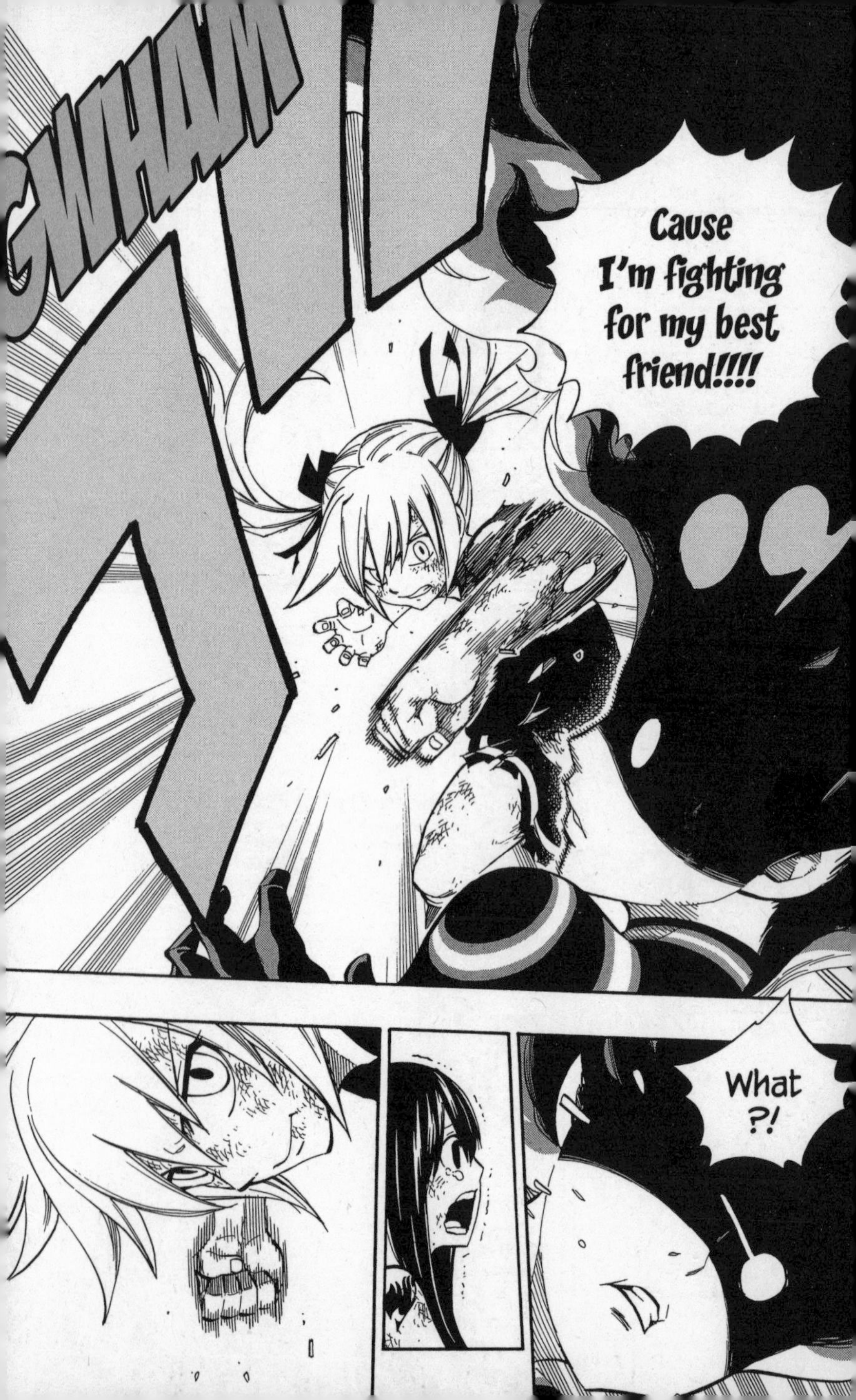
Cause I'm fighting for my best friend!!!!
GWHAM
What ?!

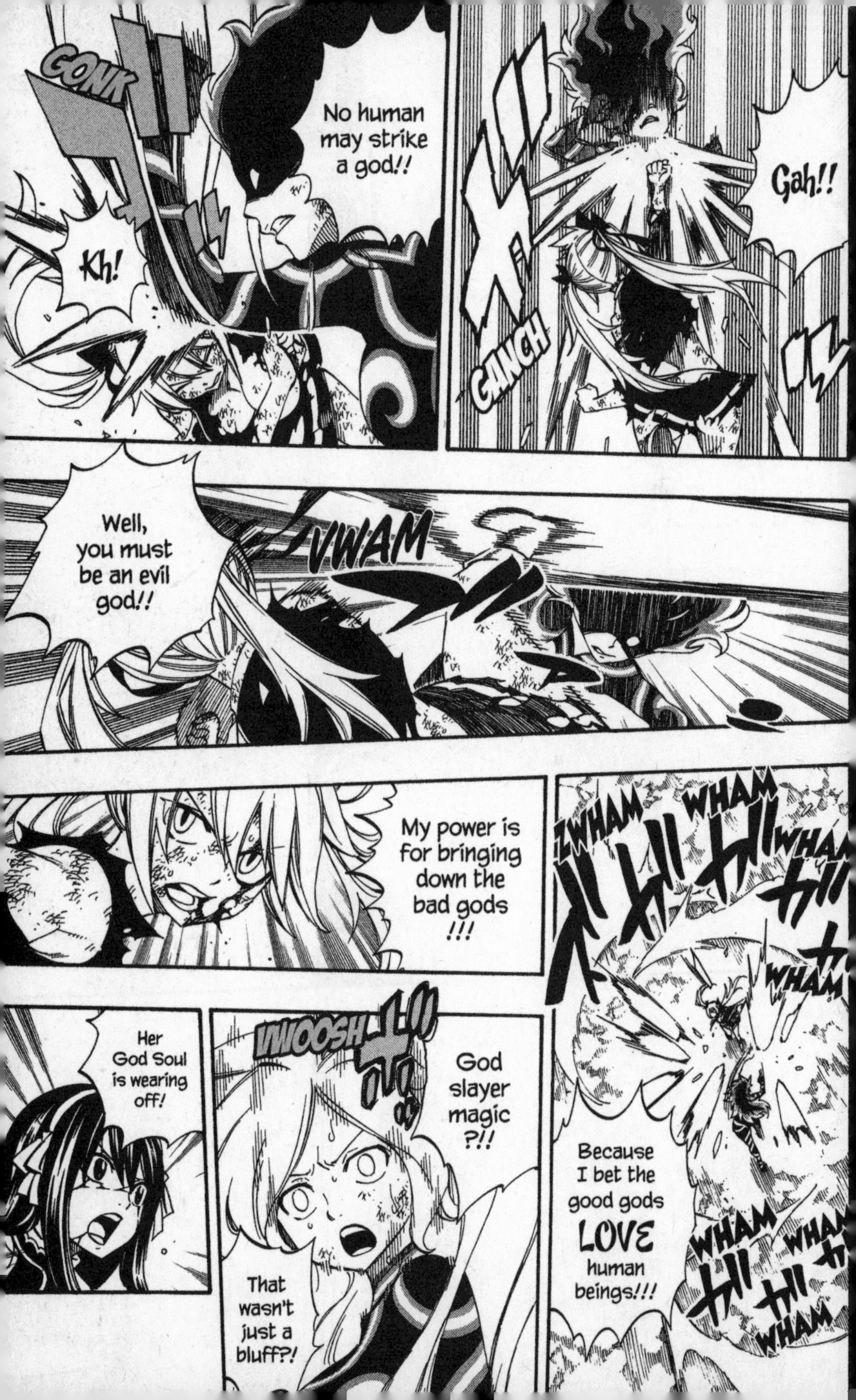
Gah!!
CANCH
GONK
No human may strike a god!!
Kh!
Well, you must be an evil god!!
VWAM
My power is for bringing down the bad gods !!!
WHAM
WHAM
WHAM
WHAM
Because I bet the good gods LOVE human beings!!!
WHAM
WHAM
WHAM
VWOOSH
God slayer magic ?!!
That wasn't just a bluff?!
Her God Soul is wearing off!

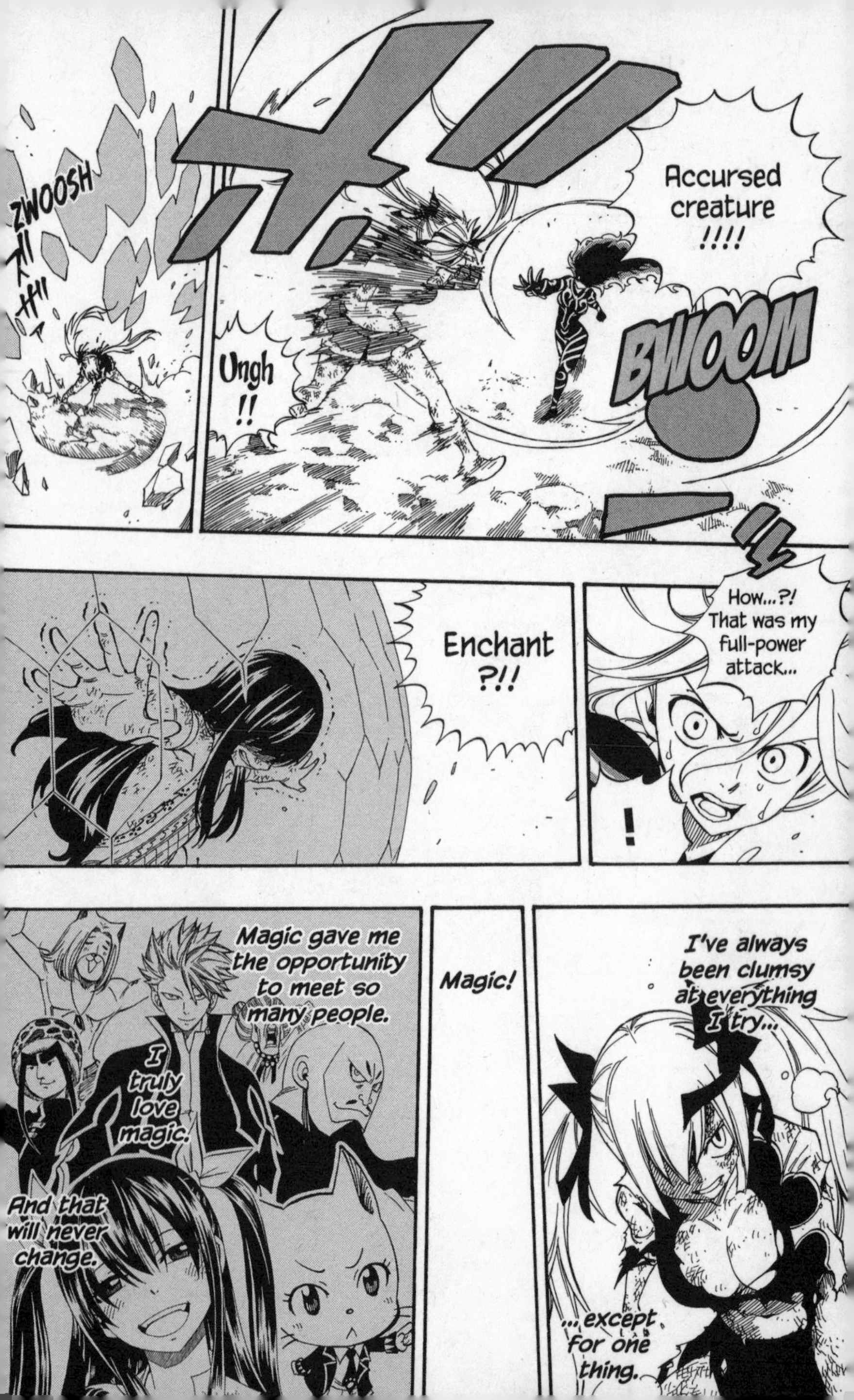
Accursed creature !!!!
BWOOM
Ungh !!
ZWOOSH
How...?! That was my full-power attack...
!
Enchant ?!!
I've always been clumsy at everything I try...
...except for one thing.
Magic!
Magic gave me the opportunity to meet so many people.
I truly love magic.
And that will never change.

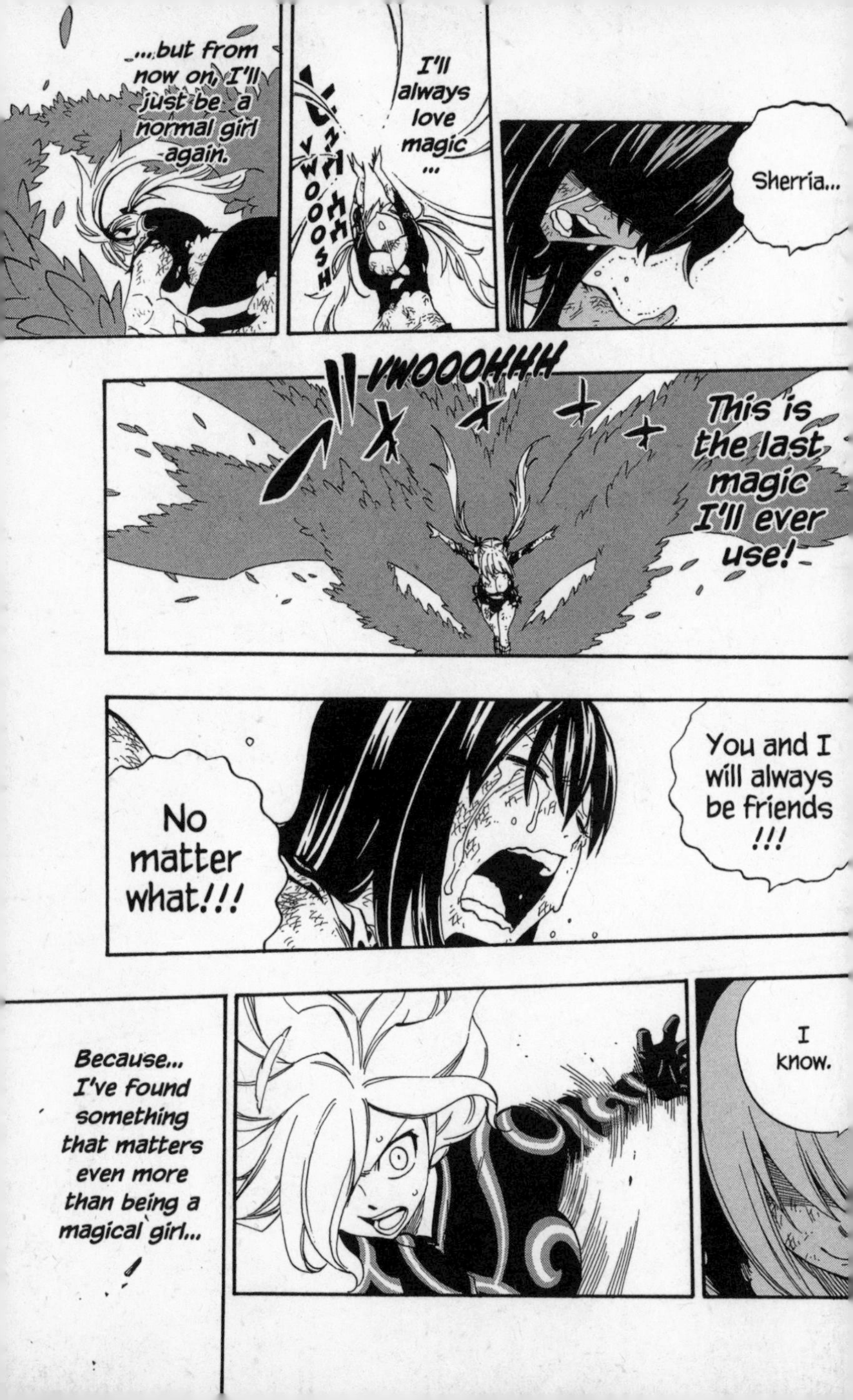
Sherria...
VWOOOSH
I'll always love magic...
...but from now on, I'll just be a normal girl again.
VWOOOHHH
This is the last magic I'll ever use!
You and I will always be friends!!!
No matter what!!!
I know.
Because... I've found something that matters even more than being a magical girl...

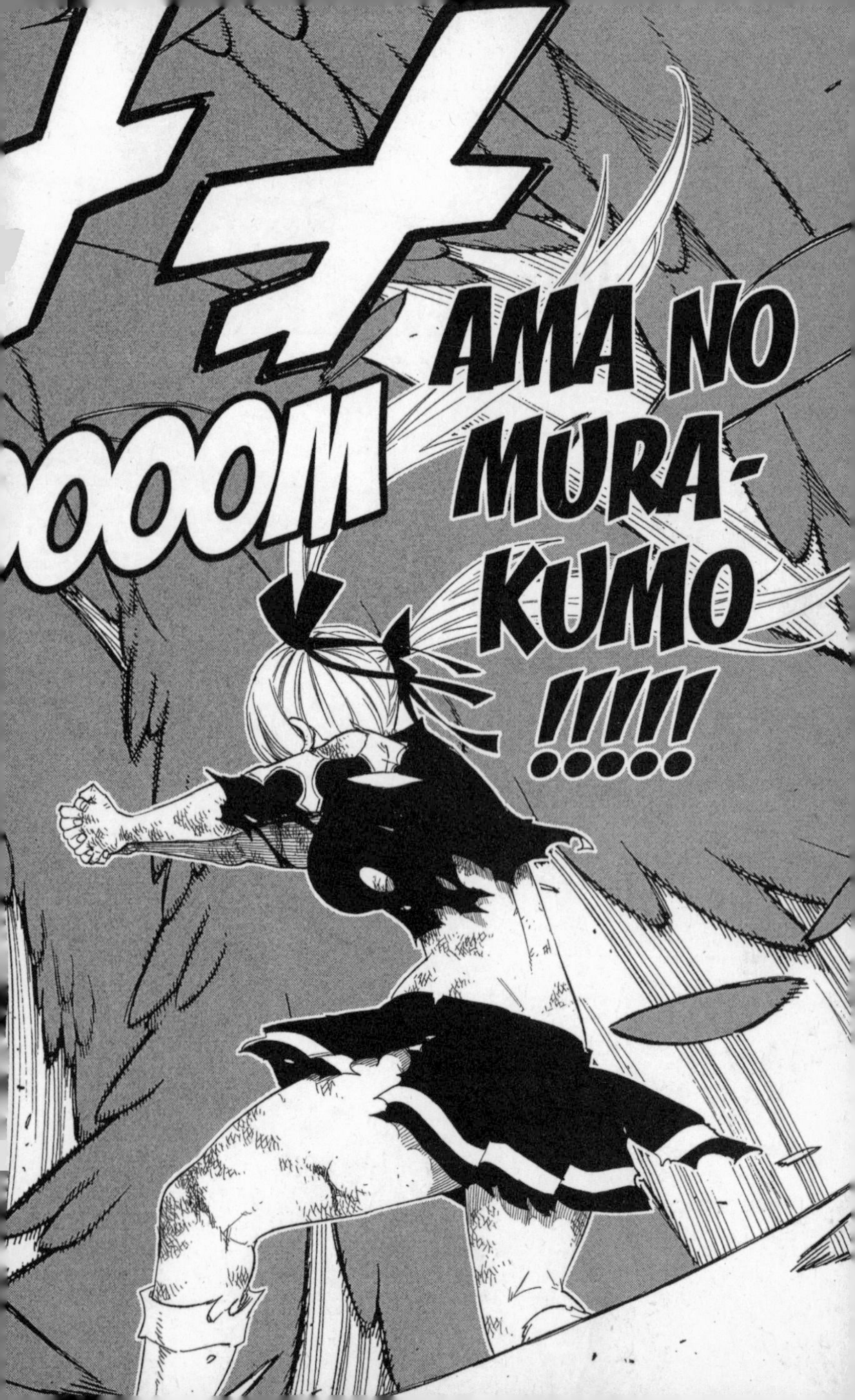
AMA NO MURA-KUMO!!!!!
OOOM

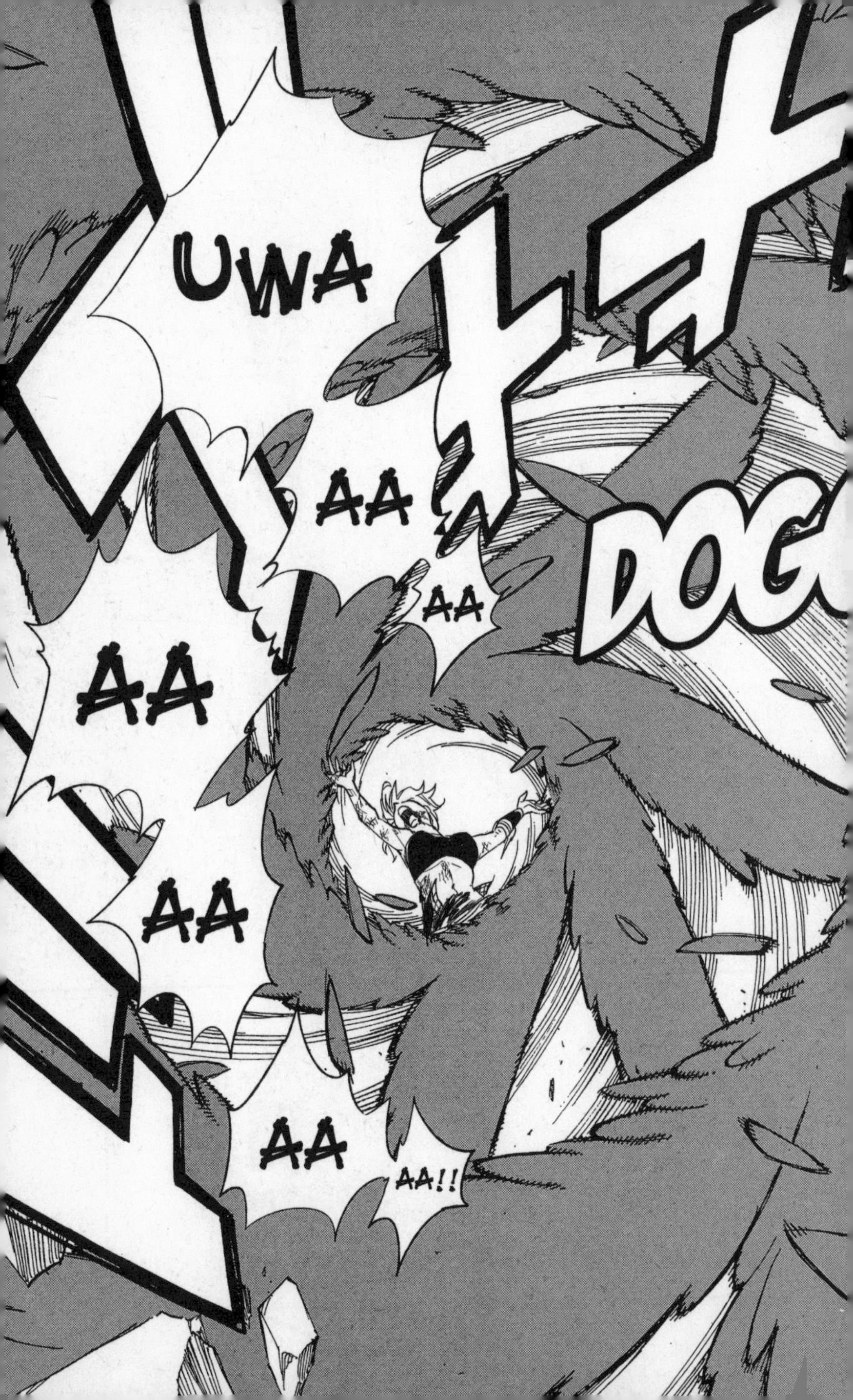
UWA
AA
AA
AA
AA
AA
AA!!
DOG

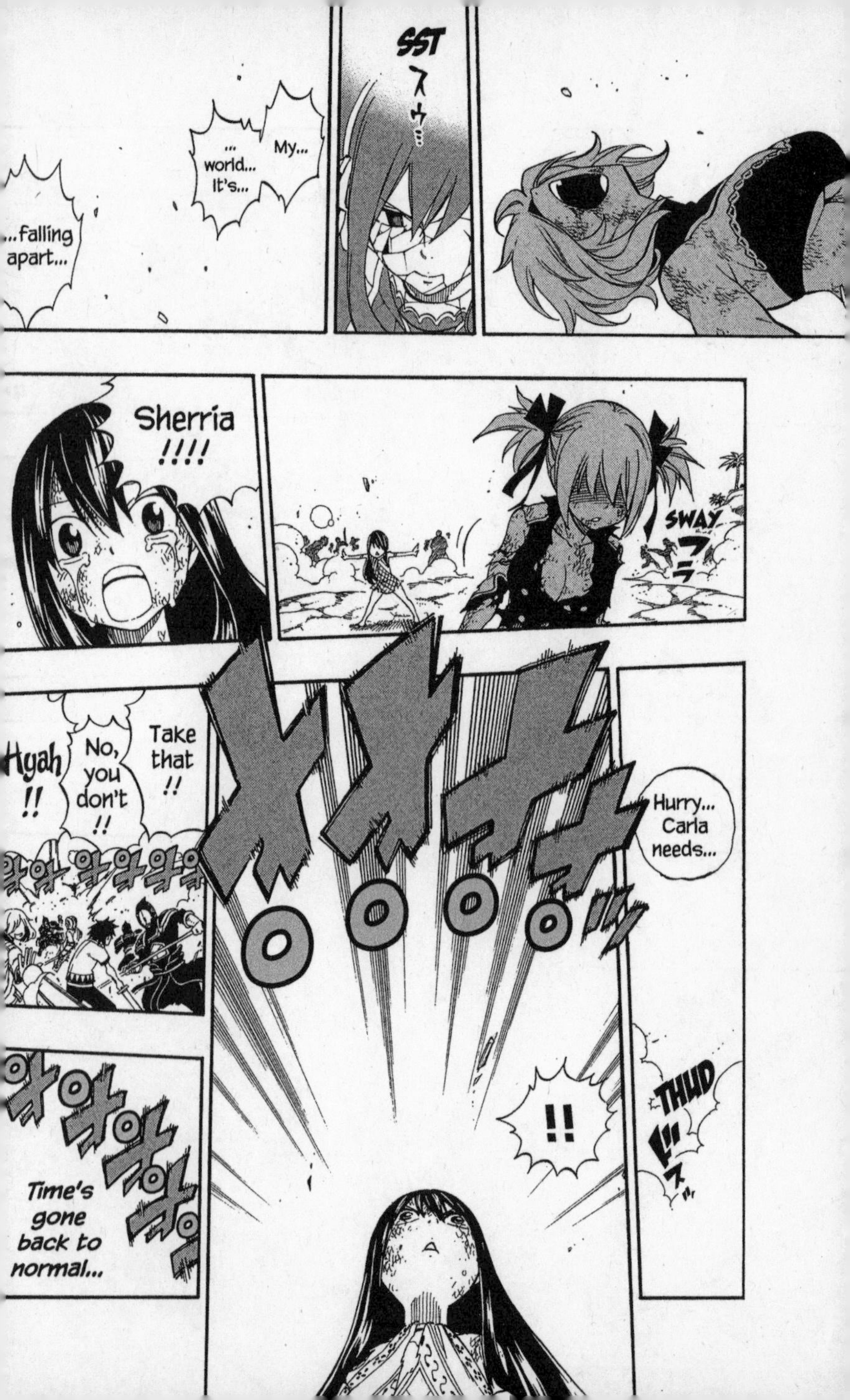
SST
My...
... world... It's...
...falling apart...
SWAY
Sherria !!!!
Hurry... Carla needs...
Take that !!
No, you don't !!
Hyah !!
THUD
!!
Time's gone back to normal...

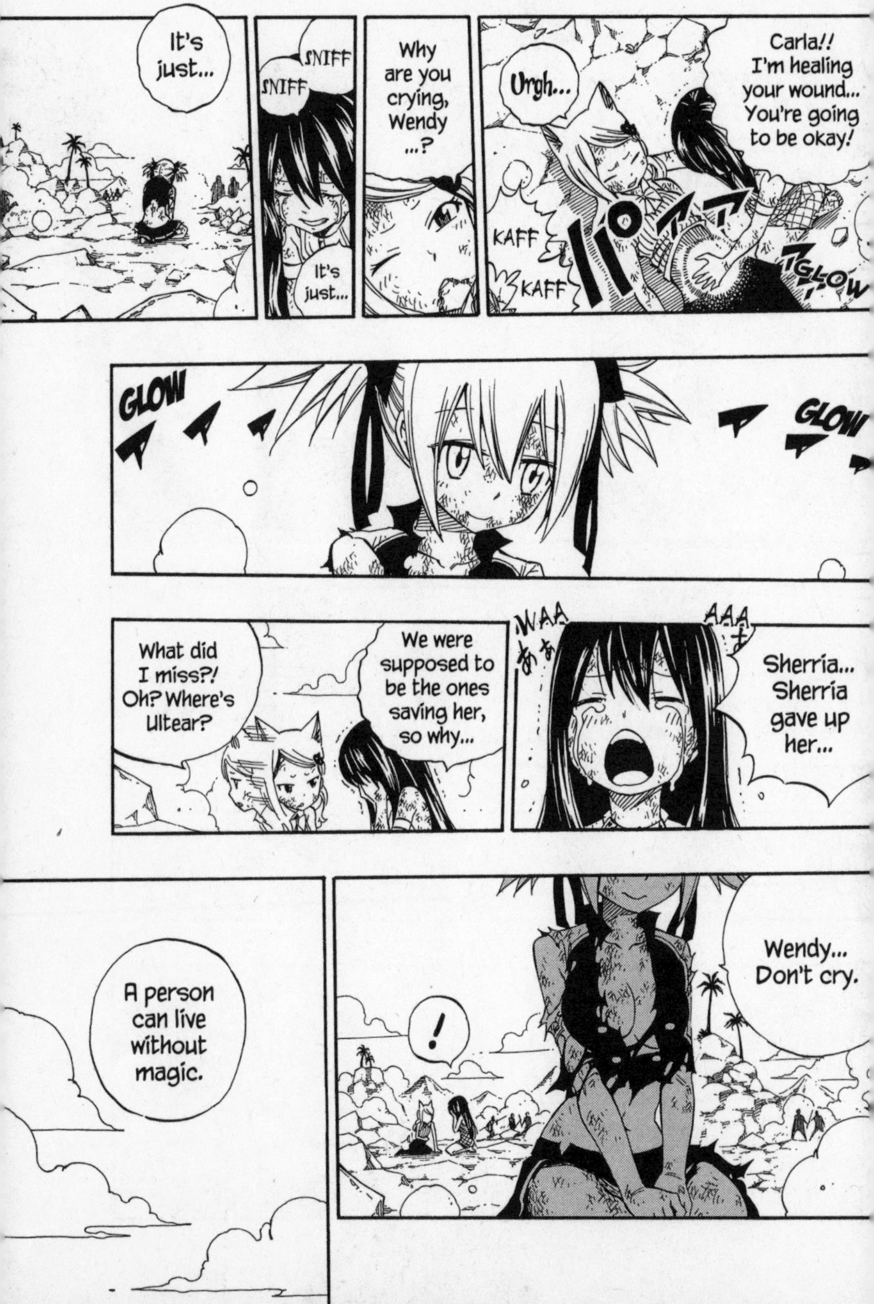
Carla!! I'm healing your wound... You're going to be okay!
Urgh...
KAFF
KAFF
GLOW
Why are you crying, Wendy ...?
SNIFF
SNIFF
It's just...
It's just...
GLOW
GLOW
WAA
AAA
Sherria... Sherria gave up her...
We were supposed to be the ones saving her, so why...
What did I miss?! Oh? Where's Ultear?
Wendy... Don't cry.
!
A person can live without magic.

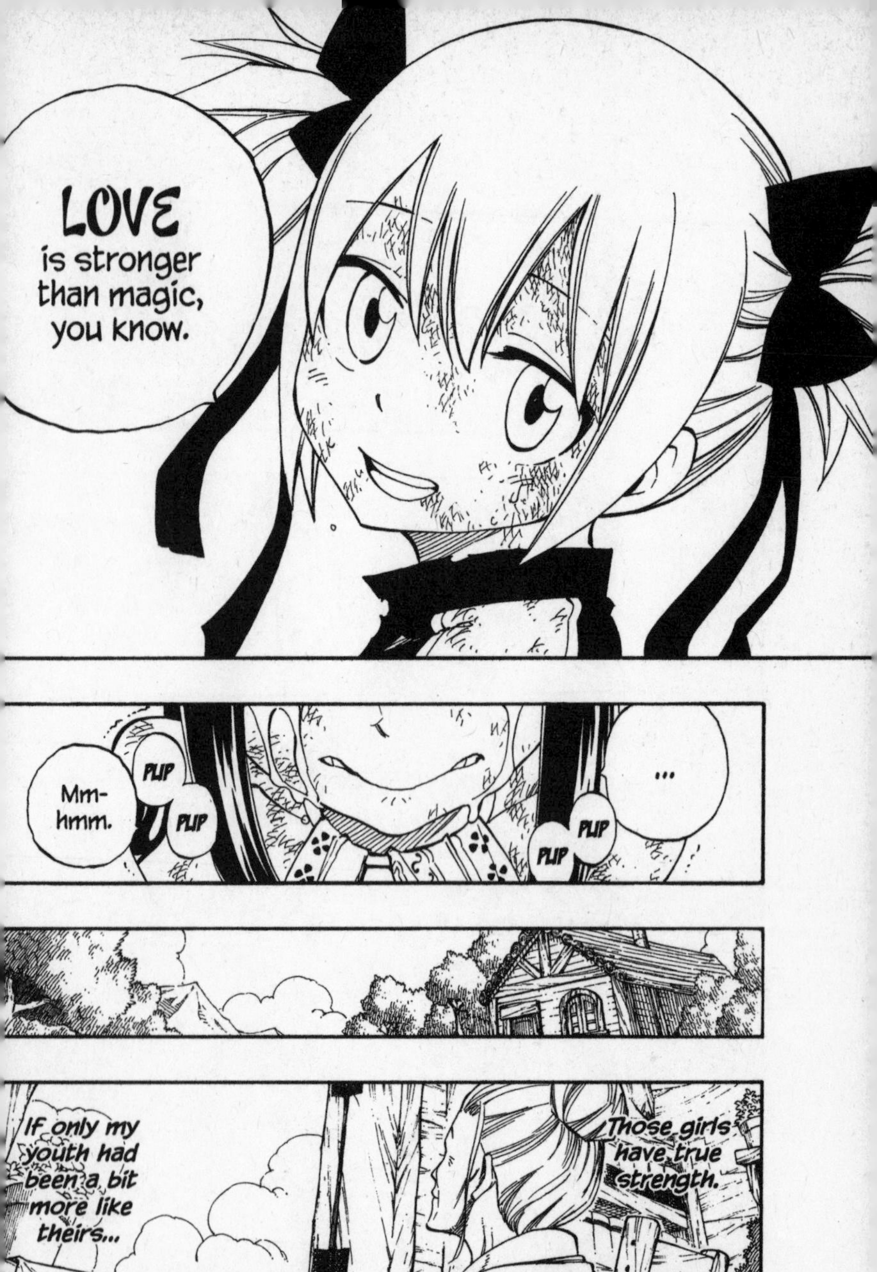
LOVE is stronger than magic, you know.
...
PLIP
PLIP
PLIP
PLIP
Mm-hmm.
Those girls have true strength.
If only my youth had been a bit more like theirs...

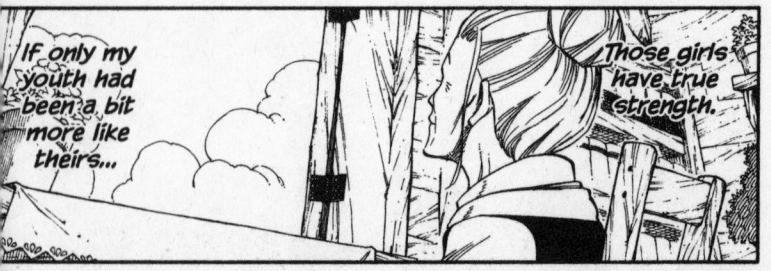

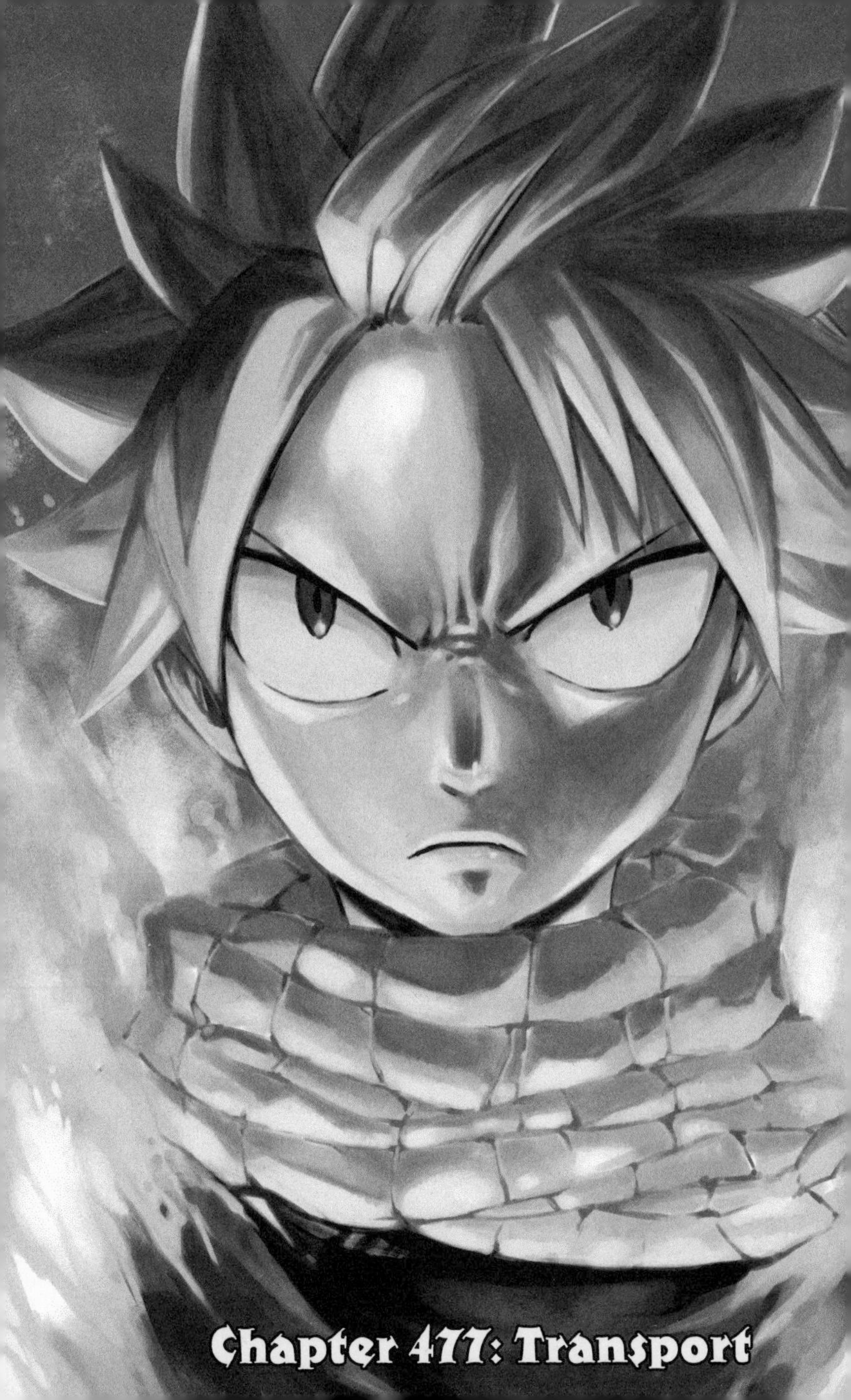

Chapter 477: Transport

FAIRY TAIL
フェアリーテイル

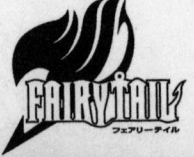

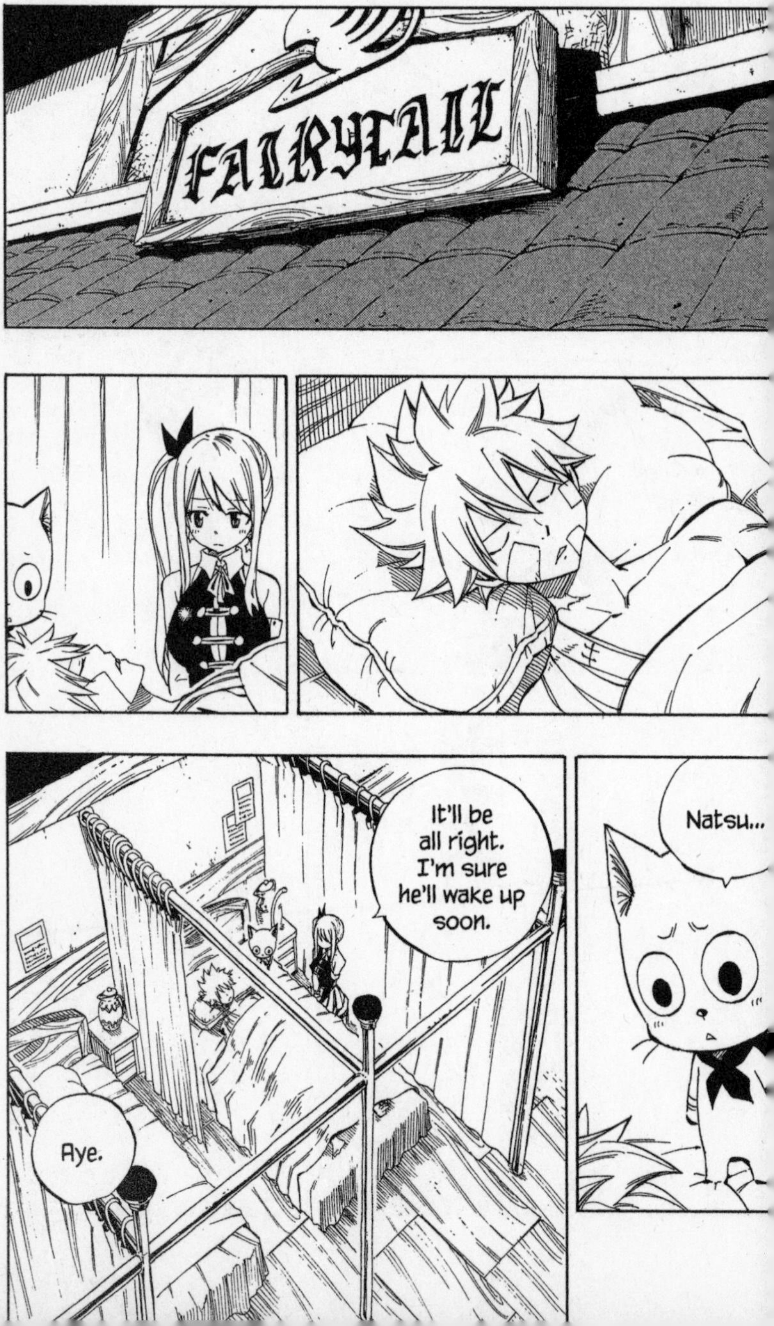
FAIRY TAIL
Natsu...
It'll be all right. I'm sure he'll wake up soon.
Aye.

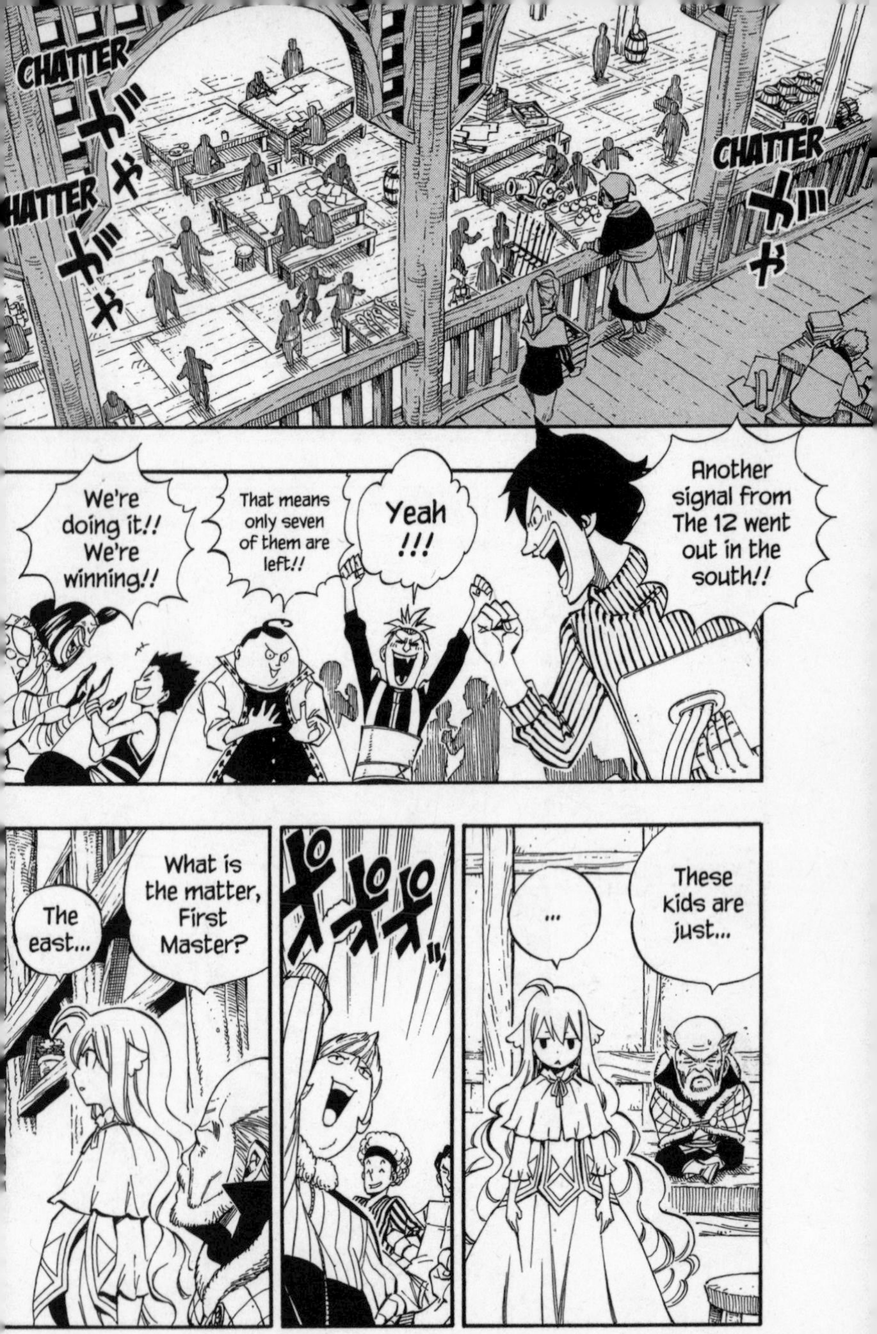
CHATTER
CHATTER
CHATTER
Another signal from The 12 went out in the south!!
Yeah!!!
That means only seven of them are left!!
We're doing it!! We're winning!!
These kids are just...
...
What is the matter, First Master?
The east...

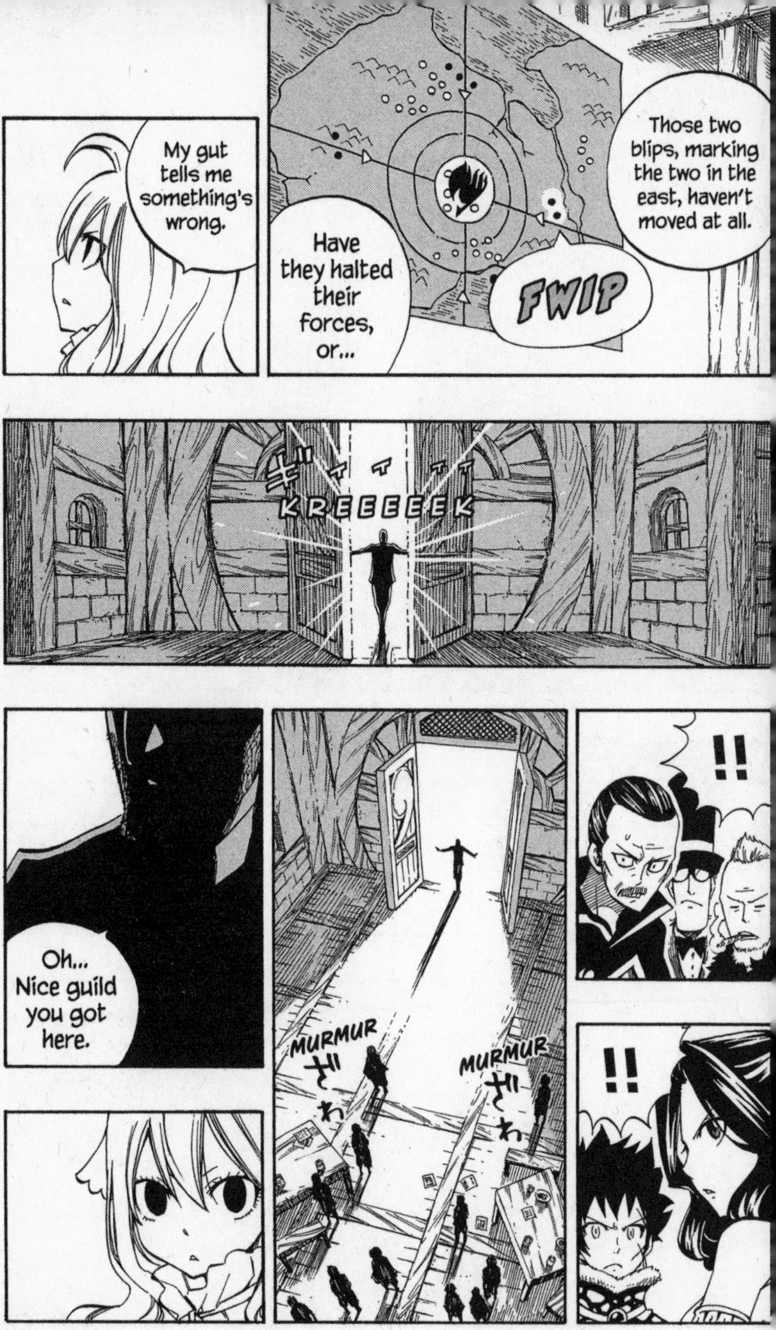
Those two blips, marking the two in the east, haven't moved at all.
FWIP
Have they halted their forces, or...
My gut tells me something's wrong.
KREEEEEEK
!!
!!
MURMUR
MURMUR
Oh... Nice guild you got here.

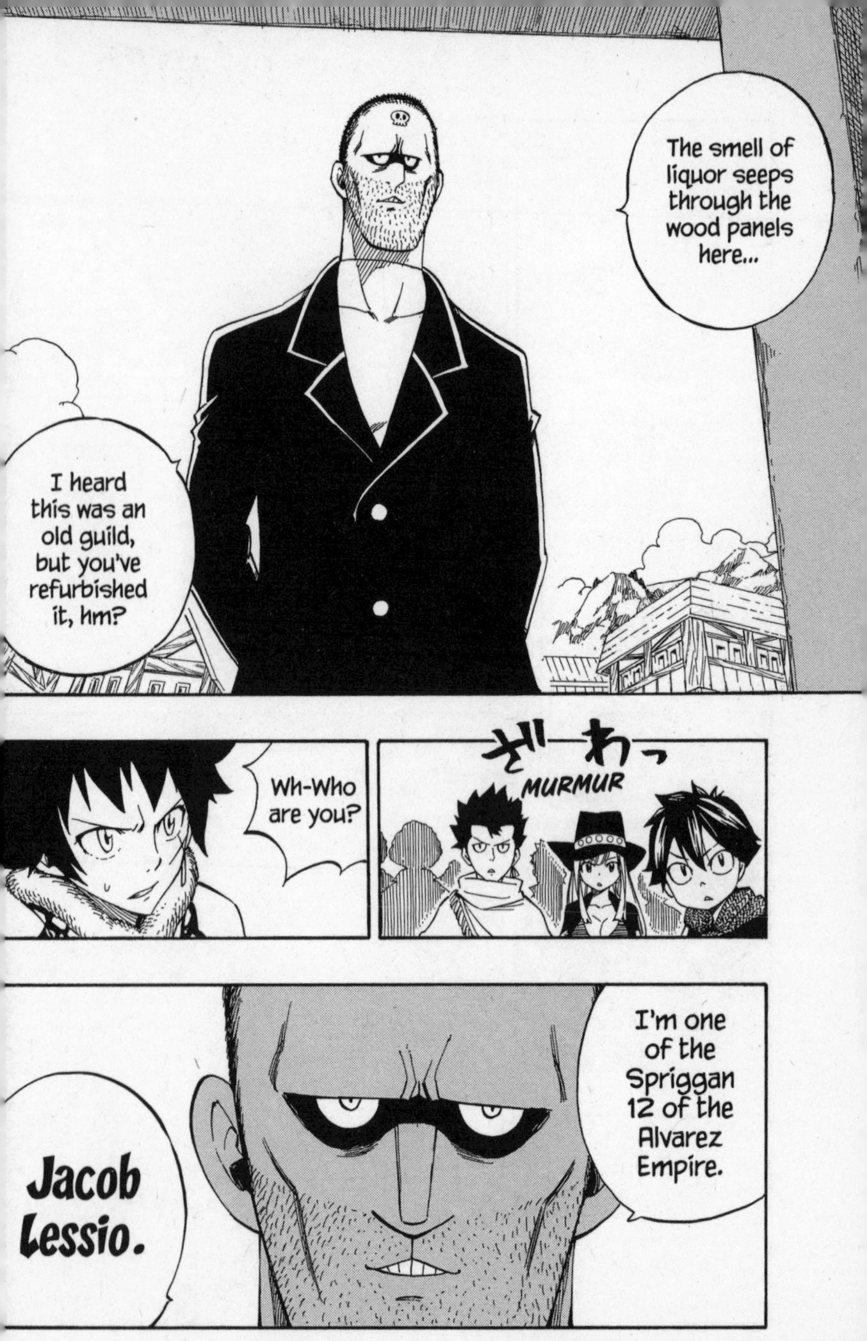
The smell of liquor seeps through the wood panels here...
I heard this was an old guild, but you've refurbished it, hm?
ざわっ
MURMUR
Wh-Who are you?
I'm one of the Spriggan 12 of the Alvarez Empire.
Jacob Lessio.

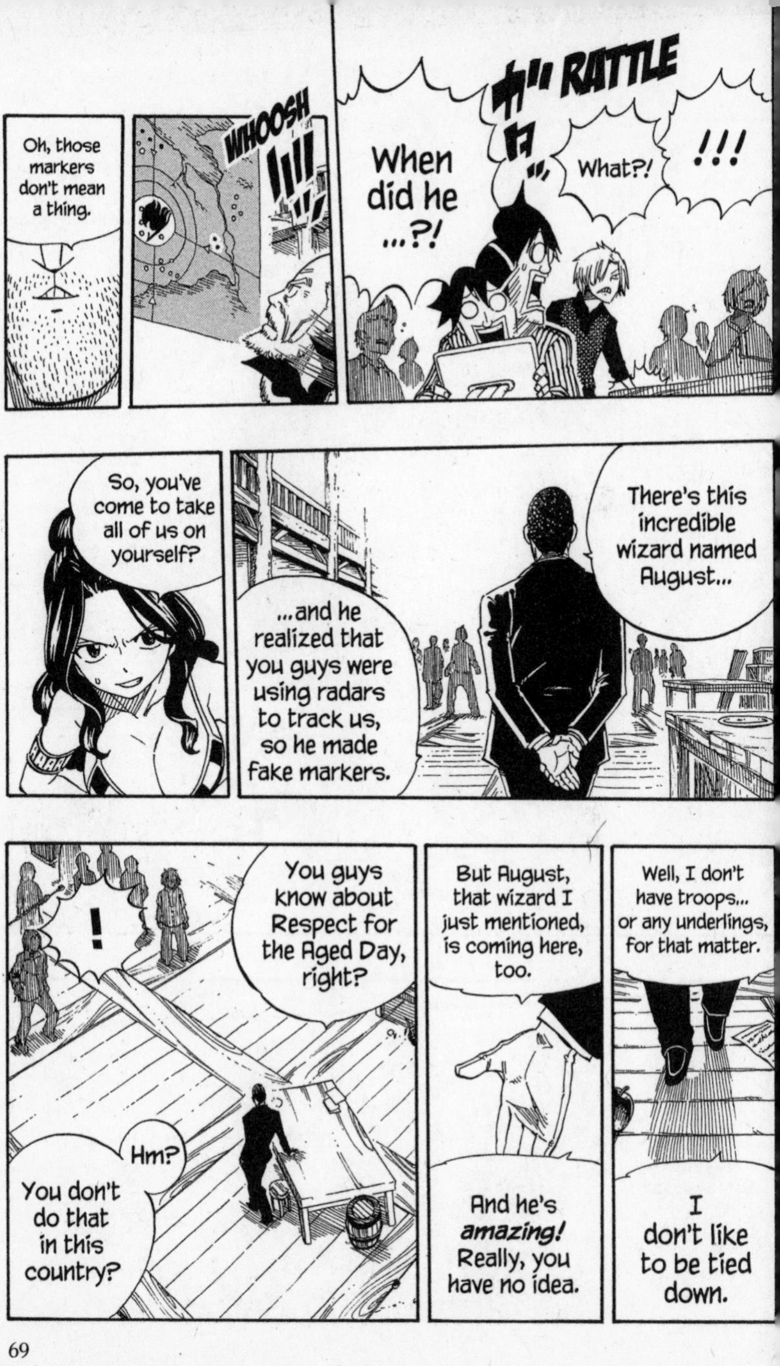
RATTLE
!!!
What?!
When did he ...?!
WHOOSH
Oh, those markers don't mean a thing.
There's this incredible wizard named August...
...and he realized that you guys were using radars to track us, so he made fake markers.
So, you've come to take all of us on yourself?
Well, I don't have troops... or any underlings, for that matter.
I don't like to be tied down.
But August, that wizard I just mentioned, is coming here, too.
And he's *amazing!* Really, you have no idea.
You guys know about Respect for the Aged Day, right?
!
Hm?
You don't do that in this country?

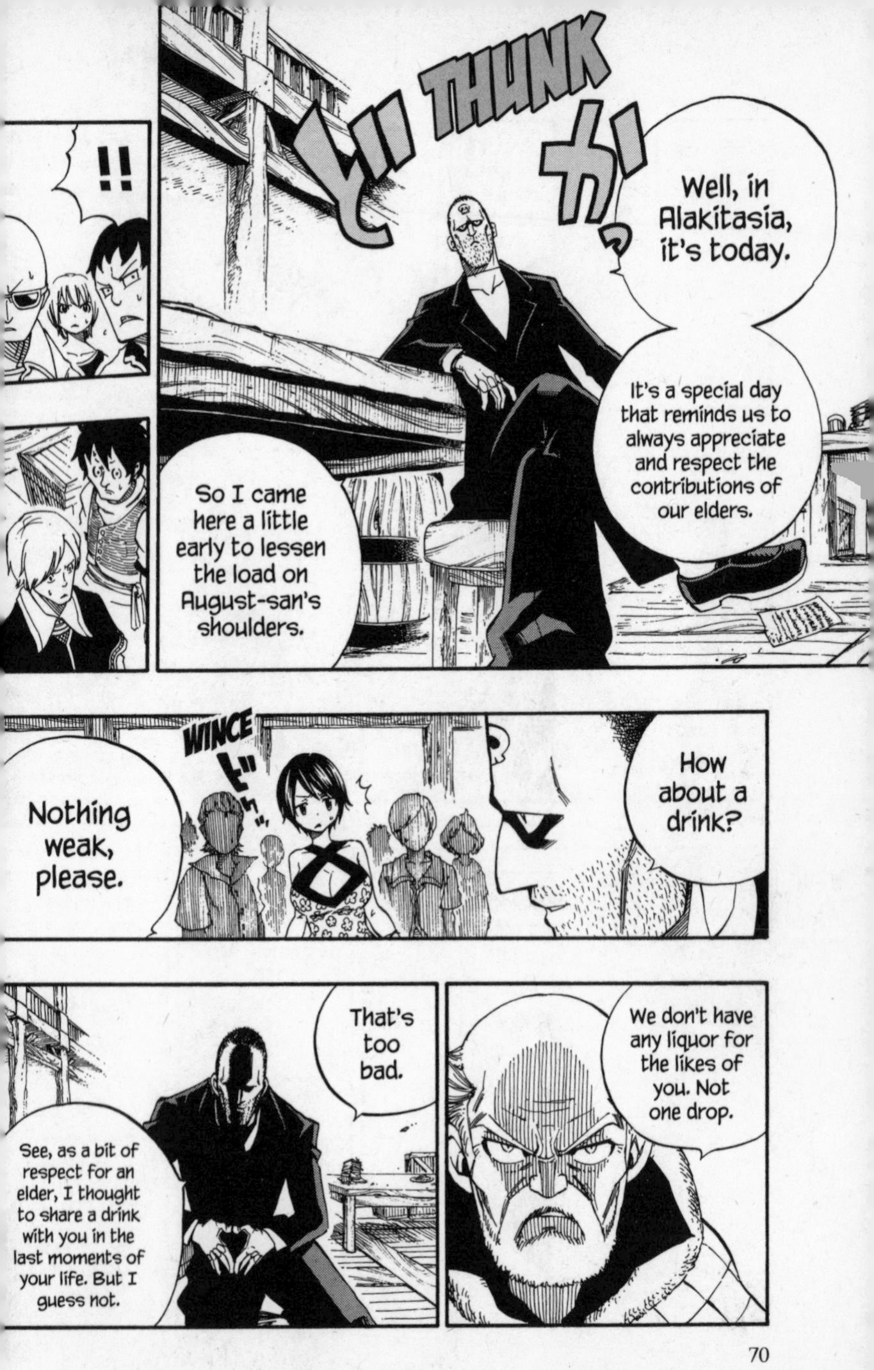
THUNK
Well, in Alakitasia, it's today.
It's a special day that reminds us to always appreciate and respect the contributions of our elders.
So I came here a little early to lessen the load on August-san's shoulders.
!!
How about a drink?
WINCE
Nothing weak, please.
We don't have any liquor for the likes of you. Not one drop.
That's too bad.
See, as a bit of respect for an elder, I thought to share a drink with you in the last moments of your life. But I guess not.

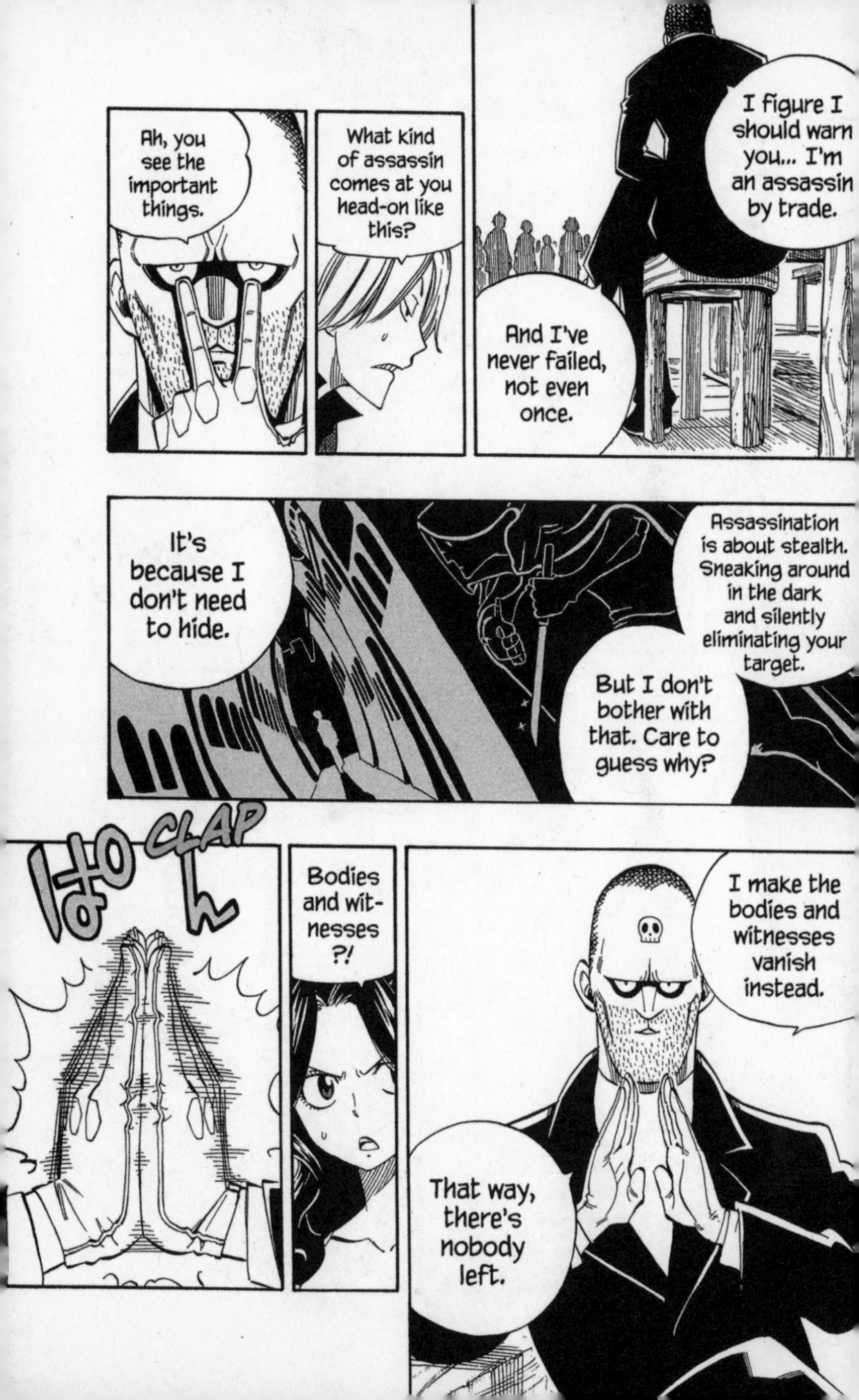
I figure I should warn you... I'm an assassin by trade.
And I've never failed, not even once.
What kind of assassin comes at you head-on like this?
Ah, you see the important things.
Assassination is about stealth. Sneaking around in the dark and silently eliminating your target.
But I don't bother with that. Care to guess why?
It's because I don't need to hide.
I make the bodies and witnesses vanish instead.
That way, there's nobody left.
Bodies and wit-nesses ?!
ぱん
CLAP

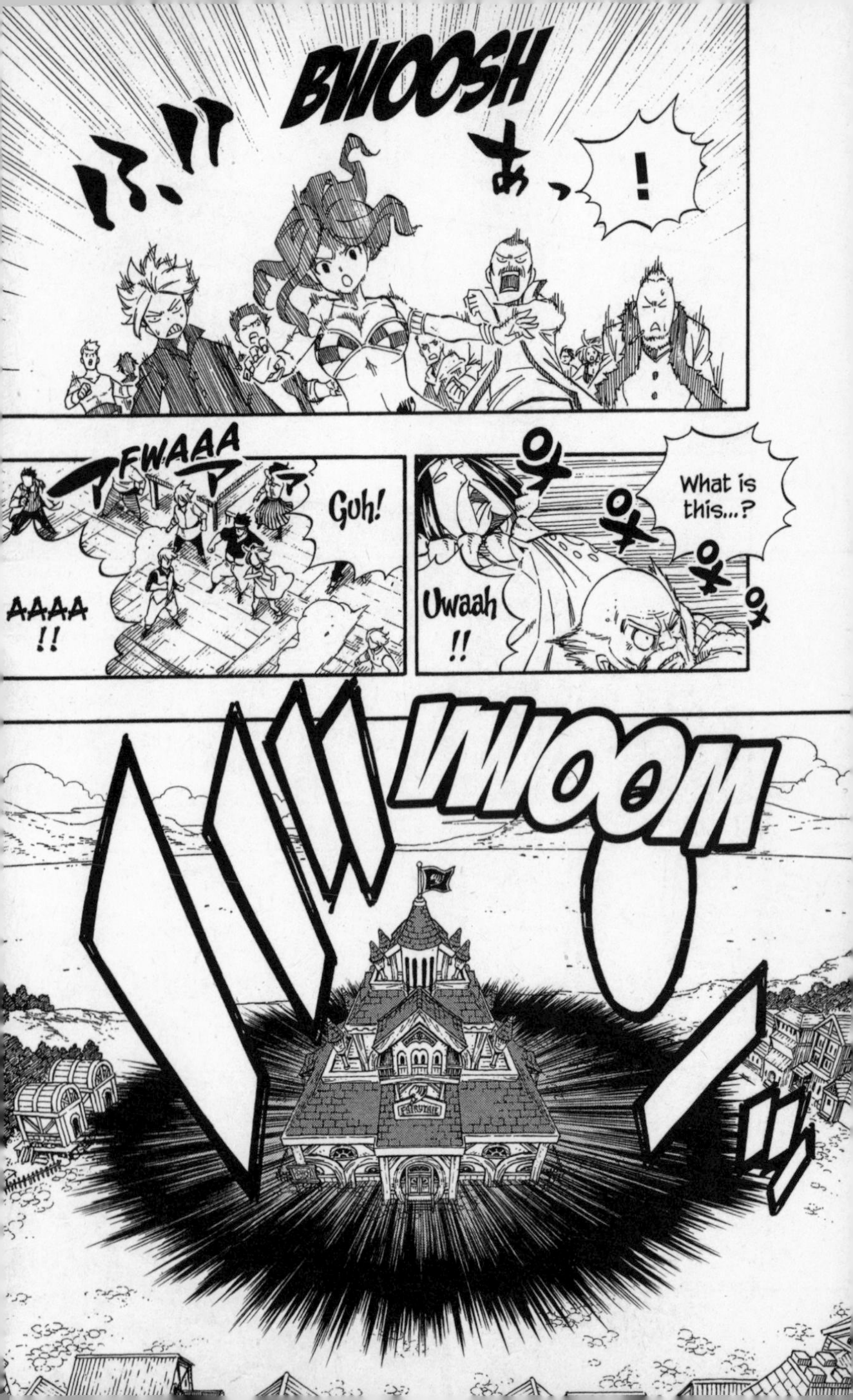
!
あっ
BWOOSH
ふ!!
What is this...?
Uwaah !!
Guh!
FWAAA
AAAA !!
VWOOM

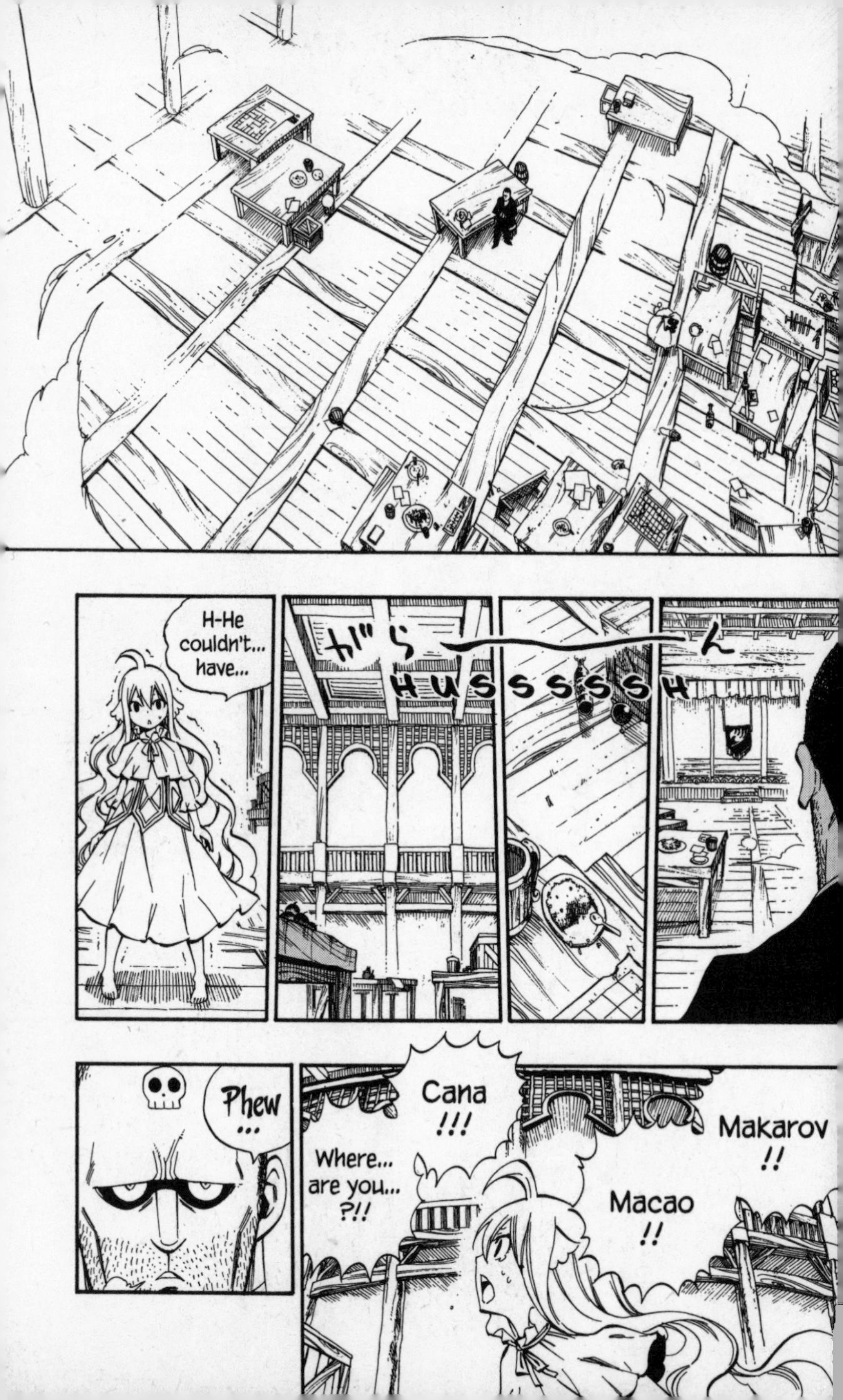

がら————ん
HUSSSSSSH
H-He couldn't... have...
Makarov !!
Cana !!!
Macao !!
Where... are you... ?!!
Phew ...

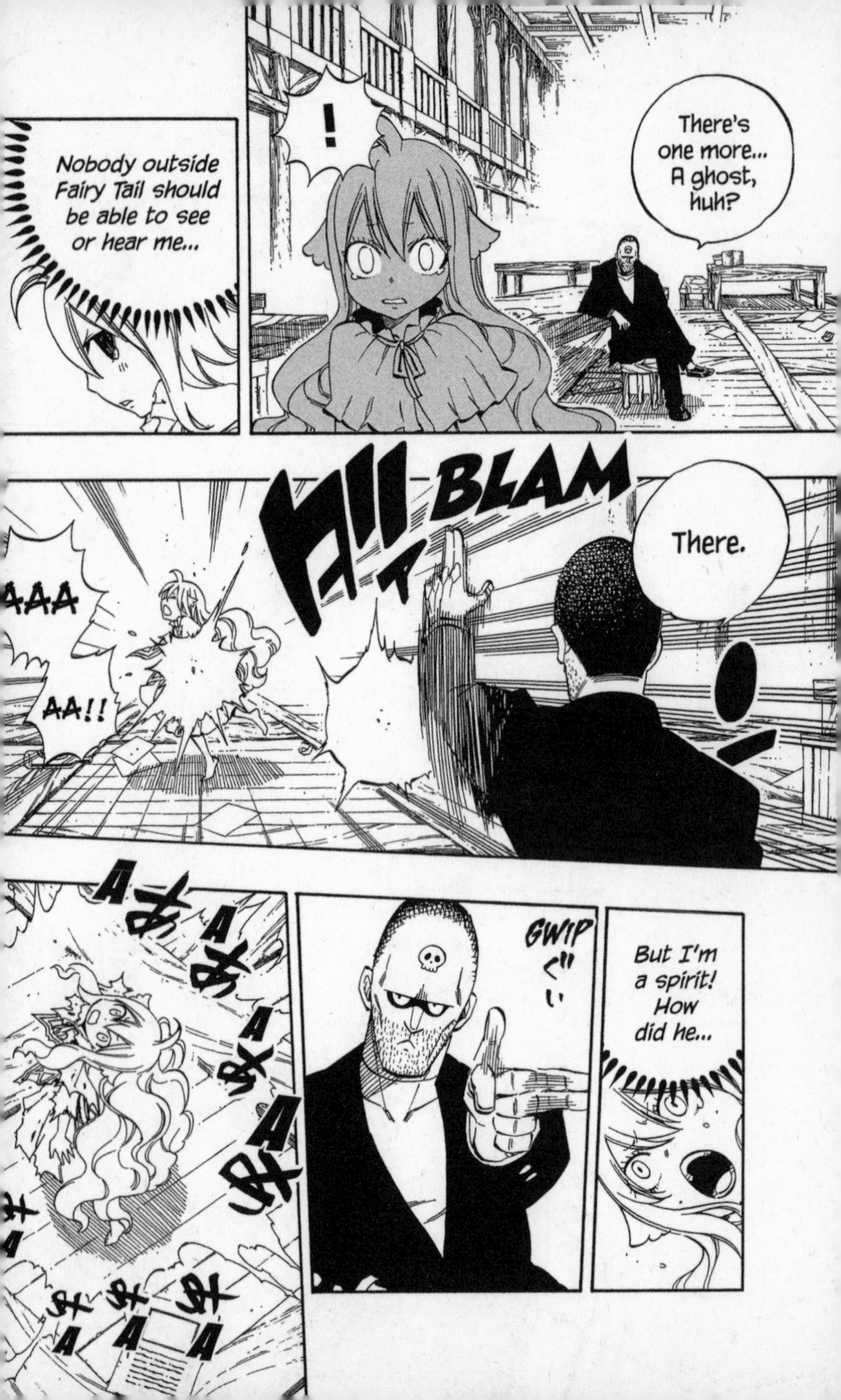
There's one more... A ghost, huh?
!
Nobody outside Fairy Tail should be able to see or hear me...
There.
BLAM
AAA
AA!!
But I'm a spirit! How did he...
GWIP
ぐい

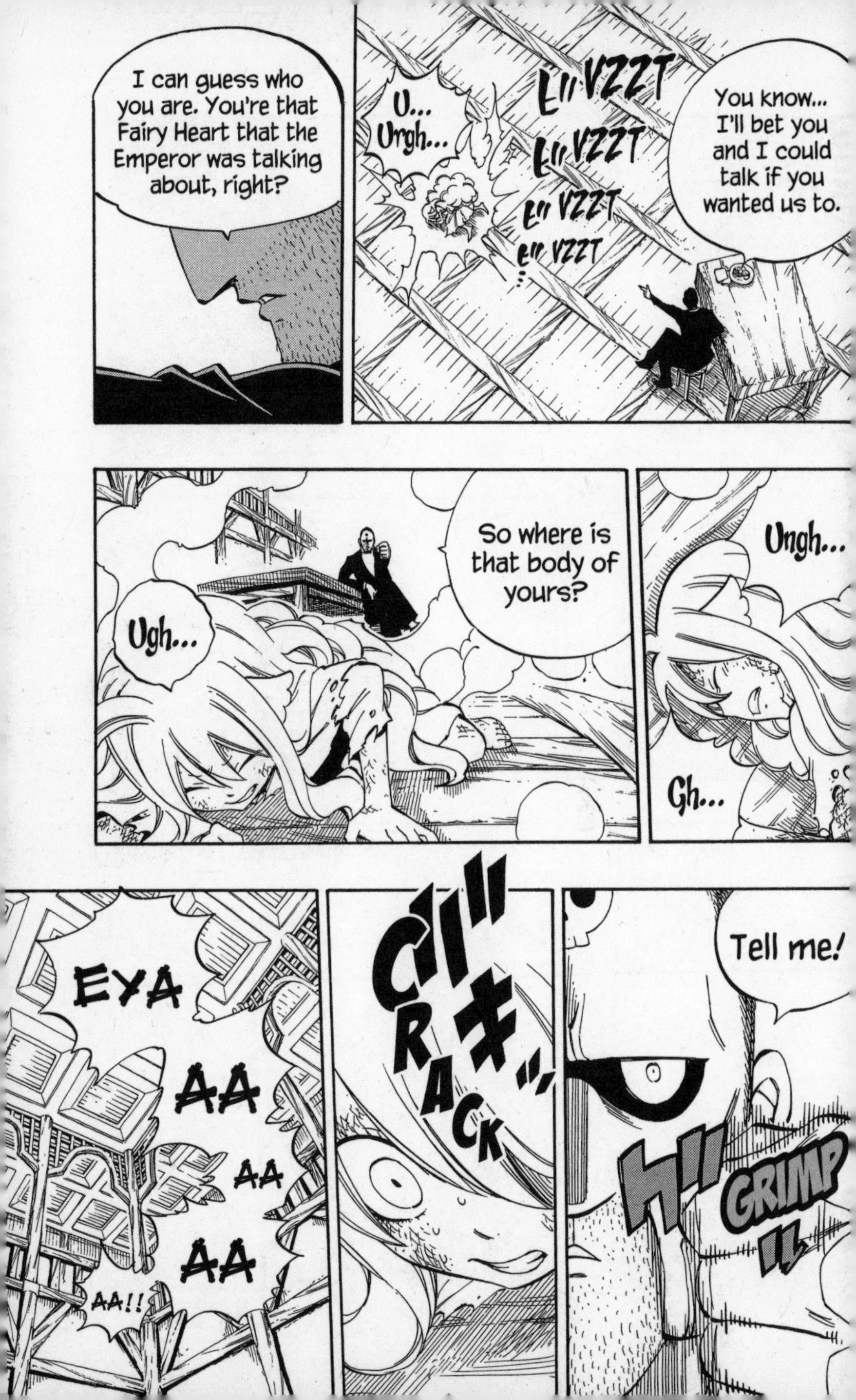

U... Urgh...
VZZT
VZZT
VZZT
VZZT
You know... I'll bet you and I could talk if you wanted us to.
I can guess who you are. You're that Fairy Heart that the Emperor was talking about, right?
Ungh...
Gh...
So where is that body of yours?
Ugh...
Tell me!
GRIMP
CRACK
EYA
AA
AA
AA
AA!!

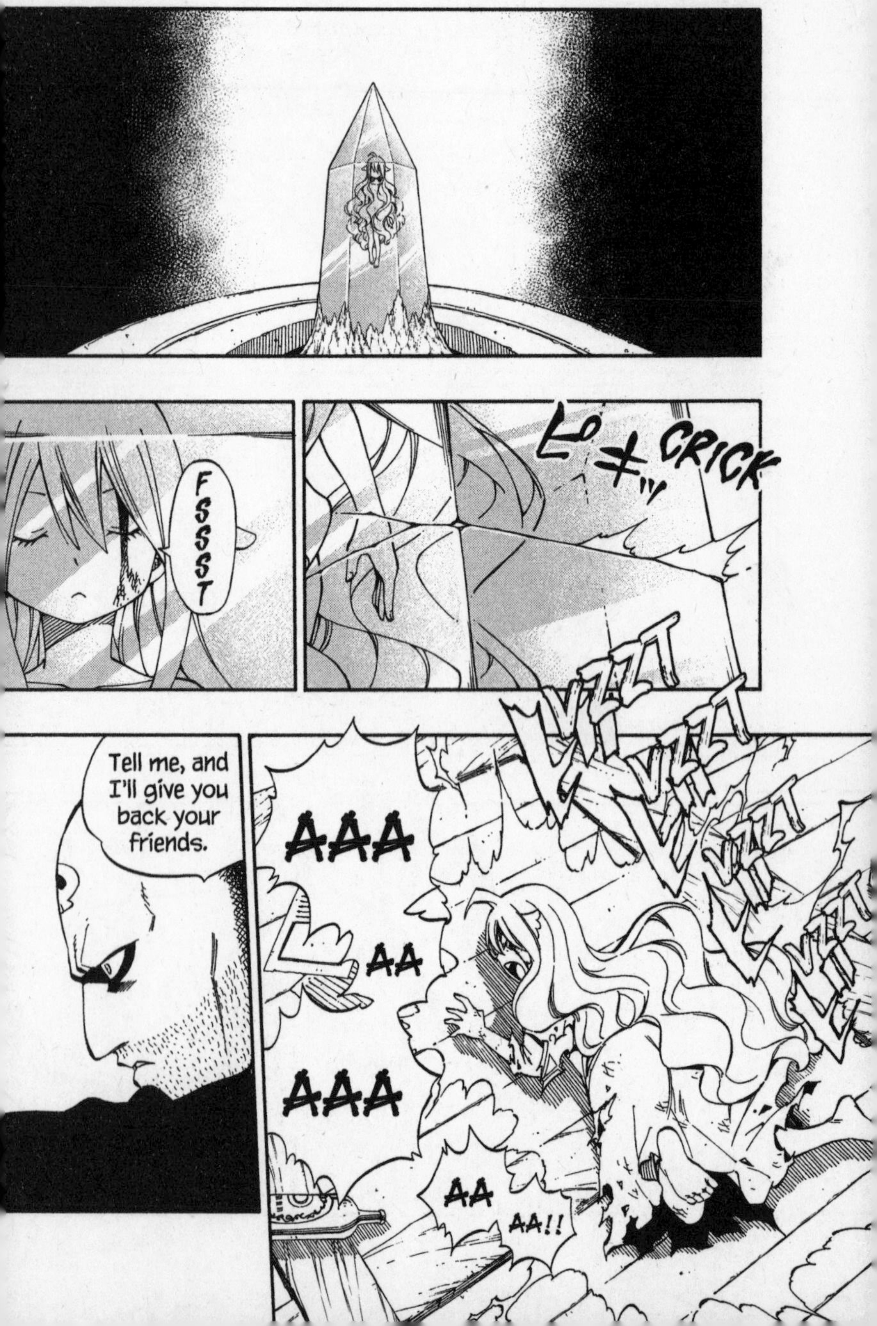
CRICK
FSSST
VZZT
VZZT
VZZT
VZZT
AAA
AA
AAA
AA
AA!!
Tell me, and I'll give you back your friends.

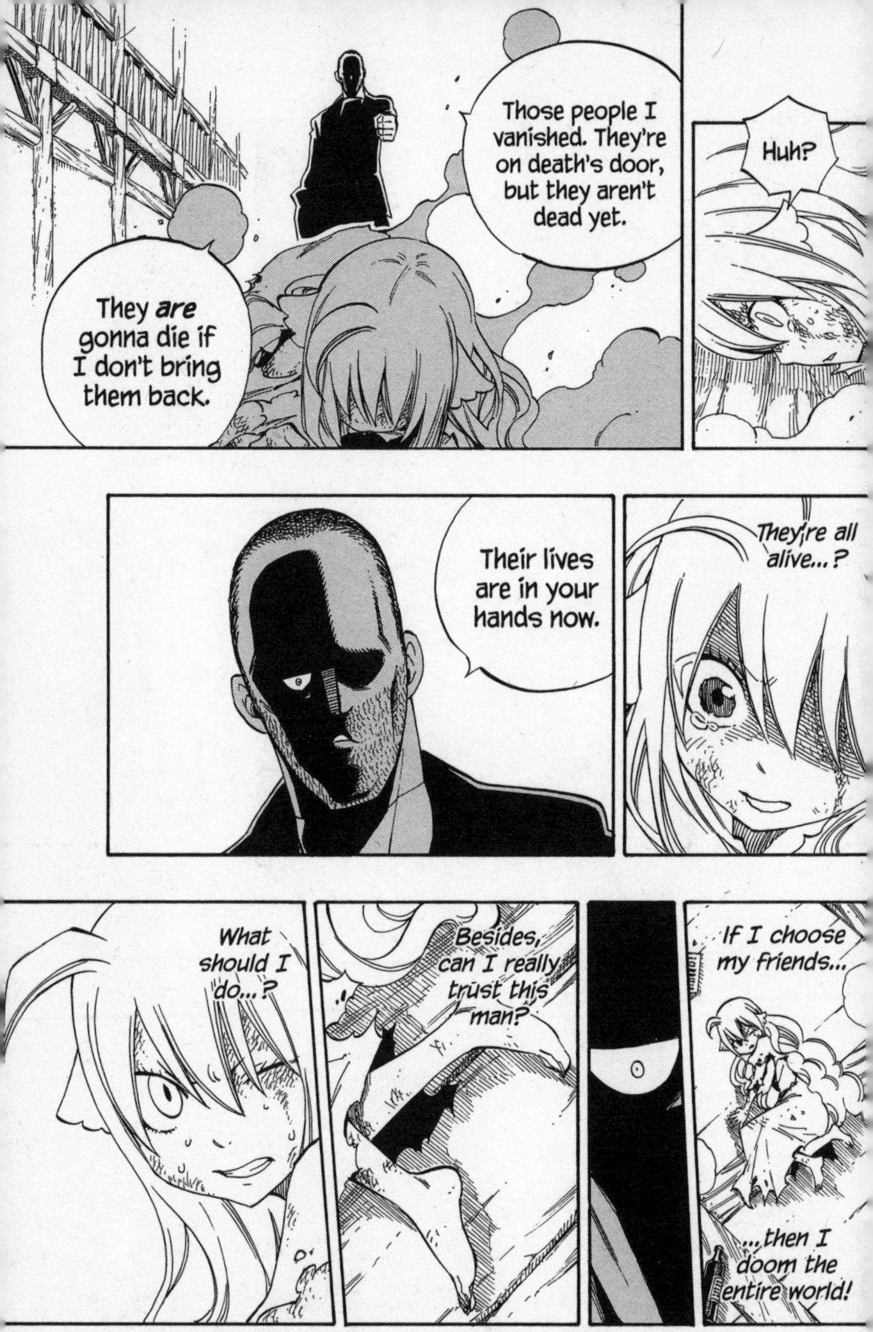

Huh?
Those people I vanished. They're on death's door, but they aren't dead yet.
They *are* gonna die if I don't bring them back.
They're all alive...?
Their lives are in your hands now.
If I choose my friends...
...then I doom the entire world!
Besides, can I really trust this man?
What should I do...?

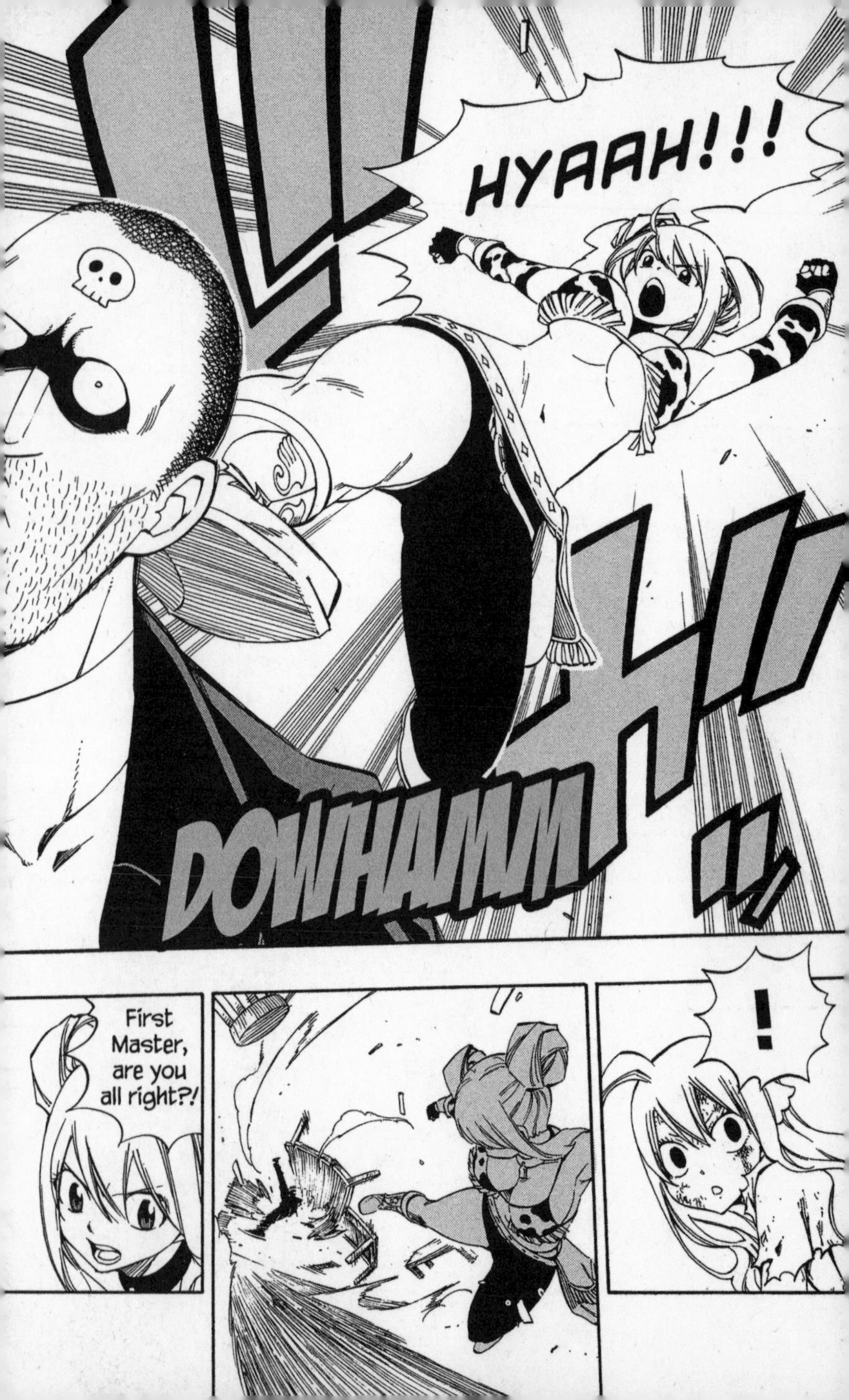
HYAAH!!!
DOWHAMM!!
!
First Master, are you all right?!

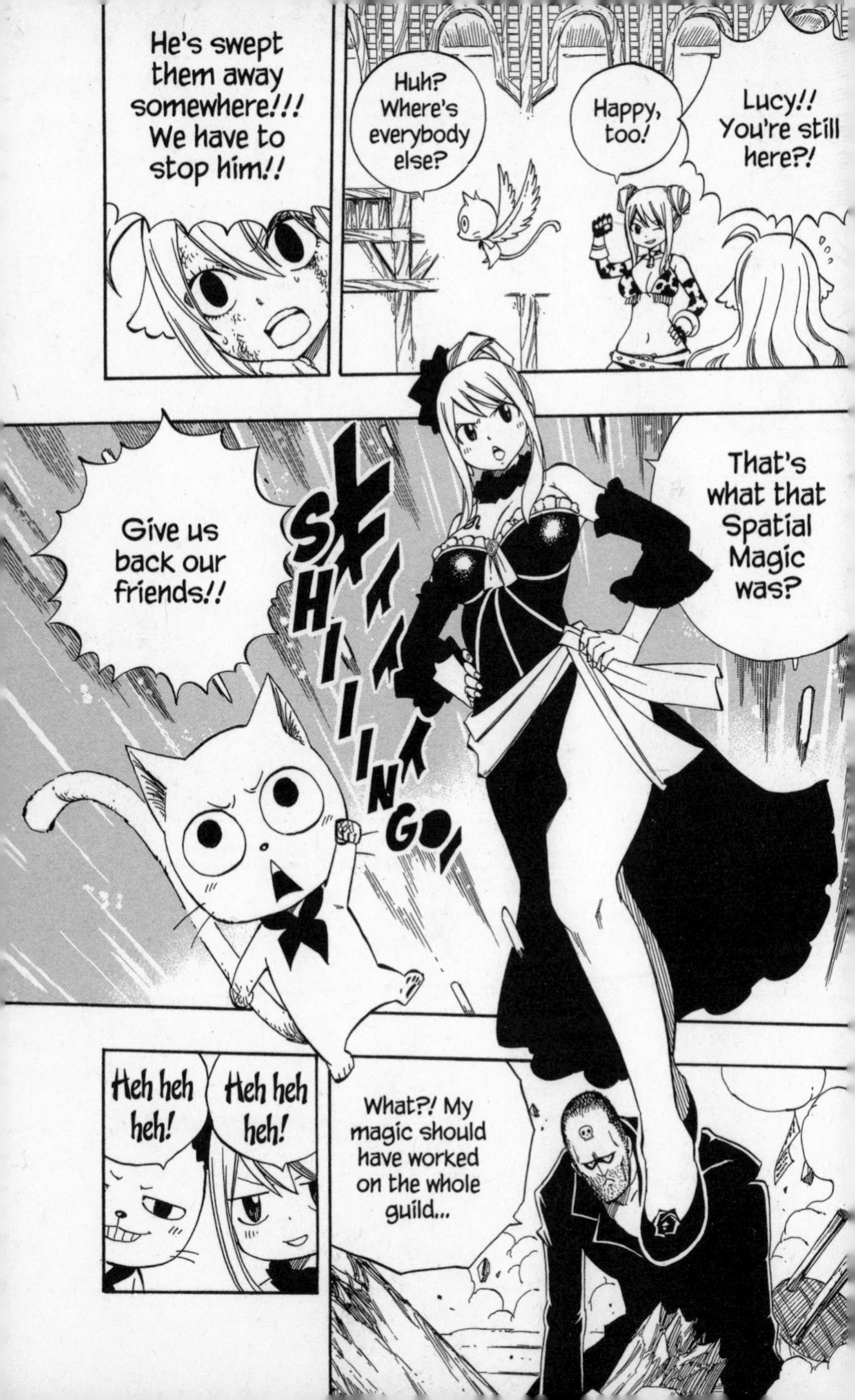
Lucy!! You're still here?!
Happy, too!
Huh? Where's everybody else?
He's swept them away somewhere!!! We have to stop him!!
That's what that Spatial Magic was?
SHIIING
Give us back our friends!!
What?! My magic should have worked on the whole guild...
Heh heh heh!
Heh heh heh!

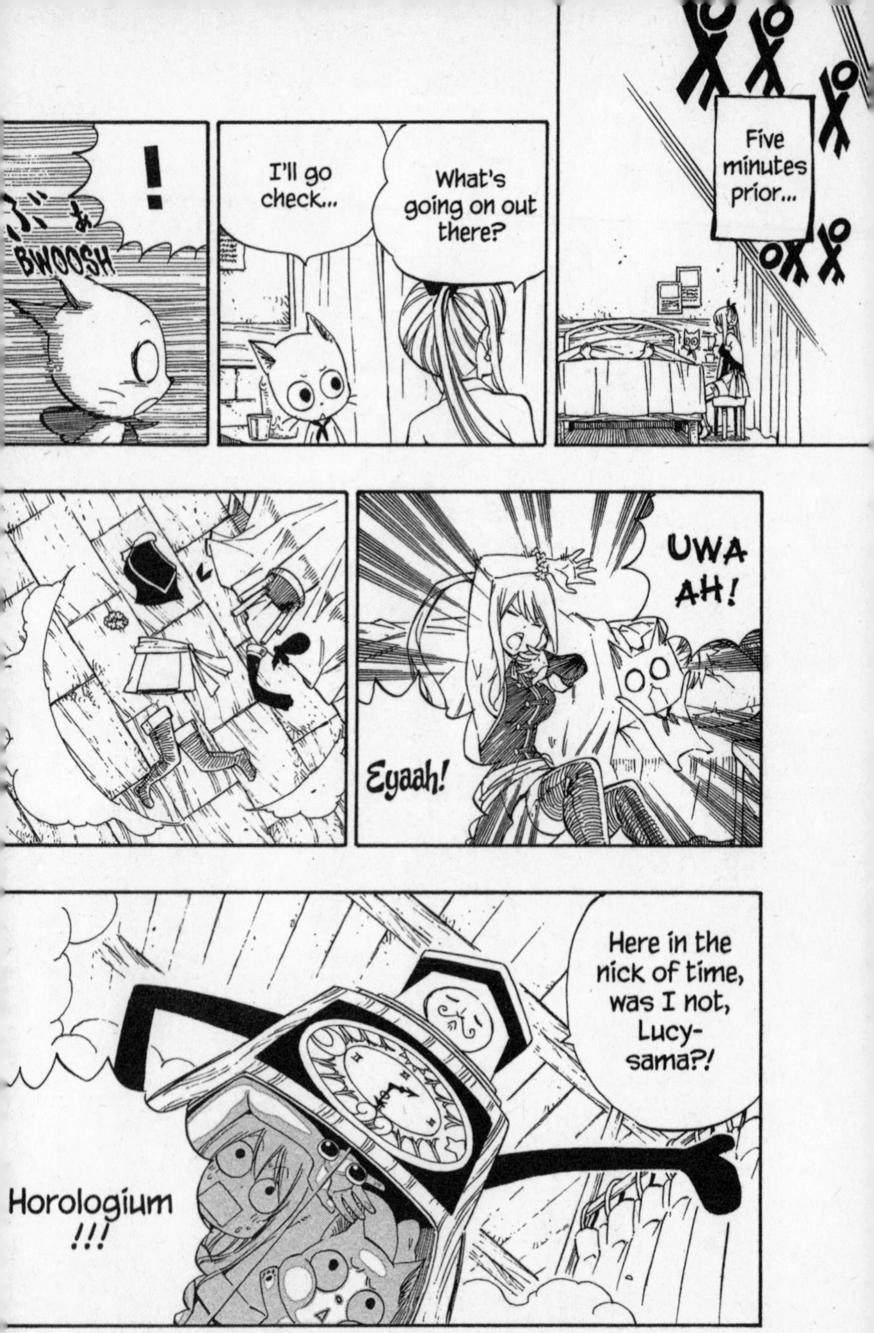
Five minutes prior...
What's going on out there?
I'll go check...
!
ぶぁ
BWOOSH
UWA AH!
Eyaah!
Here in the nick of time, was I not, Lucy-sama?!
Horologium !!!

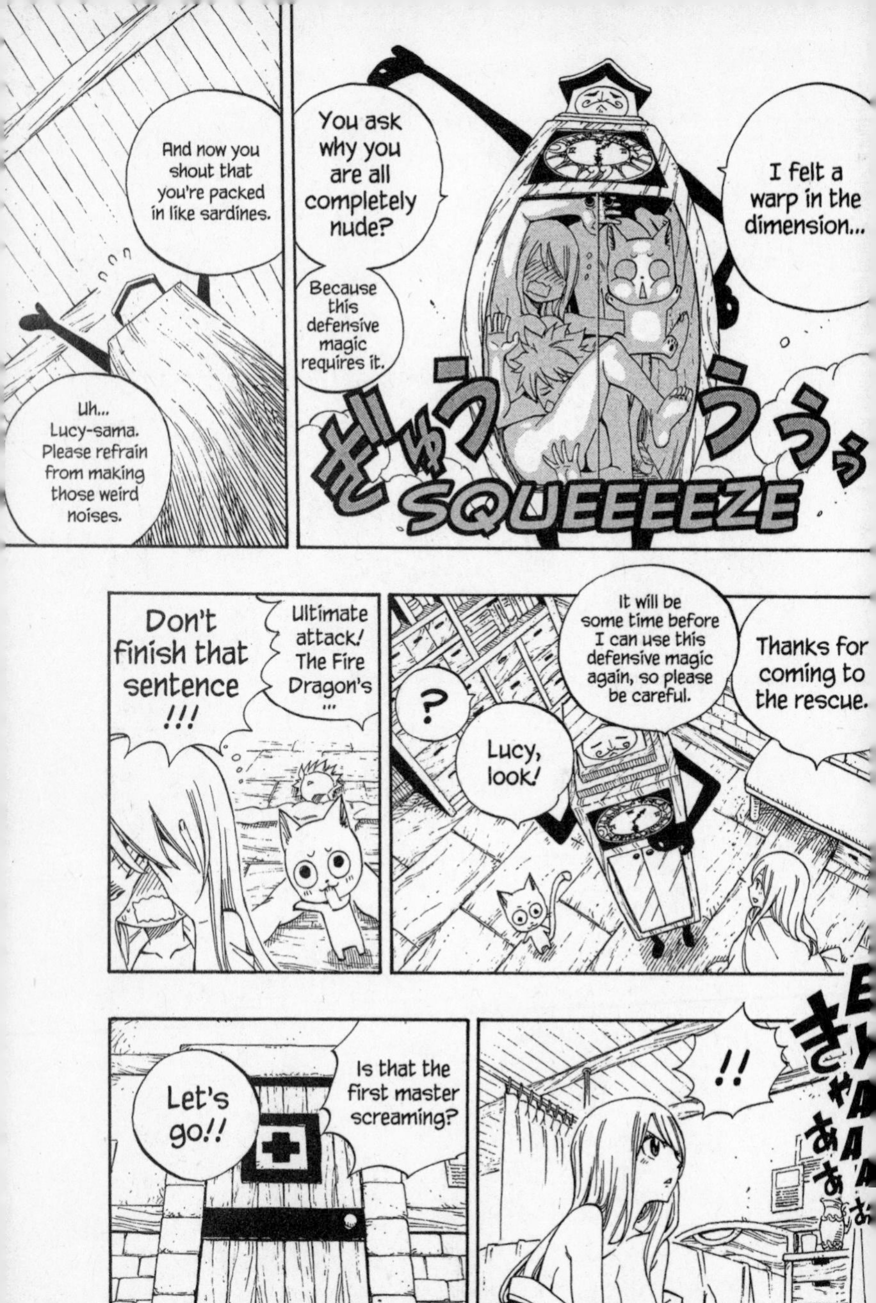

I felt a warp in the dimension...
You ask why you are all completely nude?
Because this defensive magic requires it.
ぎゅううぅぅ
SQUEEEEEZE
And now you shout that you're packed in like sardines.
Uh... Lucy-sama. Please refrain from making those weird noises.
Thanks for coming to the rescue.
It will be some time before I can use this defensive magic again, so please be careful.
?
Lucy, look!
Ultimate attack! The Fire Dragon's ...
Don't finish that sentence !!!
!!
きゃあああ
Is that the first master screaming?
Let's go!!

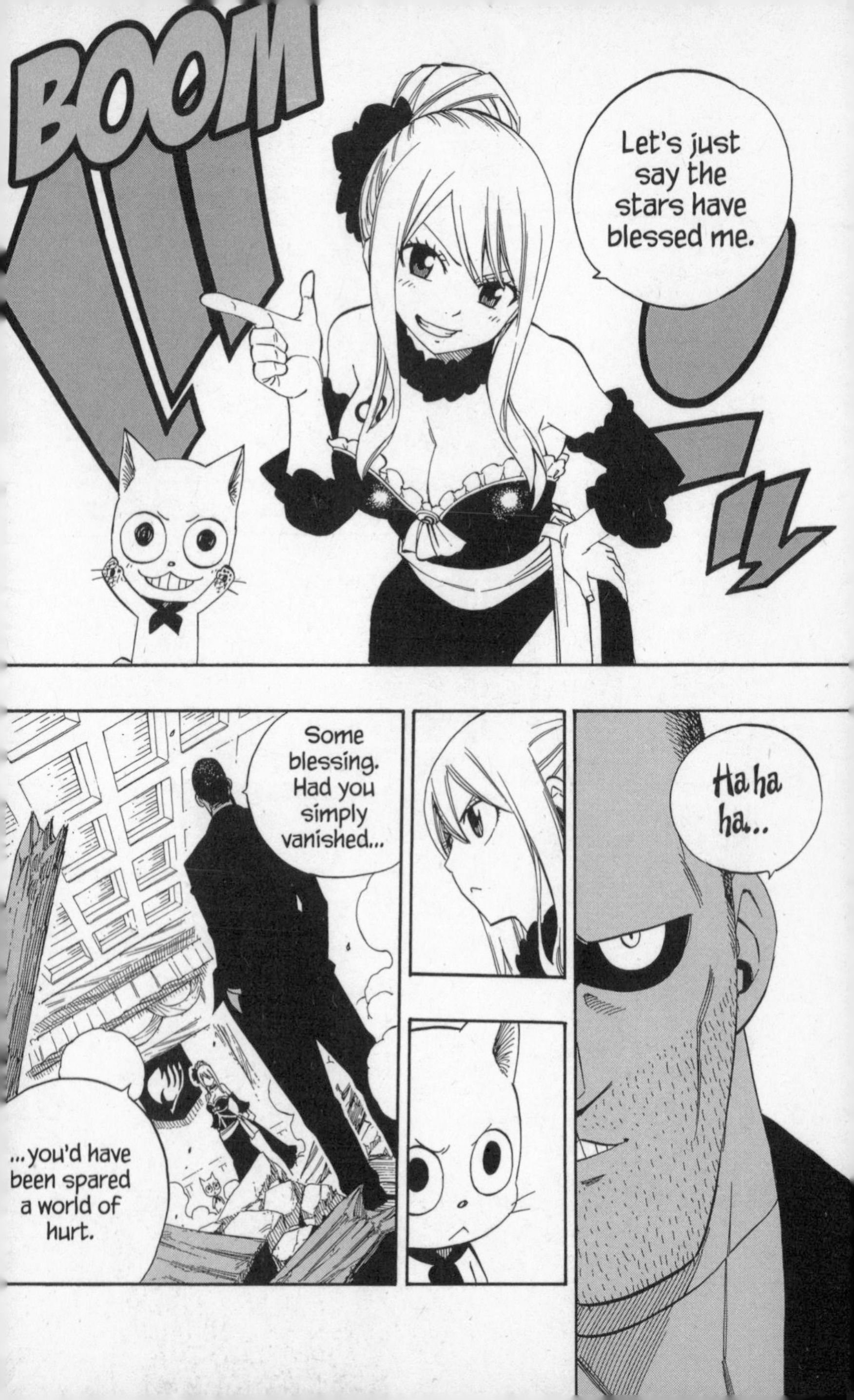
BOOM
Let's just say the stars have blessed me.
Ha ha ha...
Some blessing. Had you simply vanished...
...you'd have been spared a world of hurt.

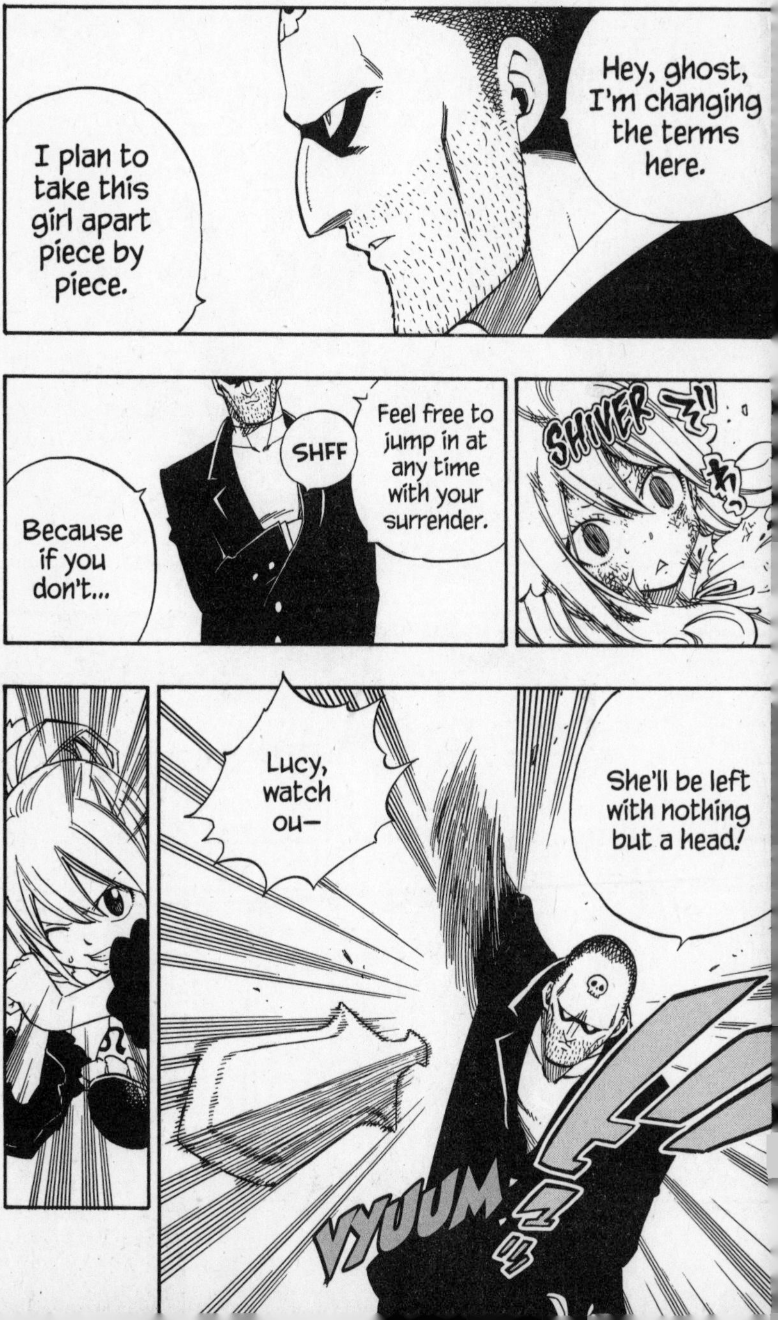
Hey, ghost, I'm changing the terms here.
I plan to take this girl apart piece by piece.
SHIVER
Feel free to jump in at any time with your surrender.
SHFF
Because if you don't...
She'll be left with nothing but a head!
Lucy, watch ou–
VYUUM

WHUNK

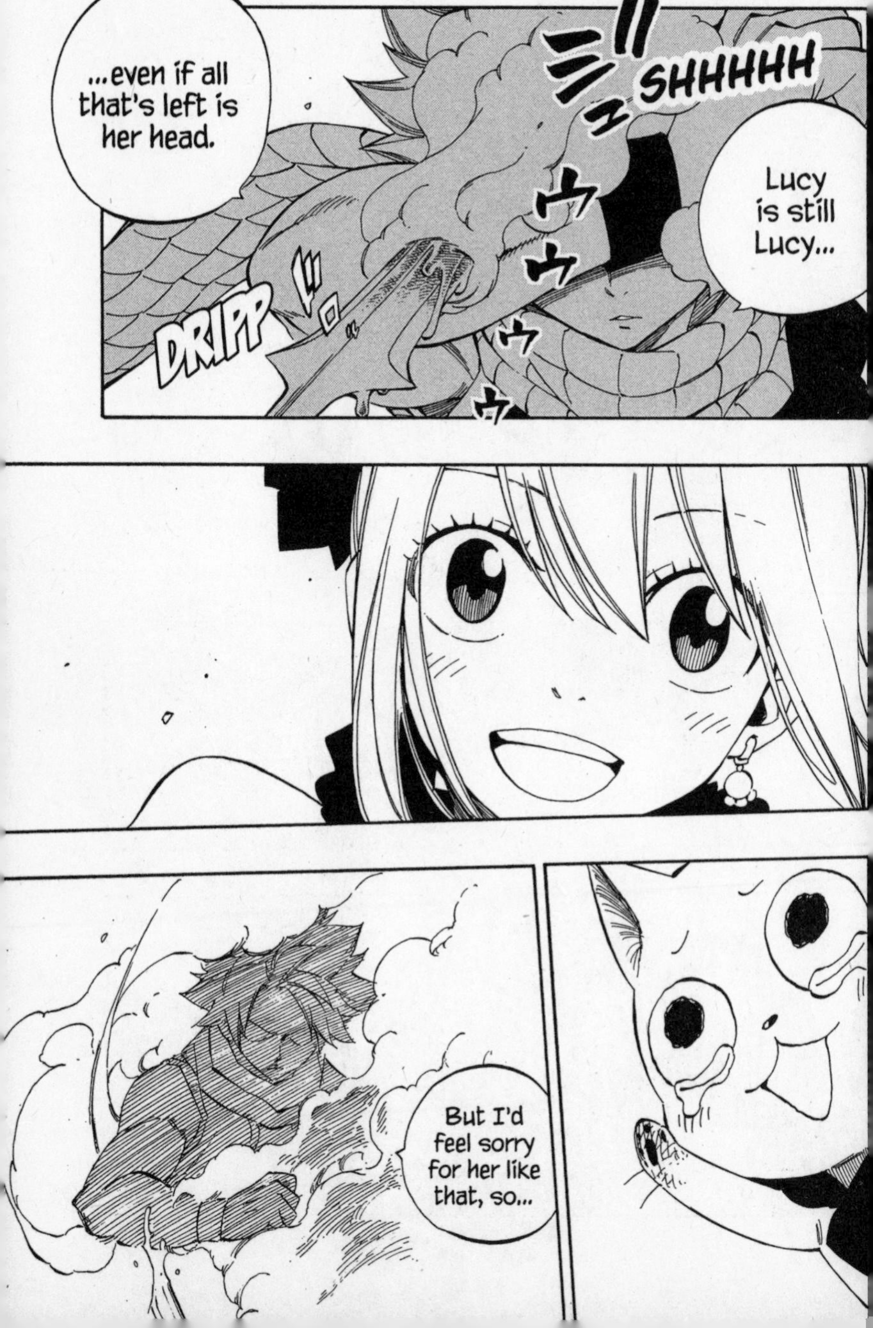
SHHHHH
Lucy is still Lucy...
...even if all that's left is her head.
DRIPP
But I'd feel sorry for her like that, so...

OM!!

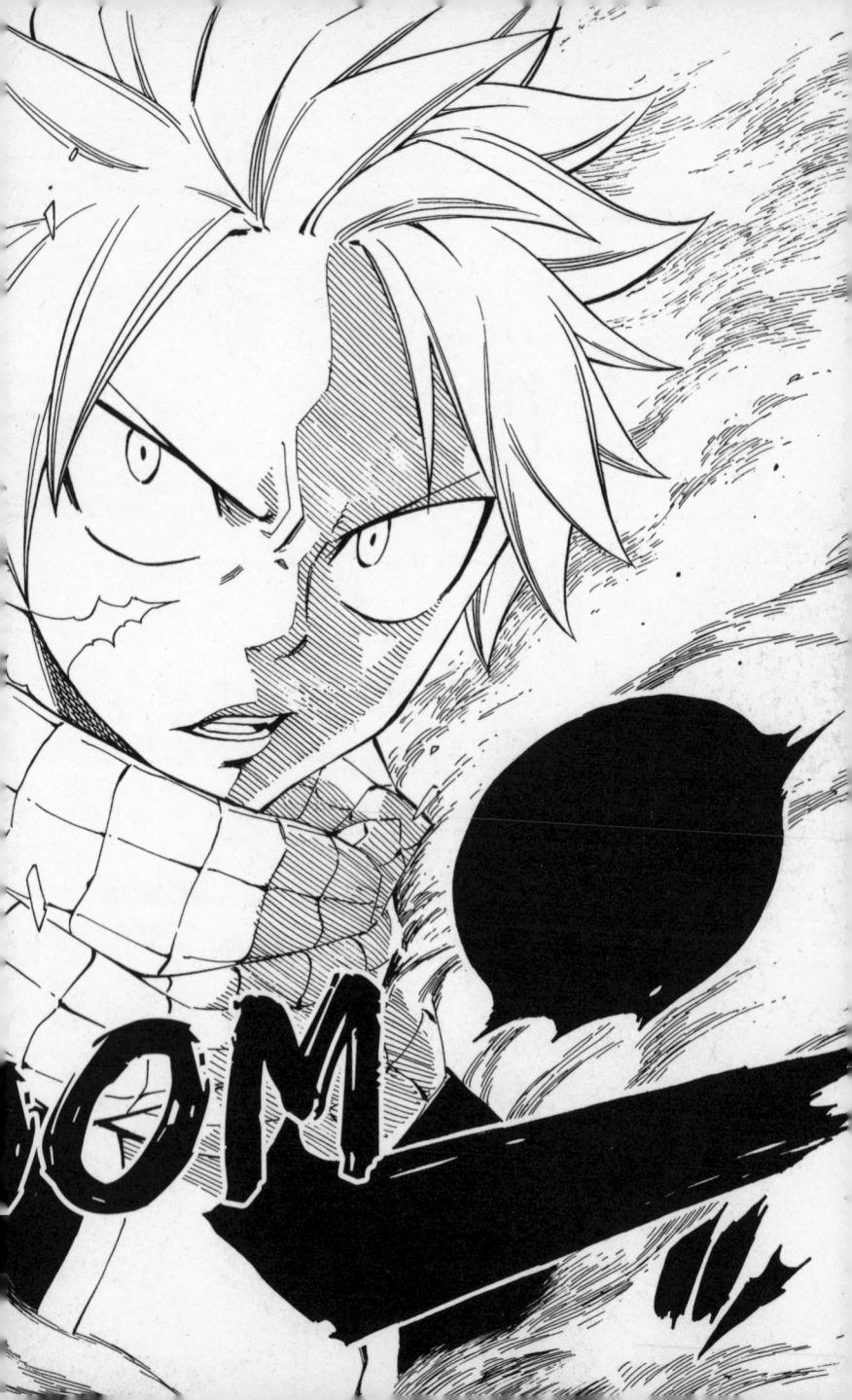

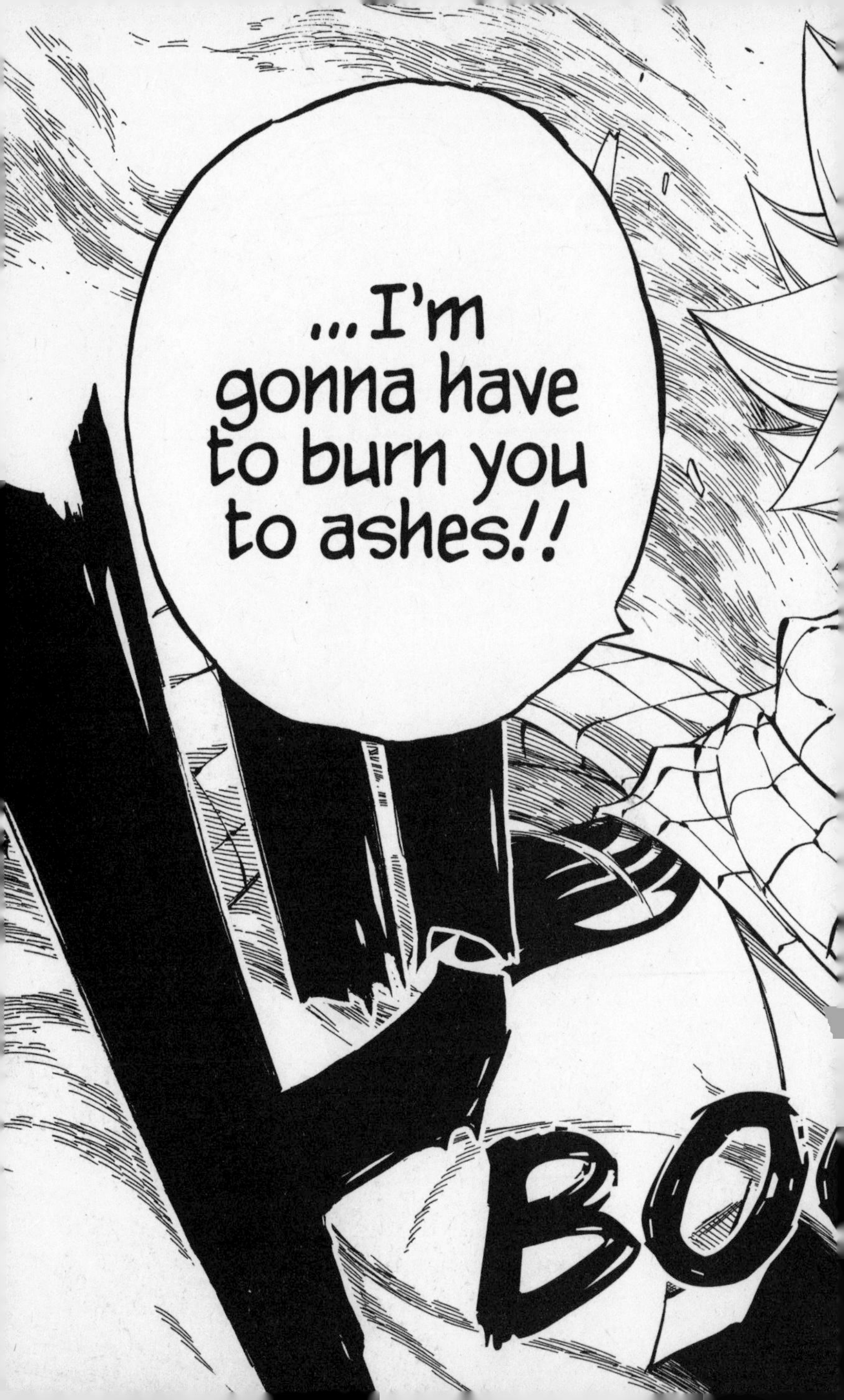
...I'm gonna have to burn you to ashes!!
BO

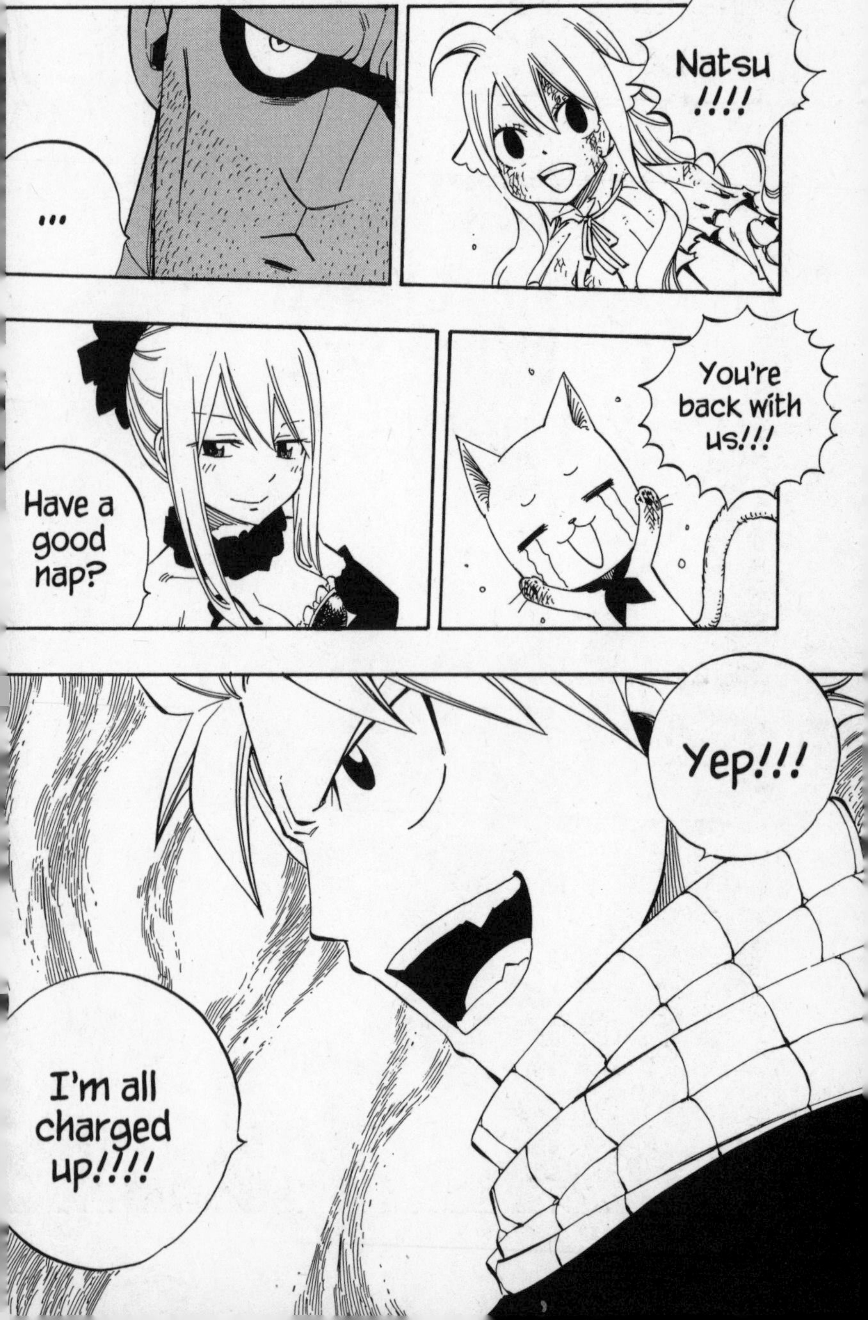
Natsu!!!!
...
You're back with us!!!
Have a good nap?
Yep!!!
I'm all charged up!!!!

FAIRY TAIL
フェアリーテイル

Chapter 478: Stealth

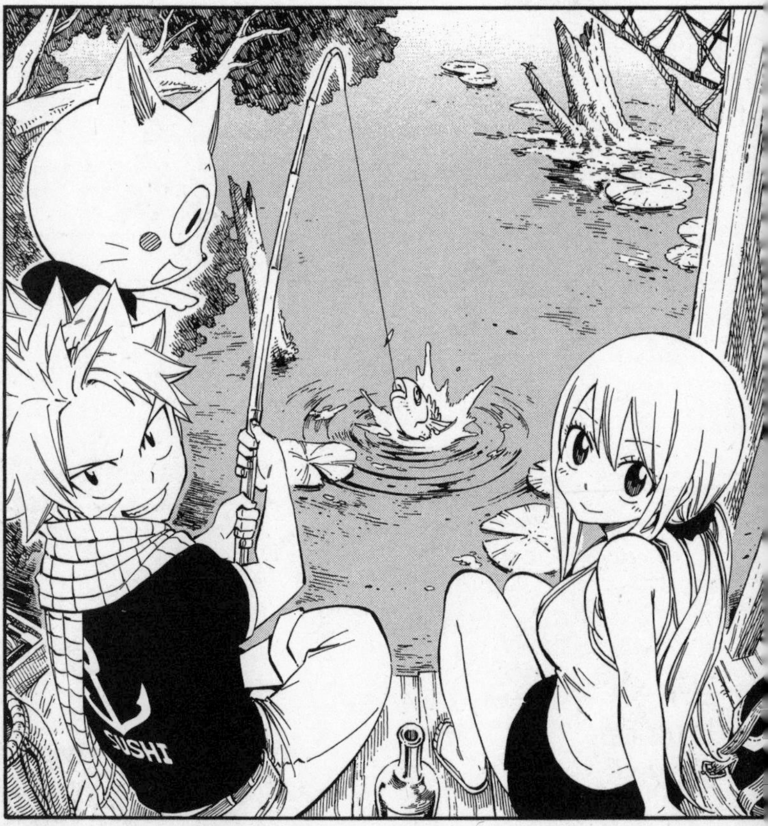
SUSHI

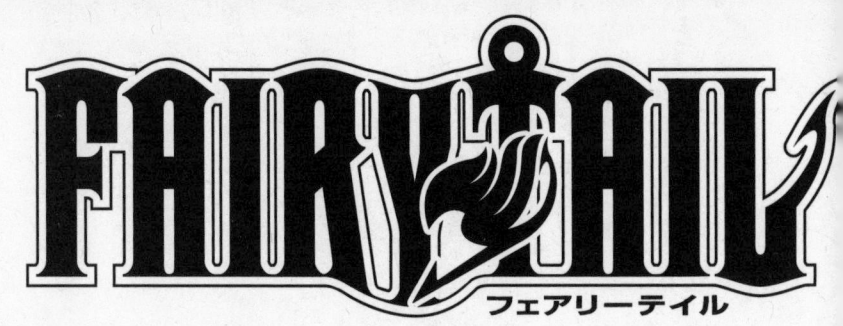

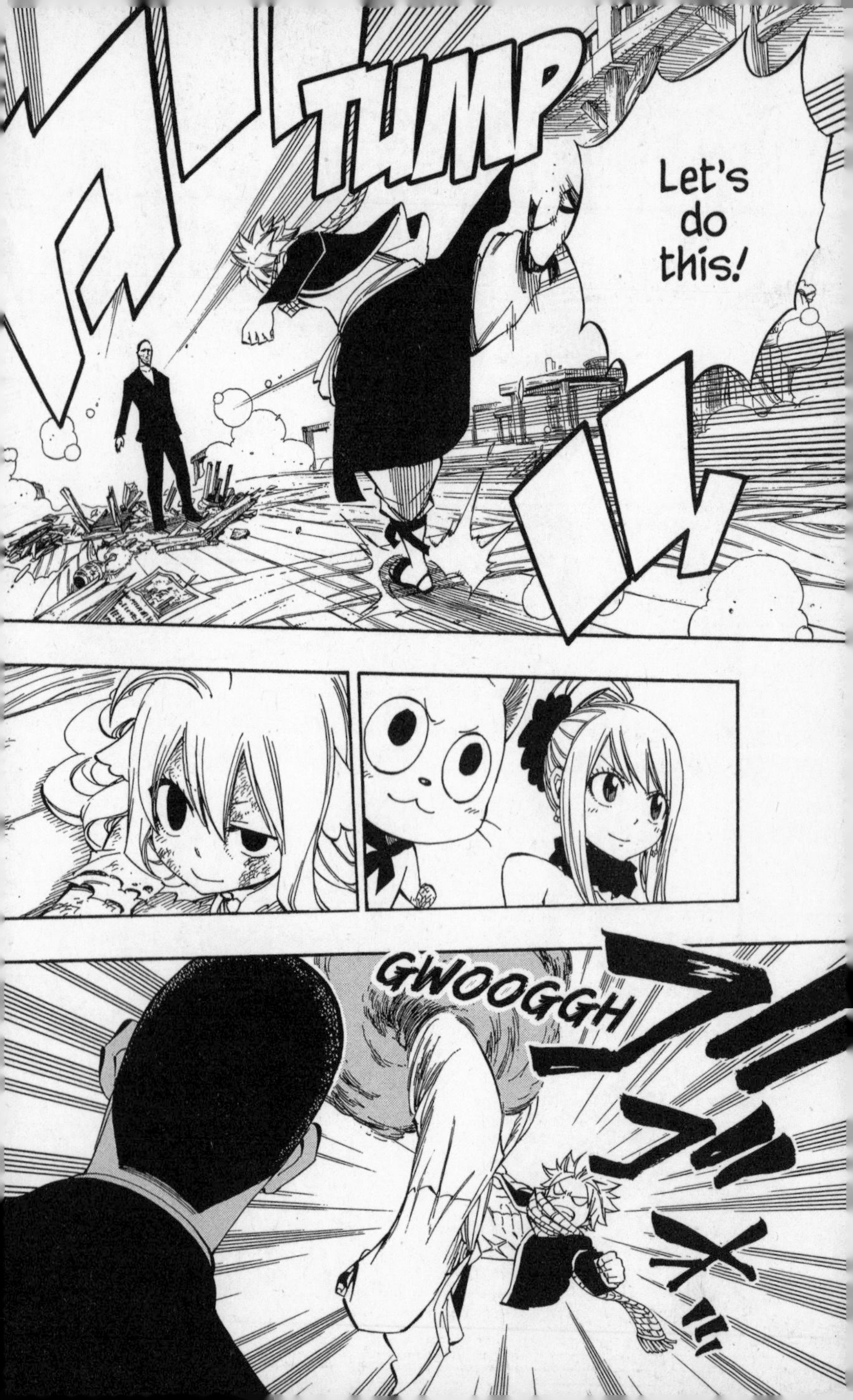
TUMP
Let's do this!
GWOOGGH

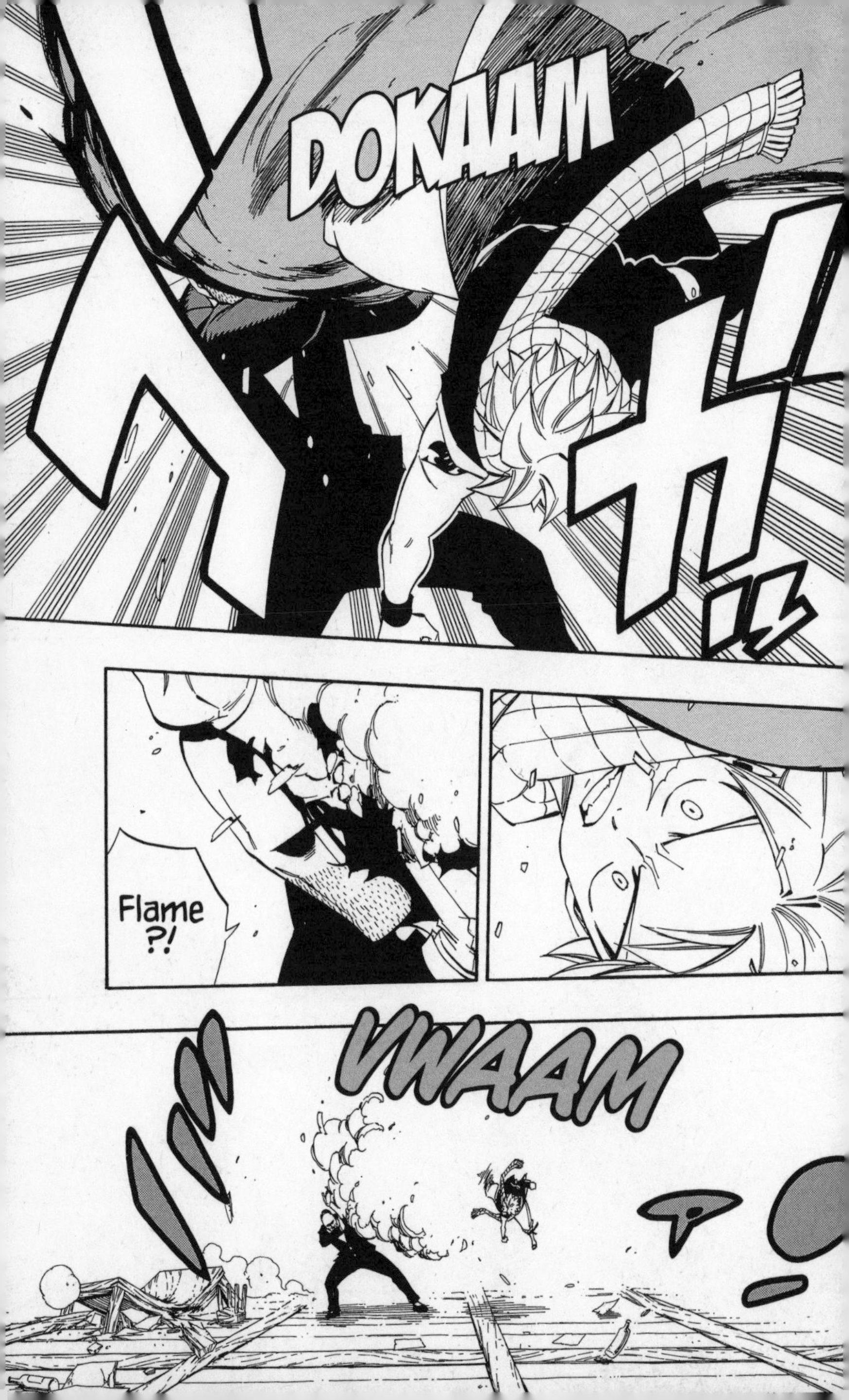
DOKAAM
Flame ?!
VWAAM

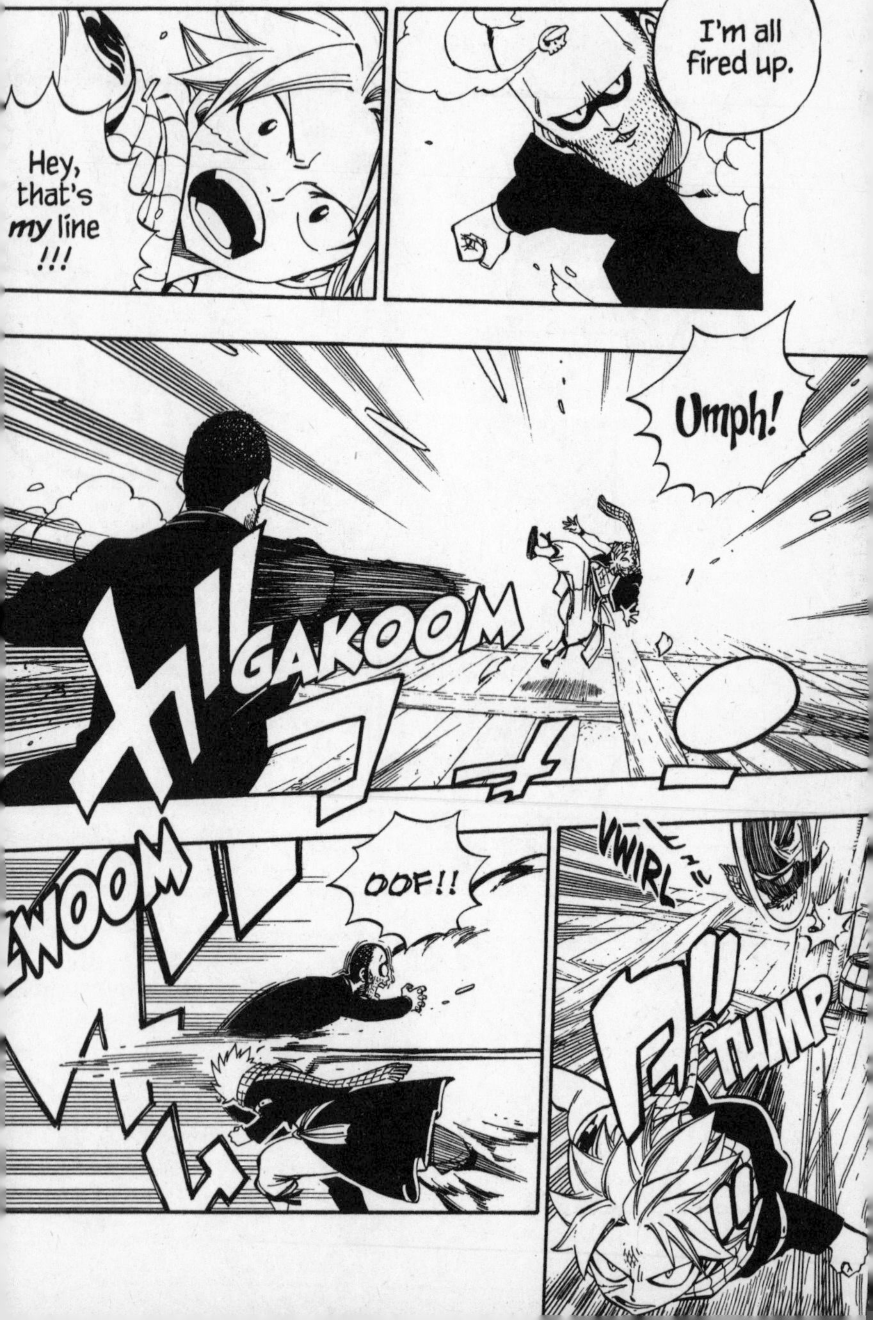
I'm all fired up.
Hey, that's my line !!!
Umph!
GAKOOM
VWIRL
TUMP
WOOM
OOF!!

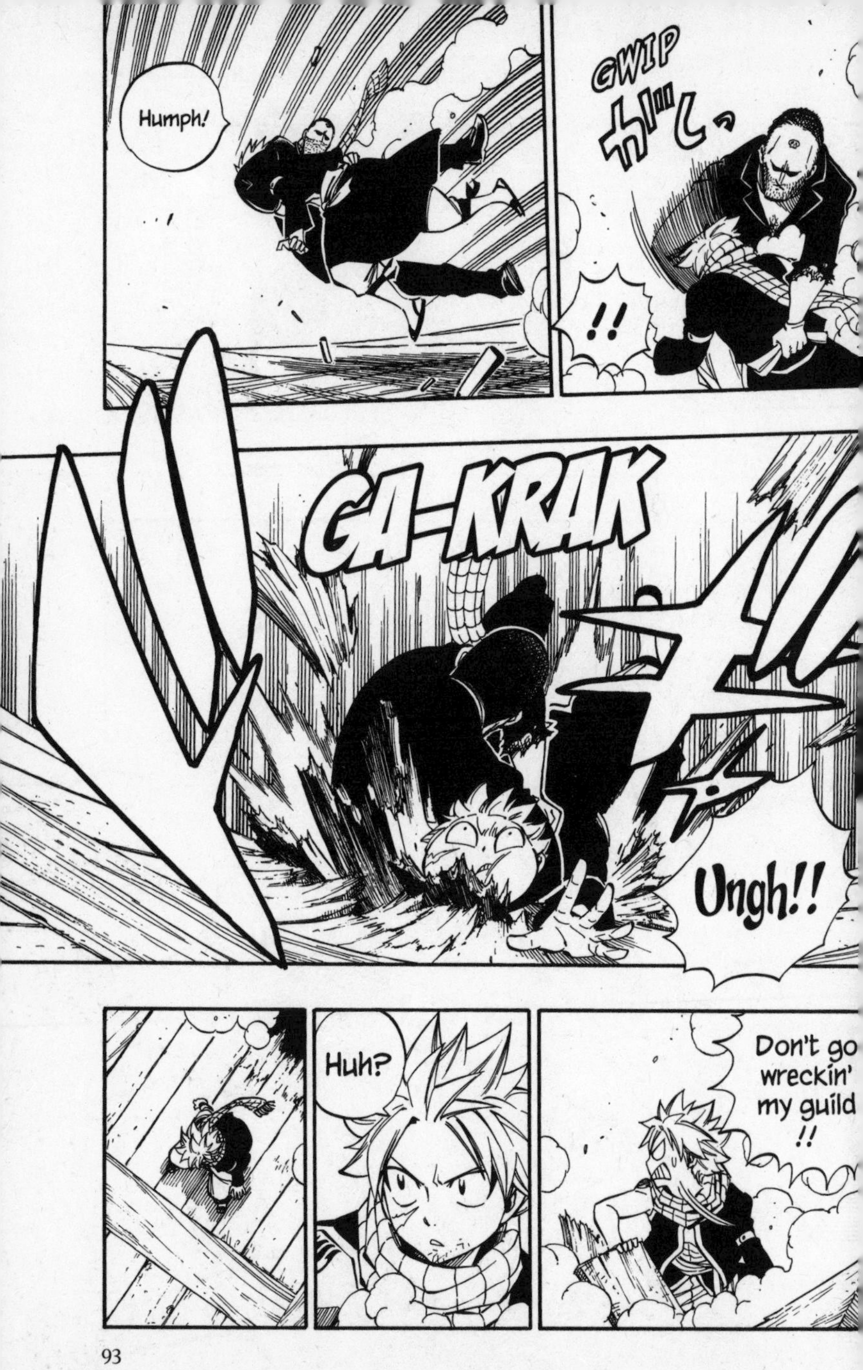
GWIP
ガしっ
!!
Humph!
GA-KRAK
Ungh!!
Don't go wreckin' my guild !!
Huh?

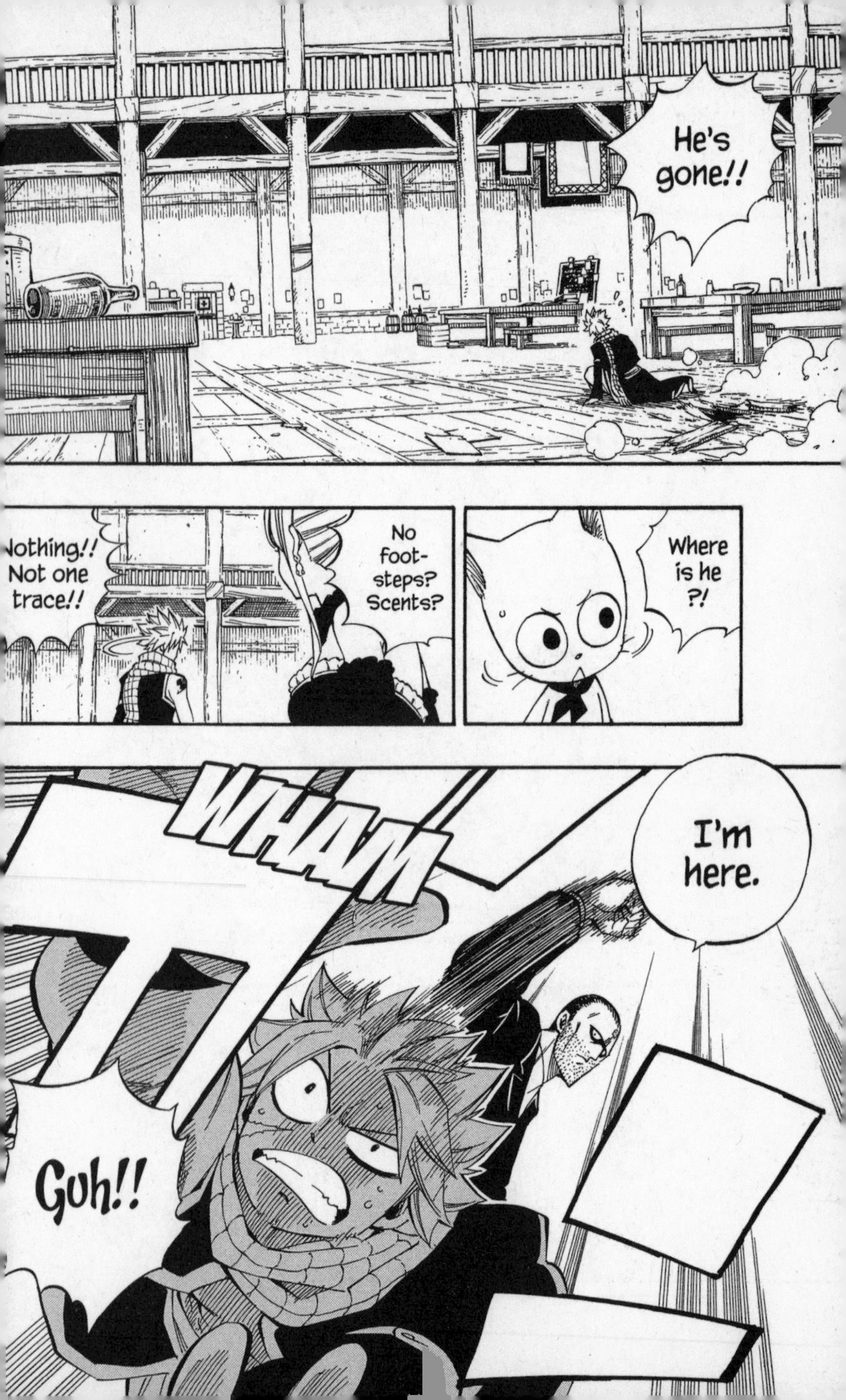
He's gone!!
Where is he ?!
No foot-steps? Scents?
Nothing!! Not one trace!!
I'm here.
WHAM
Guh!!

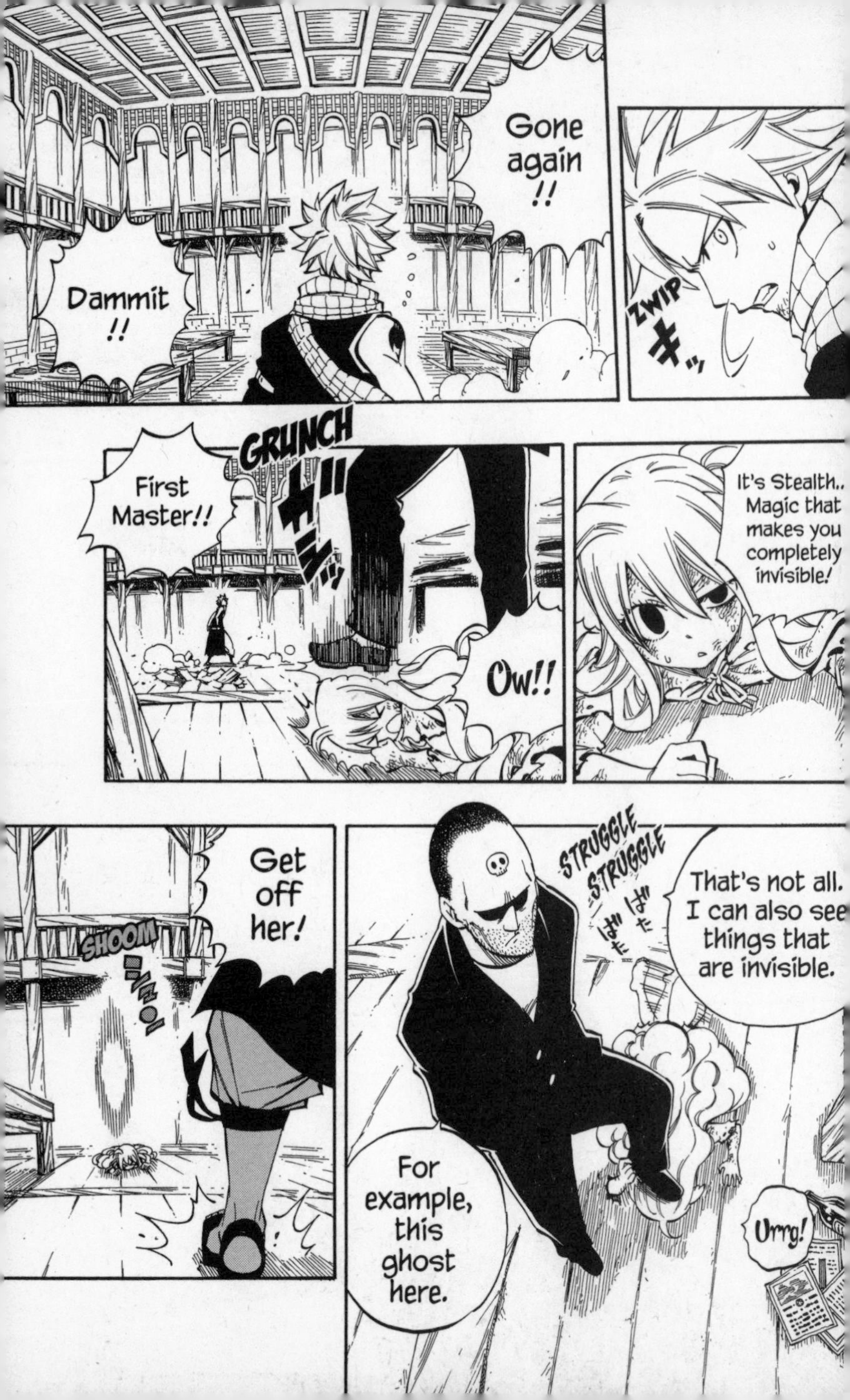
ZWIP
Gone again!!
Dammit!!
It's Stealth.. Magic that makes you completely invisible!
GRUNCH
First Master!!
Ow!!
STRUGGLE STRUGGLE
ばたばた
That's not all. I can also see things that are invisible.
For example, this ghost here.
Urrg!
Get off her!
SHOOM

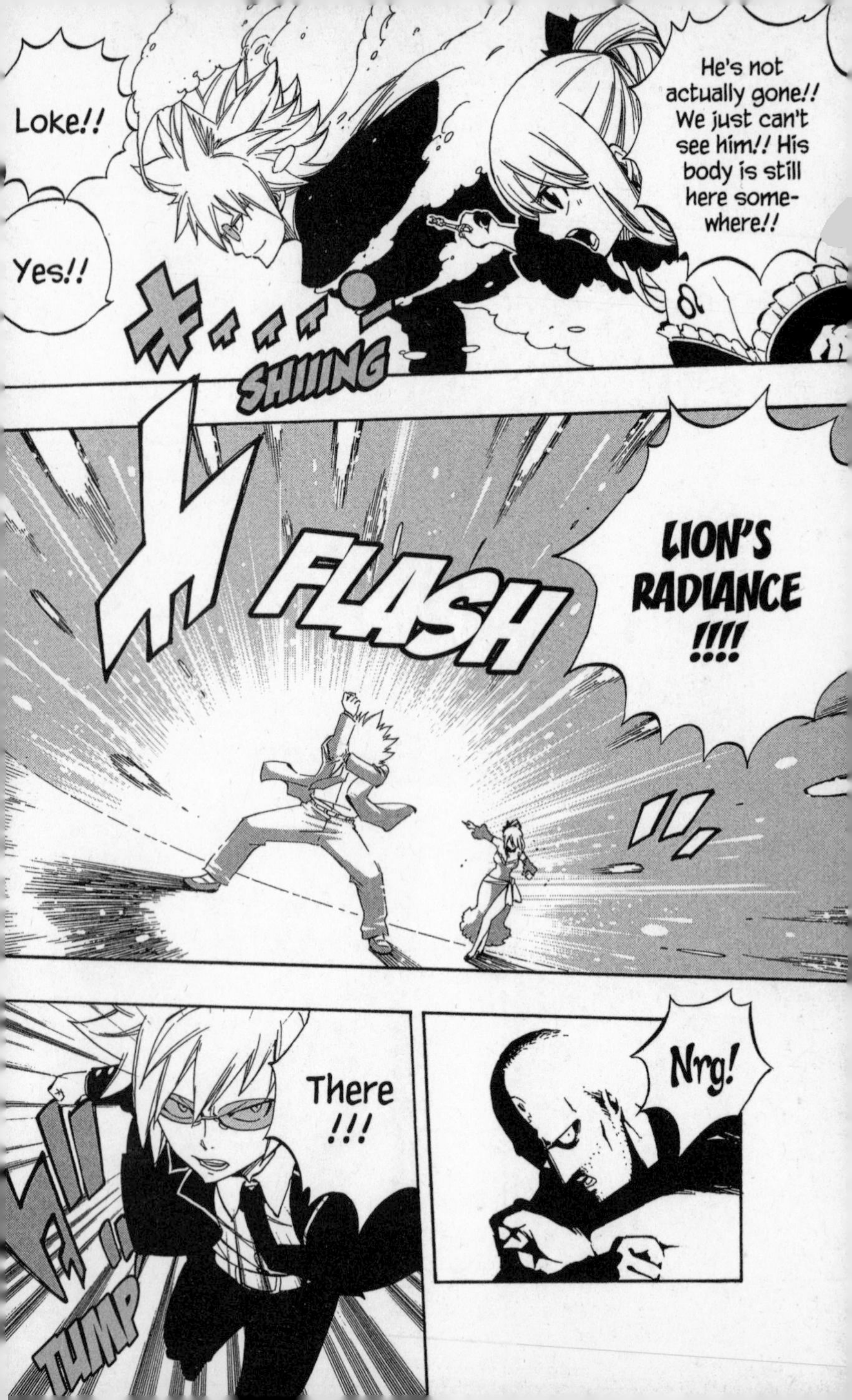
He's not actually gone!! We just can't see him!! His body is still here some-where!!
Loke!!
Yes!!
SHIIING
LION'S RADIANCE !!!!
FLASH
Nrg!
There !!!
THUMP

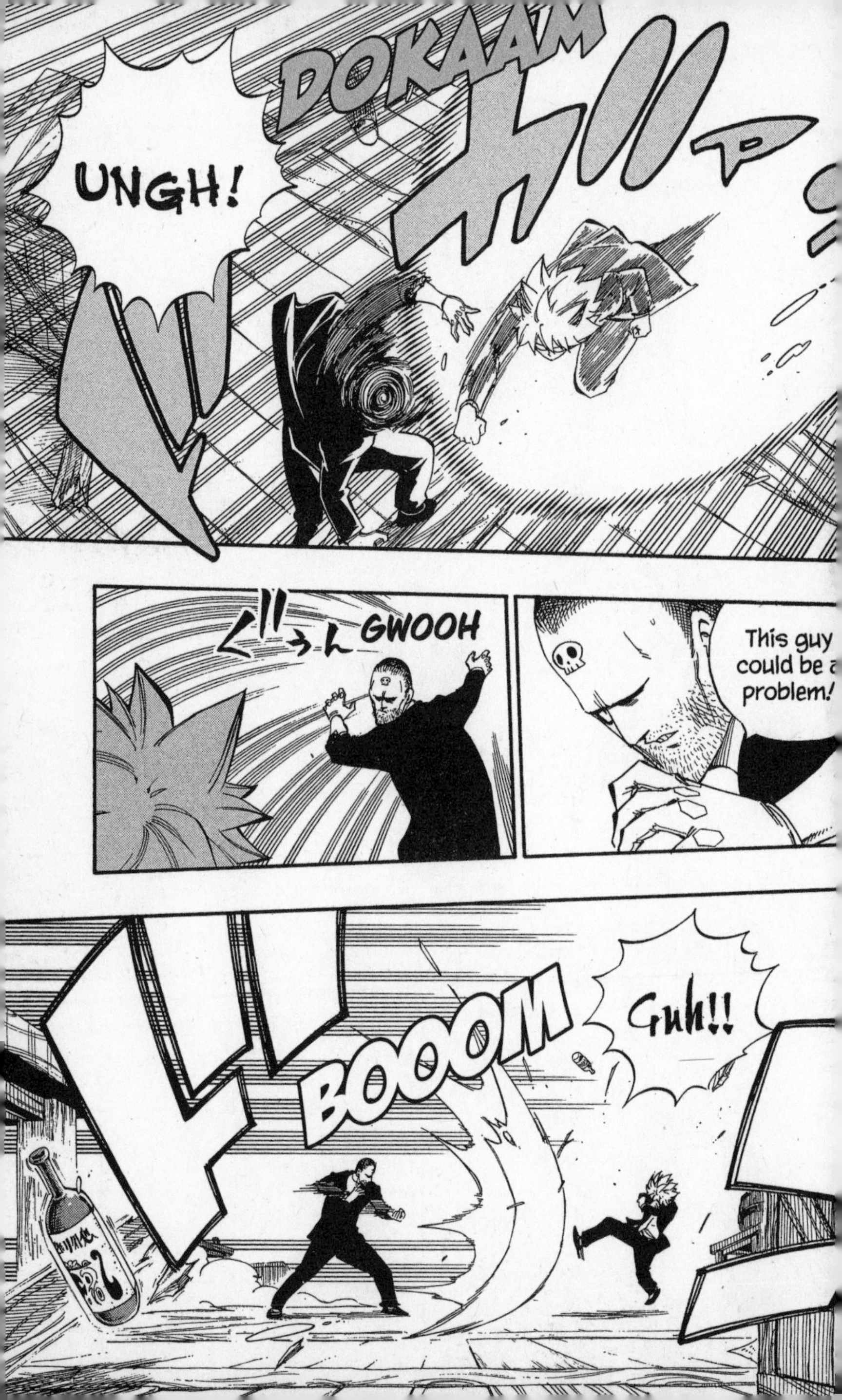
DOKAAM
UNGH!
This guy could be a problem!
GWOOH
Guh!!
BOOOM

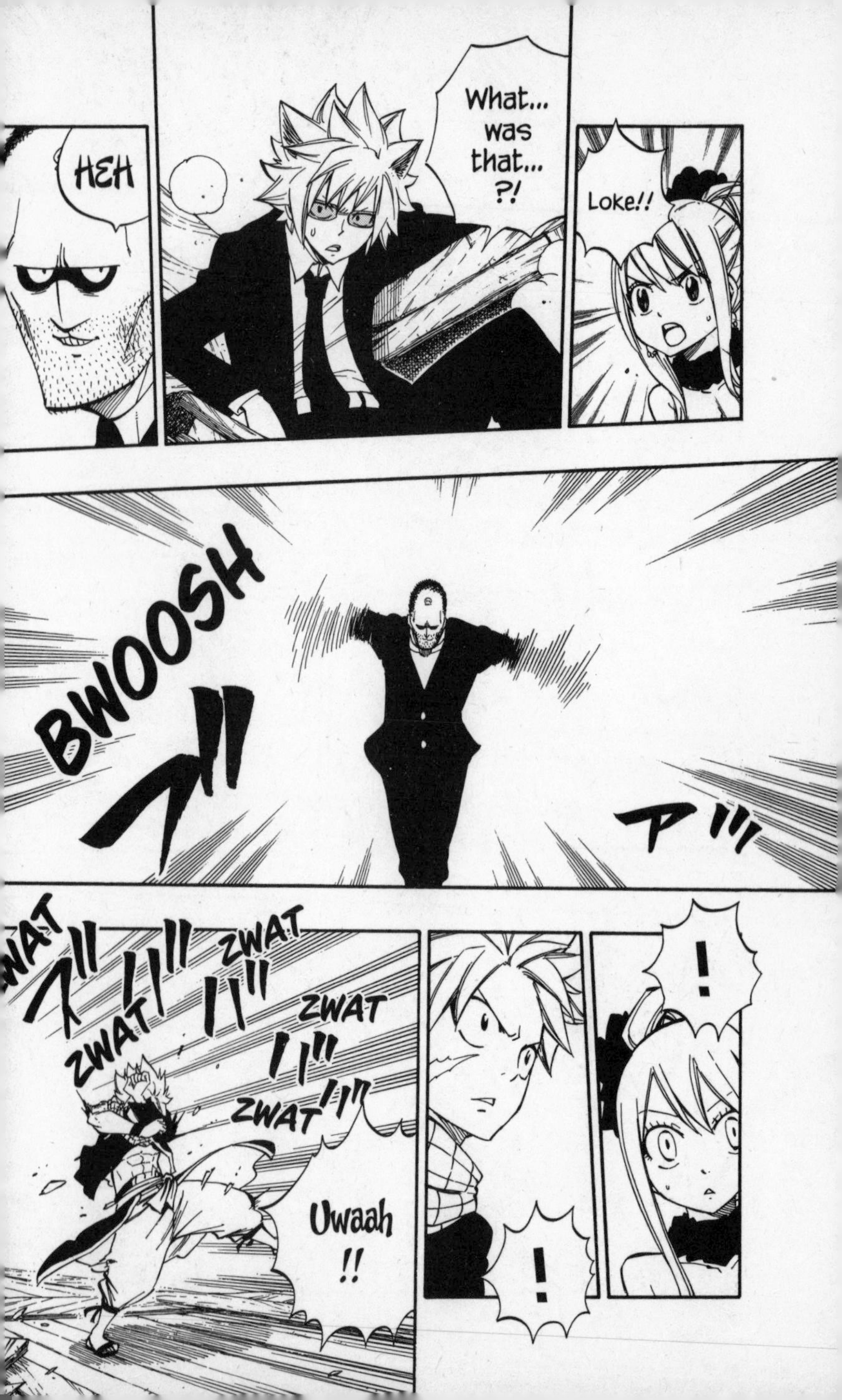
Loke!!
What... was that...?!
HEH
BWOOSH
!
!
WAT
ZWAT
ZWAT
ZWAT
ZWAT
Uwaah!!

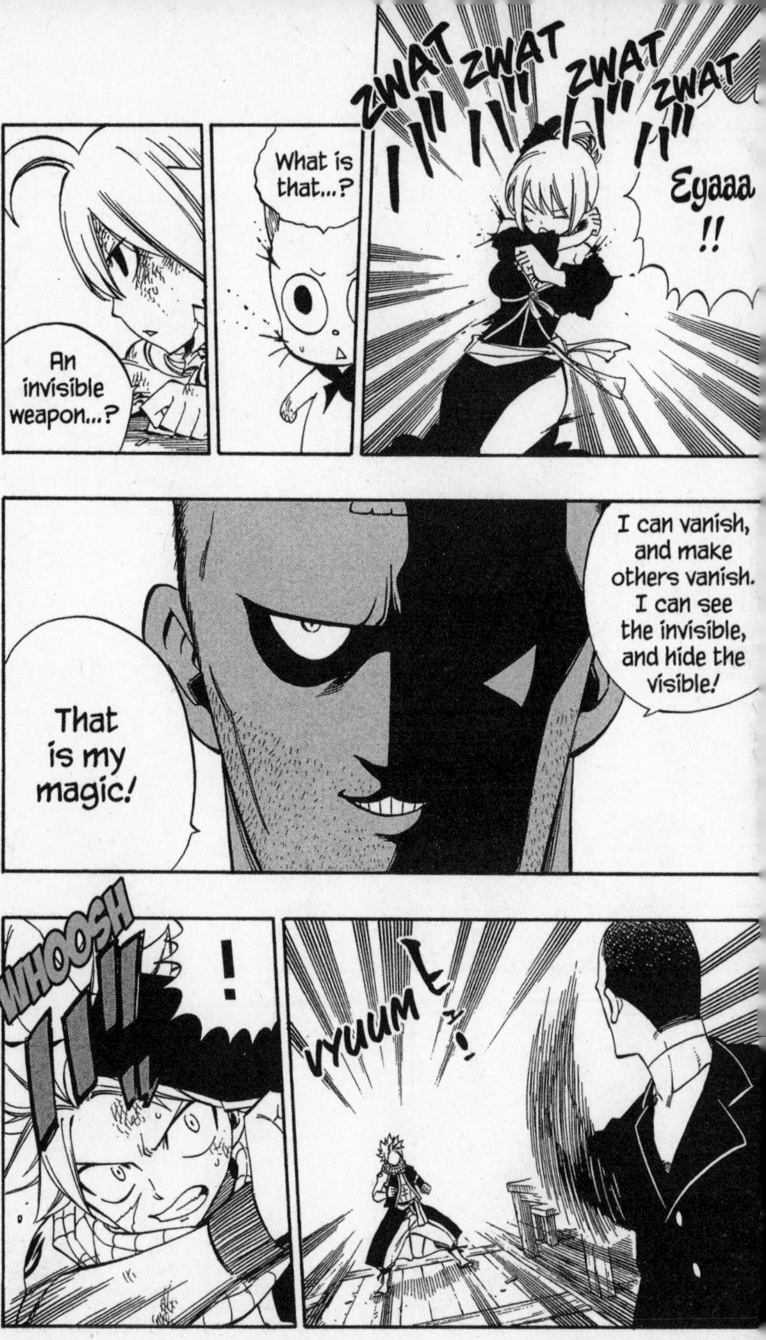
ZWAT ZWAT ZWAT ZWAT
Eyaaa !!
What is that...?
An invisible weapon...?
I can vanish, and make others vanish. I can see the invisible, and hide the visible!
That is my magic!
VYUUM
!
WHOOSH
!

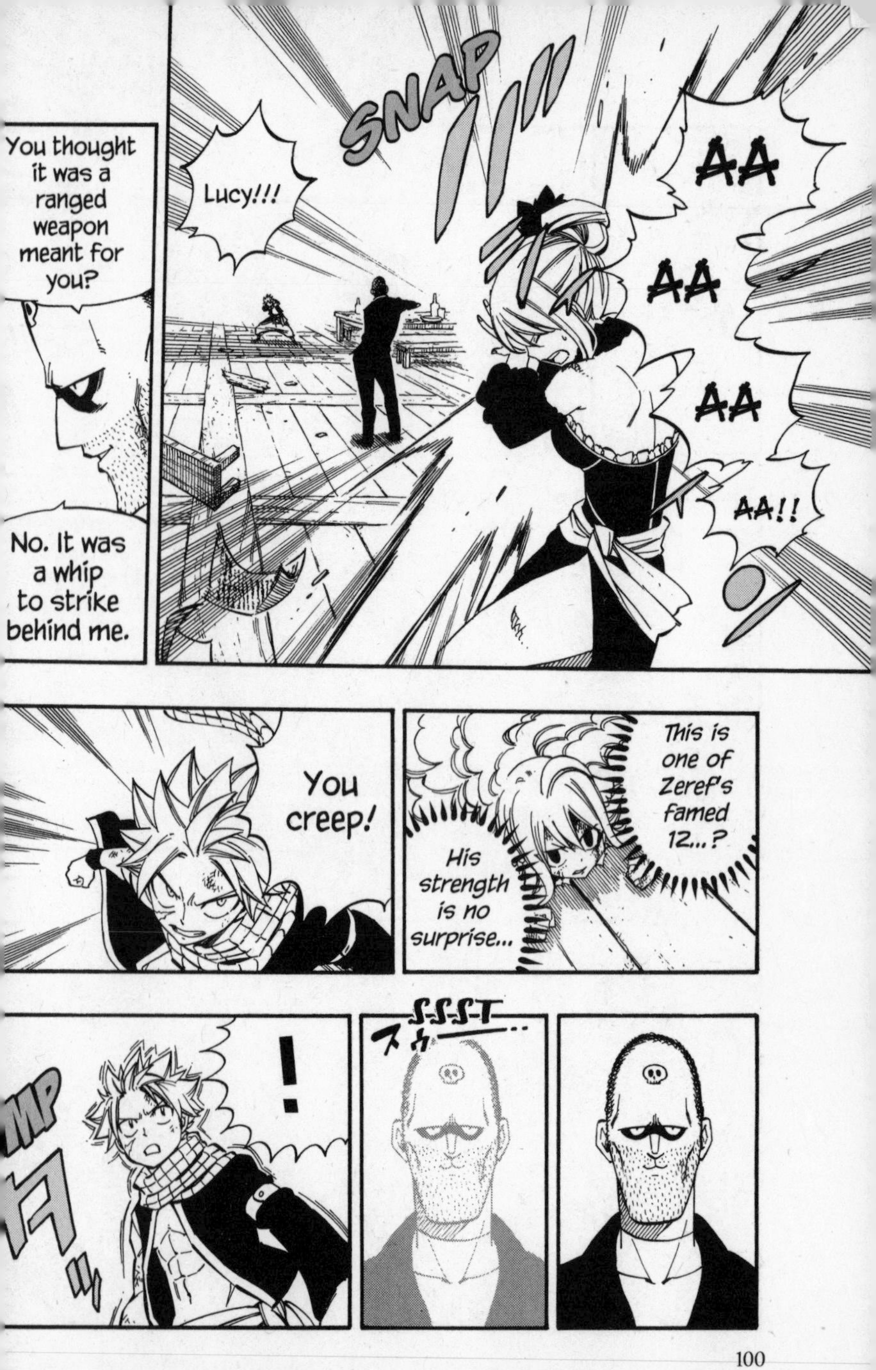
SNAP
AA AA AA AA!!
Lucy!!!
You thought it was a ranged weapon meant for you?
No. It was a whip to strike behind me.
This is one of Zeref's famed 12...?
His strength is no surprise...
You creep!
S-S-S-T
!

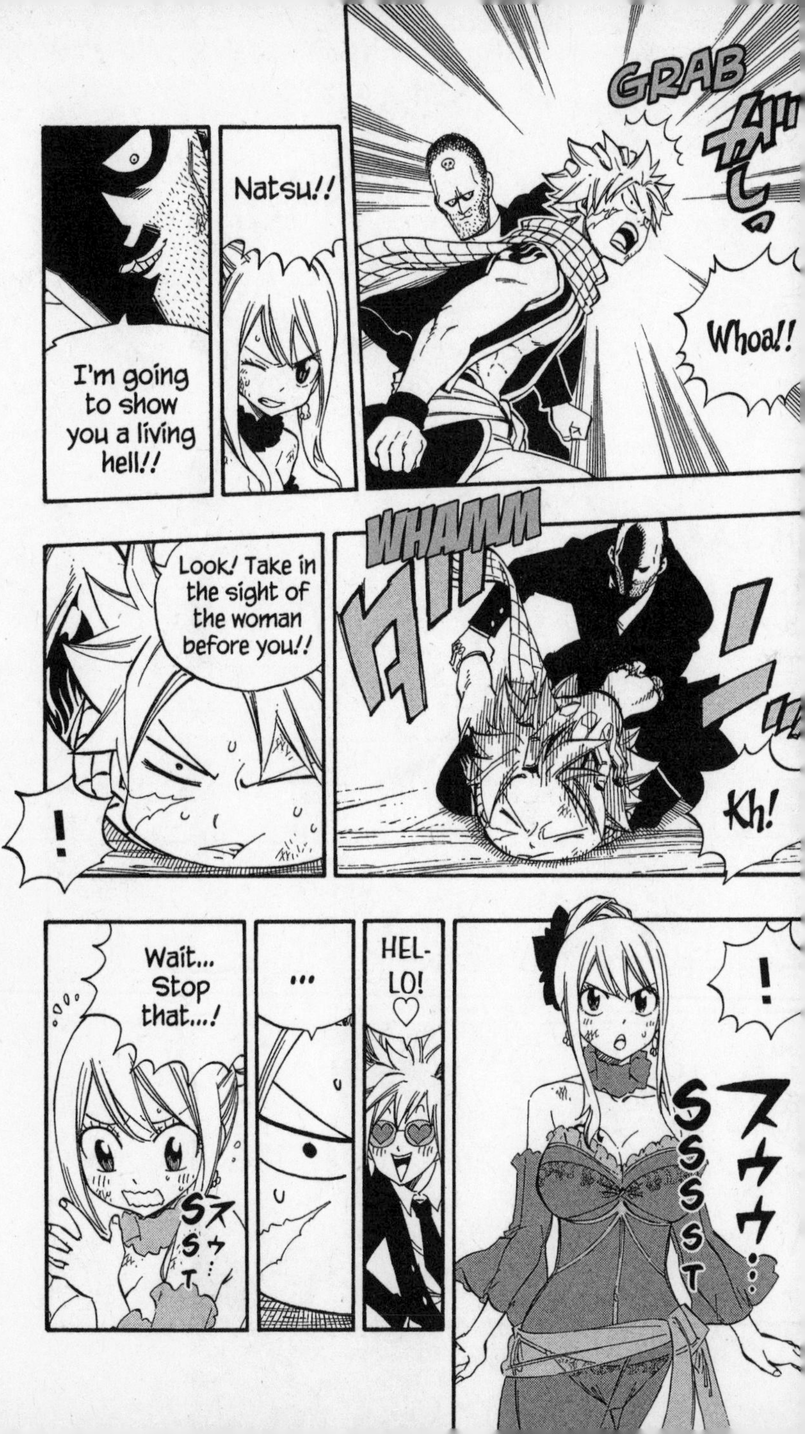
GRAB
Whoa!!
Natsu!!
I'm going to show you a living hell!!
WHAMM
Kh!
Look! Take in the sight of the woman before you!!
!
!
SSSST
HEL-LO! ♡
...
Wait... Stop that...!
SST

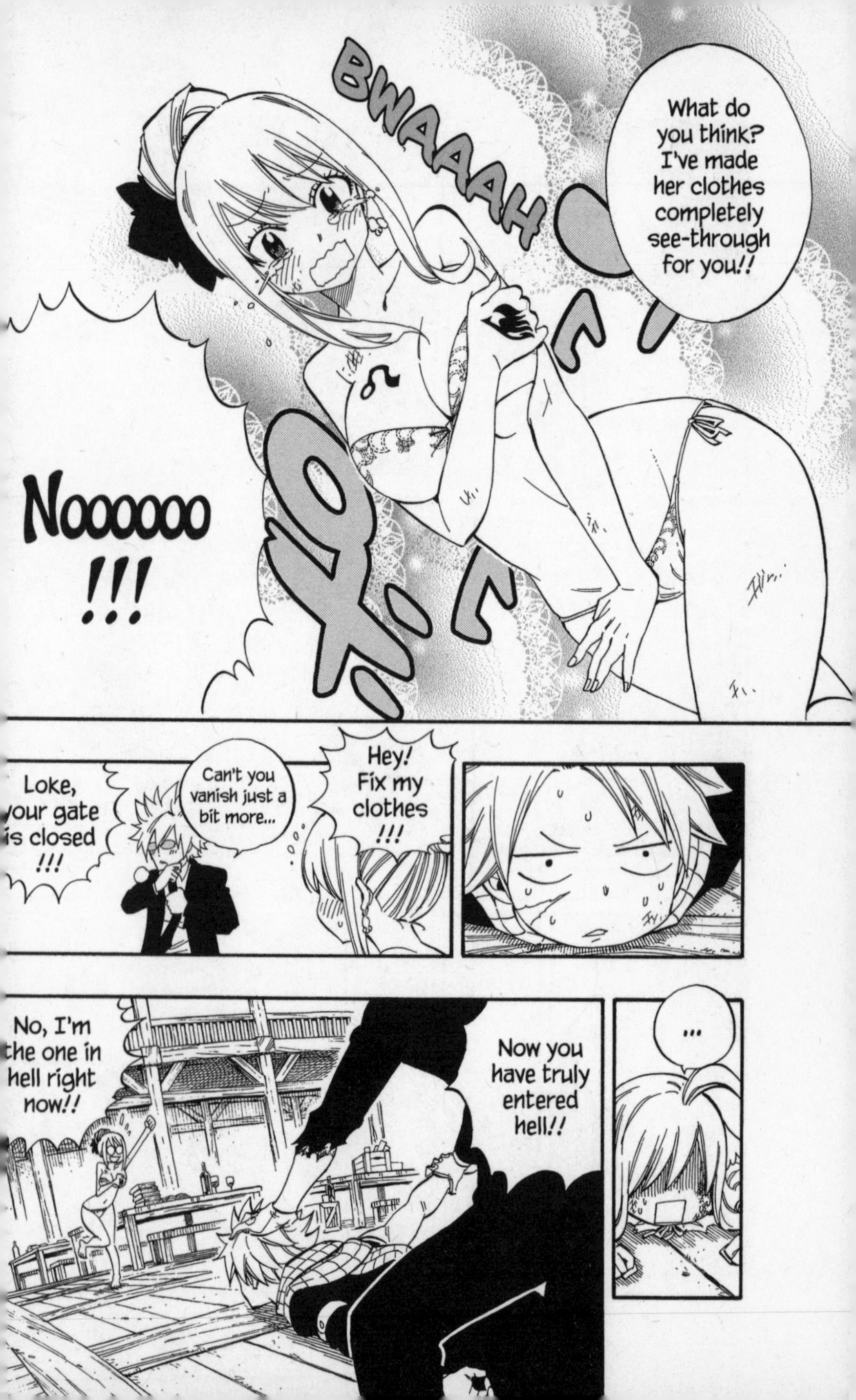
What do you think? I've made her clothes completely see-through for you!!
BWAAAAH
Nooooooo!!!
Hey! Fix my clothes!!!
Can't you vanish just a bit more...
Loke, your gate is closed!!!
...
Now you have truly entered hell!!
No, I'm the one in hell right now!!

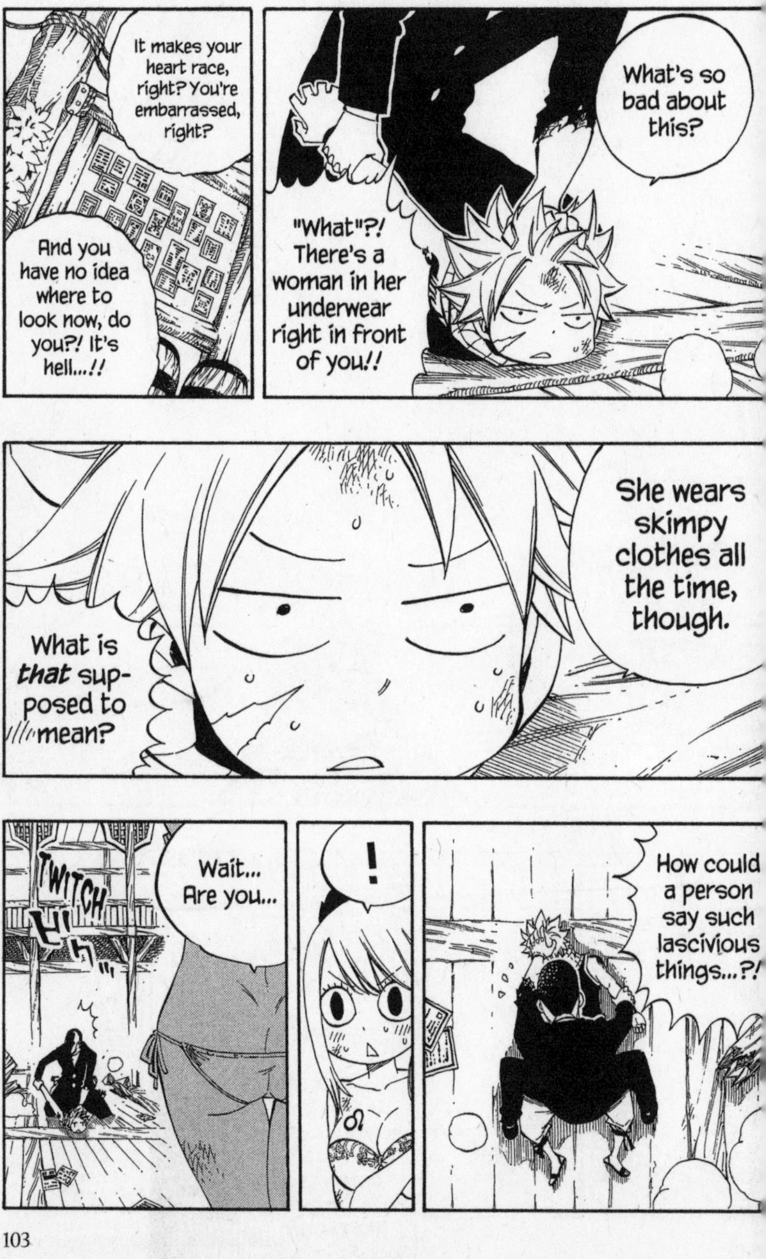
What's so bad about this?
"What"?! There's a woman in her underwear right in front of you!!
It makes your heart race, right? You're embarrassed, right?
And you have no idea where to look now, do you?! It's hell...!!
She wears skimpy clothes all the time, though.
What is *that* supposed to mean?
How could a person say such lascivious things...?!
!
Wait... Are you...
TWITCH

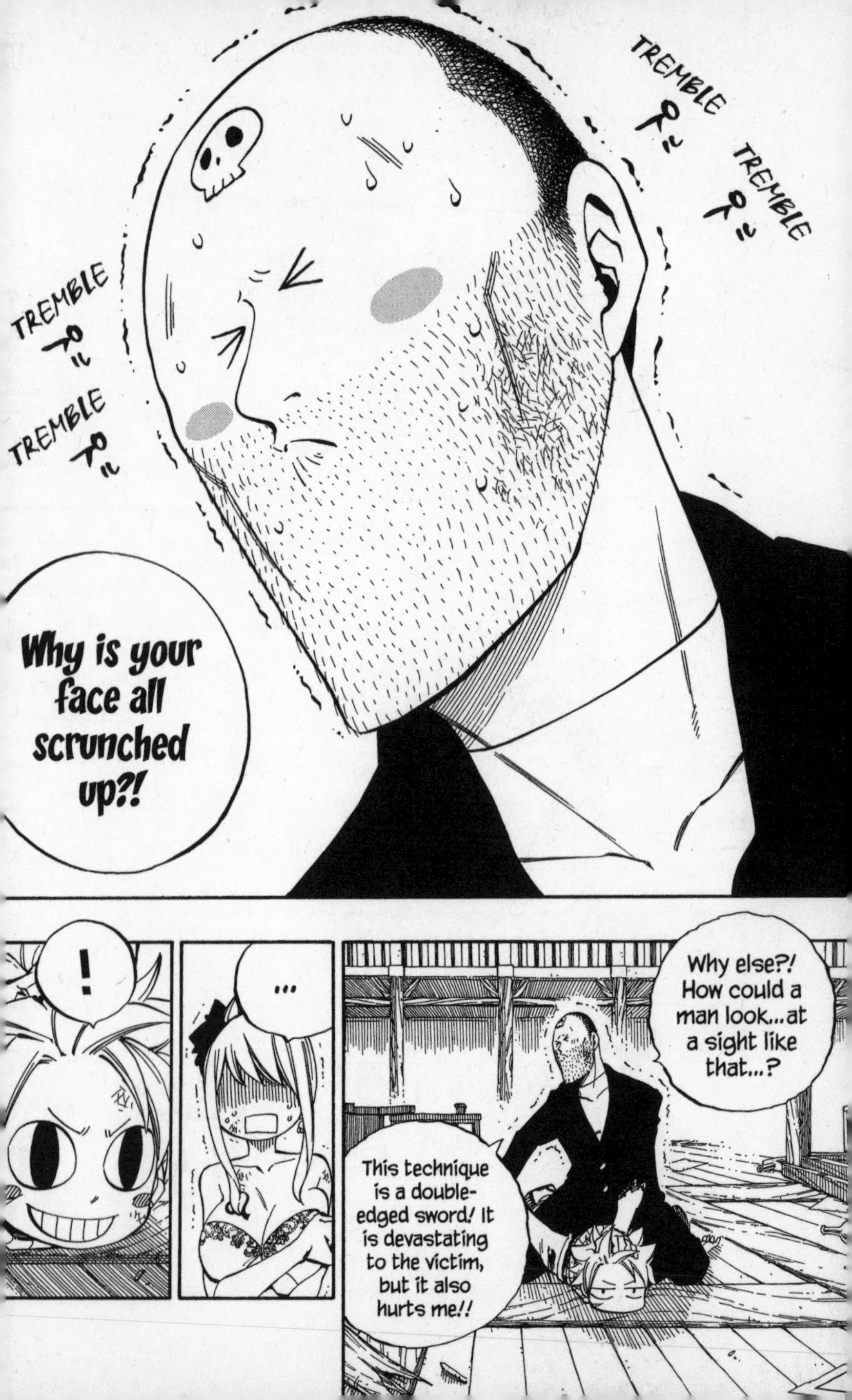
TREMBLE
TREMBLE
TREMBLE
TREMBLE
Why is your face all scrunched up?!
Why else?! How could a man look...at a sight like that...?
This technique is a double-edged sword! It is devastating to the victim, but it also hurts me!!
...
!

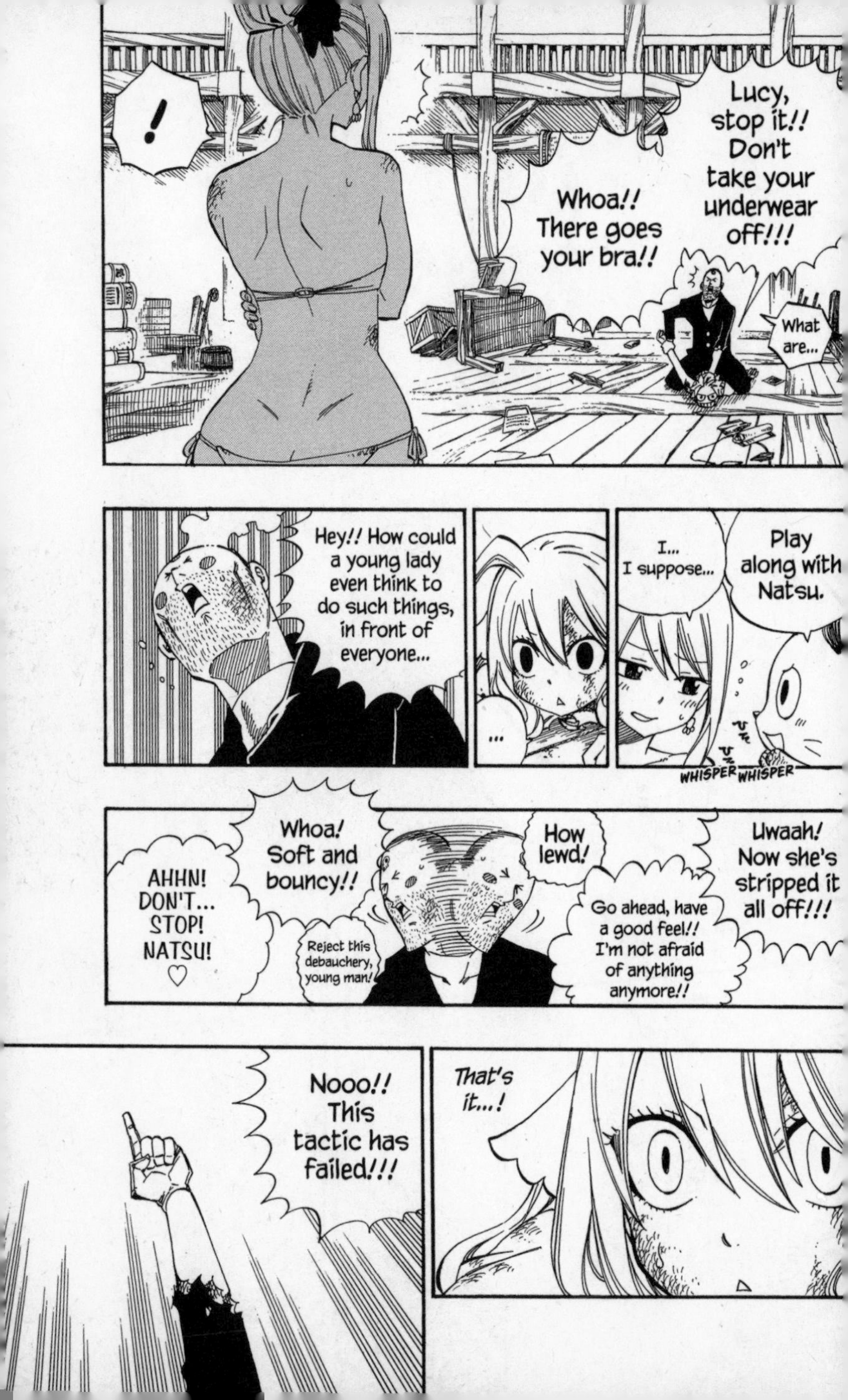
Lucy, stop it!! Don't take your underwear off!!!
Whoa!! There goes your bra!!
What are...
!
Play along with Natsu.
I... I suppose...
WHISPER WHISPER
...
Hey!! How could a young lady even think to do such things, in front of everyone...
Uwaah! Now she's stripped it all off!!!
How lewd!
Go ahead, have a good feel!! I'm not afraid of anything anymore!!
Whoa! Soft and bouncy!!
Reject this debauchery, young man!
AHHN! DON'T... STOP! NATSU! ♡
That's it...!
Nooo!! This tactic has failed!!!

!
... LUCY KICK !!!!
REGULUS ...
KARYÛ NO* ...
*Fire Dragon's...

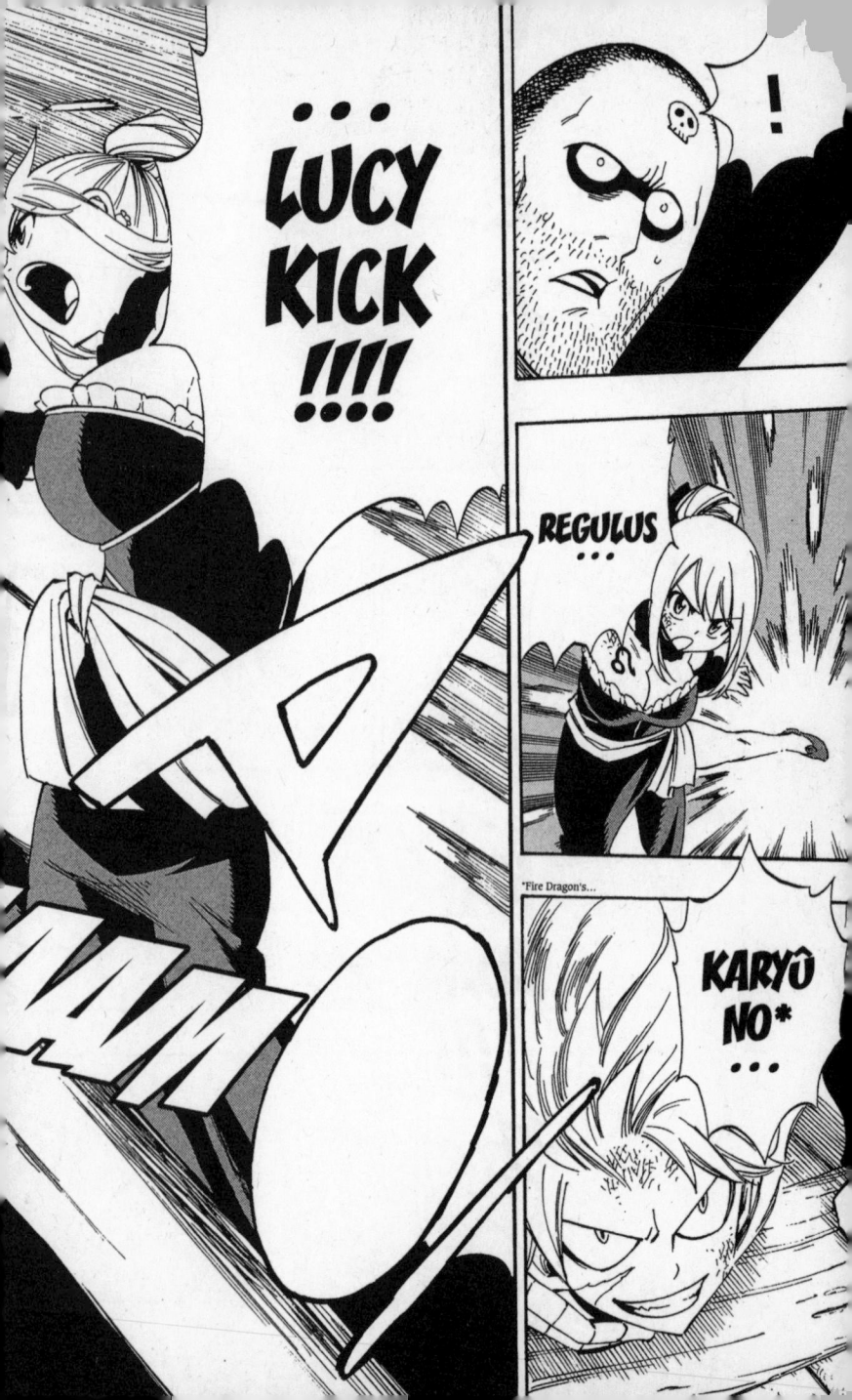

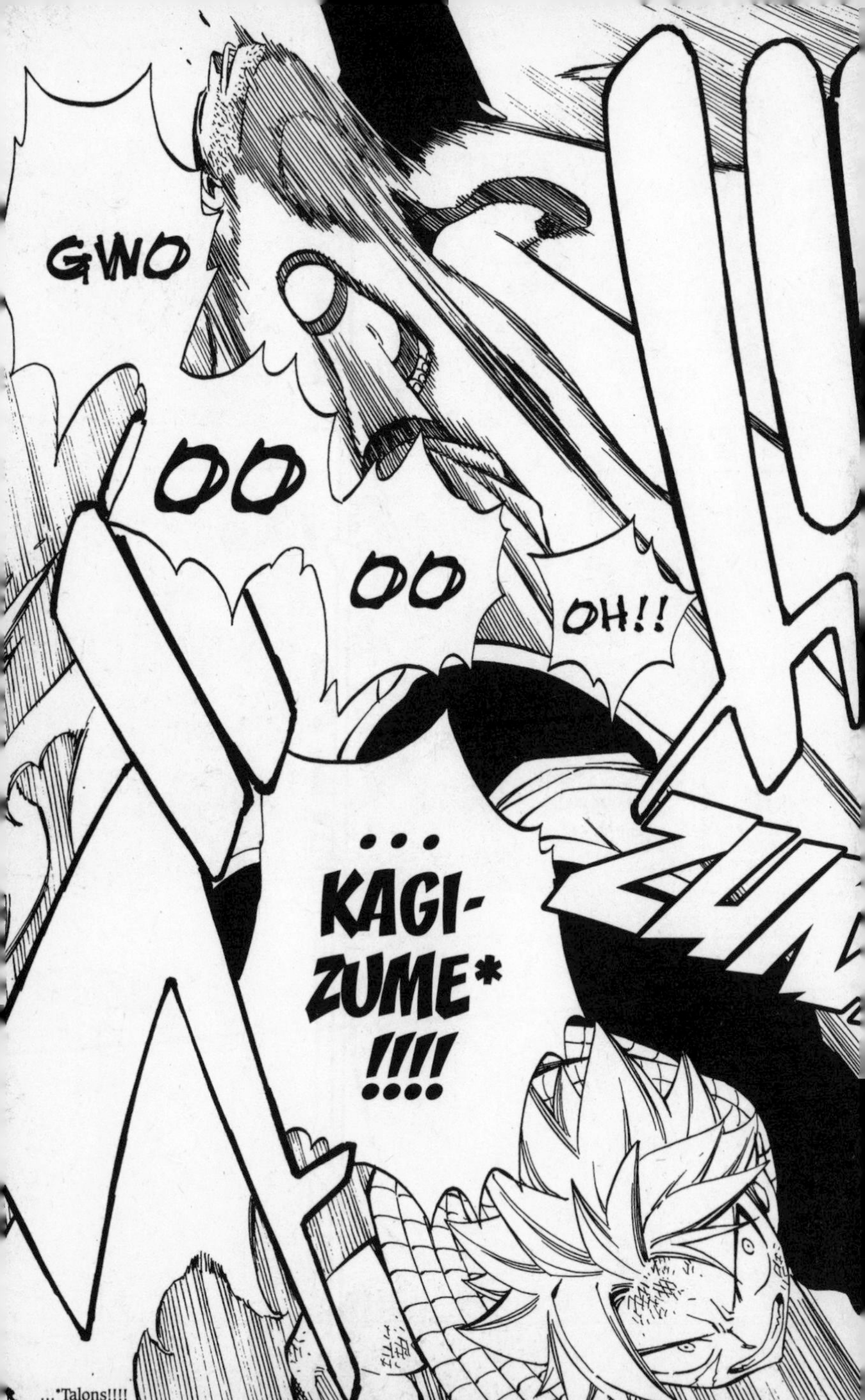
GWO
OO
OO
OH!!
...KAGI-ZUME*!!!!

...*Talons!!!!

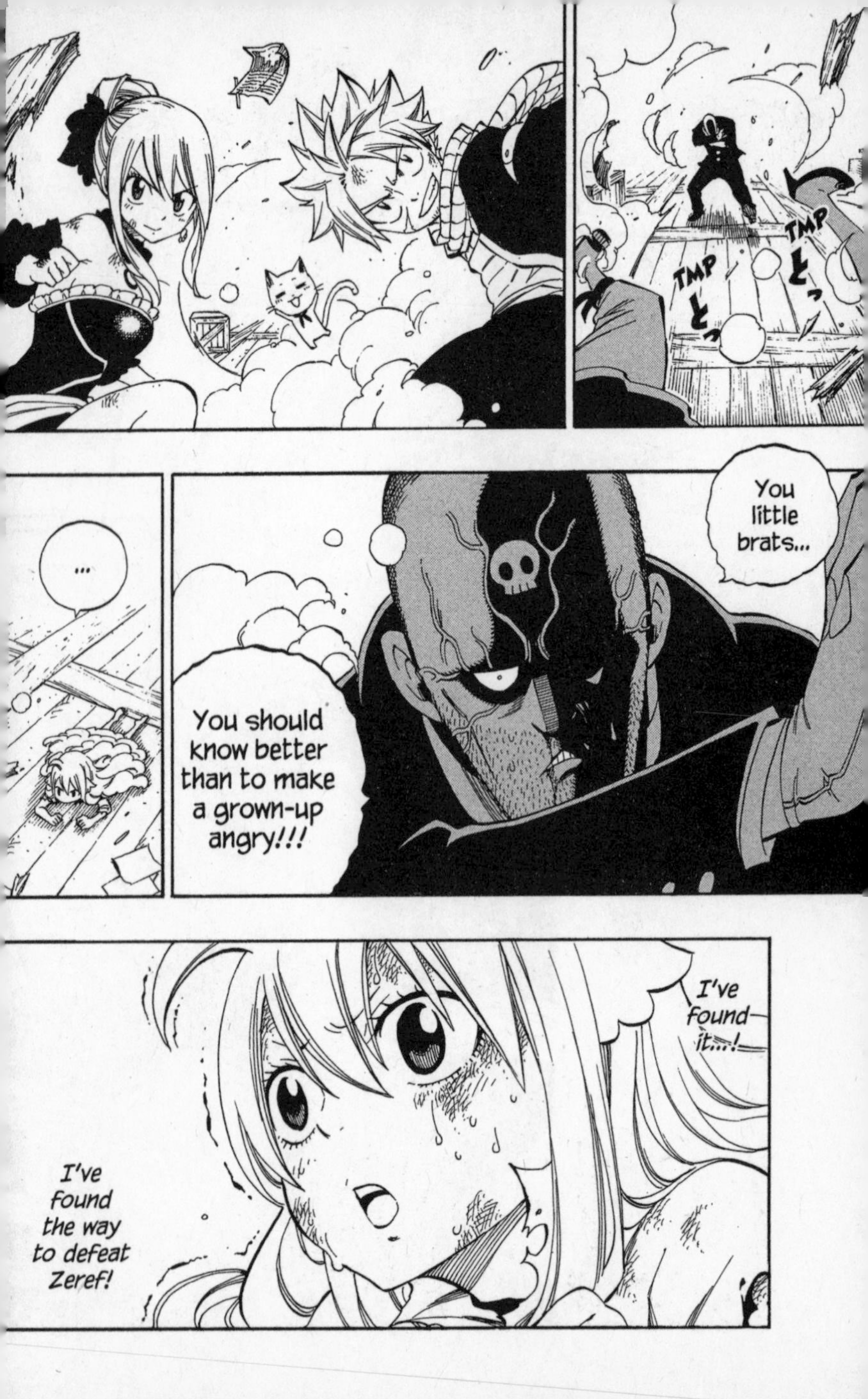
TMP
TMP
You little brats...
You should know better than to make a grown-up angry!!!
...
I've found it...!
I've found the way to defeat Zeref!

FAIRY TAIL

フェアリーテイル

Chapter 479: The One Most Respected

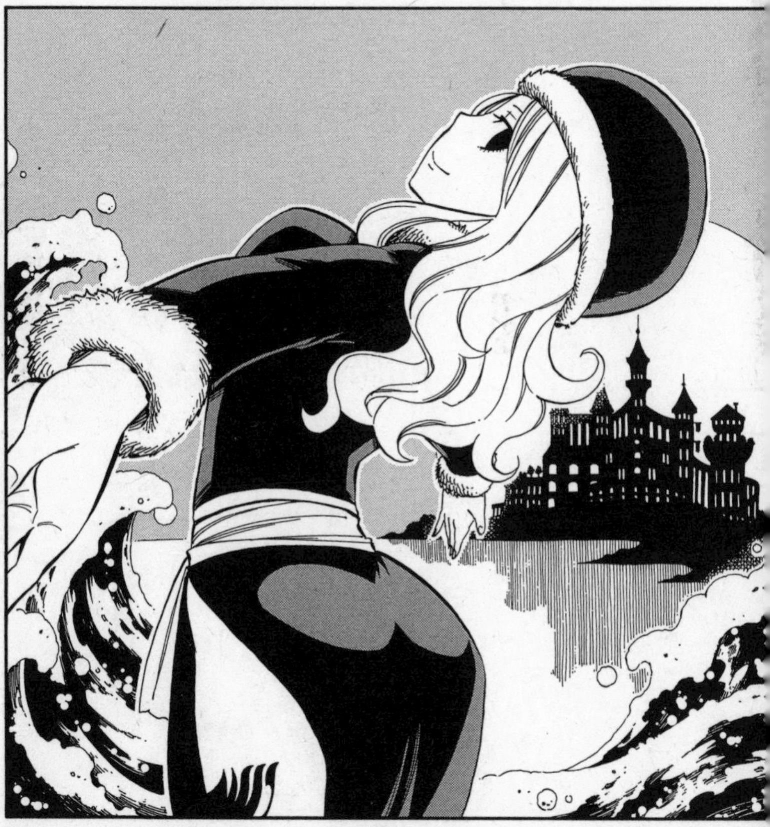

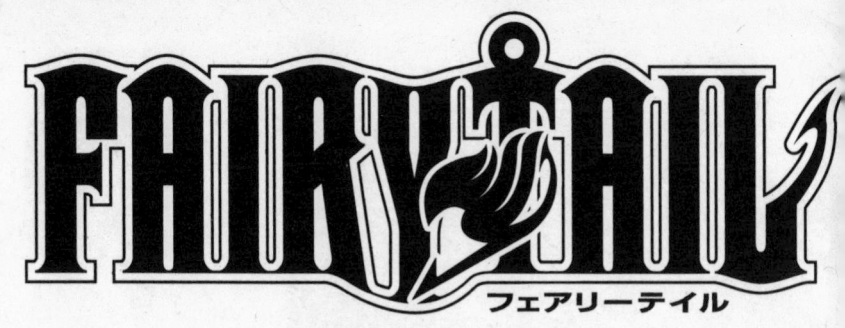

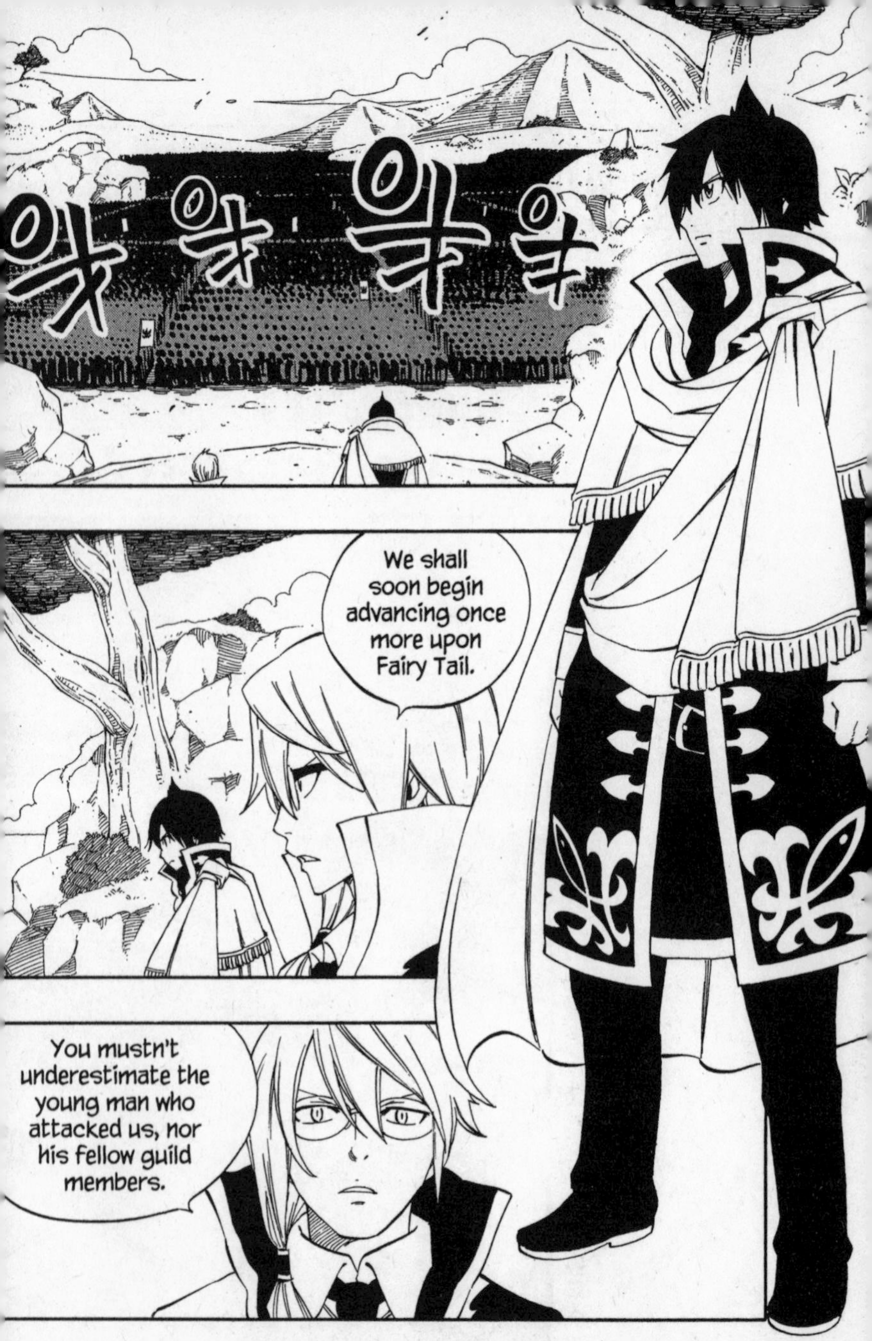
ワォ ワォ ワォ ワォ
We shall soon begin advancing once more upon Fairy Tail.
You mustn't underestimate the young man who attacked us, nor his fellow guild members.

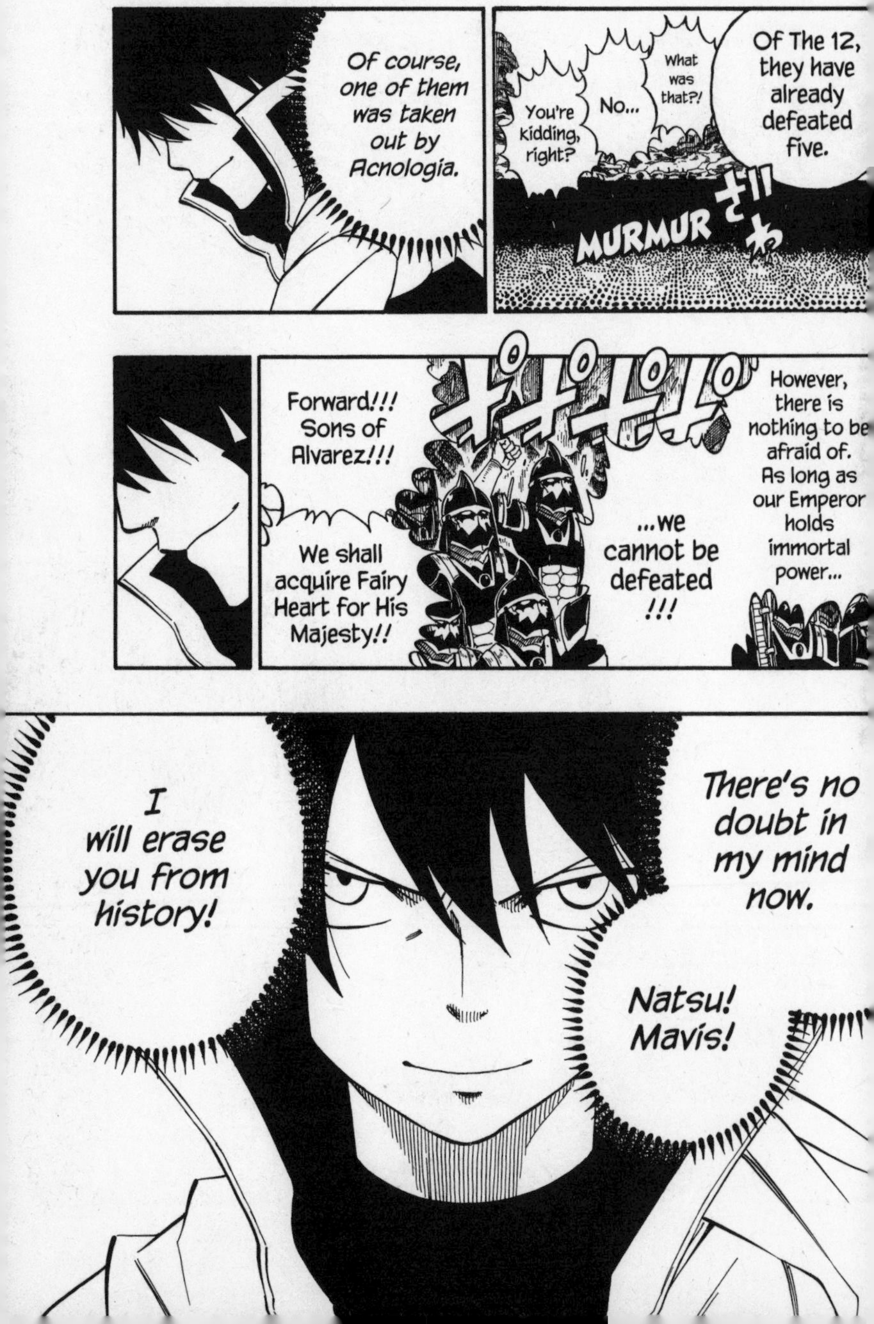
Of The 12, they have already defeated five.
What was that?!
No...
You're kidding, right?
MURMUR ざわ
Of course, one of them was taken out by Acnologia.
However, there is nothing to be afraid of. As long as our Emperor holds immortal power...
...we cannot be defeated!!!
Forward!!! Sons of Alvarez!!!
We shall acquire Fairy Heart for His Majesty!!
There's no doubt in my mind now.
Natsu! Mavis!
I will erase you from history!

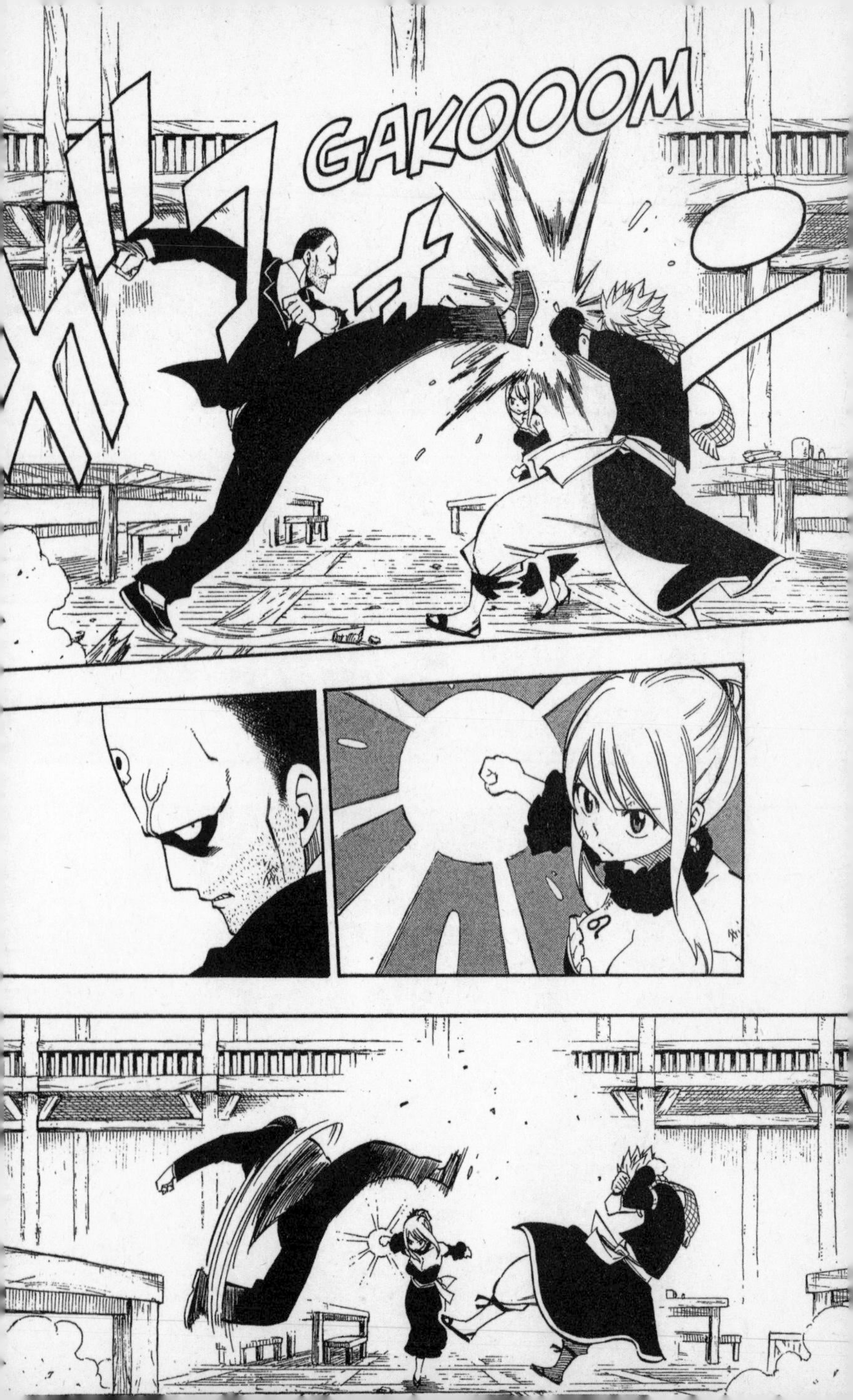
GAKOOOM

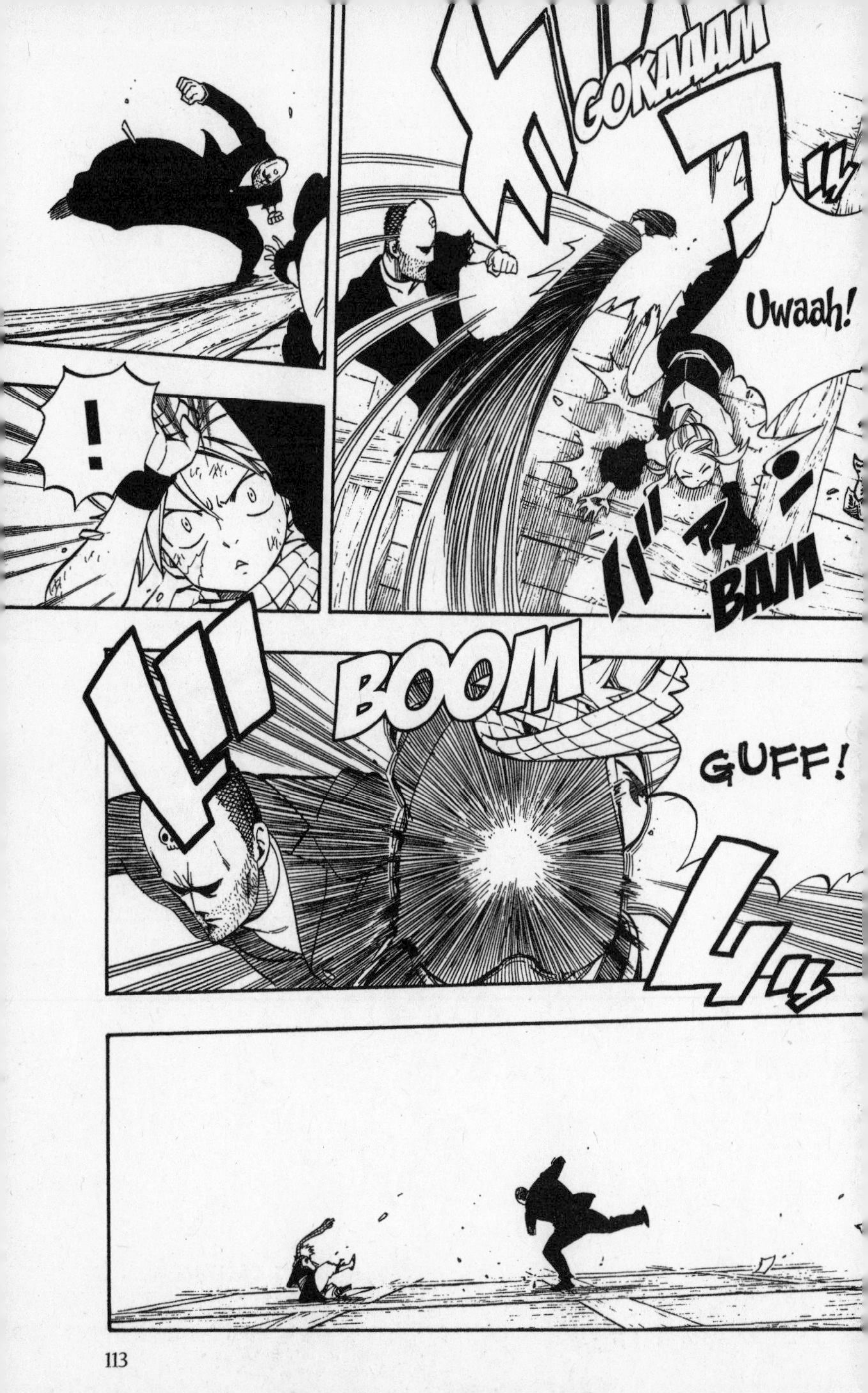
GOKAAAM
Uwaah!
BAM
!
BOOM
GUFF!

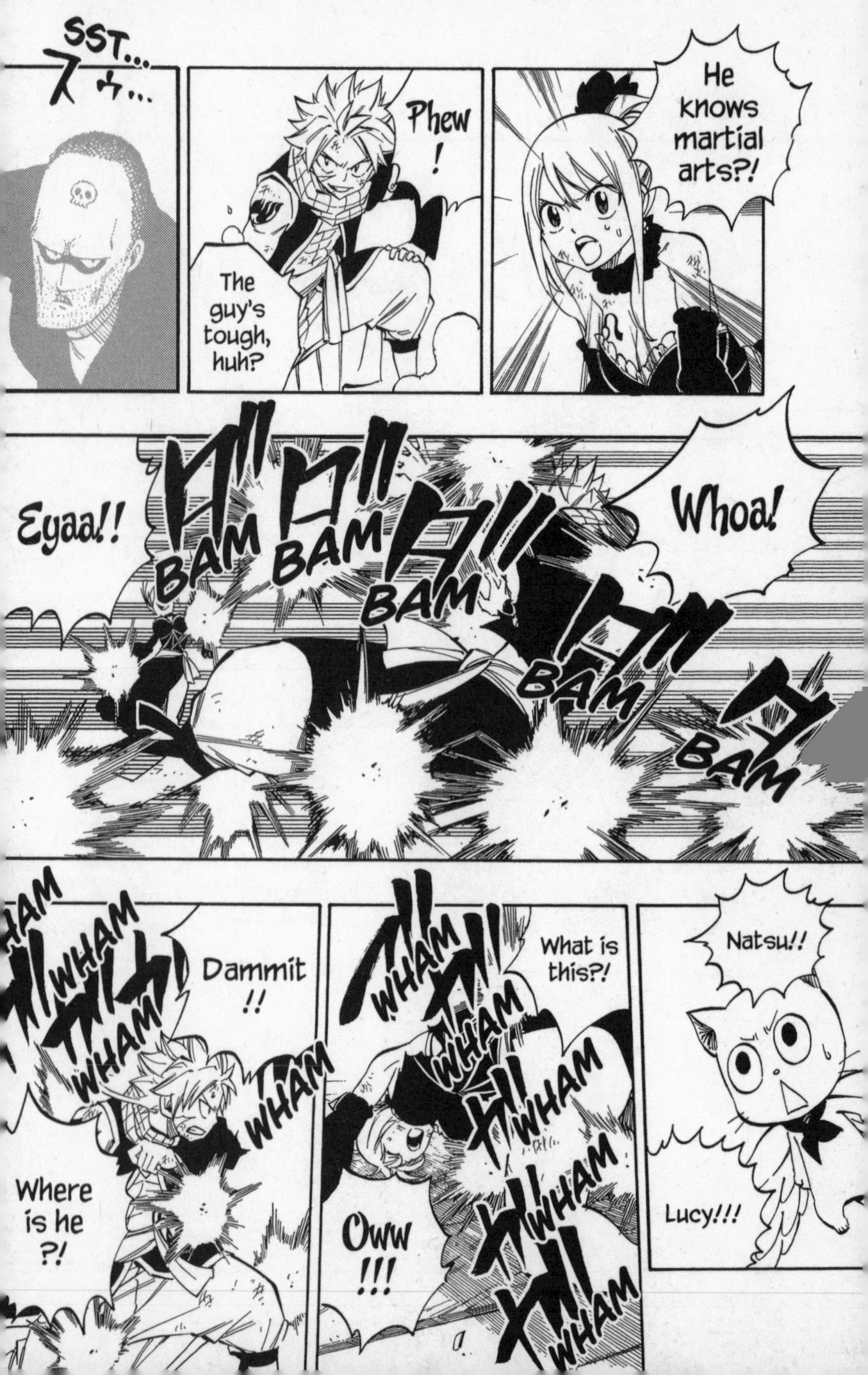
He knows martial arts?!
Phew!
The guy's tough, huh?
SST...
Whoa!
BAM
BAM
BAM
BAM
BAM
BAM
Eyaa!!
Natsu!!
Lucy!!!
What is this?!
WHAM
WHAM
WHAM
WHAM
WHAM
WHAM
Oww!!!
Dammit!!
WHAM
WHAM
WHAM
WHAM
HAM
Where is he?!

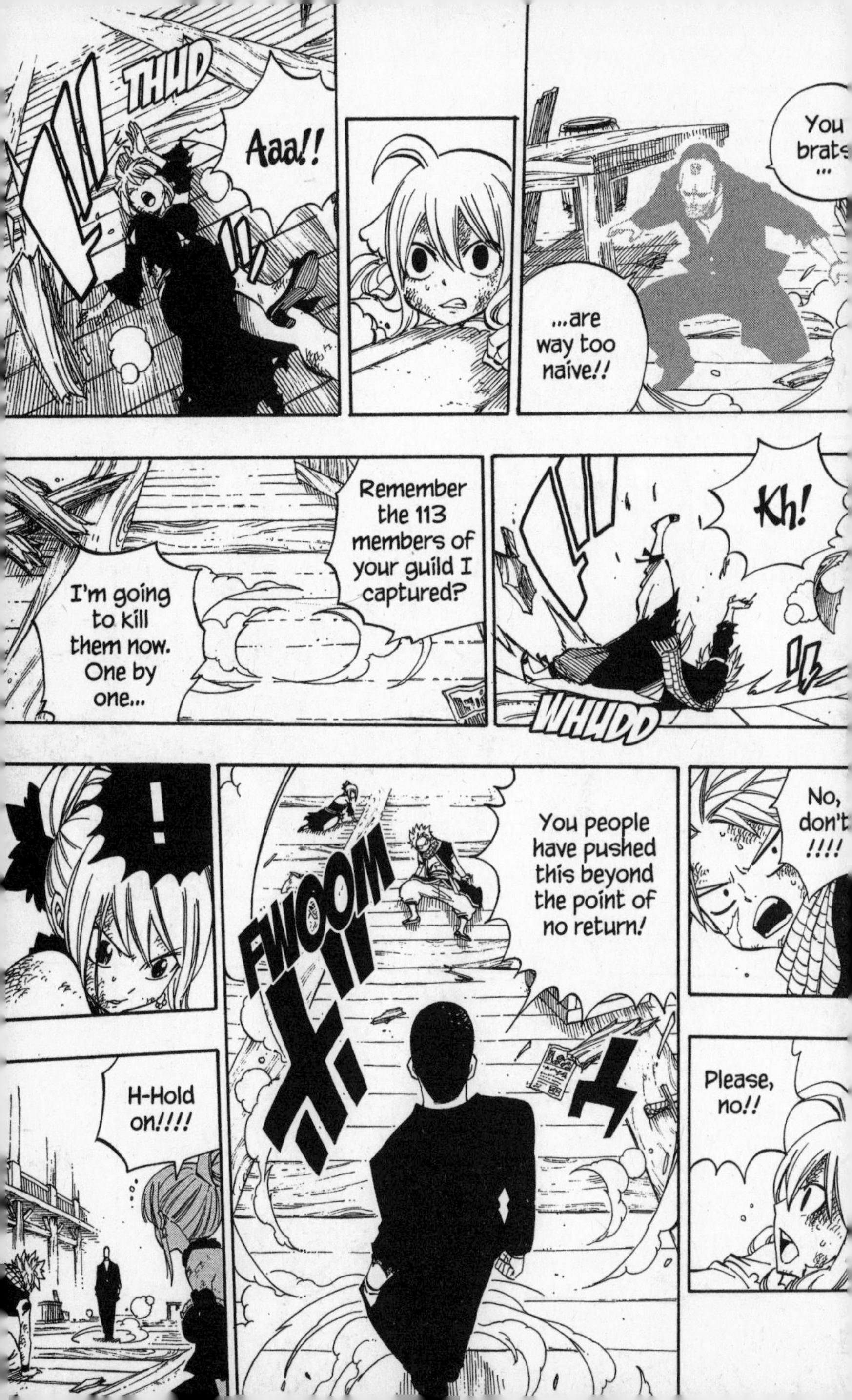
You brats ...
...are way too naive!!
THUD
Aaa!!
Kh!
WHUDD
Remember the 113 members of your guild I captured?
I'm going to kill them now. One by one...
No, don't !!!!
Please, no!!
You people have pushed this beyond the point of no return!
FWOOM
!
H-Hold on!!!!

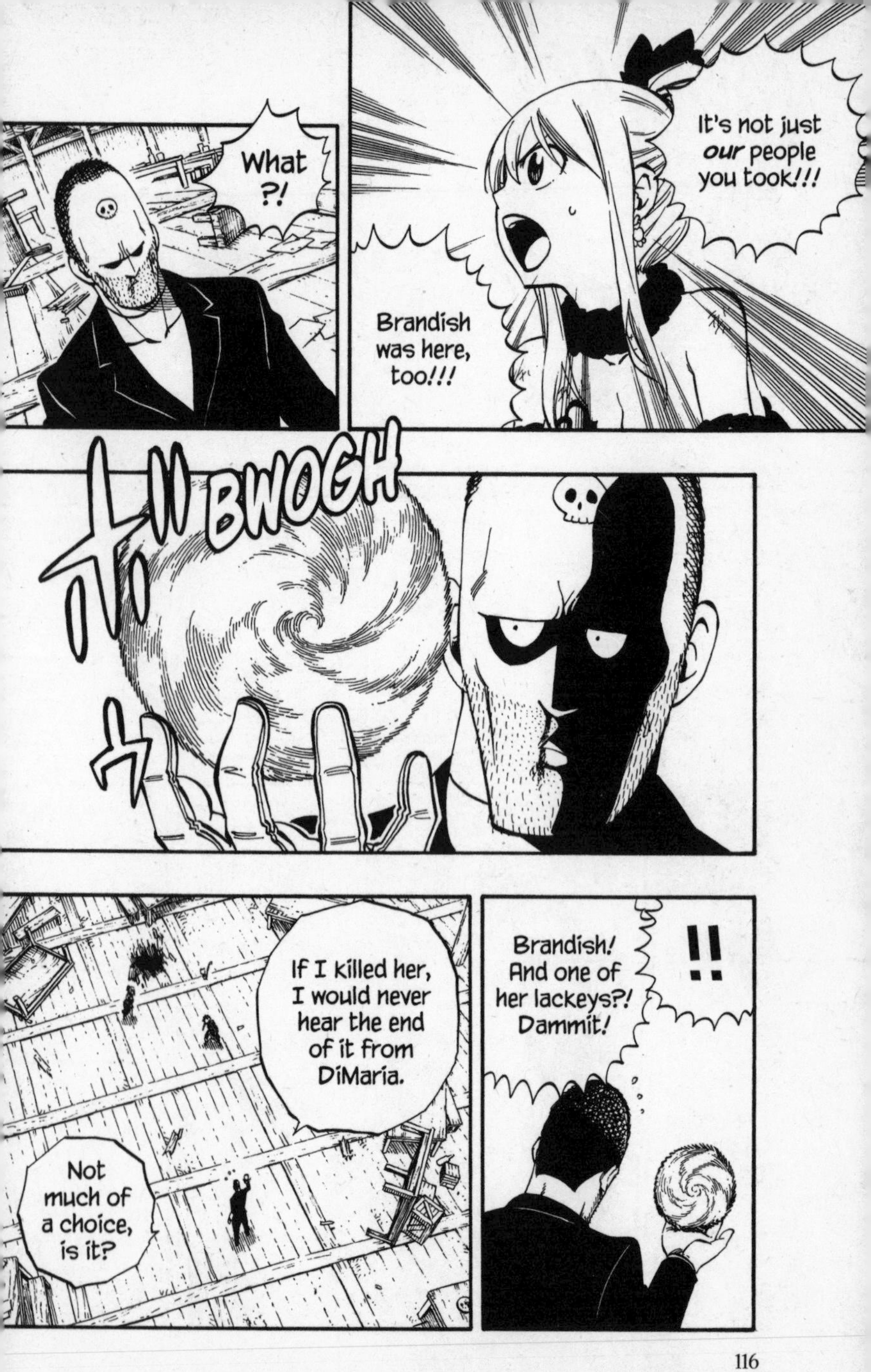

It's not just *our* people you took!!!
Brandish was here, too!!!
What ?!
BWOGH
!!
Brandish! And one of her lackeys?! Dammit!
If I killed her, I would never hear the end of it from DiMaria.
Not much of a choice, is it?

Pathetic!
Oof!
BWUMPH
Urg!
Is that you, Jacob?!
CRIKK
CRIKK
Ohh! I can't thank you enough, Jacob-san!!
...
There's another one of me?!
We pass! ♥

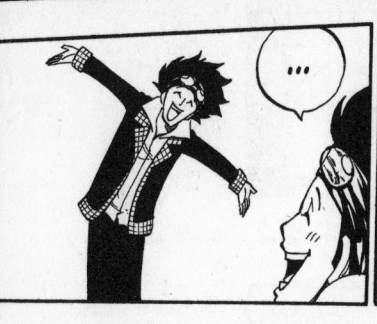

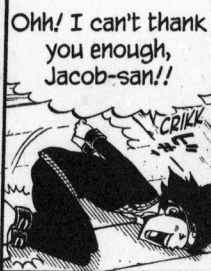

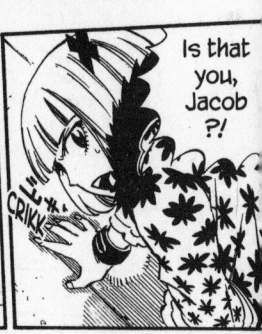

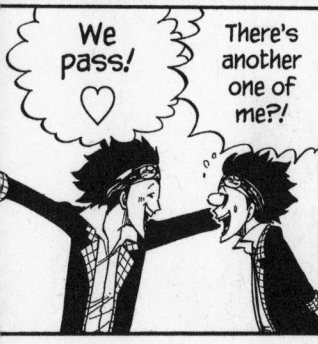

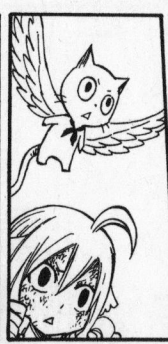

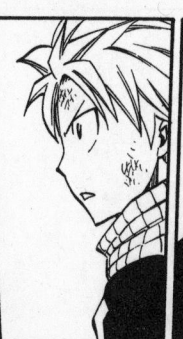

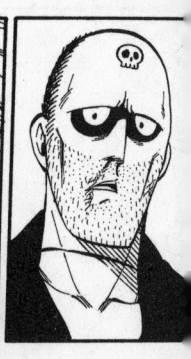

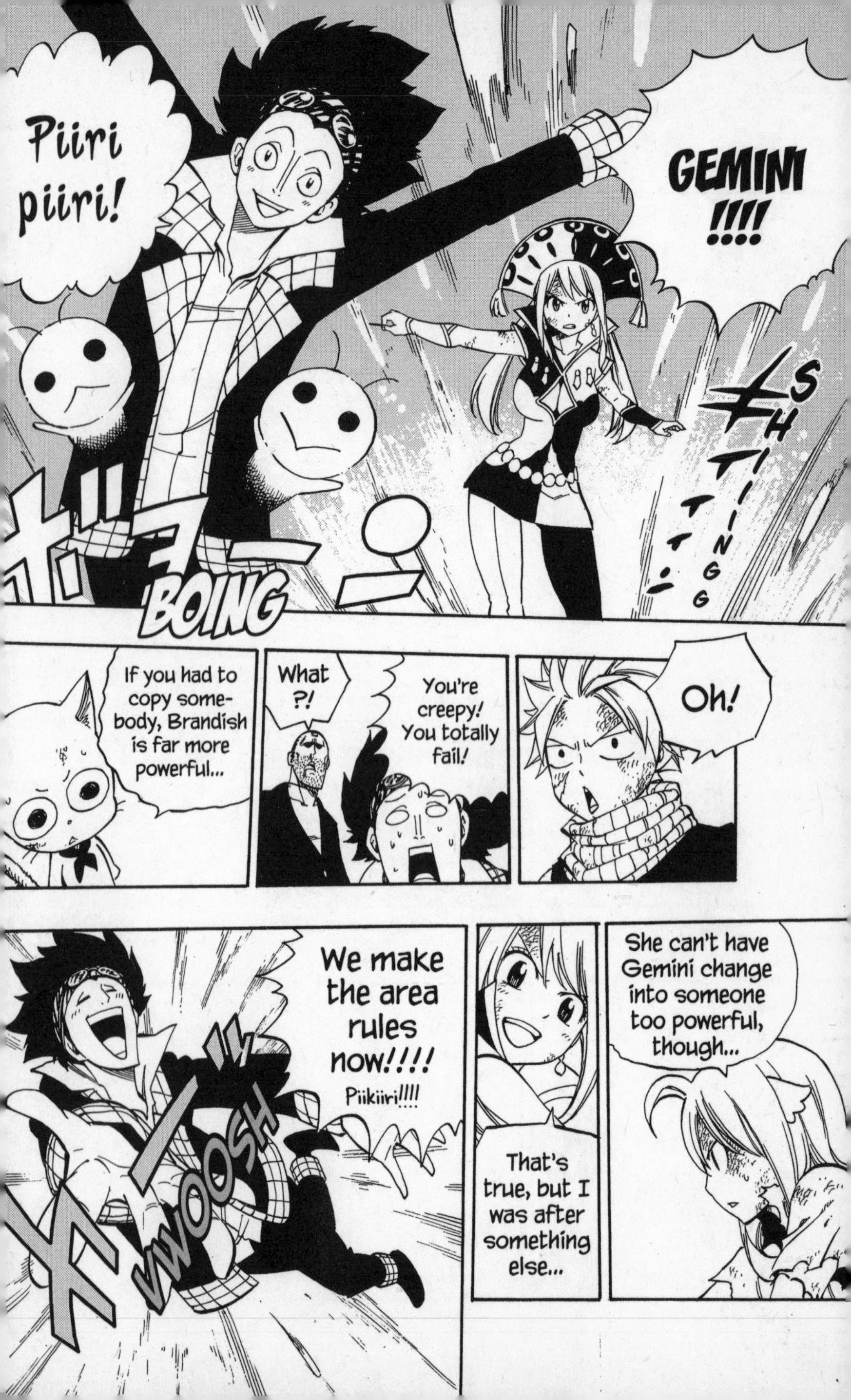
GEMINI!!!!
SHTIIING
Piiri piiri!
BOING
Oh!
You're creepy! You totally fail!
What?!
If you had to copy somebody, Brandish is far more powerful...
She can't have Gemini change into someone too powerful, though...
That's true, but I was after something else...
We make the area rules now!!!!
Piikiiri!!!!
WOOSH

And there goes my Star Dress, too.
But it's okay.
Ah! We have to vanish now!
POPP
Ah!
That just reversed all the Spatial Magic in our vicinity!
...
My Transport is...
D-Dammit!!!
In other words...
POP
POP
POP
POP
POP
POP

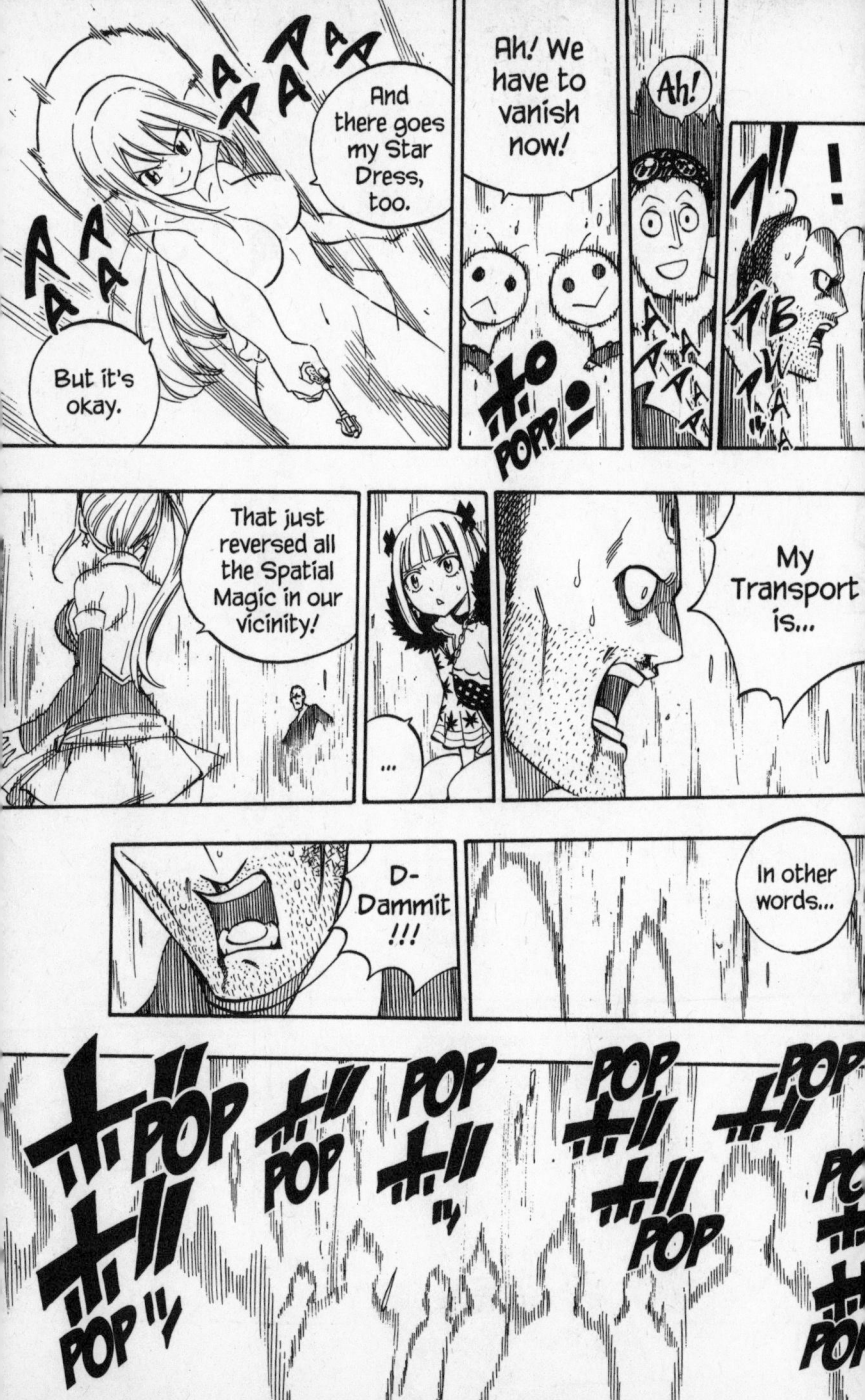

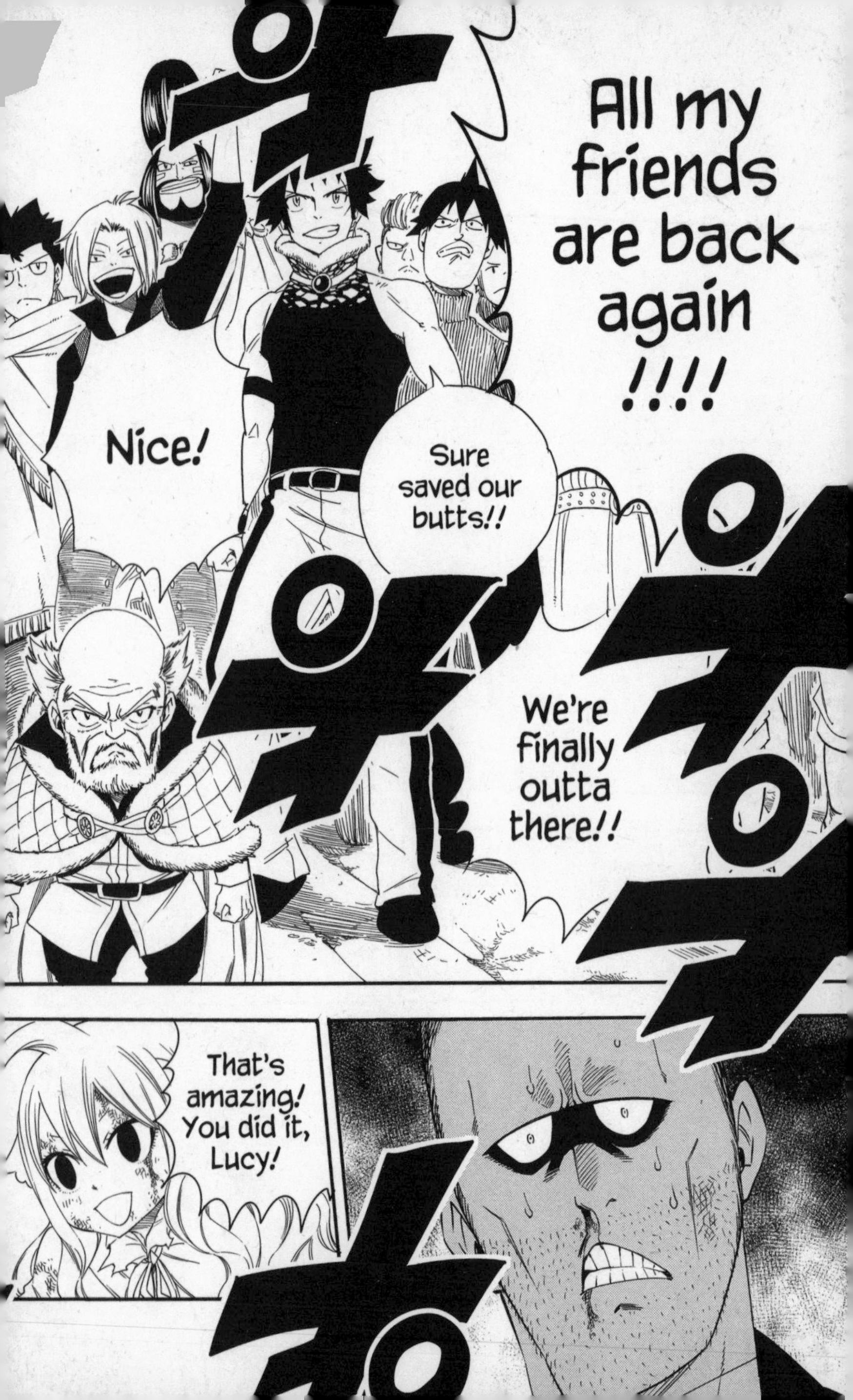
All my friends are back again!!!!
Sure saved our butts!!
Nice!
We're finally outta there!!
That's amazing! You did it, Lucy!

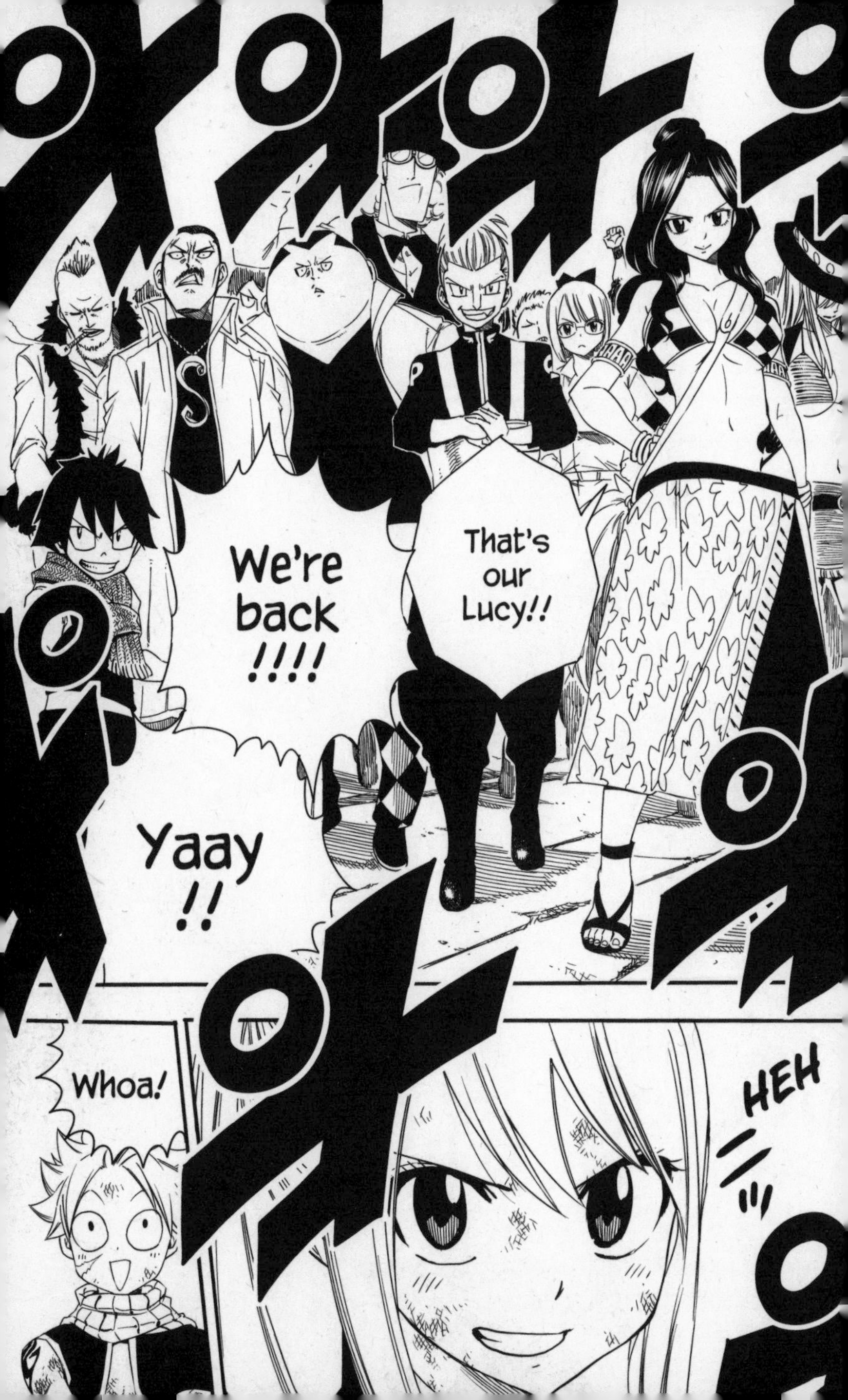
That's our Lucy!!
We're back!!!!
Yaay!!
HEH
Whoa!

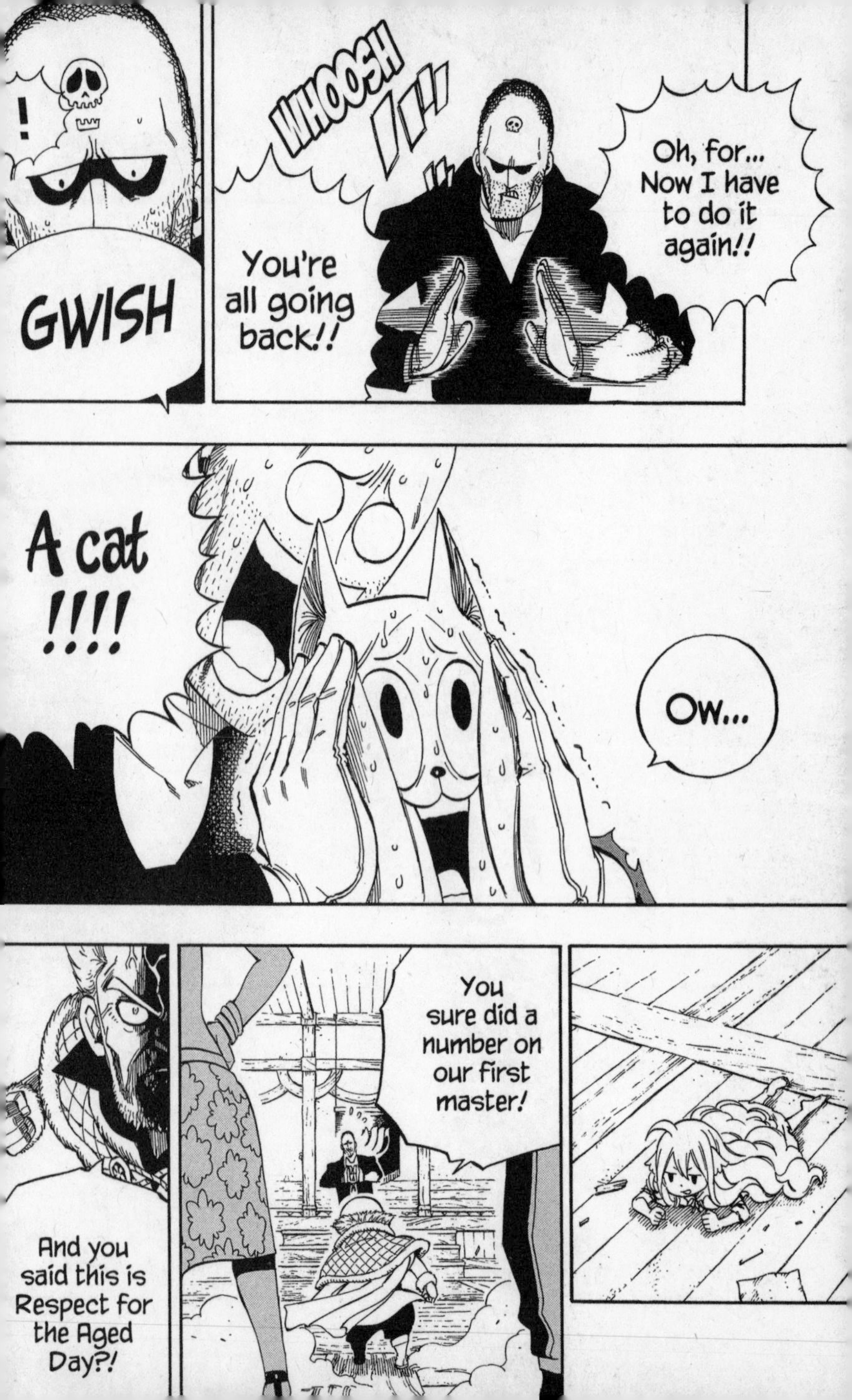
Oh, for... Now I have to do it again!!
WHOOSH
You're all going back!!
!
GWISH
Ow...
A cat !!!!
You sure did a number on our first master!
And you said this is Respect for the Aged Day?!

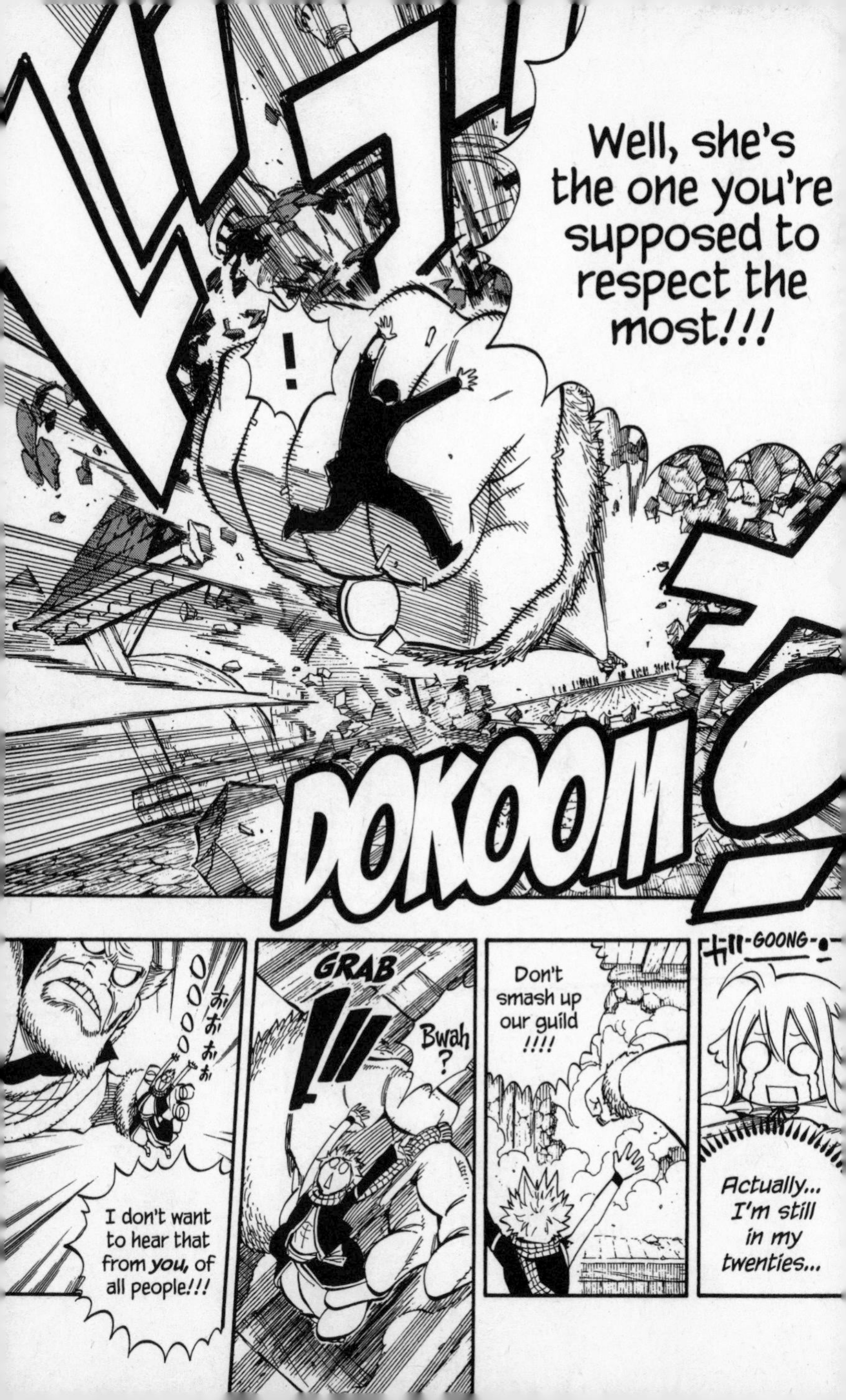
Well, she's the one you're supposed to respect the most!!!
!
DOKOOM
-GOONG-
Actually... I'm still in my twenties...
Don't smash up our guild !!!!
GRAB
!!
Bwah ?
OOOOO
I don't want to hear that from *you*, of all people!!!

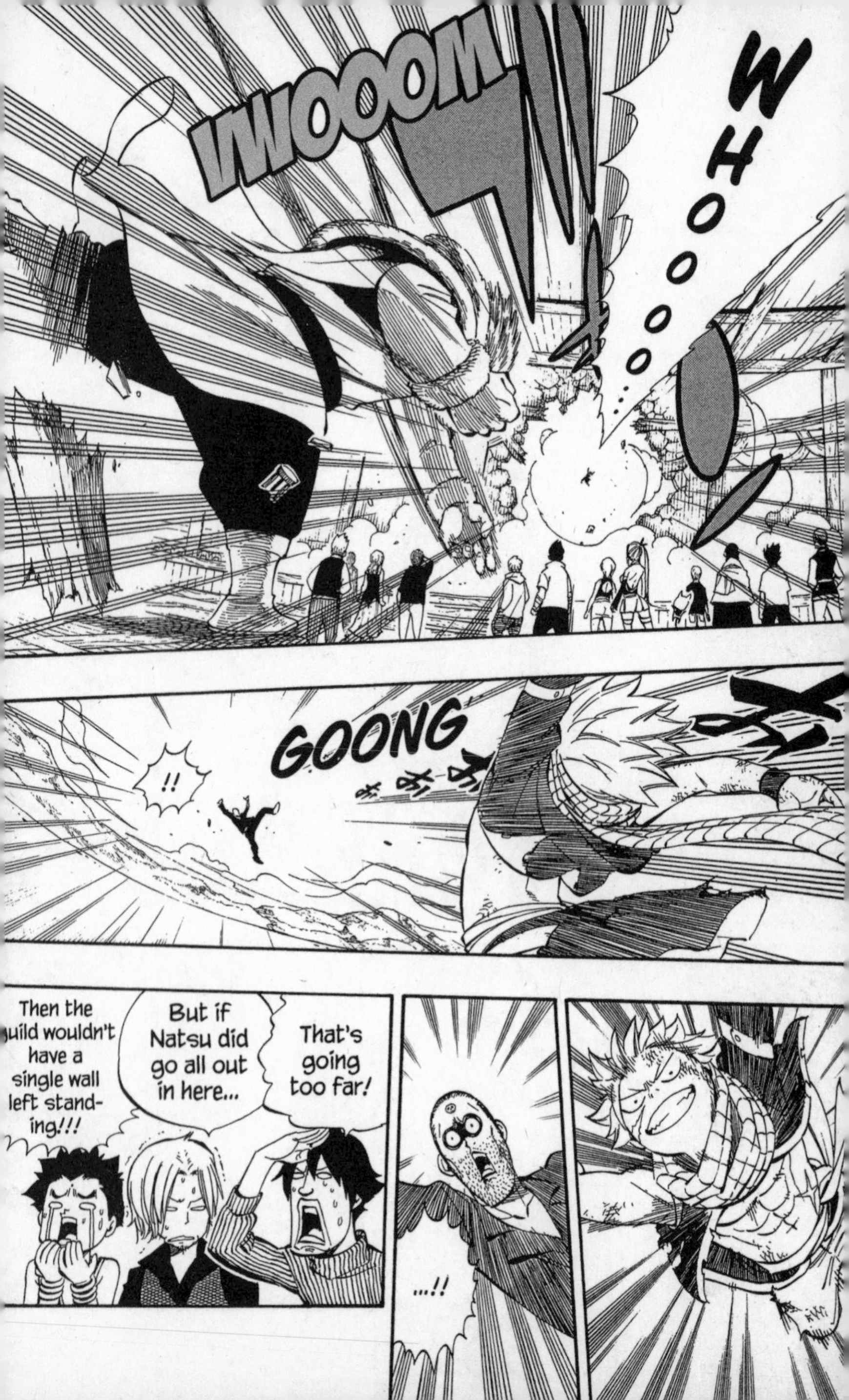
WHOOOO...
VWOOOM
GOONG
!!
...!!
That's going too far!
But if Natsu did go all out in here...
Then the uild wouldn't have a single wall left standing!!!

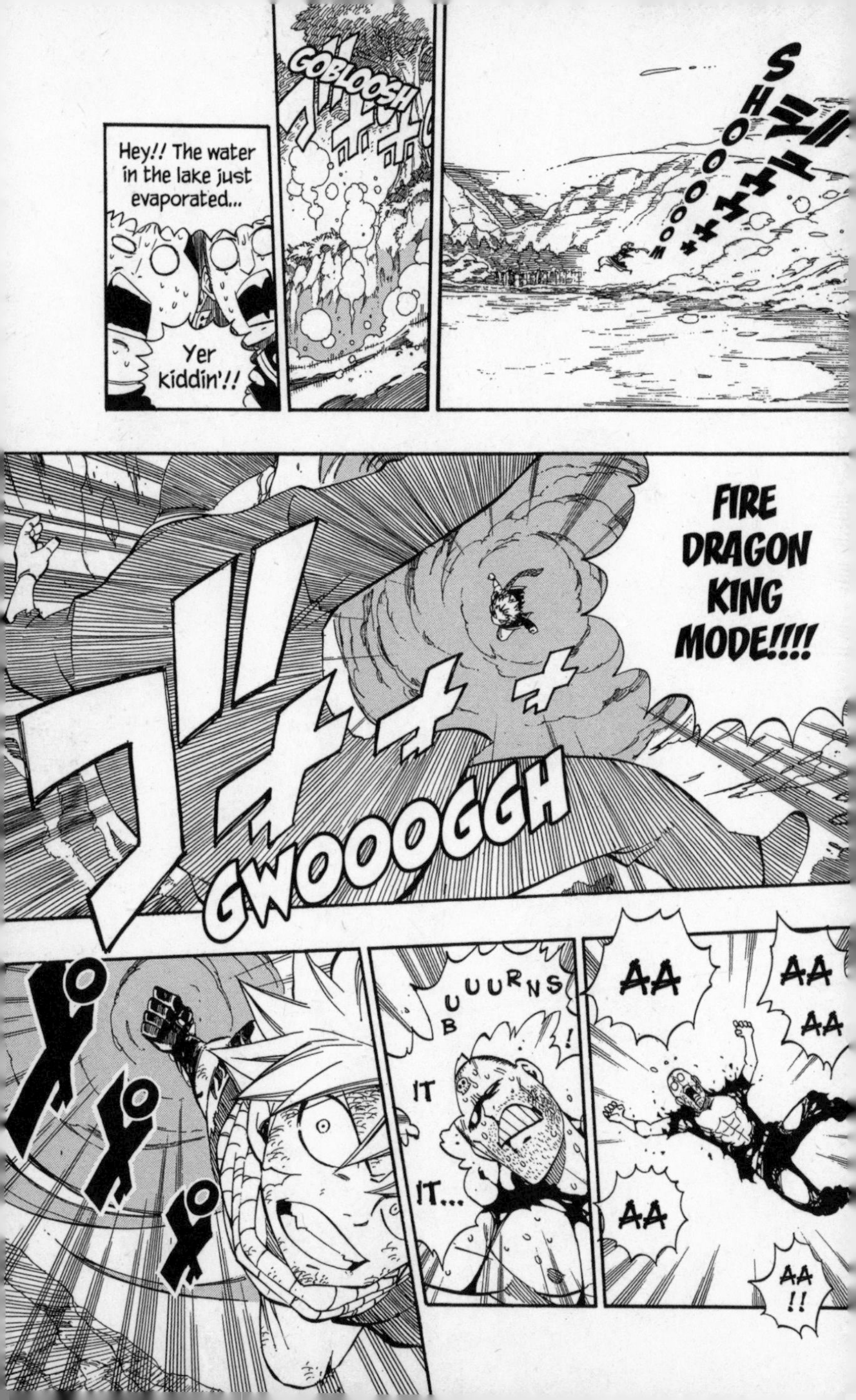
SHOOOOOOM
GOBLOOSH
Hey!! The water in the lake just evaporated...
Yer kiddin'!!
FIRE DRAGON KING MODE!!!!
GWOOOGGH
AA
AA
AA
AA
AA!!
BUUURNS!
IT
IT...

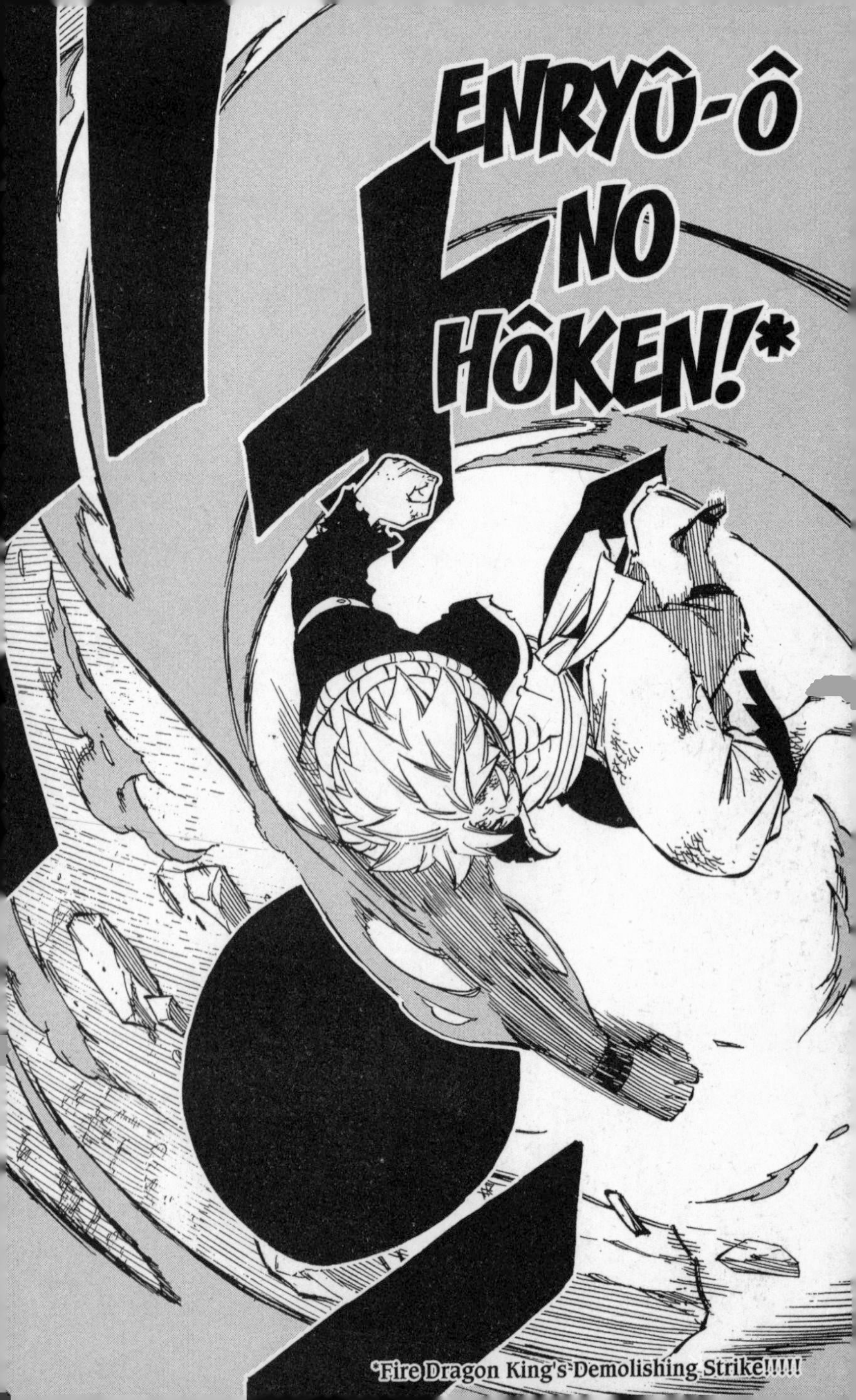
ENRYÛ-Ô NO HÔKEN!*

*Fire Dragon King's Demolishing Strike!!!!!

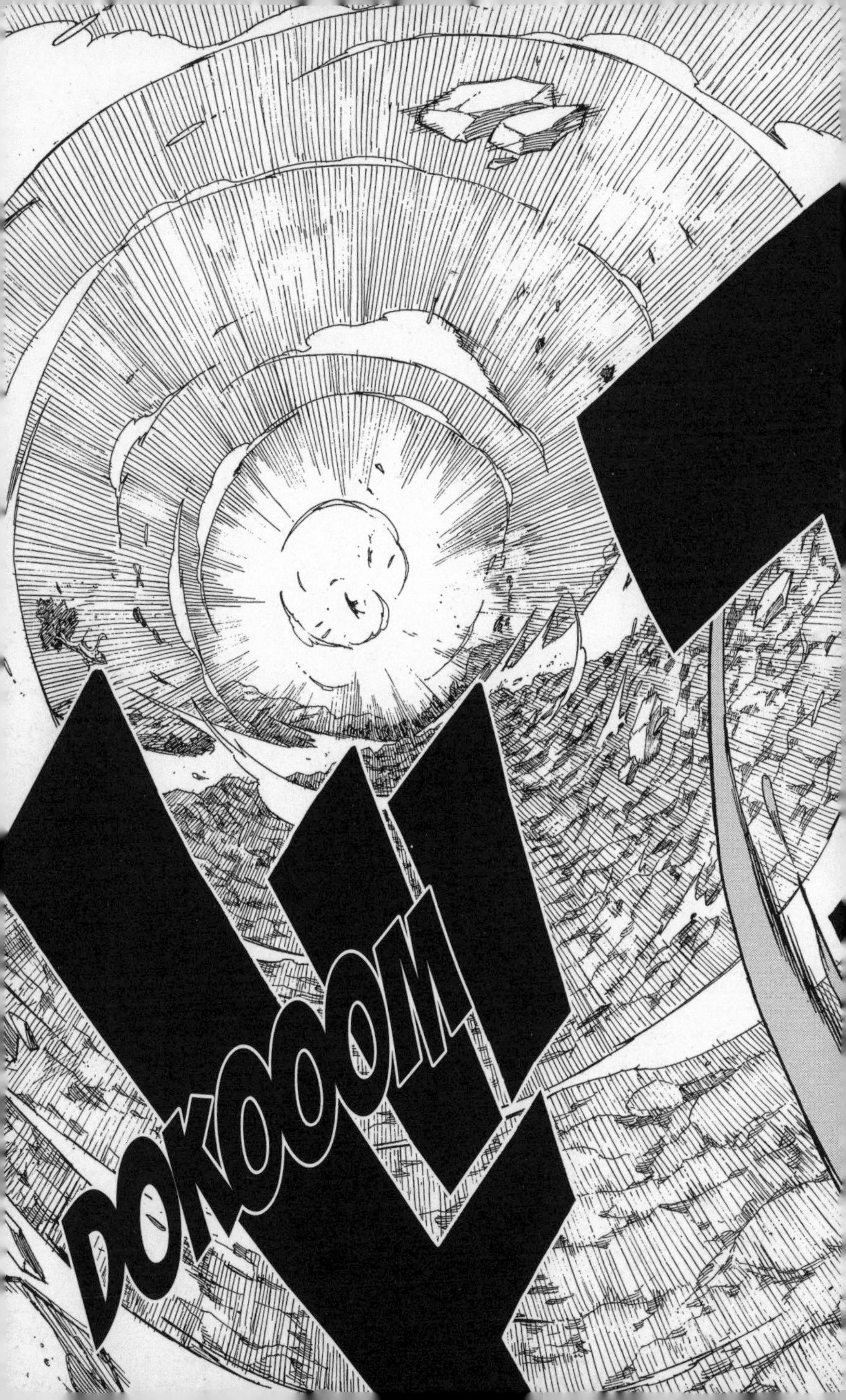
DOKOOOM

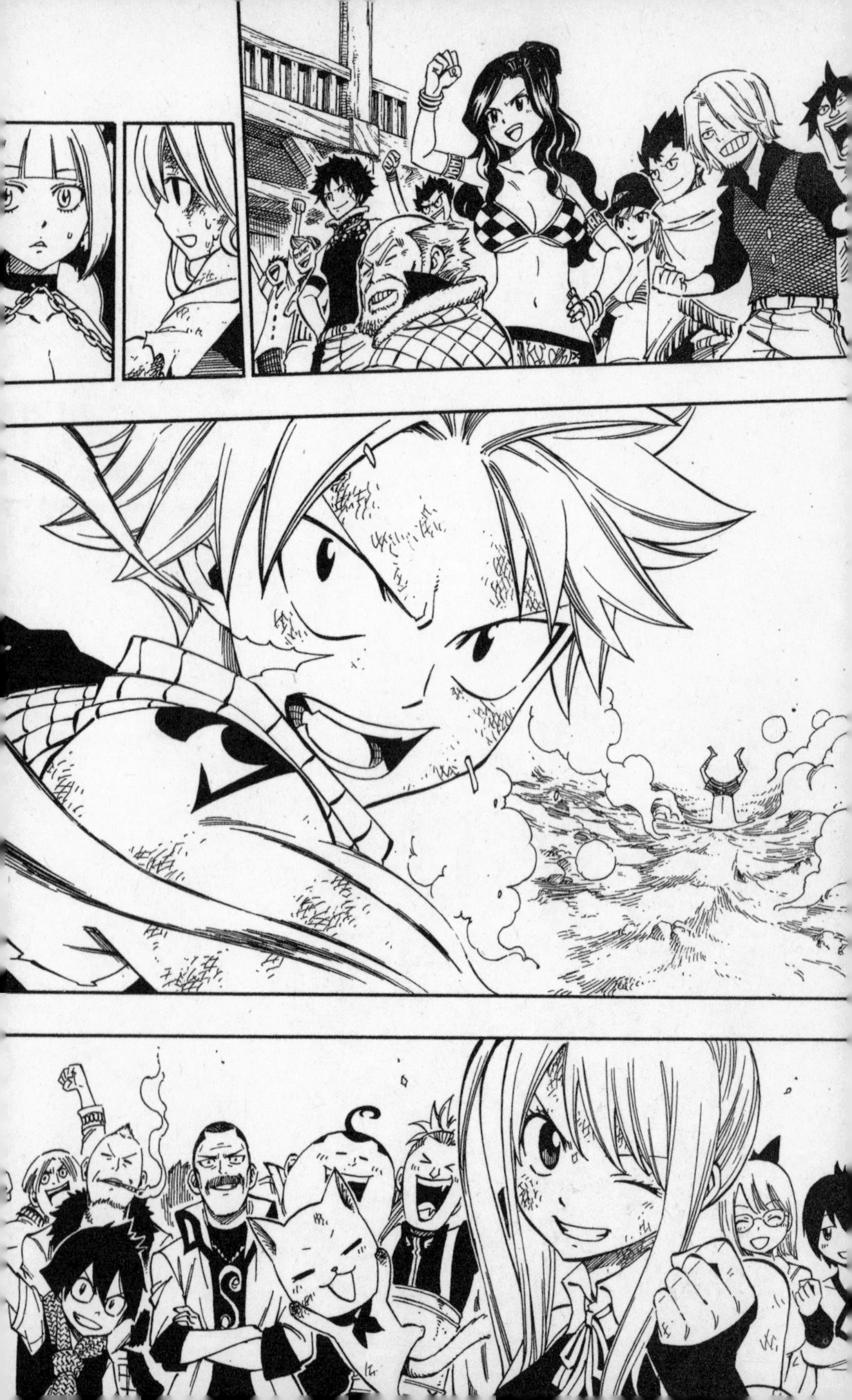

FAIRY TAIL

フェアリーテイル

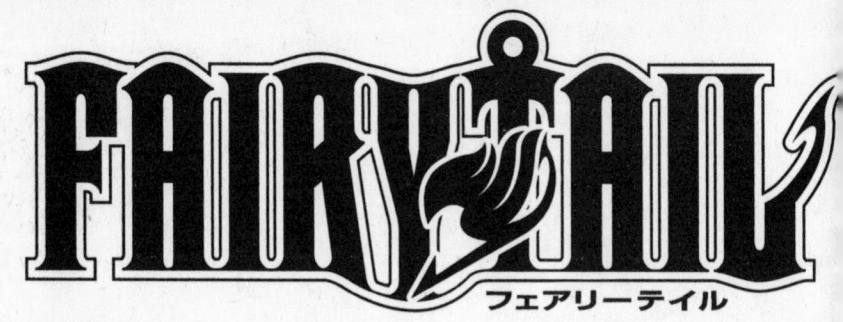

Chapter 480: Grave Markers of the North

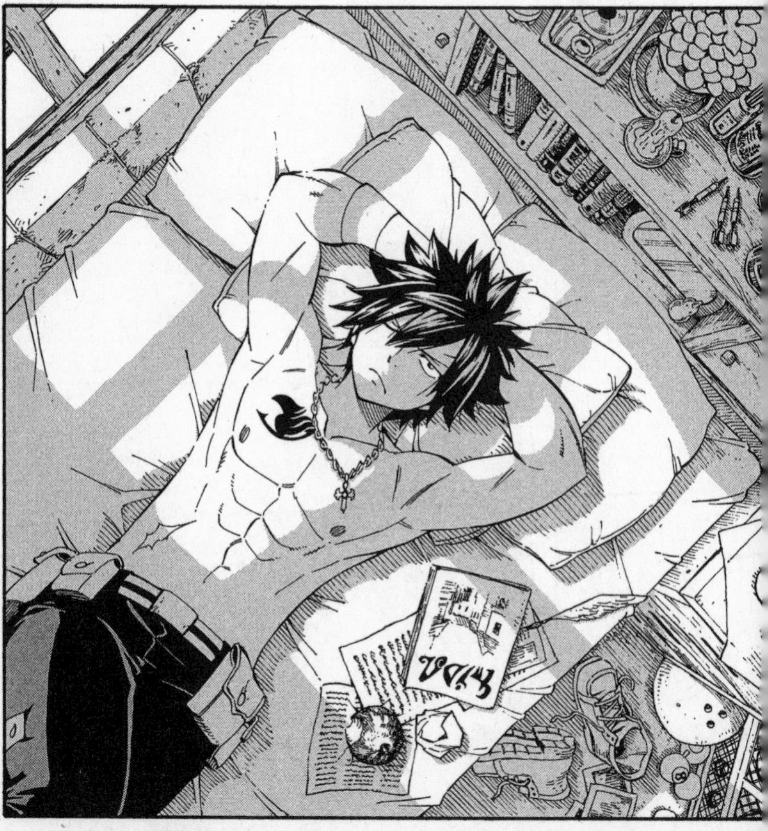

Hey, I hear you went and saved my life!
Thanks a lot!
...
You didn't have to go back to your cell...
We really appreciate what you did!
I never expected you to defeat Jacob.
I now realize what the Emperor meant when he told us not to underestimate you.

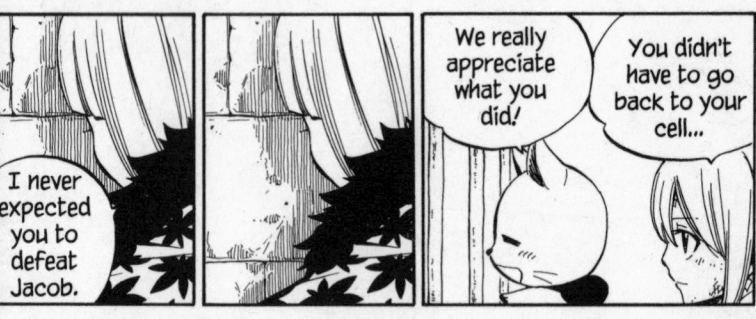

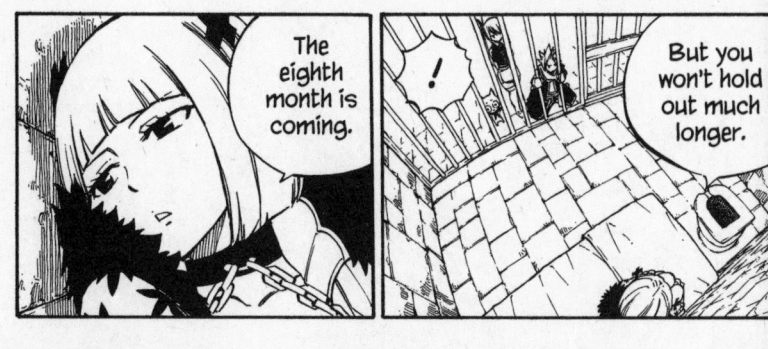

The eighth month is coming.
!
But you won't hold out much longer.
Eighth month?
No, that was *last* month.
In Alakitasia, we see the eighth month as the month of natural disasters.
So everybody makes sure to pray, take more care, and live a more upright life during that month.
August is the month of fear.
Everybody knows it. It's in our legends.

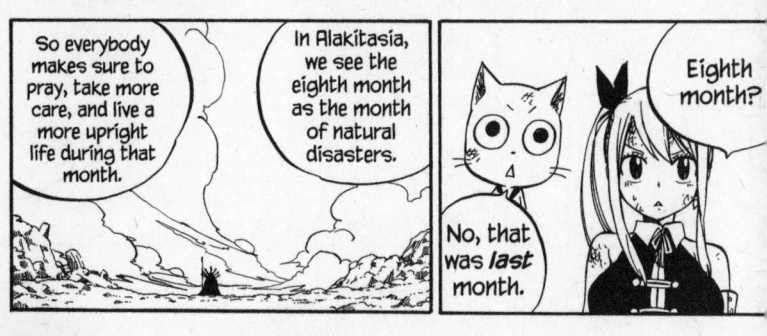

Don't go punching holes in the guild, Master!!
KLANG!
KRANK!
CHANK!
Hey, get me a wooden board up here!
Aren't old guys supposed to have more restraint?
I've got Wood Make Magic! I can fix it in no time!
Please forgive me...
Warren! How're the other regions?
I don't know... It looks like the radar's busted!
That could have been my fault, too...
GLARE
No... There's a really strong jamming signal.
Somebody's blocking my radar!

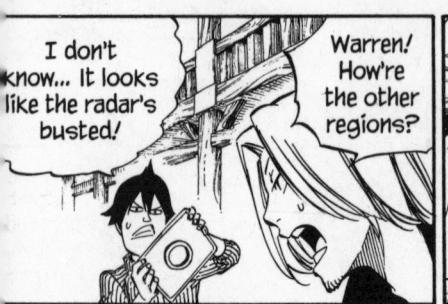

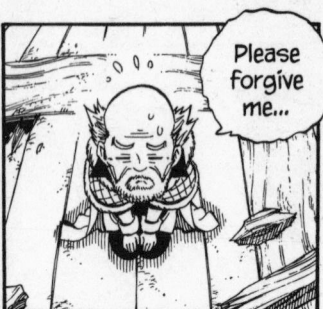

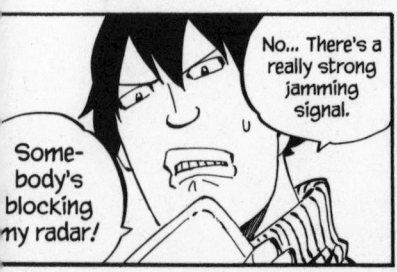

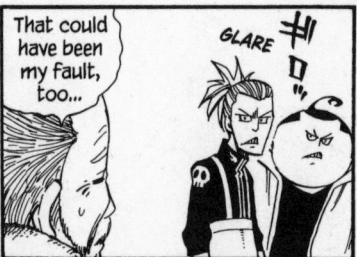

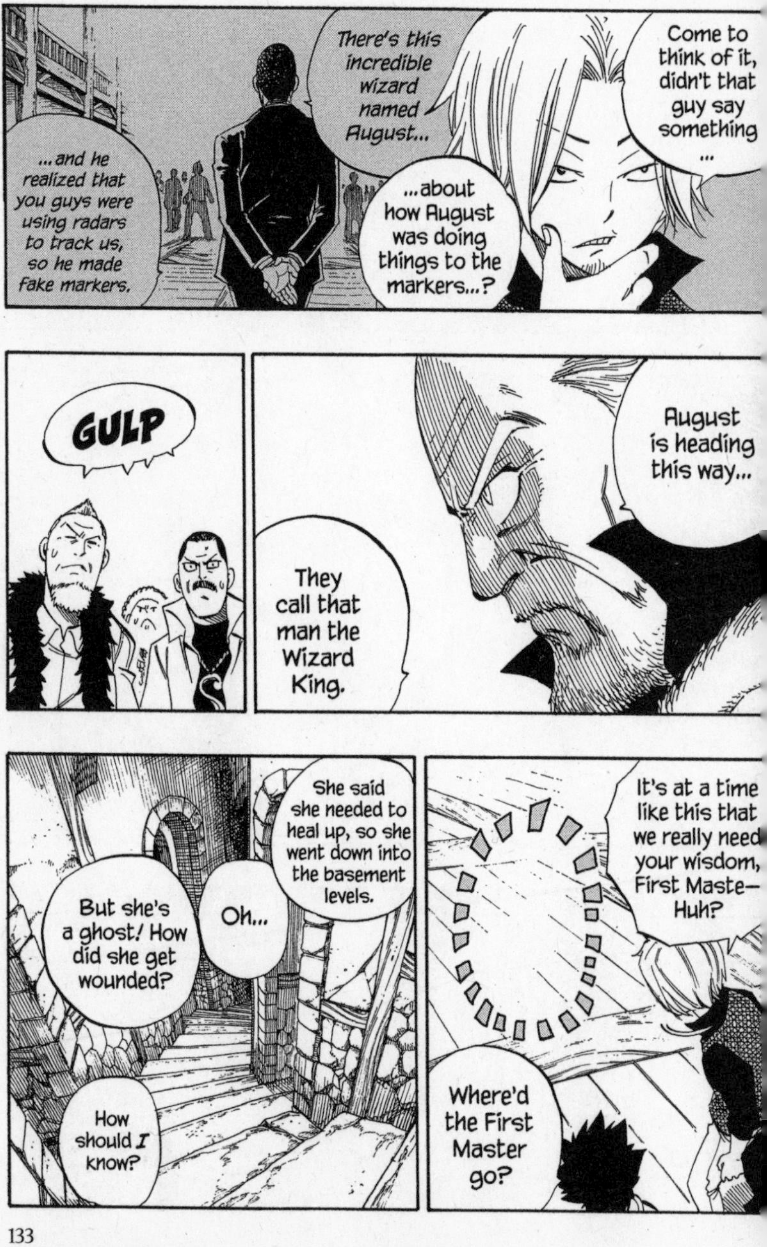
Come to think of it, didn't that guy say something ...
...about how August was doing things to the markers...?
There's this incredible wizard named August...
...and he realized that you guys were using radars to track us, so he made fake markers.
August is heading this way...
They call that man the Wizard King.
GULP
It's at a time like this that we really need your wisdom, First Maste— Huh?
Where'd the First Master go?
She said she needed to heal up, so she went down into the basement levels.
Oh...
But she's a ghost! How did she get wounded?
How should I know?

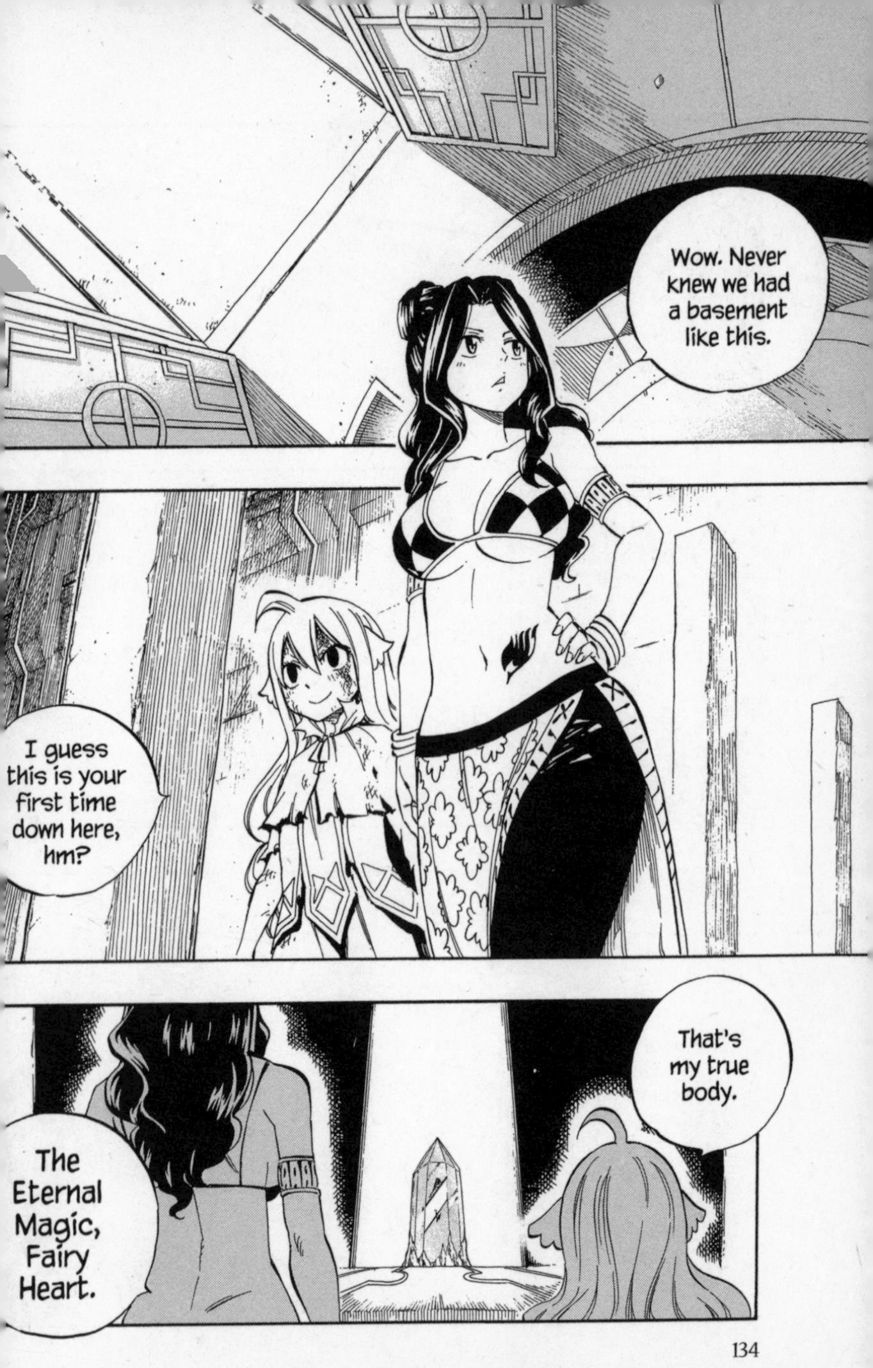
Wow. Never knew we had a basement like this.
I guess this is your first time down here, hm?
That's my true body.
The Eternal Magic, Fairy Heart.

Yes...

That's what Zeref is after?

When I saw Natsu and Lucy fighting Jacob's magic...

...I figured out a plan to defeat Zeref.

I can't give you any details yet, but...

Huh?

...the first step is to get my body out of that lacrima.

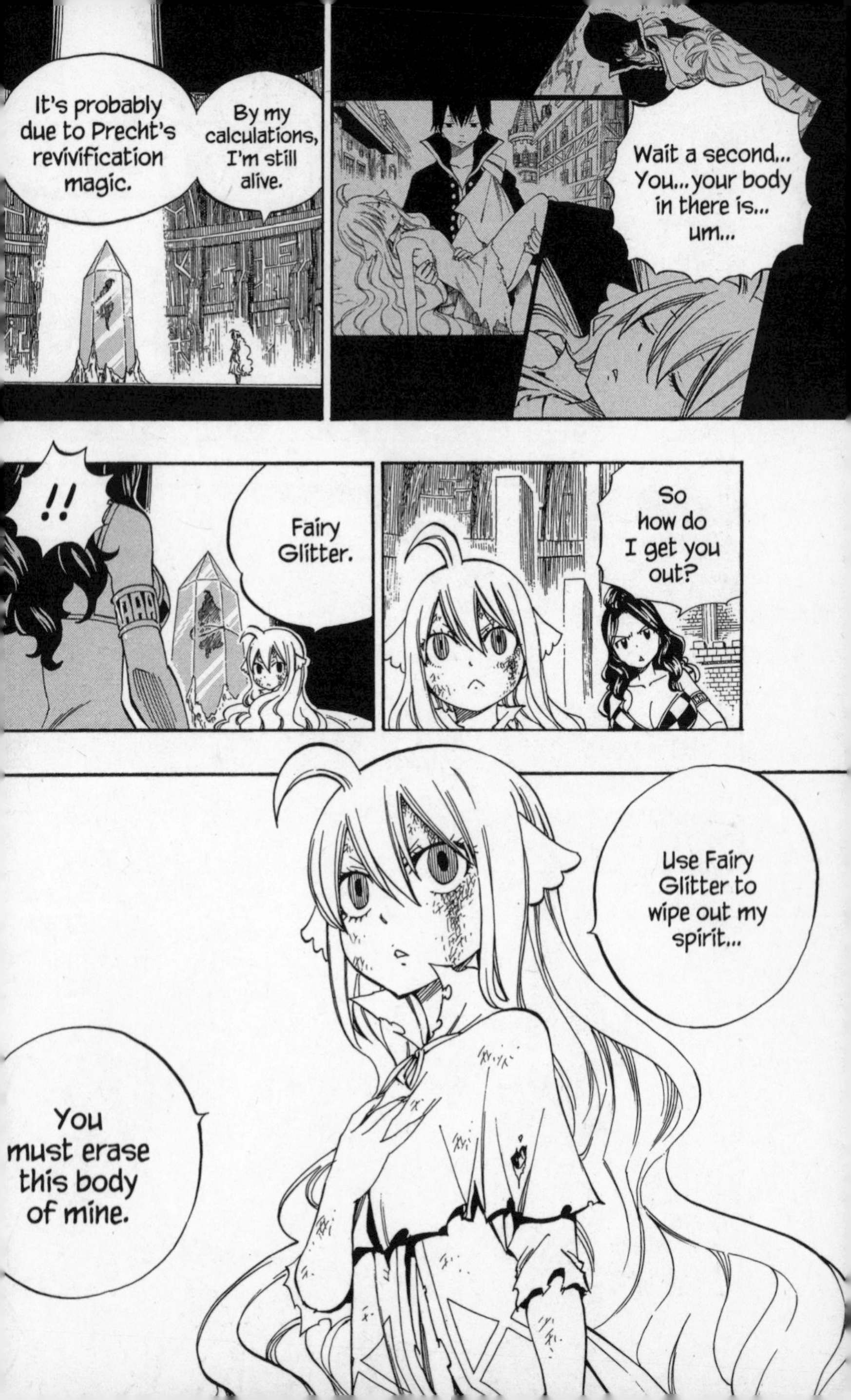

It's probably due to Precht's revivification magic.
By my calculations, I'm still alive.
Wait a second... You...your body in there is... um...
!!
Fairy Glitter.
So how do I get you out?
Use Fairy Glitter to wipe out my spirit...
You must erase this body of mine.

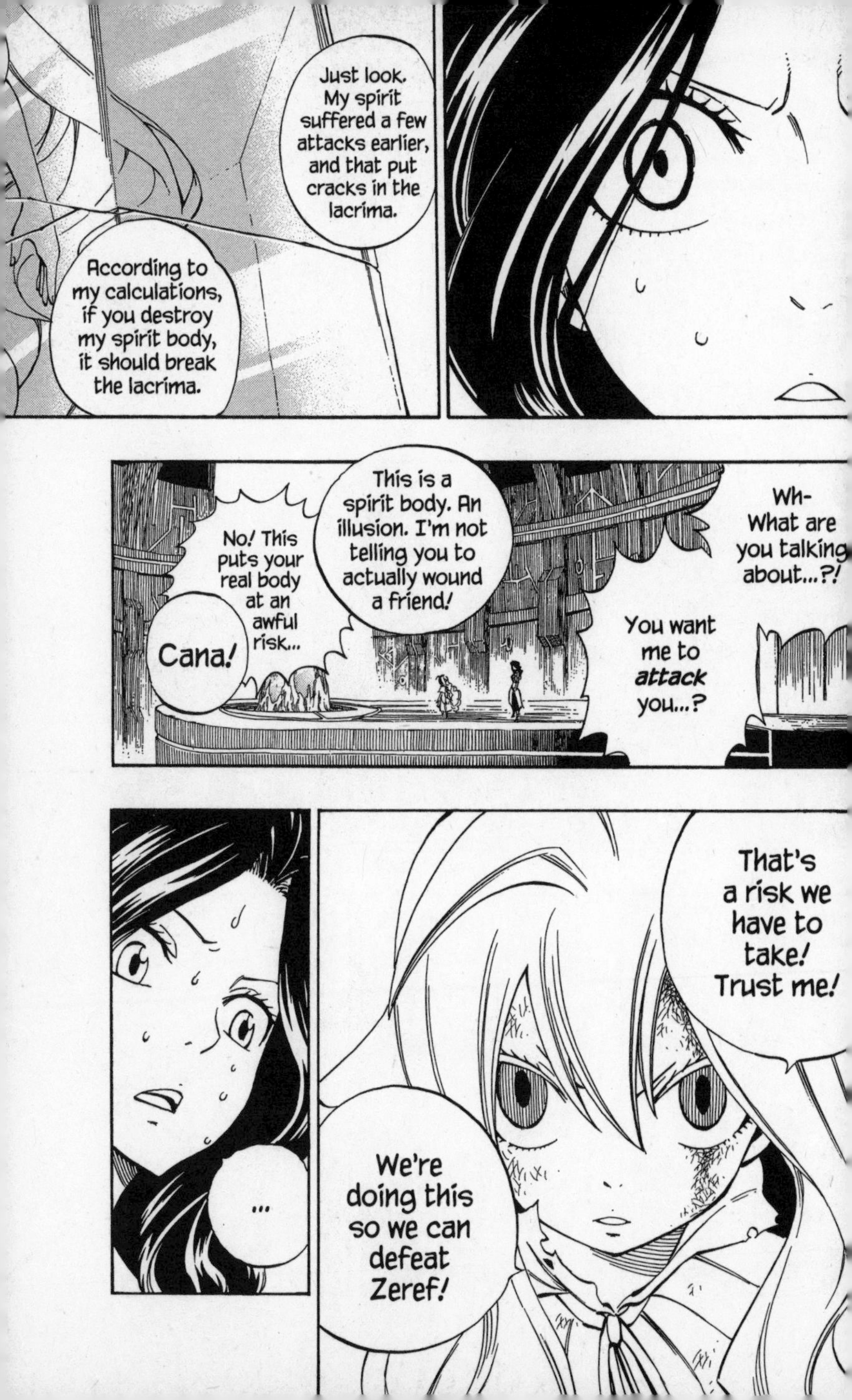
Just look. My spirit suffered a few attacks earlier, and that put cracks in the lacrima.
According to my calculations, if you destroy my spirit body, it should break the lacrima.
Wh- What are you talking about...?!
You want me to *attack* you...?
This is a spirit body. An illusion. I'm not telling you to actually wound a friend!
No! This puts your real body at an awful risk...
Cana!
That's a risk we have to take! Trust me!
We're doing this so we can defeat Zeref!
...

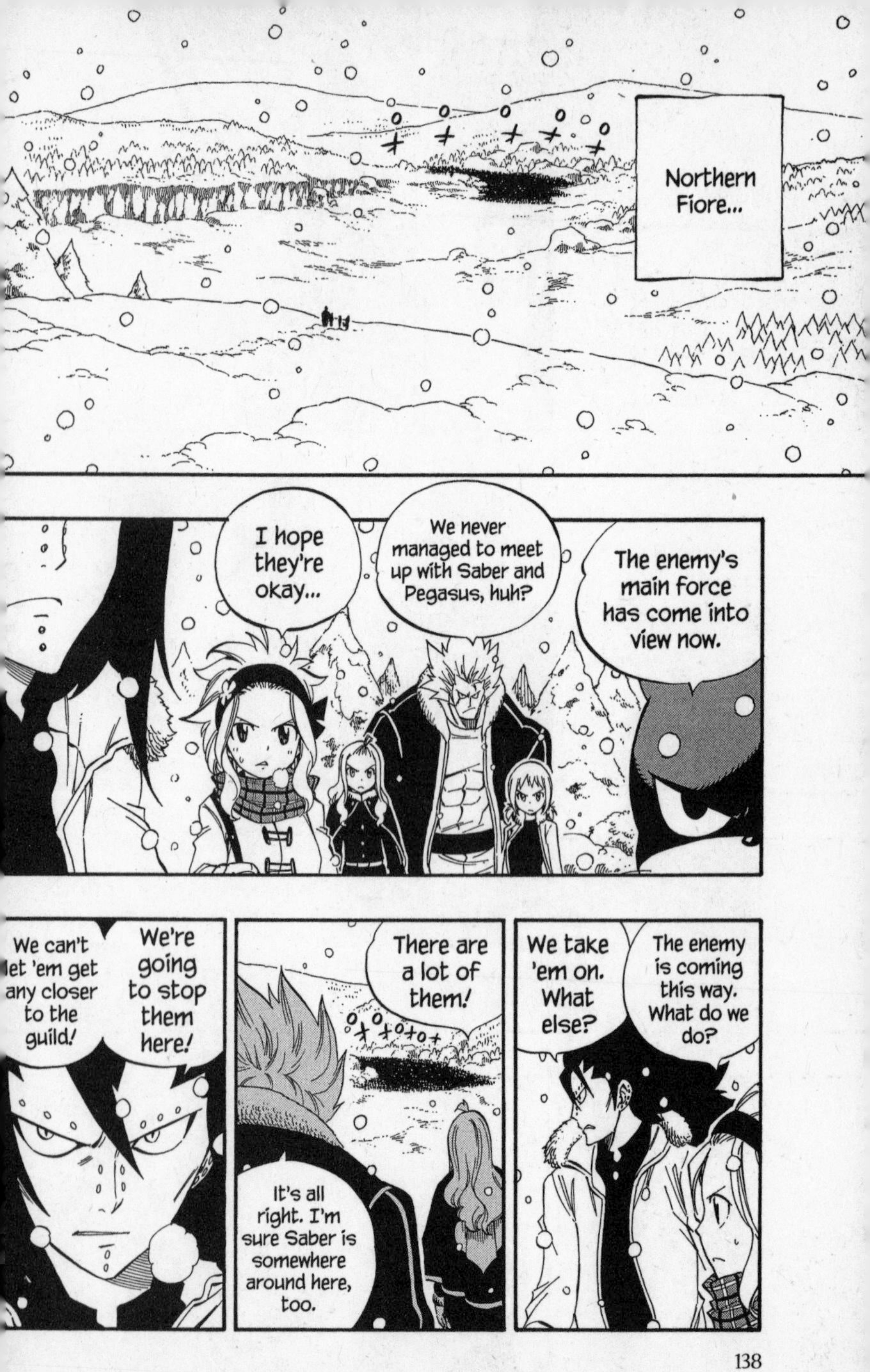
Northern Fiore...
The enemy's main force has come into view now.
We never managed to meet up with Saber and Pegasus, huh?
I hope they're okay...
The enemy is coming this way. What do we do?
We take 'em on. What else?
There are a lot of them!
It's all right. I'm sure Saber is somewhere around here, too.
We're going to stop them here!
We can't let 'em get any closer to the guild!

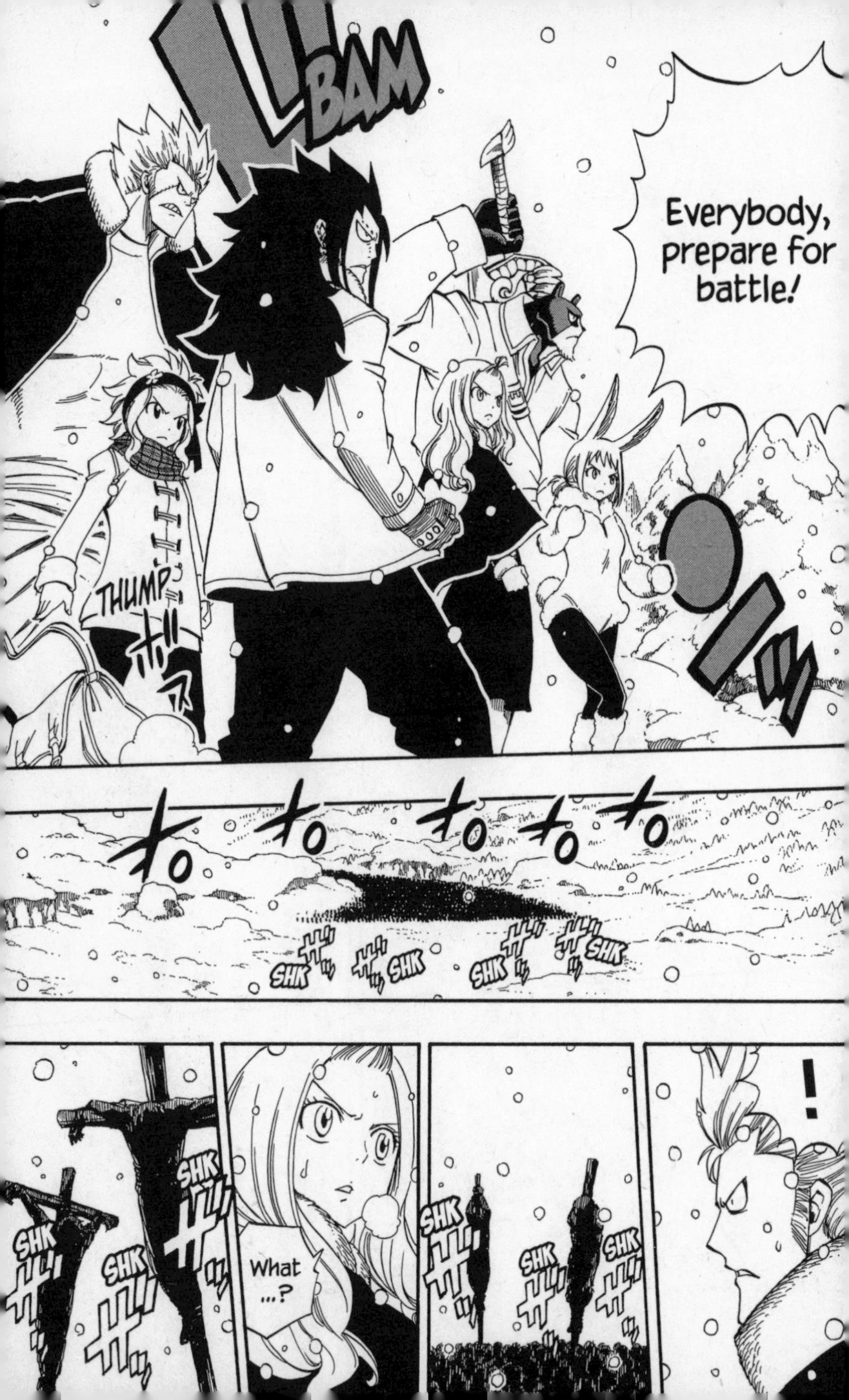
BAM
Everybody, prepare for battle!
THUMP
SHK
SHK
SHK
SHK
!
SHK
SHK
What ...?
SHK
SHK
SHK

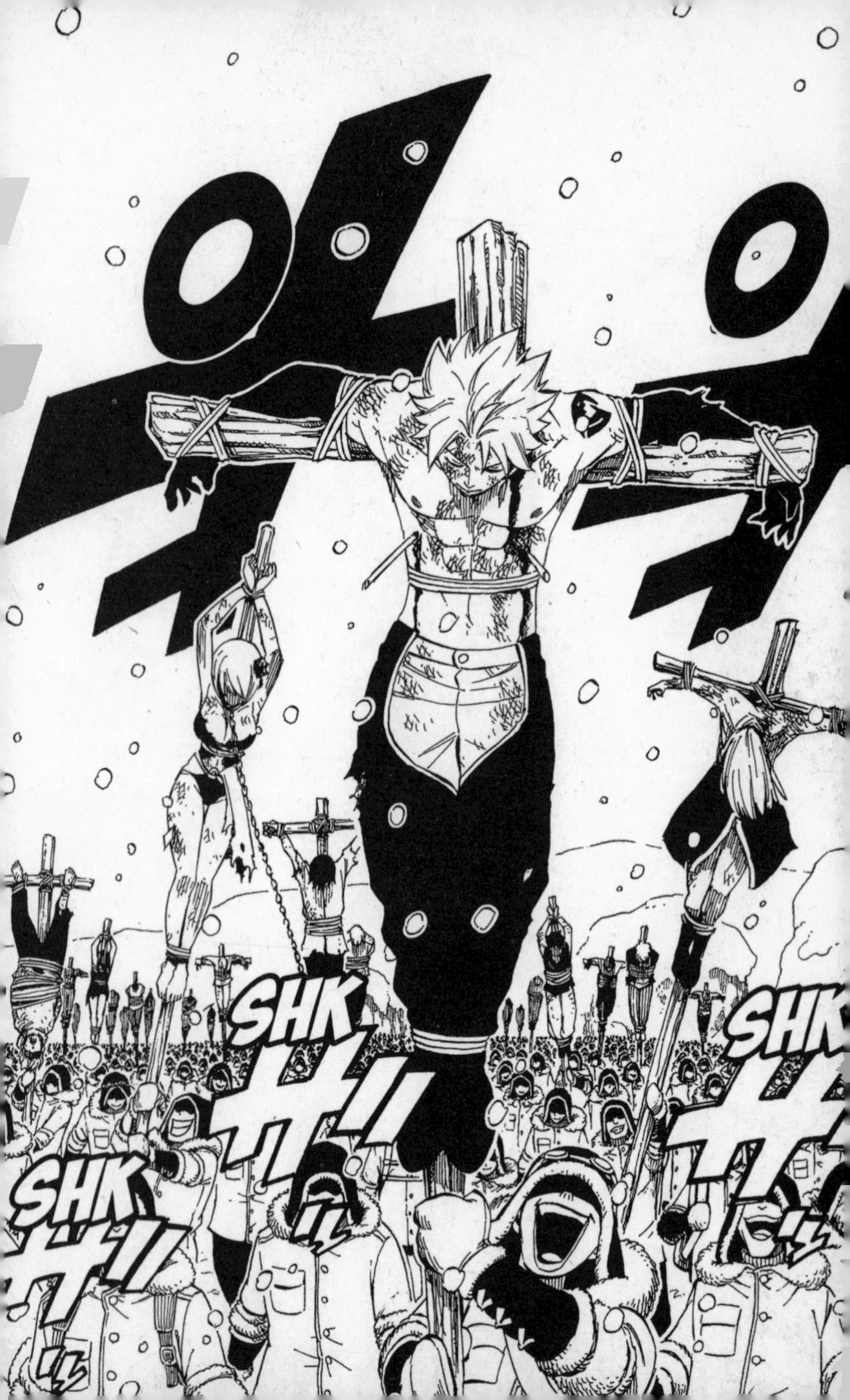
SHK
SHK
SHK

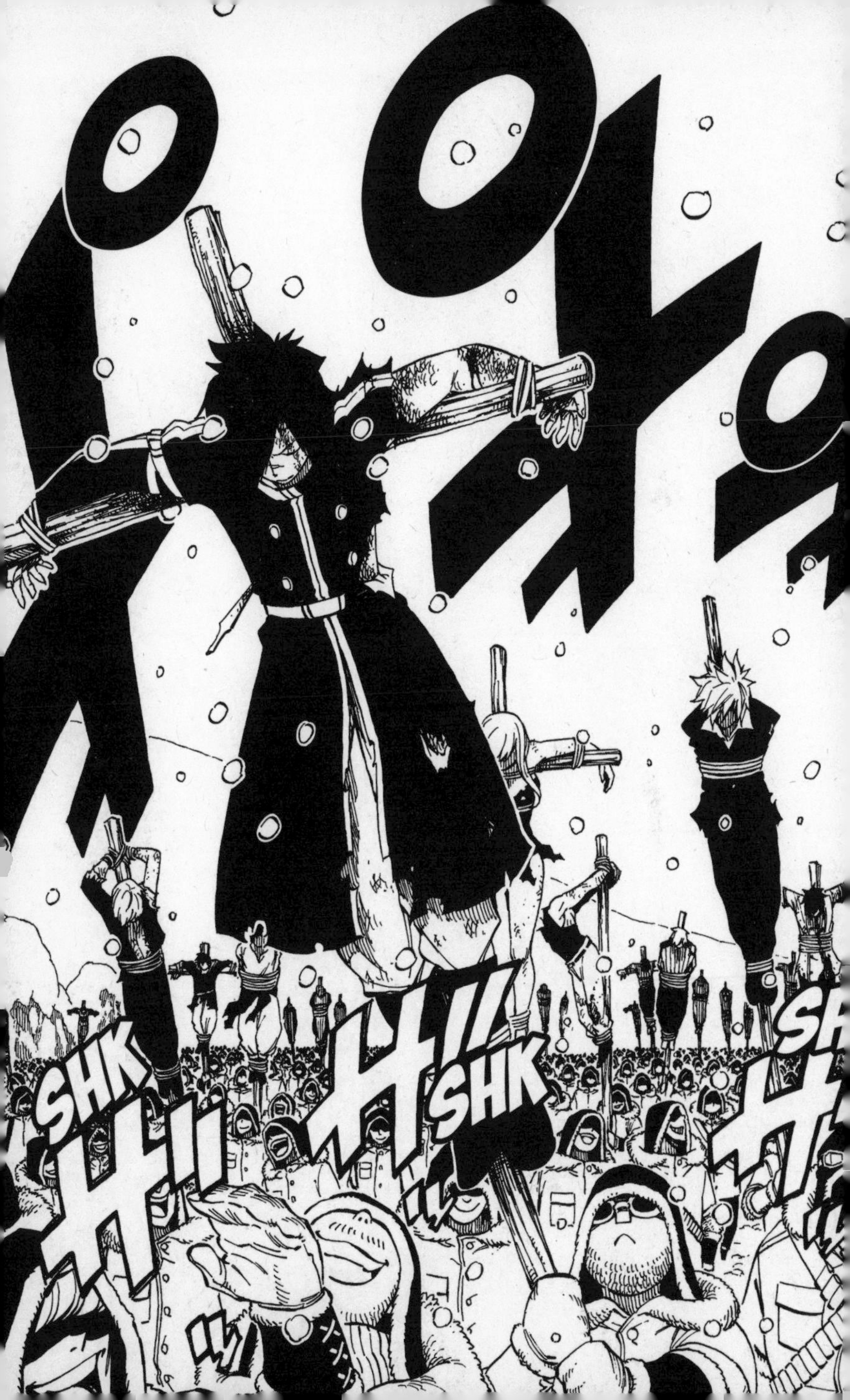
SHK
SHK

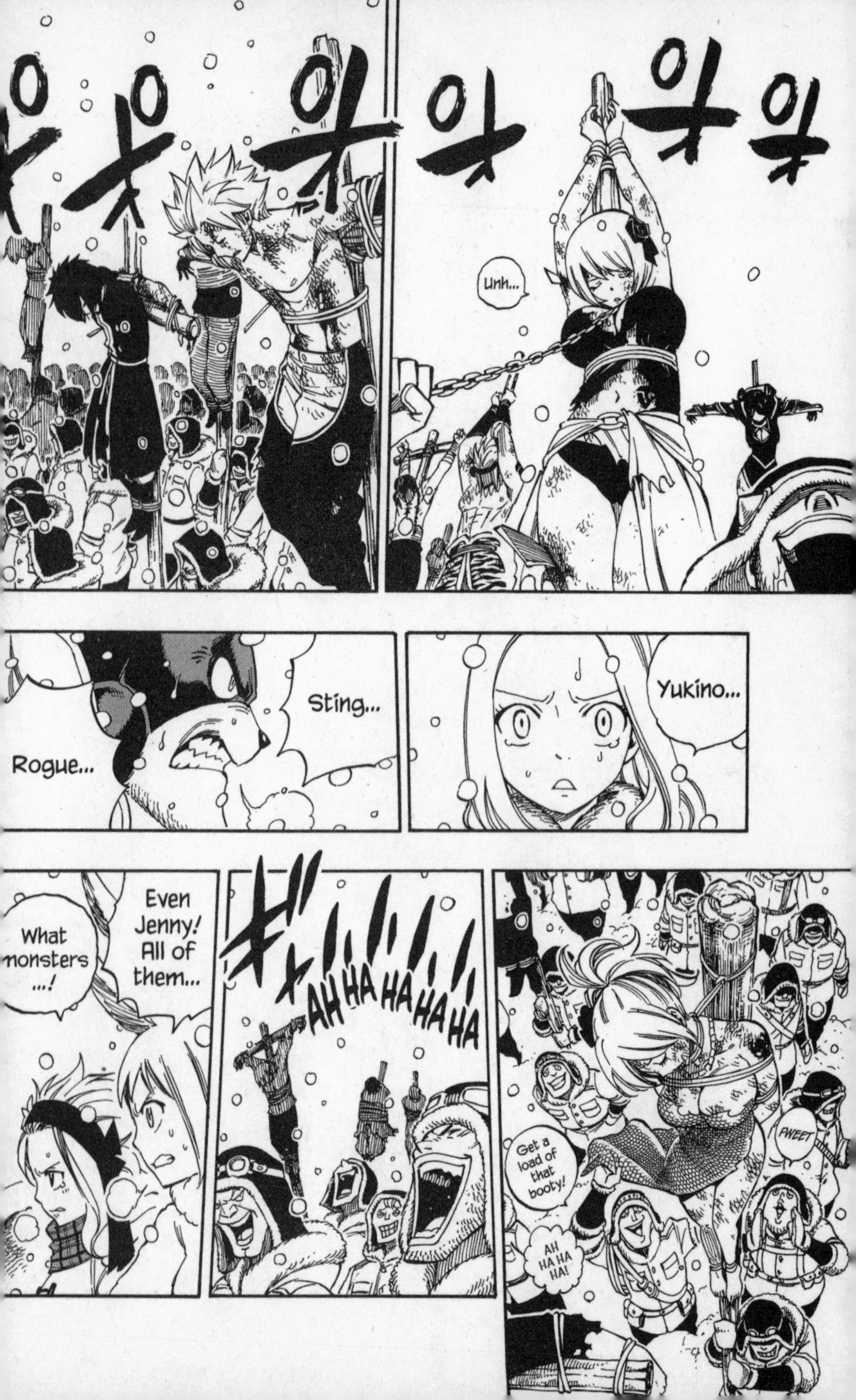
Unh...
Yukino...
Sting...
Rogue...
PWEET
Get a load of that booty!
AH HA HA HA!
AH HA HA HA HA HA
Even Jenny! All of them...
What monsters ...!

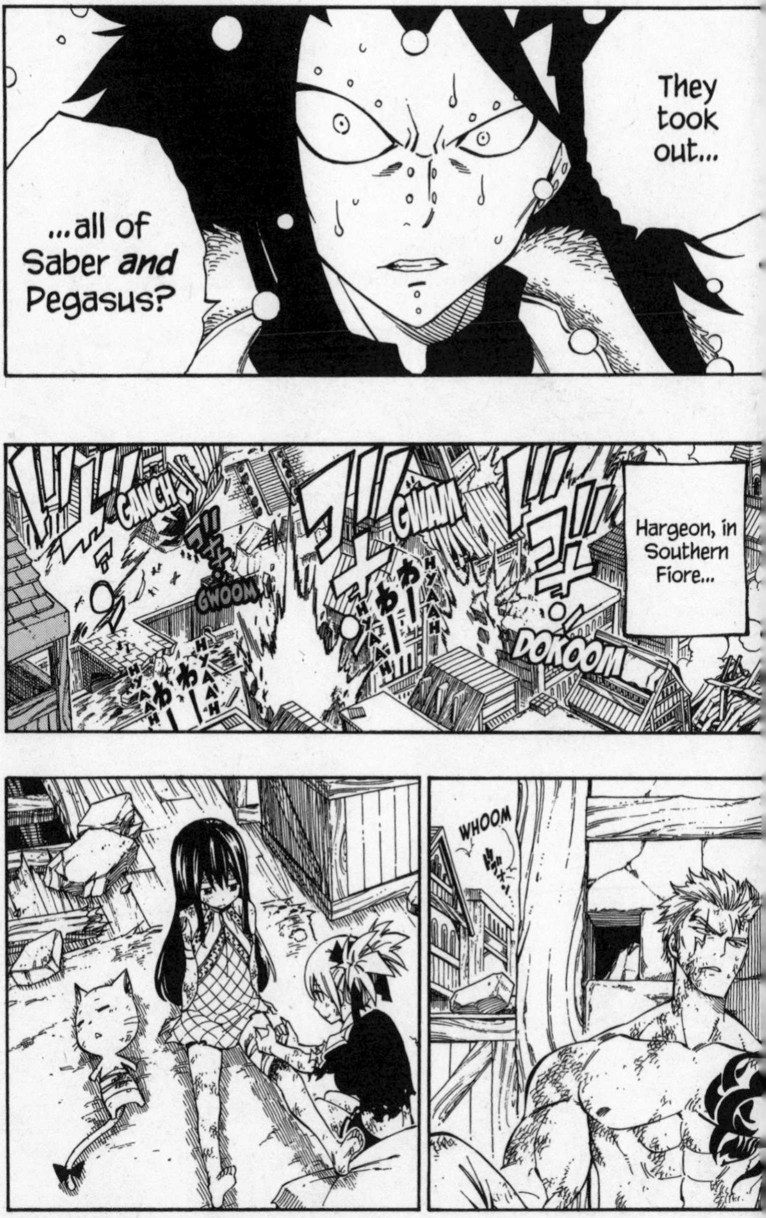
They took out...
...all of Saber *and* Pegasus?
Hargeon, in Southern Fiore...
DOKOOM
HYAAH
GWAM
GWOOM
GANCH
WHOOM

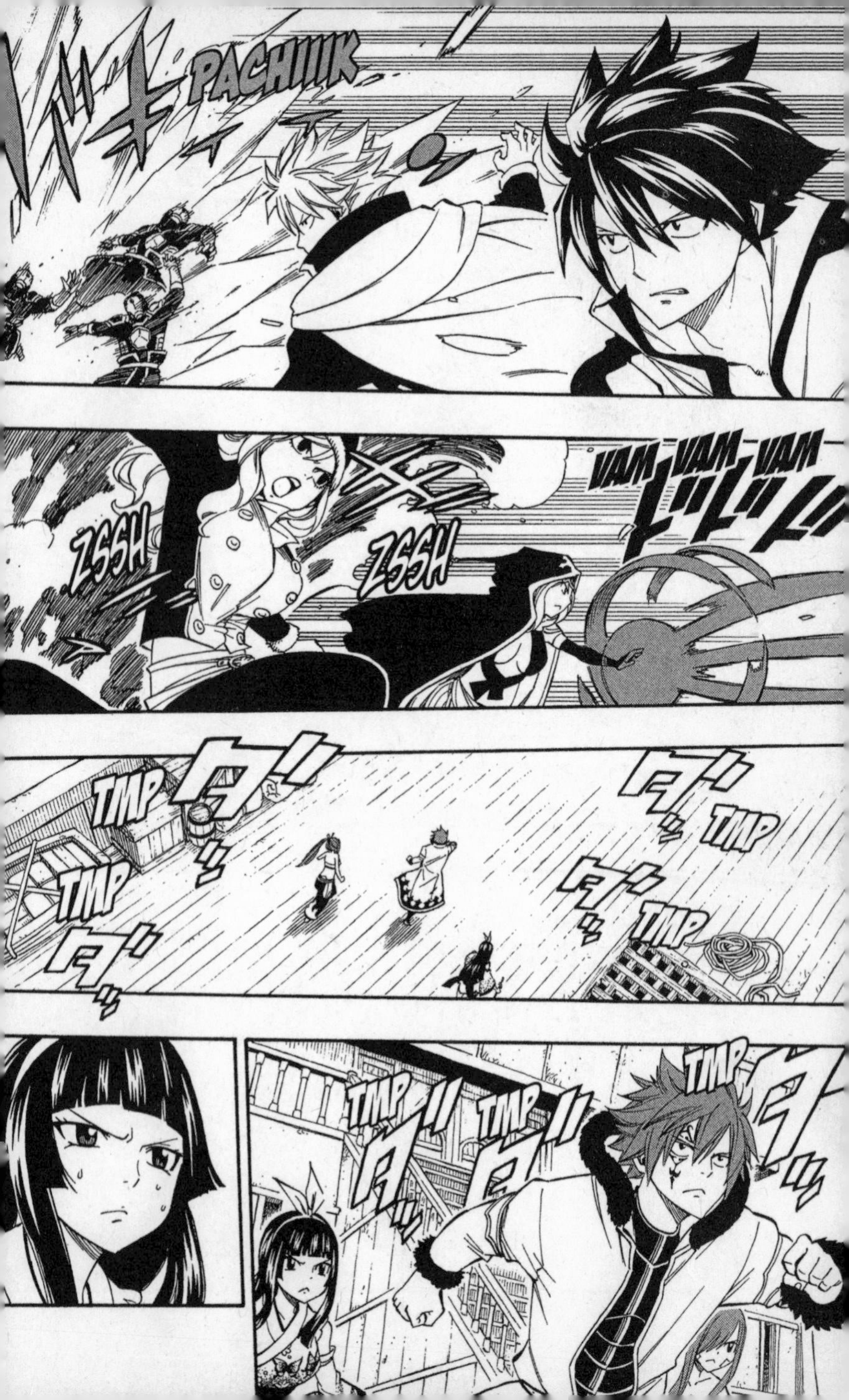
PACHIIIK
VAM VAM VAM
ZSSH
ZSSH
TMP
TMP
TMP
TMP
TMP
TMP
TMP

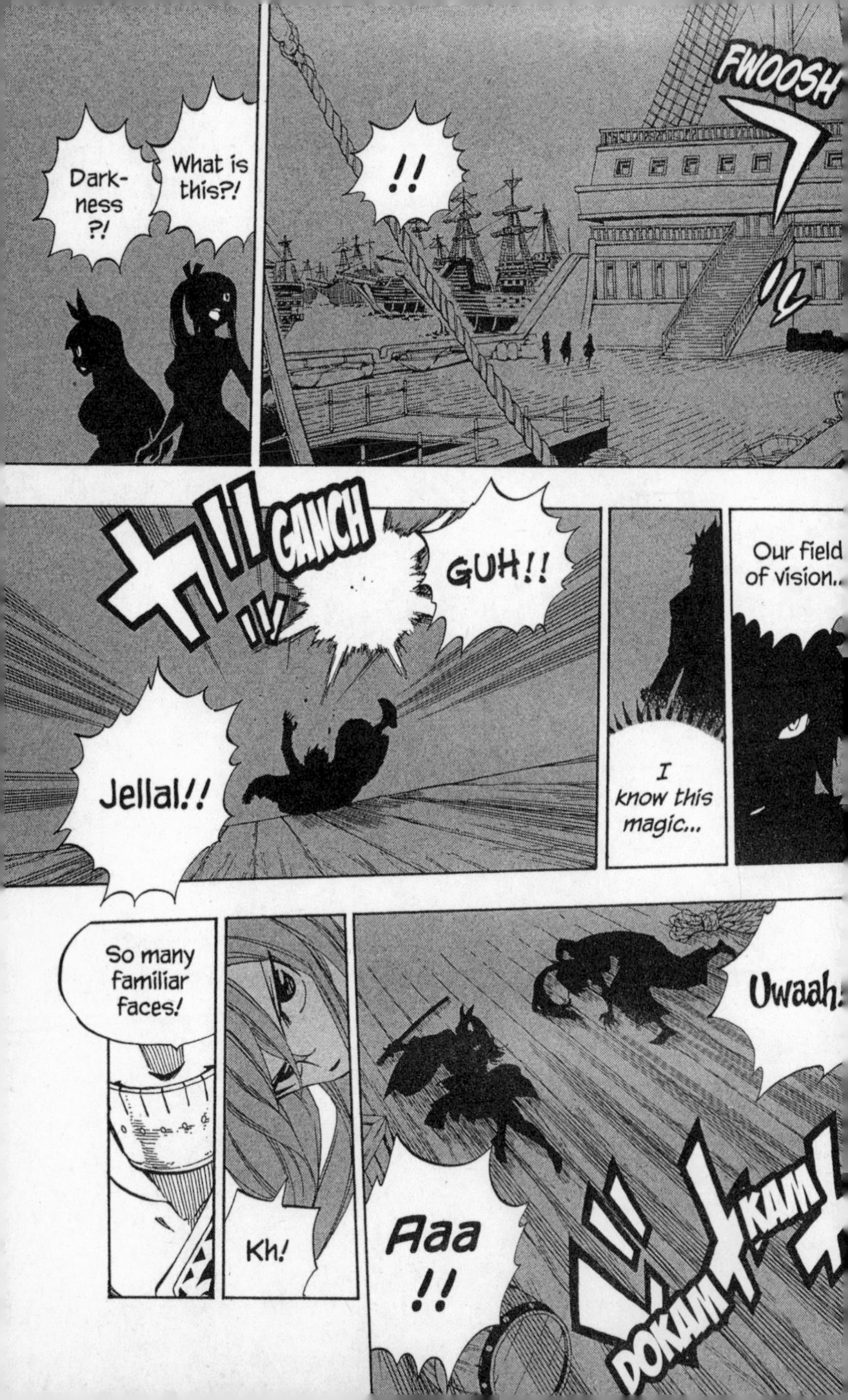
FWOOSH
!!
What is this?!
Dark-ness?!
Our field of vision...
I know this magic...
GUH!!
GANCH
Jellal!!
Uwaah!
KAM
DOKAM
Aaa!!
Kh!
So many familiar faces!

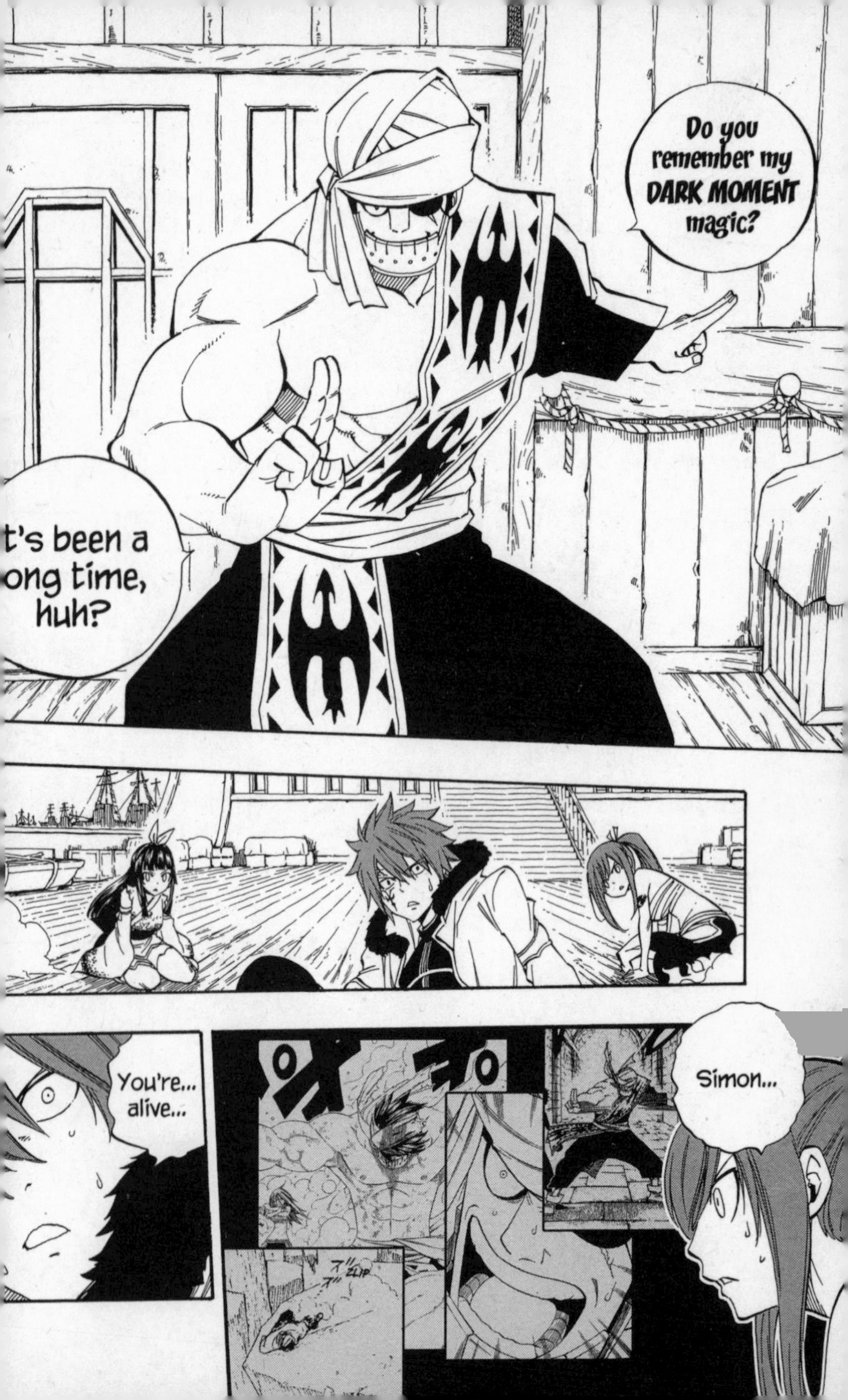
Do you remember my DARK MOMENT magic?
t's been a ong time, huh?
Simon...
ZLIP
You're... alive...

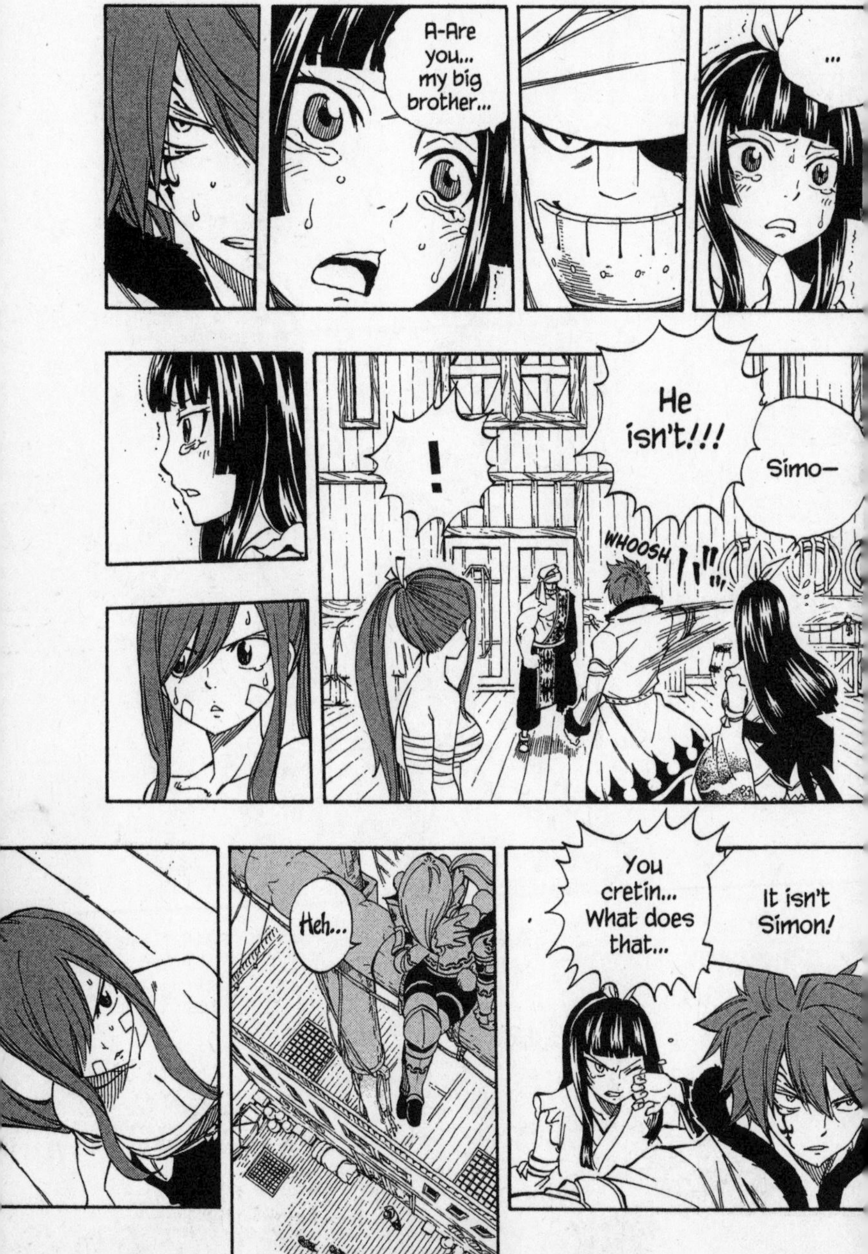
...
A-Are you... my big brother...
Simo–
He isn't!!!
!
WHOOSH
It isn't Simon!
You cretin... What does that...
Heh...

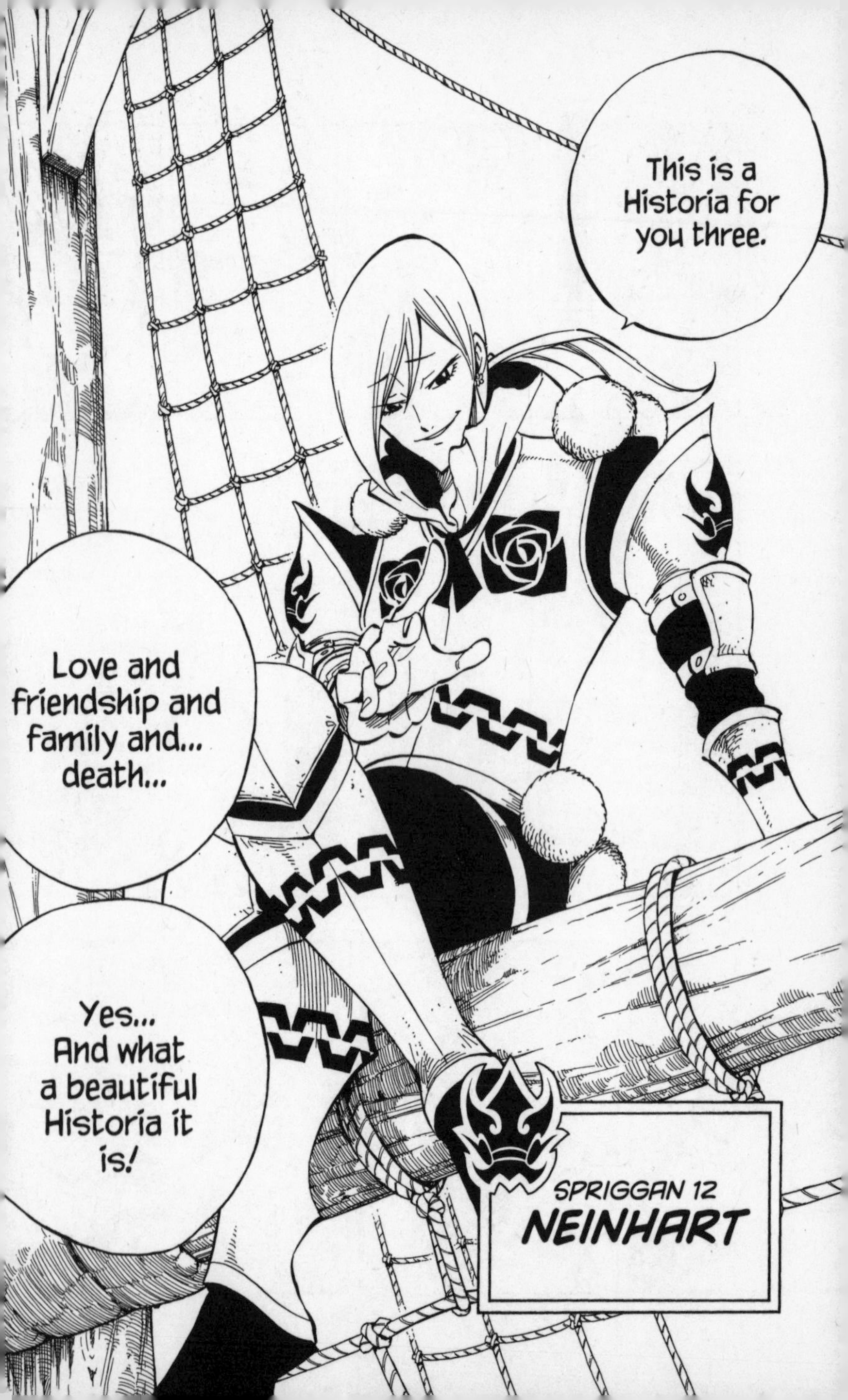
This is a Historia for you three.
Love and friendship and family and... death...
Yes... And what a beautiful Historia it is!
SPRIGGAN 12
NEINHART

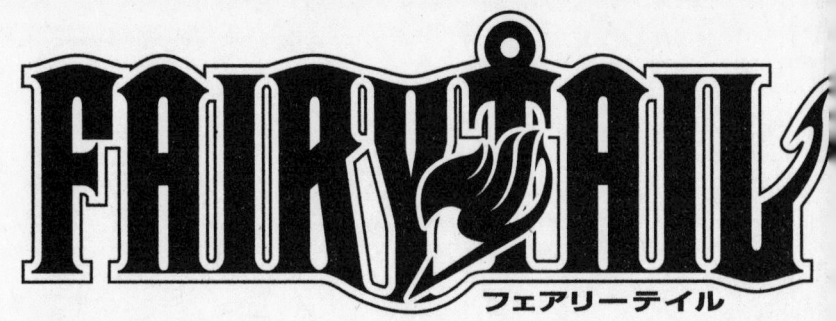

FAIRY TAIL

フェアリーテイル

Chapter 481: The Historia of the Dea

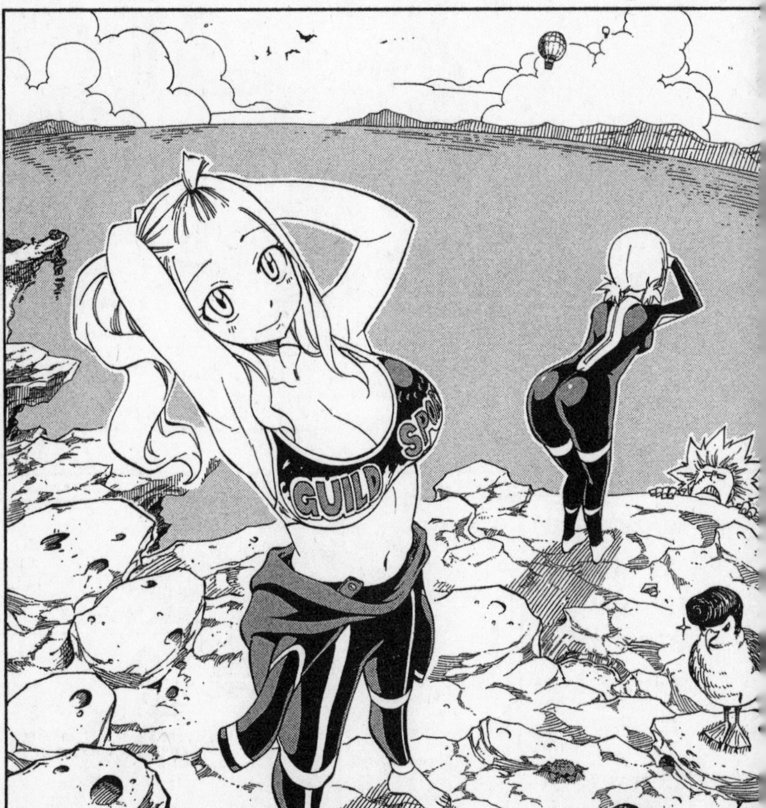
GUILD

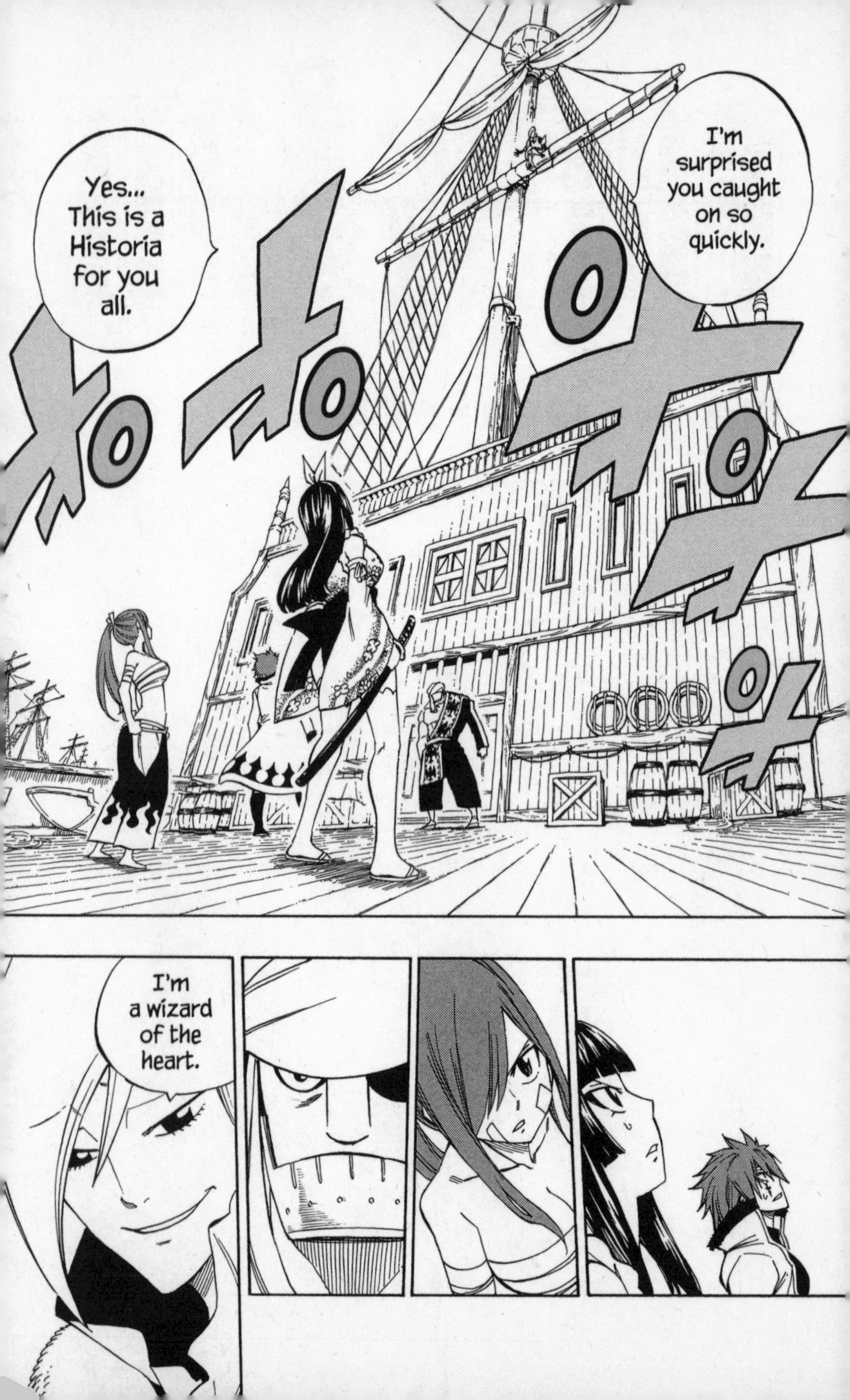
I'm surprised you caught on so quickly.
Yes... This is a Historia for you all.
I'm a wizard of the heart.

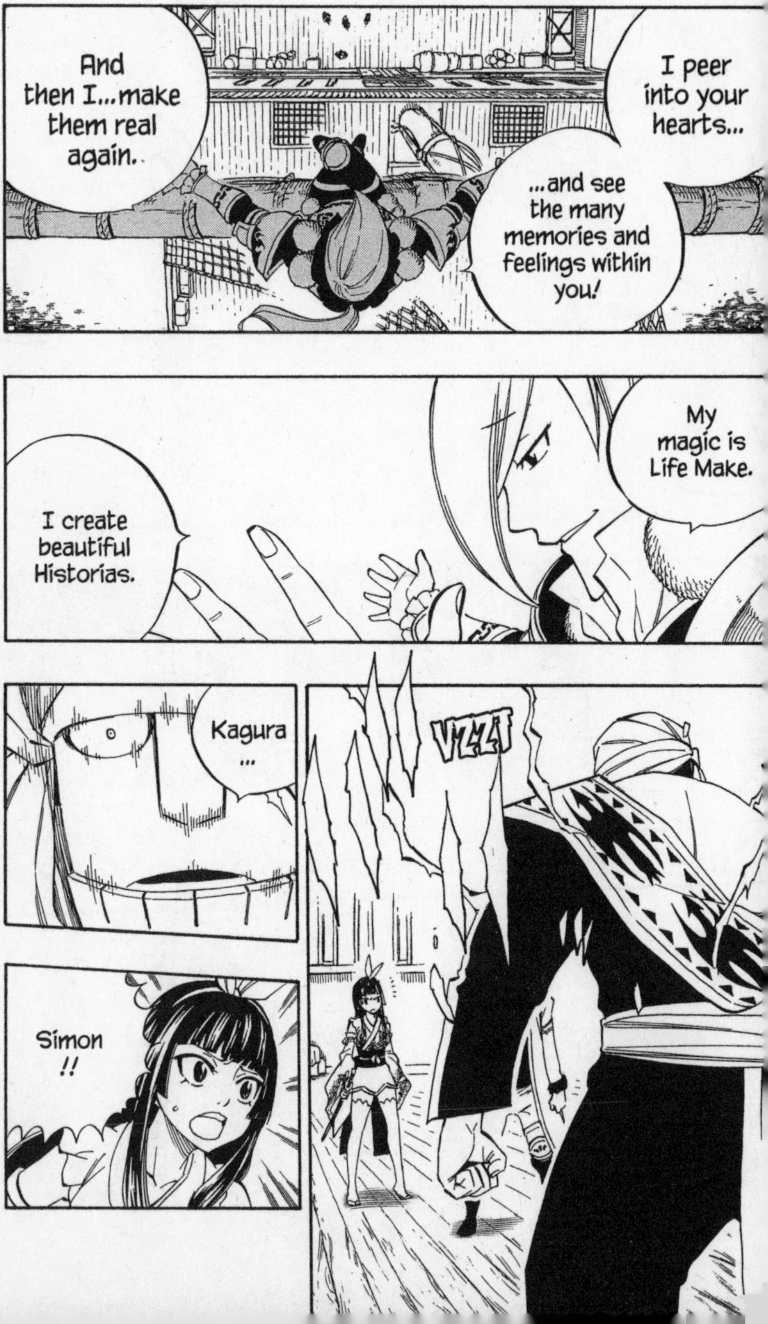
I peer into your hearts...
...and see the many memories and feelings within you!
And then I...make them real again..
My magic is Life Make.
I create beautiful Historias.
VZZZT
Kagura ...
Simon !!

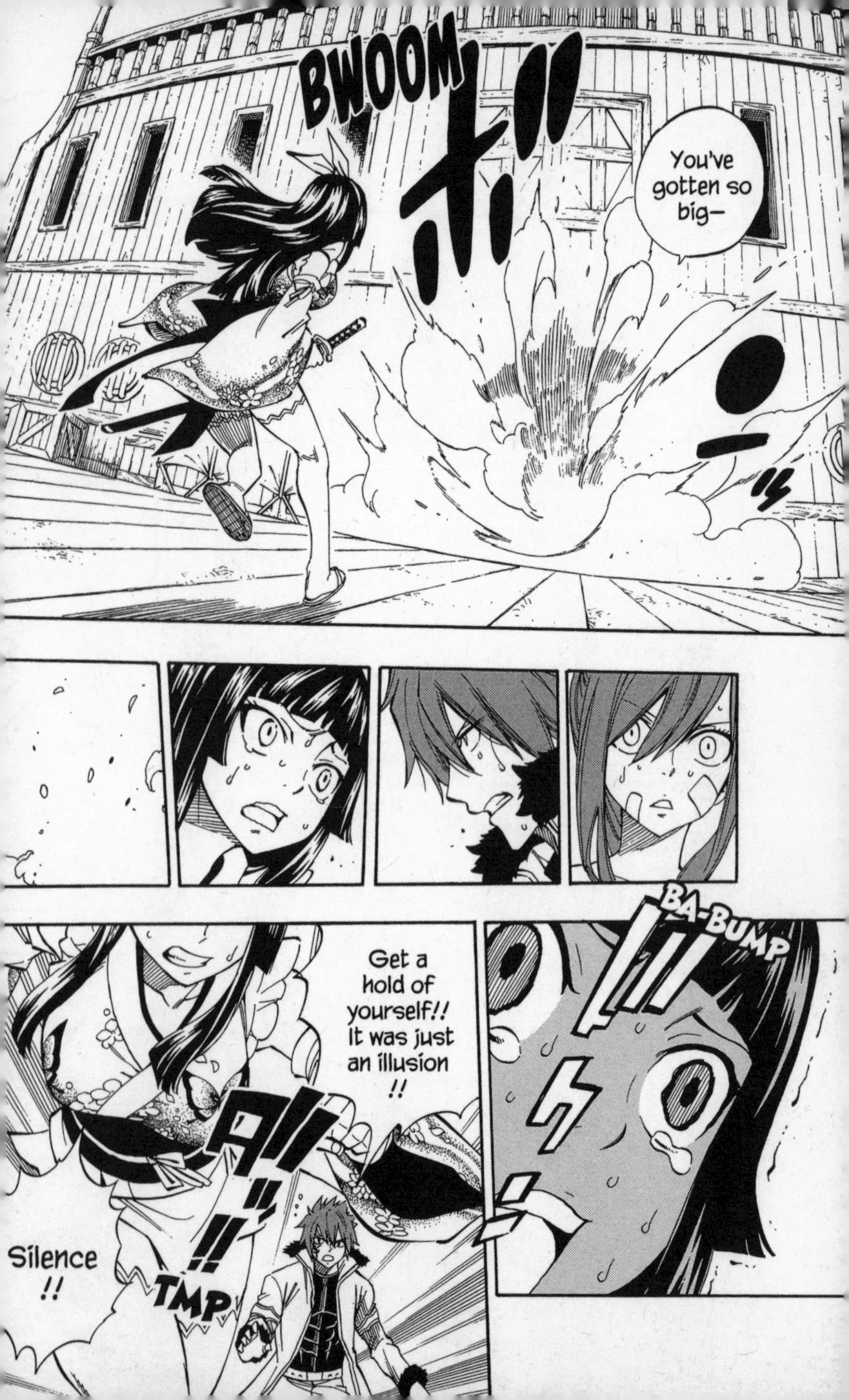
BWOOM
You've gotten so big–
BA-BUMP
Get a hold of yourself!! It was just an illusion!!
TMP
Silence!!

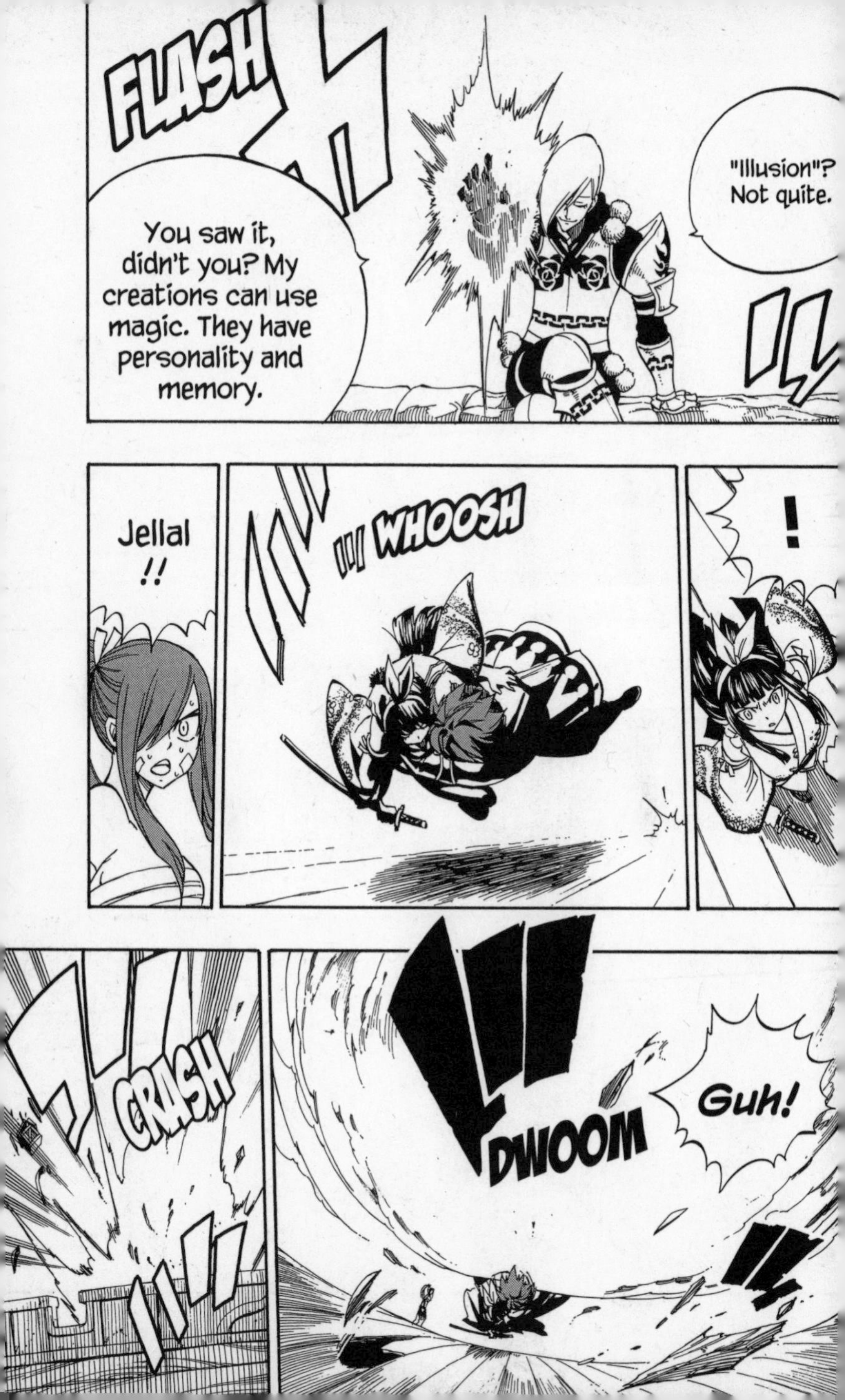
"Illusion"? Not quite.
FLASH
You saw it, didn't you? My creations can use magic. They have personality and memory.
!
WHOOSH
Jellal !!
Guh!
DWOOM
CRASH

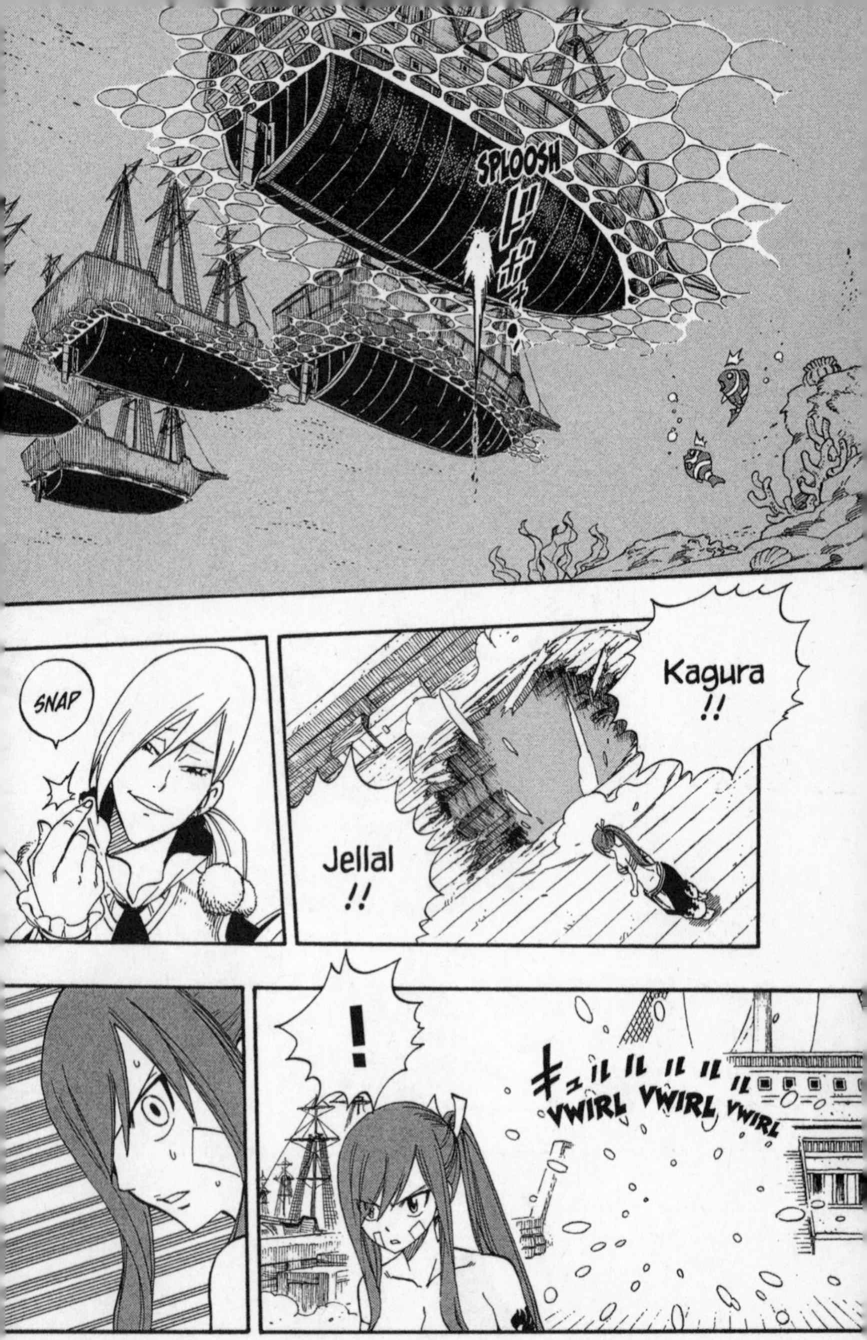
SPLOOSH
Kagura !!
Jellal !!
SNAP
!
VWIRL VWIRL VWIRL

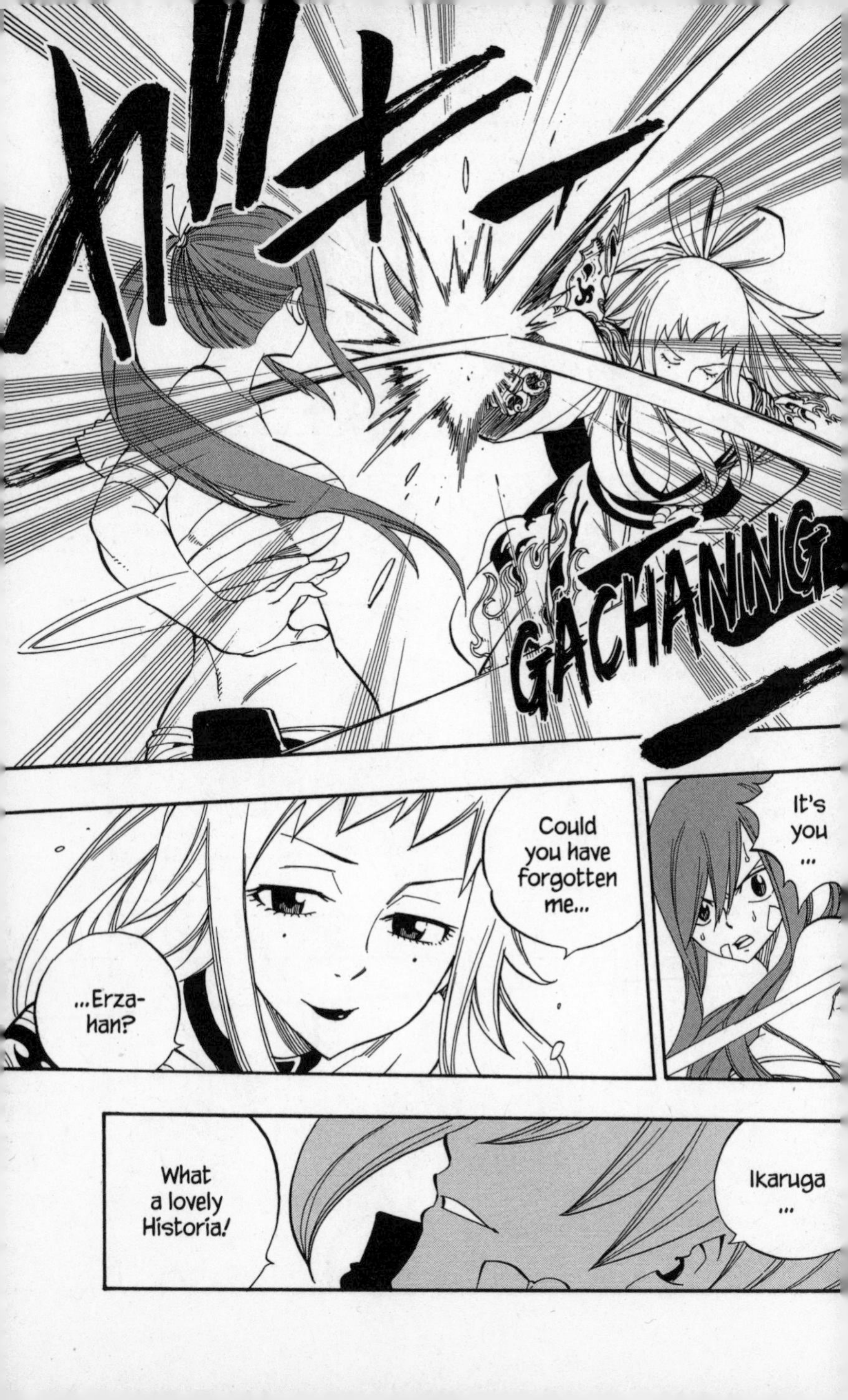

ガキィ
GACHANNG
It's you ...
Could you have forgotten me...
...Erza-han?
Ikaruga ...
What a lovely Historia!

Get off of me!!

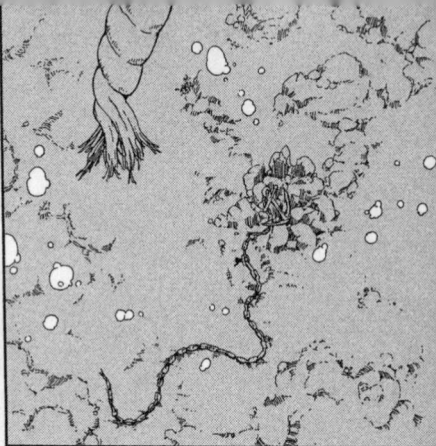

I must go help Erza!!

He's the man who murdered my big brother...

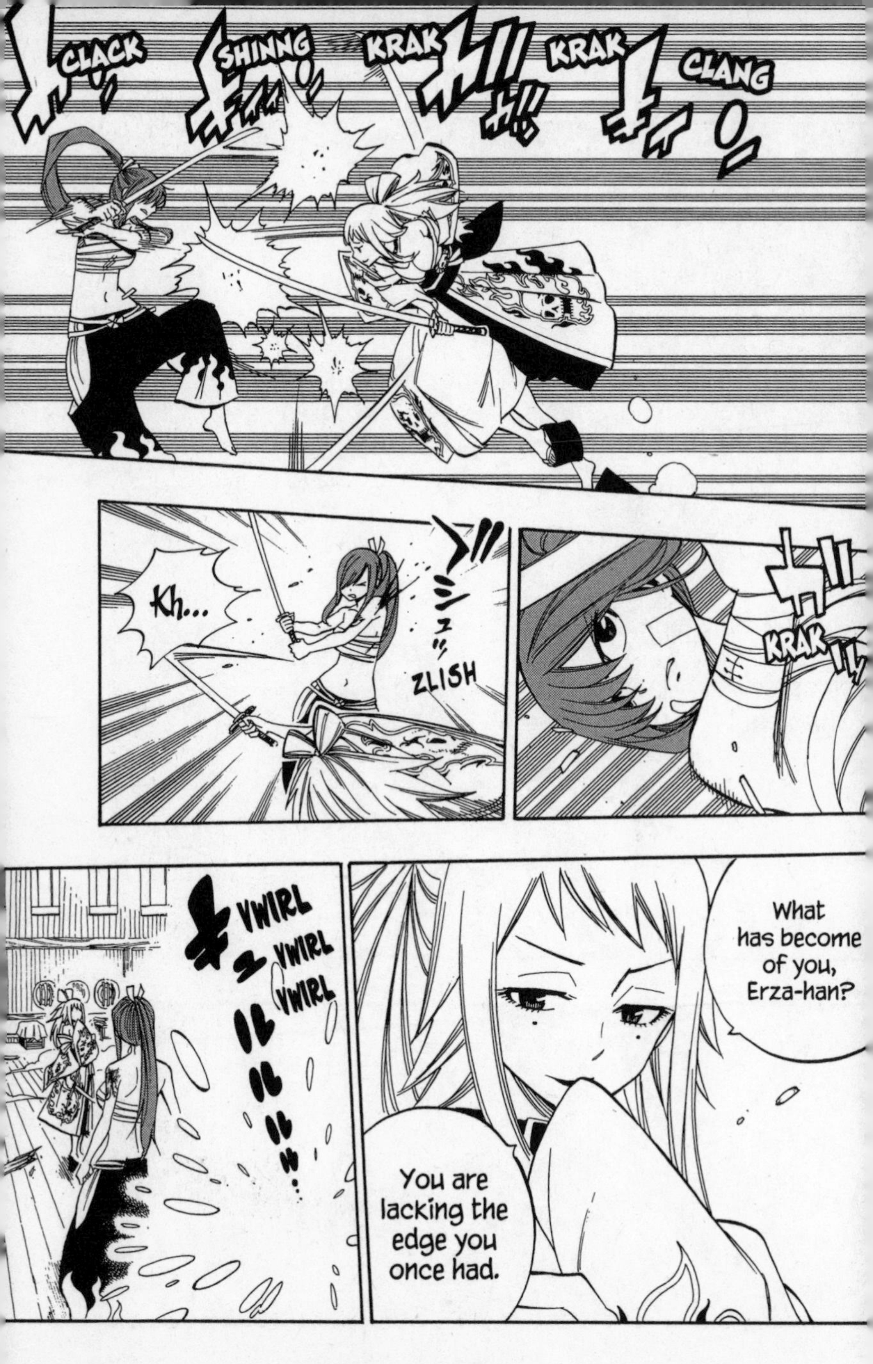
CLACK
SHINNG
KRAK
KRAK
CLANG
KRAK
ZLISH
Kh...
VWIRL
VWIRL
VWIRL
What has become of you, Erza-han?
You are lacking the edge you once had.

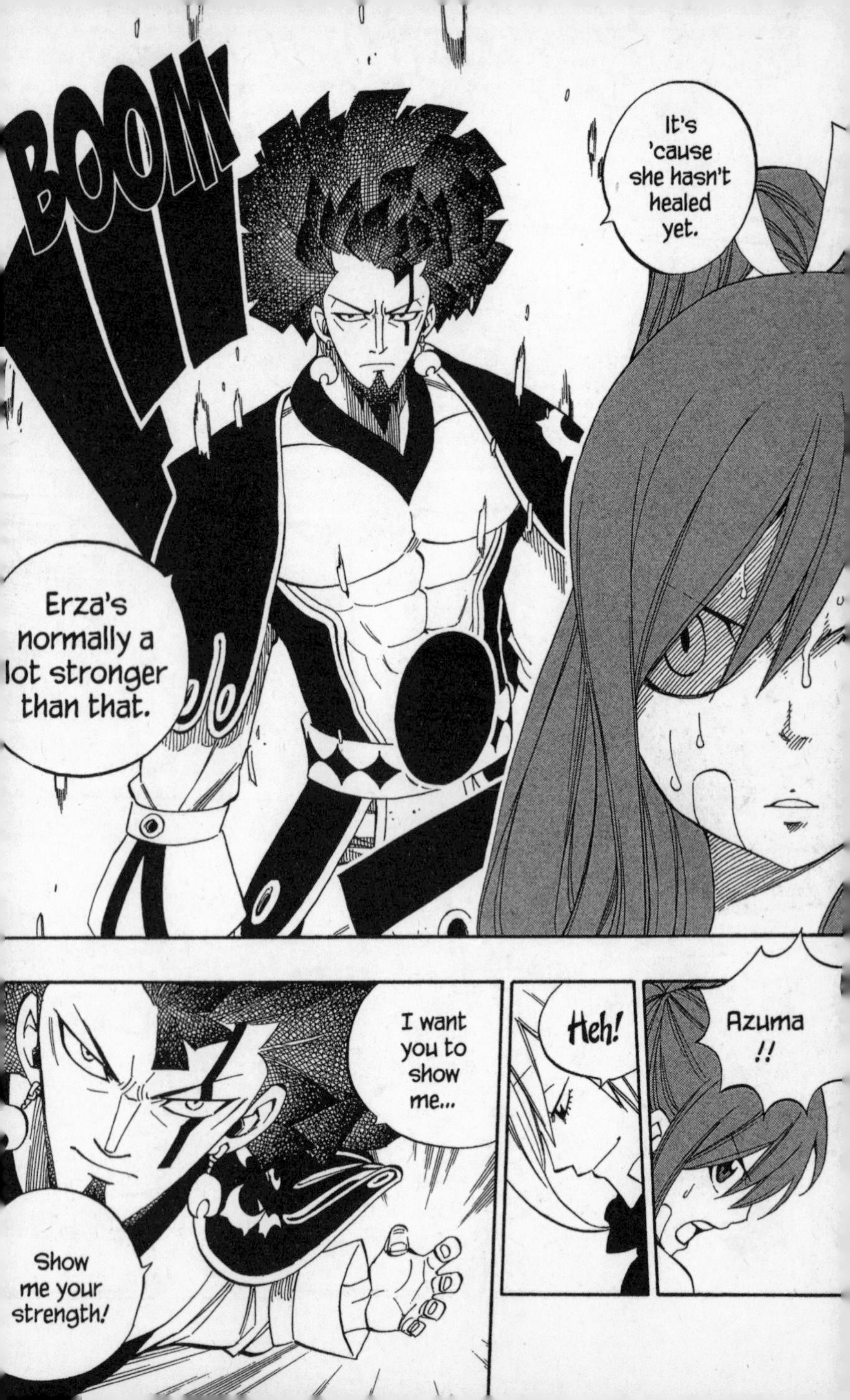
BOOM
It's 'cause she hasn't healed yet.
Erza's normally a lot stronger than that.
Azuma !!
Heh!
I want you to show me...
Show me your strength!

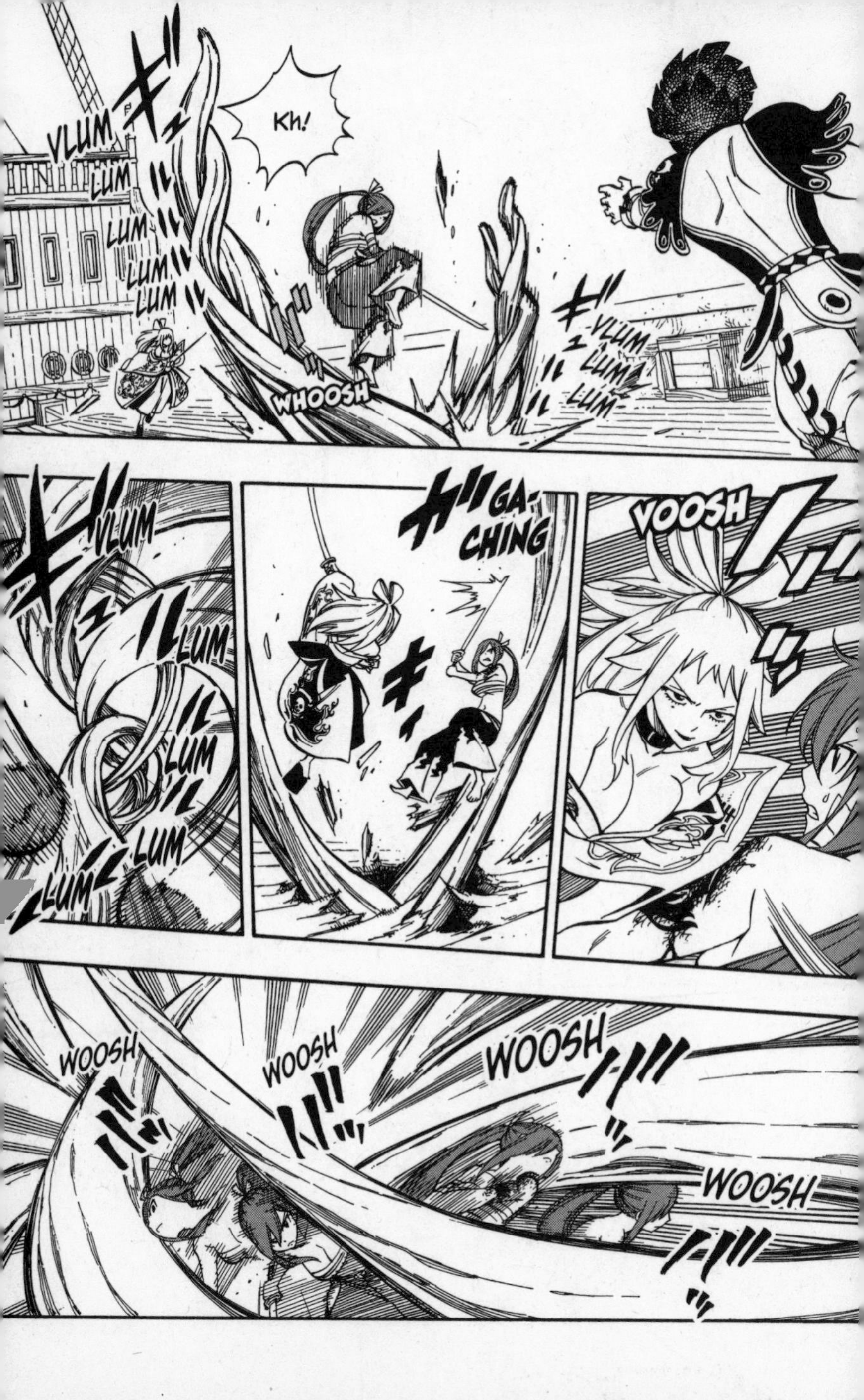
Kh!
VLUM LUM LUM
WHOOSH
VLUM LUM LUM LUM LUM
VOOSH
GA-CHING
VLUM LUM LUM LUM LUM
WOOSH
WOOSH
WOOSH
WOOSH

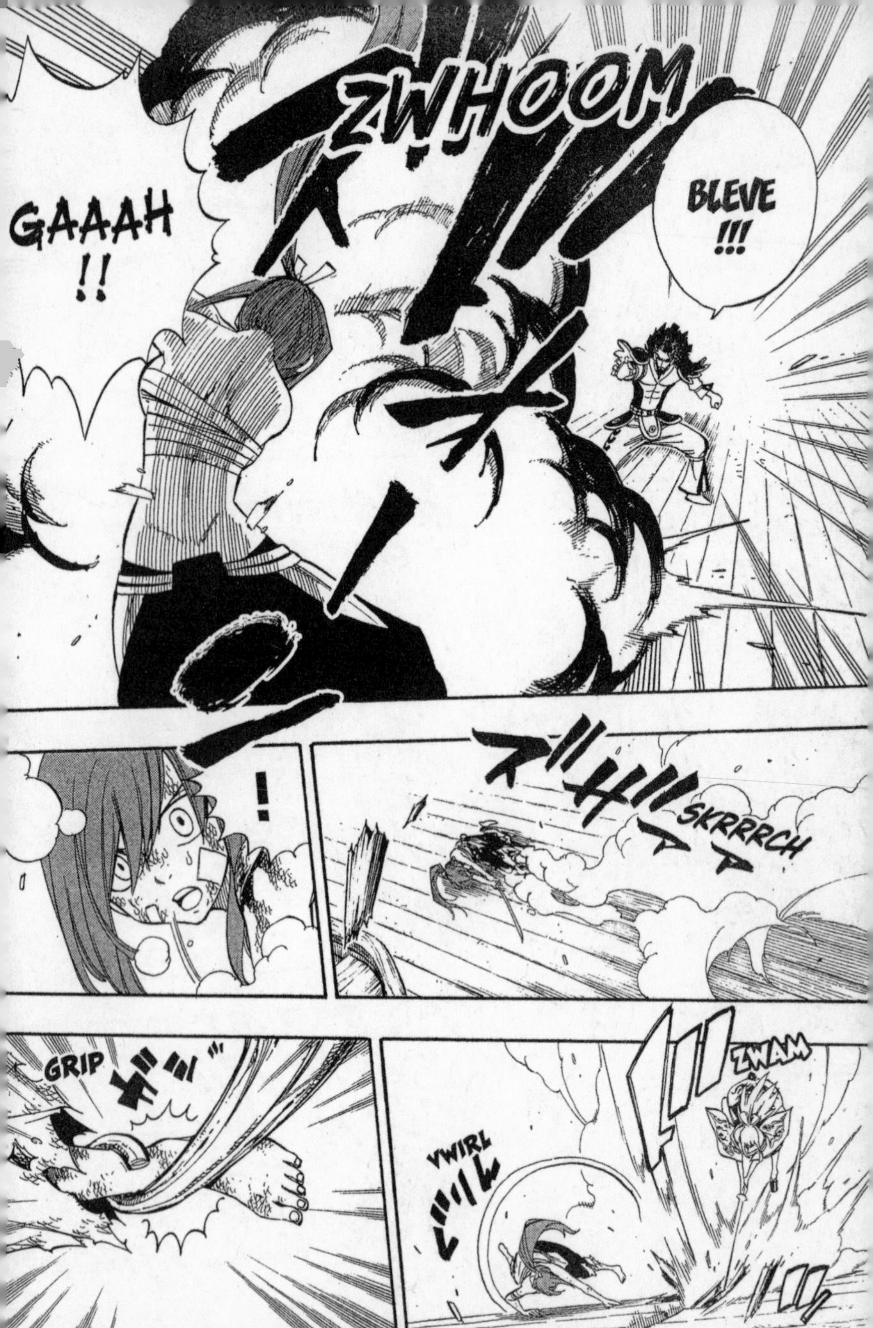
ZWHOOM
BLEVE !!!
GAAAH !!
SKRRRCH
!
ZWAM
VWIRL
GRIP

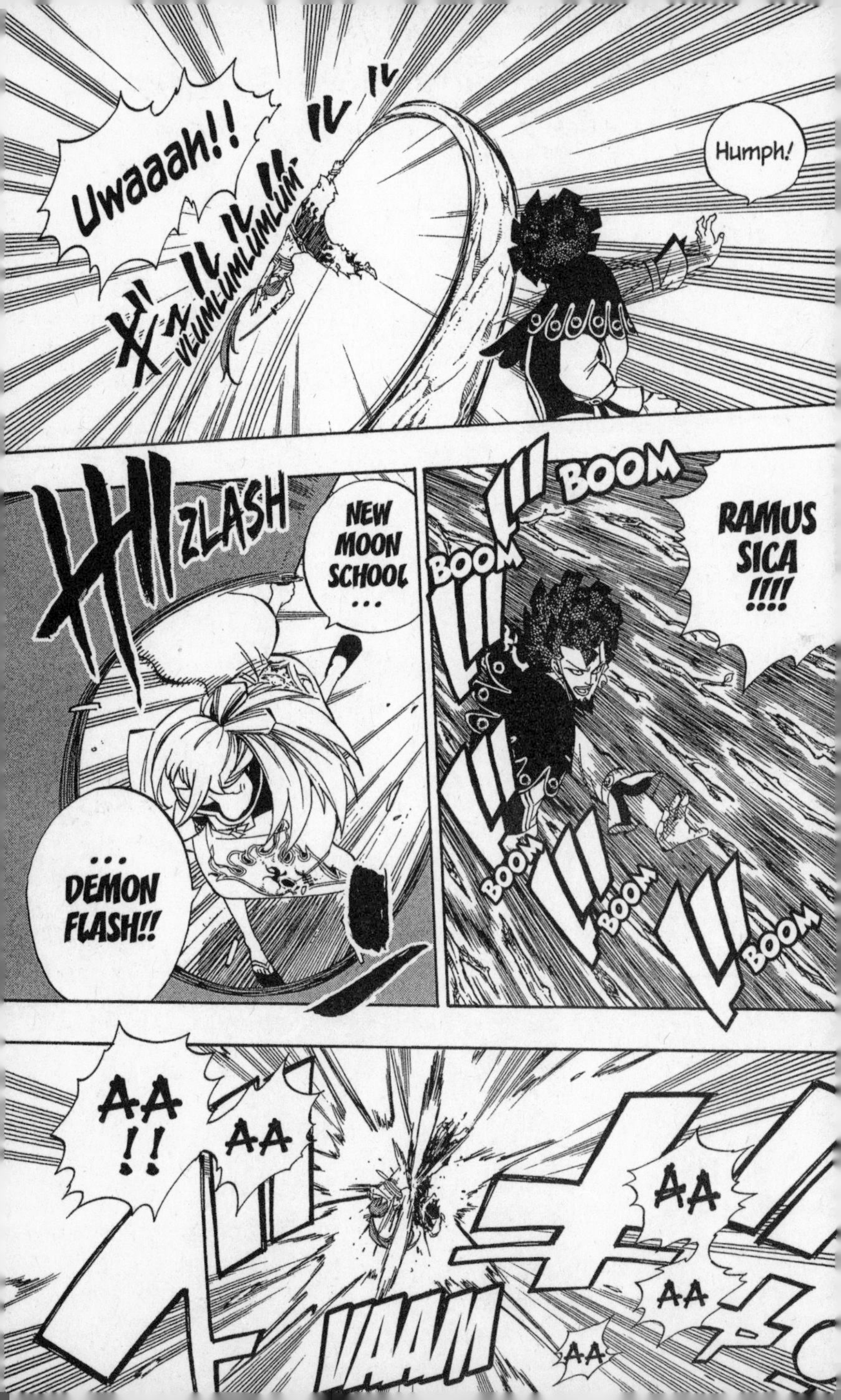
Humph!
Uwaaah!!
VLUMLUMLUMLUM
BOOM
BOOM
RAMUS SICA!!!!
BOOM
BOOM
BOOM
ZLASH
NEW MOON SCHOOL...
...DEMON FLASH!!
AA
AA
AA!!
AA
AA
VAAM

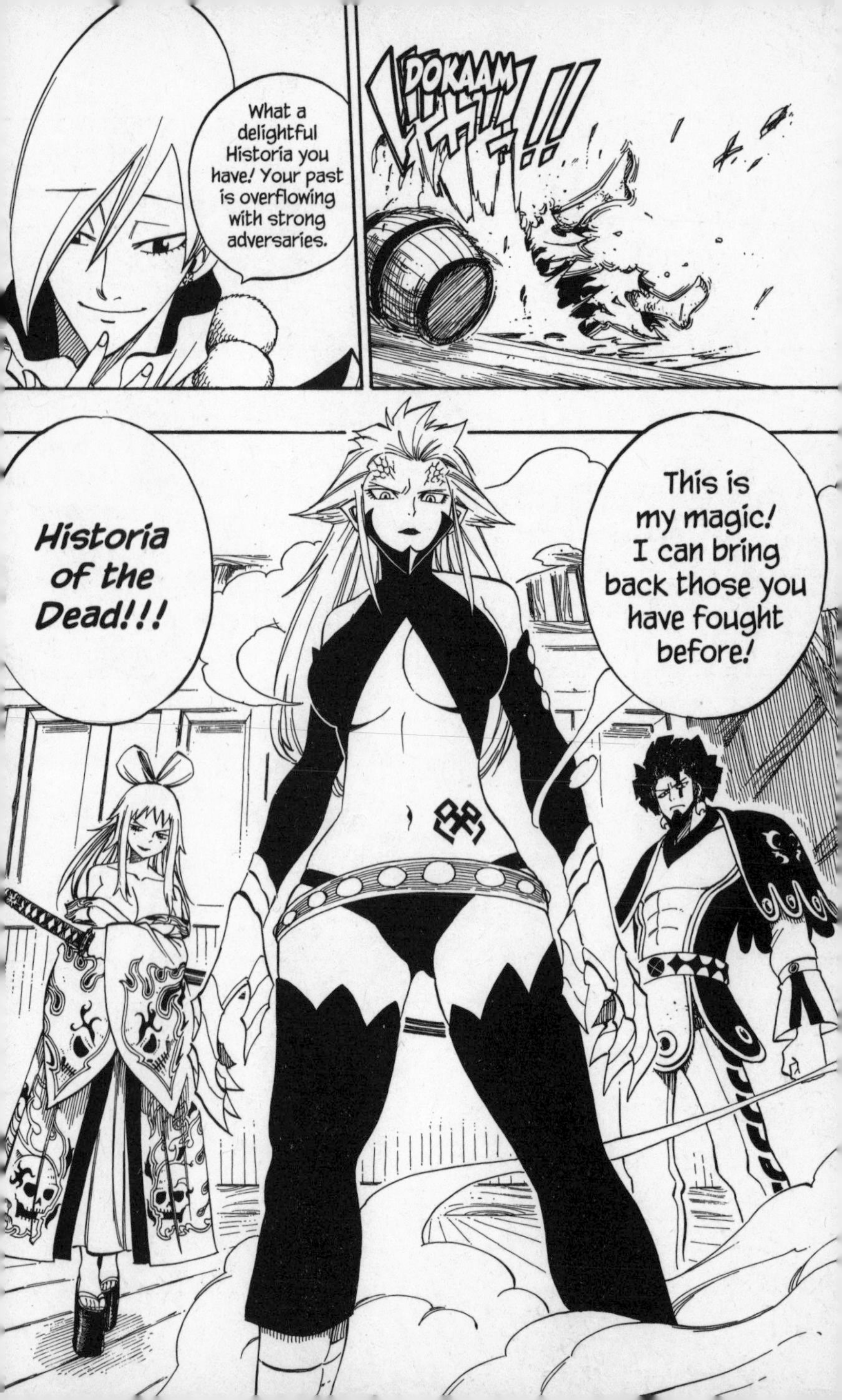
DOKAAM
What a delightful Historia you have! Your past is overflowing with strong adversaries.
This is my magic! I can bring back those you have fought before!
Historia of the Dead!!!

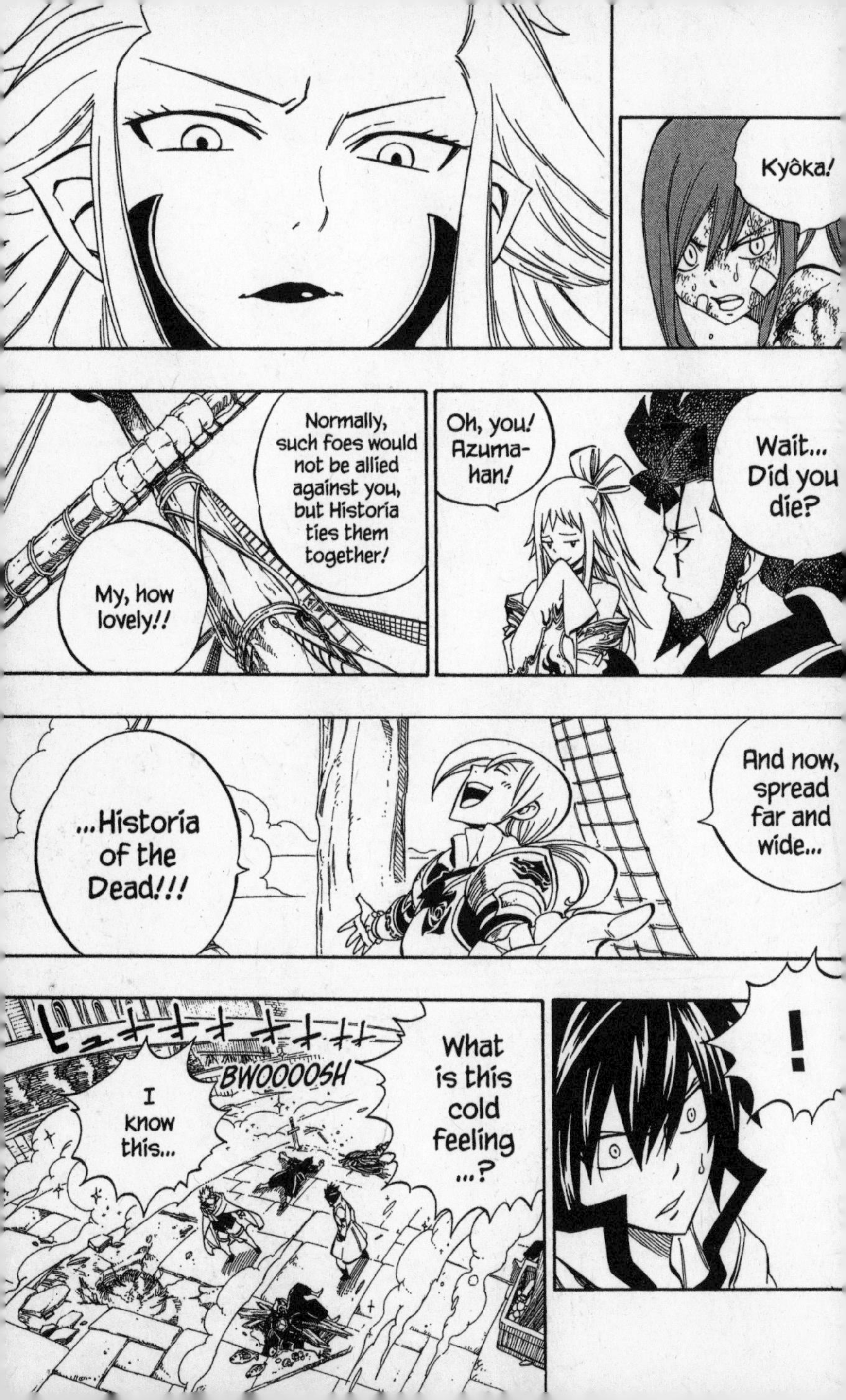
Kyôka!
Wait... Did you die?
Oh, you! Azuma-han!
Normally, such foes would not be allied against you, but Historia ties them together!
My, how lovely!!
And now, spread far and wide...
...Historia of the Dead!!!
!
What is this cold feeling ...?
BWOOOOSH
I know this...

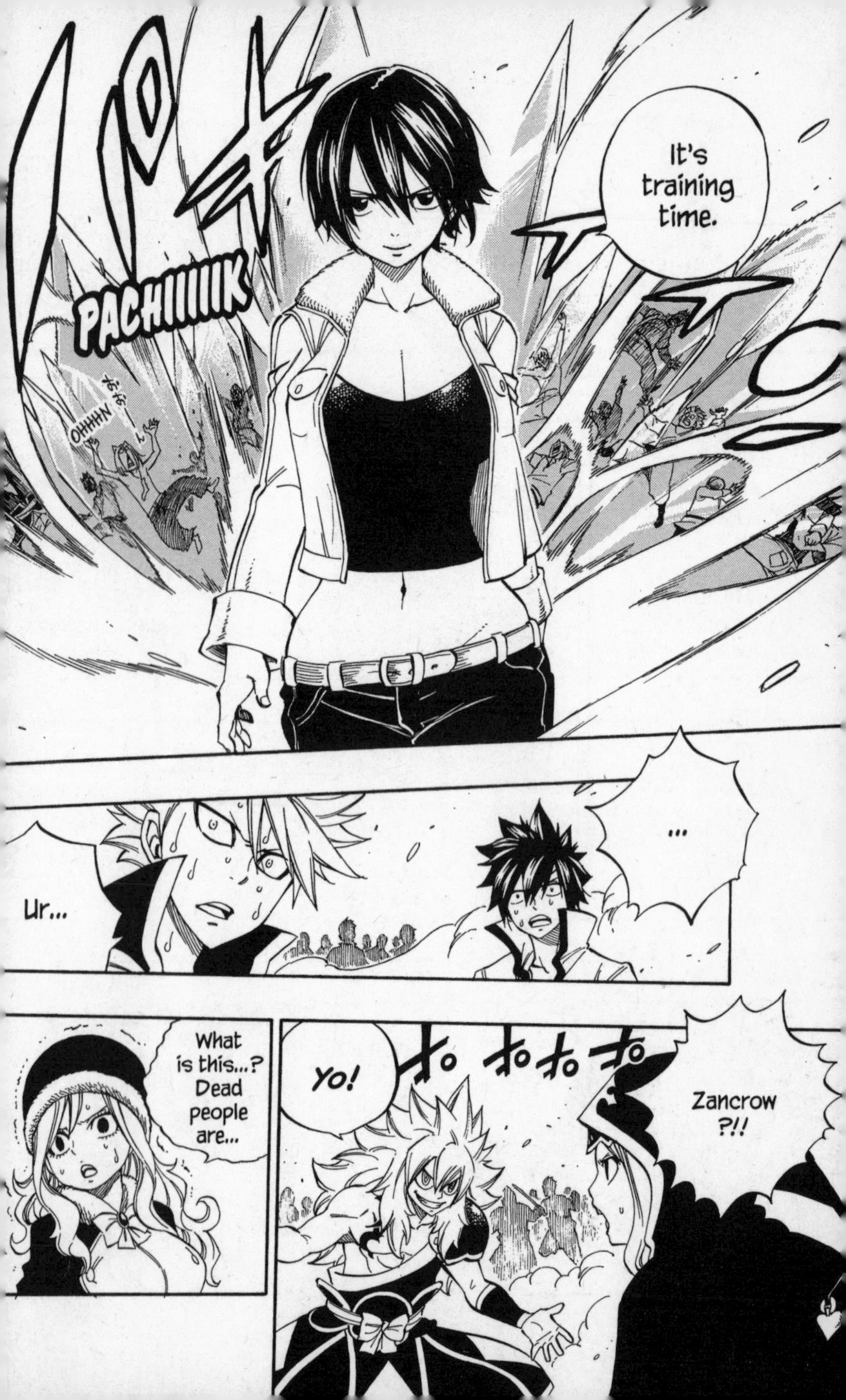
It's training time.
PACHIIIIIK
OHHHN
...
Ur...
Zancrow ?!!
Yo!
What is this...? Dead people are...

This magic is somewhat different to necromancy, th
manipulation of the dead.
FWOOM
!!
It is truly fascinating. This wizard pulls particularly strong individuals from memories and makes them flesh.
ZNN
ZNN
ZNN
What?
What is this ...?
We meet again, Shorty!!
Sherria, take Carla and run!!!
Now !!!
I can't even laugh at this.

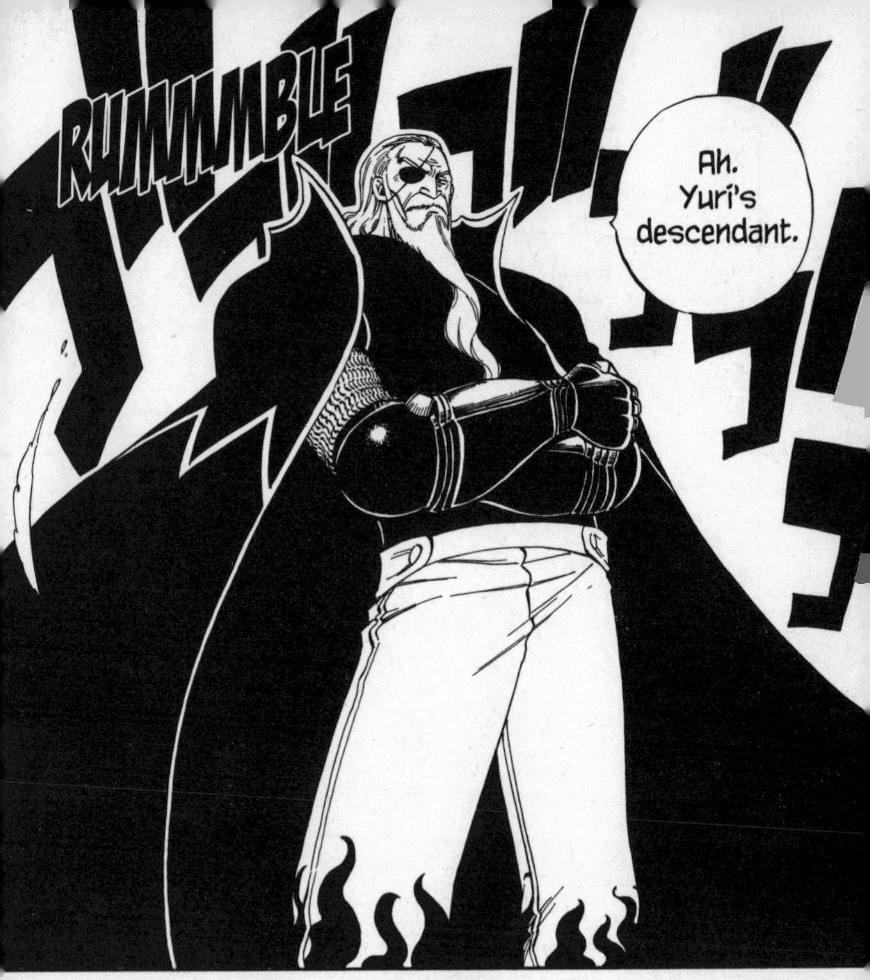
RUMMMBLE
Ah. Yuri's descendant.
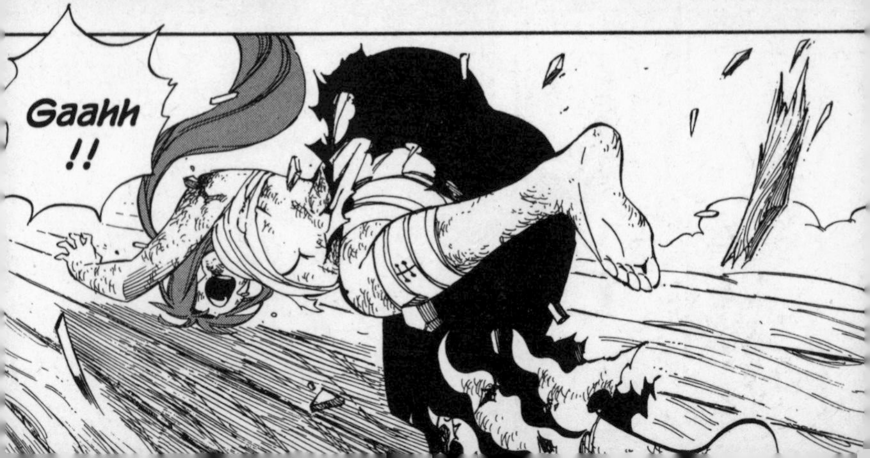
Gaahh !!

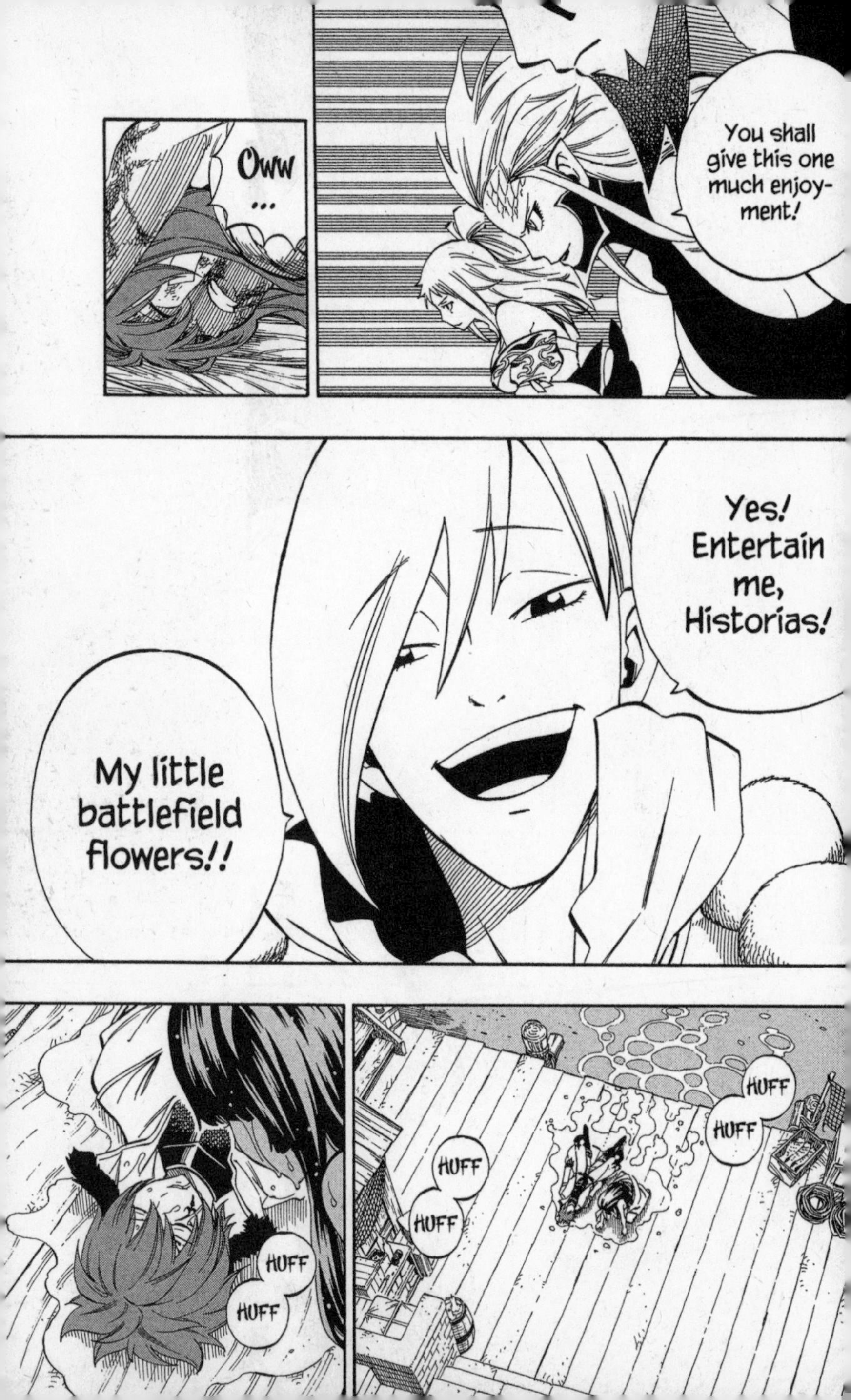
You shall give this one much enjoyment!
Oww ...
Yes! Entertain me, Historias!
My little battlefield flowers!!
HUFF
HUFF
HUFF
HUFF
HUFF
HUFF

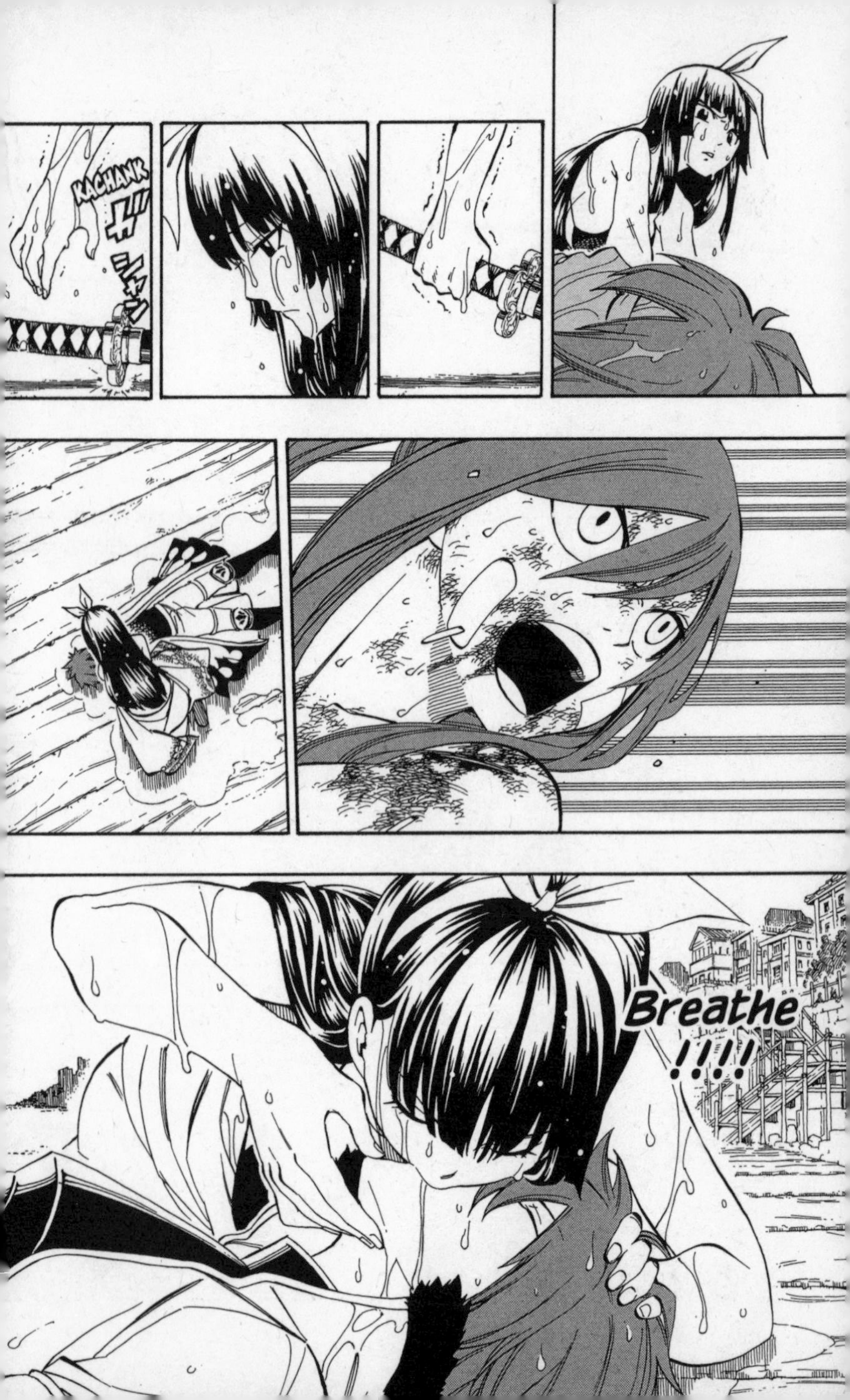
KACHANK
Breathe
!!!!

FAIRY TAIL

フェアリーテイル

Chapter 482: Fighting Spirit

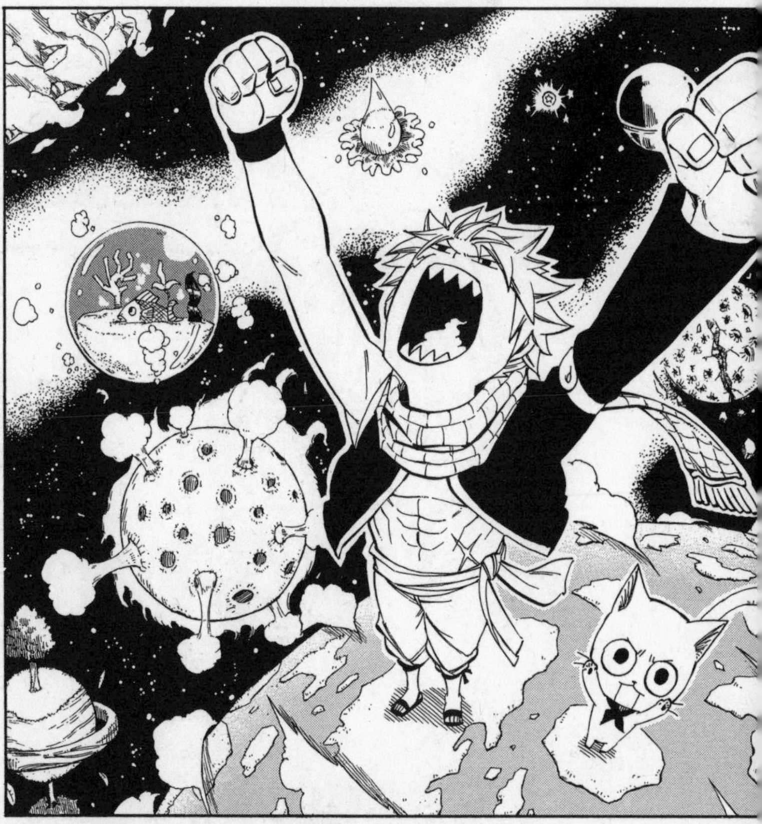

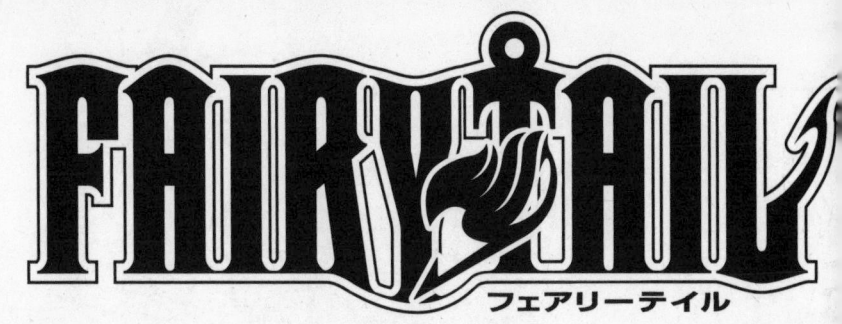

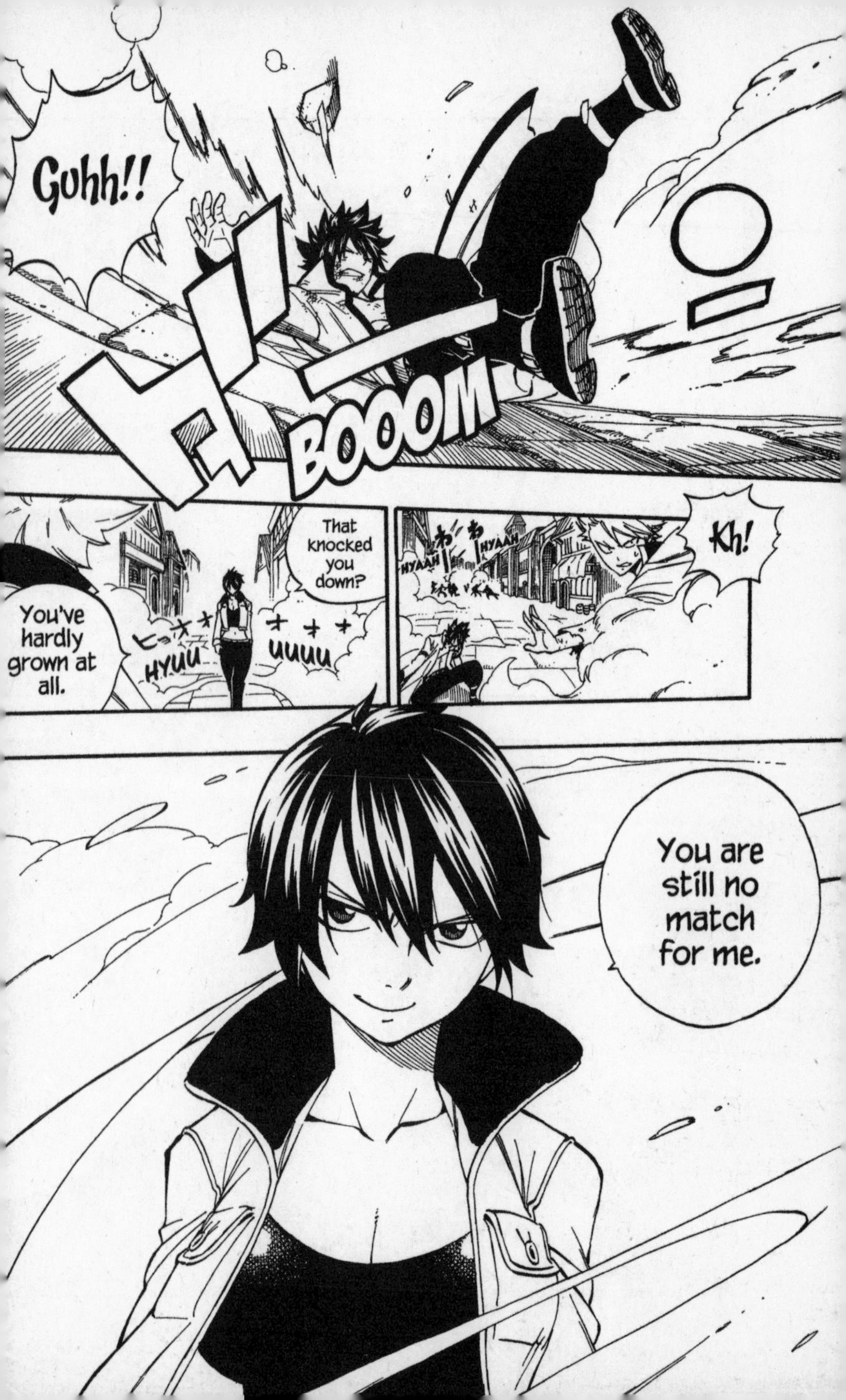
Guhh!!
BOOOM
Kh!
HYAAH
HYAAH
That knocked you down?
UUUU
HYUU
You've hardly grown at all.
You are still no match for me.

...
Wake up!! That isn't Ur!!
Ur...
I know...
It's just the enemy's magic...
But...
This thing's even got Ur's magic...?
SHK-H!!
But we're not the kids we used to be!!
ROSEN KRONE!!!!
PA-CHIK
AAGH!!
GUH!

WHOOSH
VSH
We can do this, Lyon!
This is just an enemy that stole Ur's form!
Gray ...
I won't let you sully Ur's name any more than you already have!!

Zancrow... On Sirius Island, you...
VWAM
You got that right! I *died* there!
That's the whole reason...
VWAM
VWAM
...I *really* hate the people who breezed through it and went on with their lives like it was nothin'!
AA AA AA
AA
AA !!
BWOOOGH
The voices of the dead echo throughout the battle-field!
RUMBLE
Now they have become my puppets! How delightful!
SWIRL
Kh!
How dare you defile the dead!

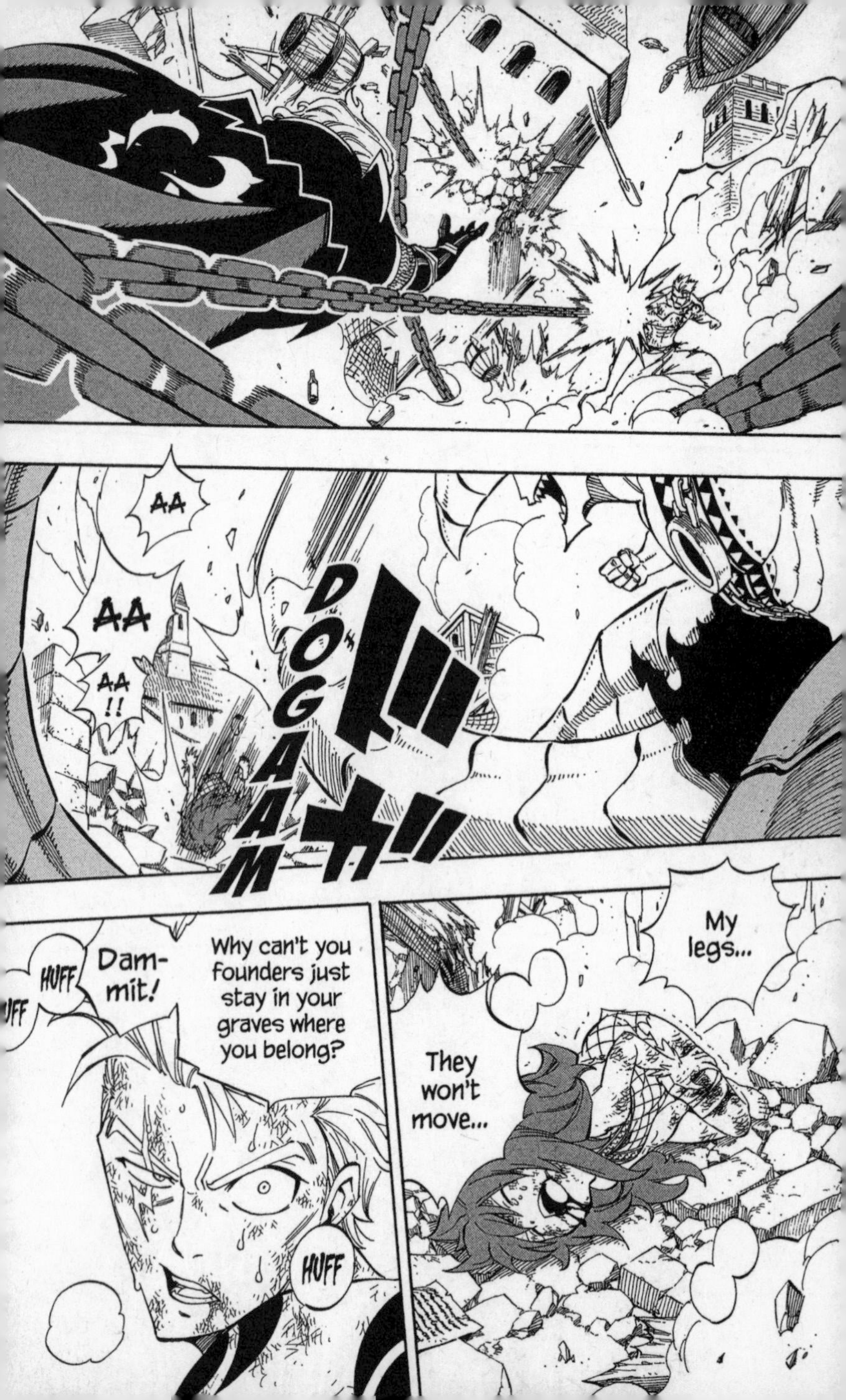
AA
AA
AA!!
DOGAAAM
My legs...
They won't move...
Why can't you founders just stay in your graves where you belong?
Dam-mit!
HUFF
HUFF

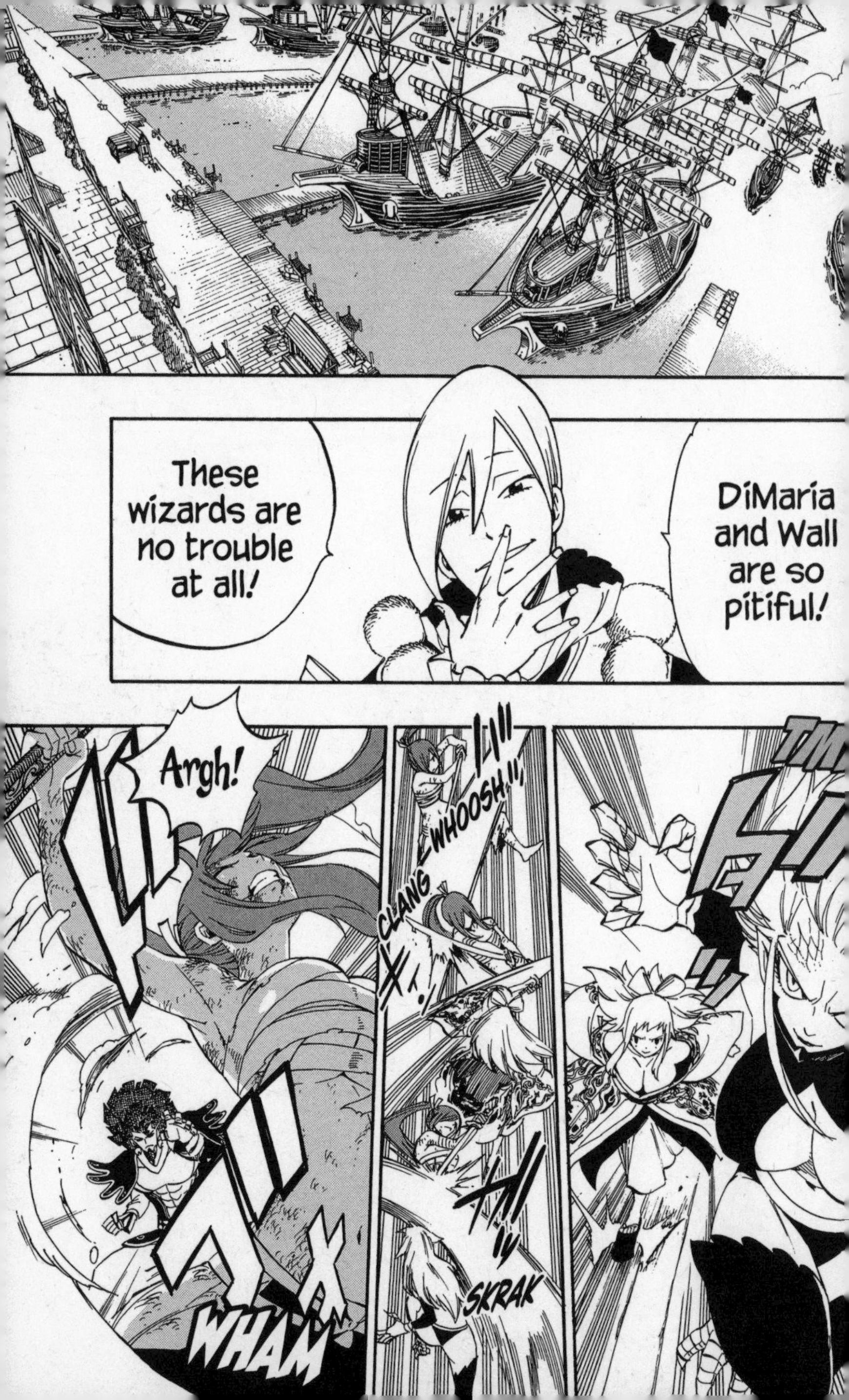
DiMaria and Wall are so pitiful!
These wizards are no trouble at all!
WHOOSH
CLANG
SKRAK
Argh!
WHAM

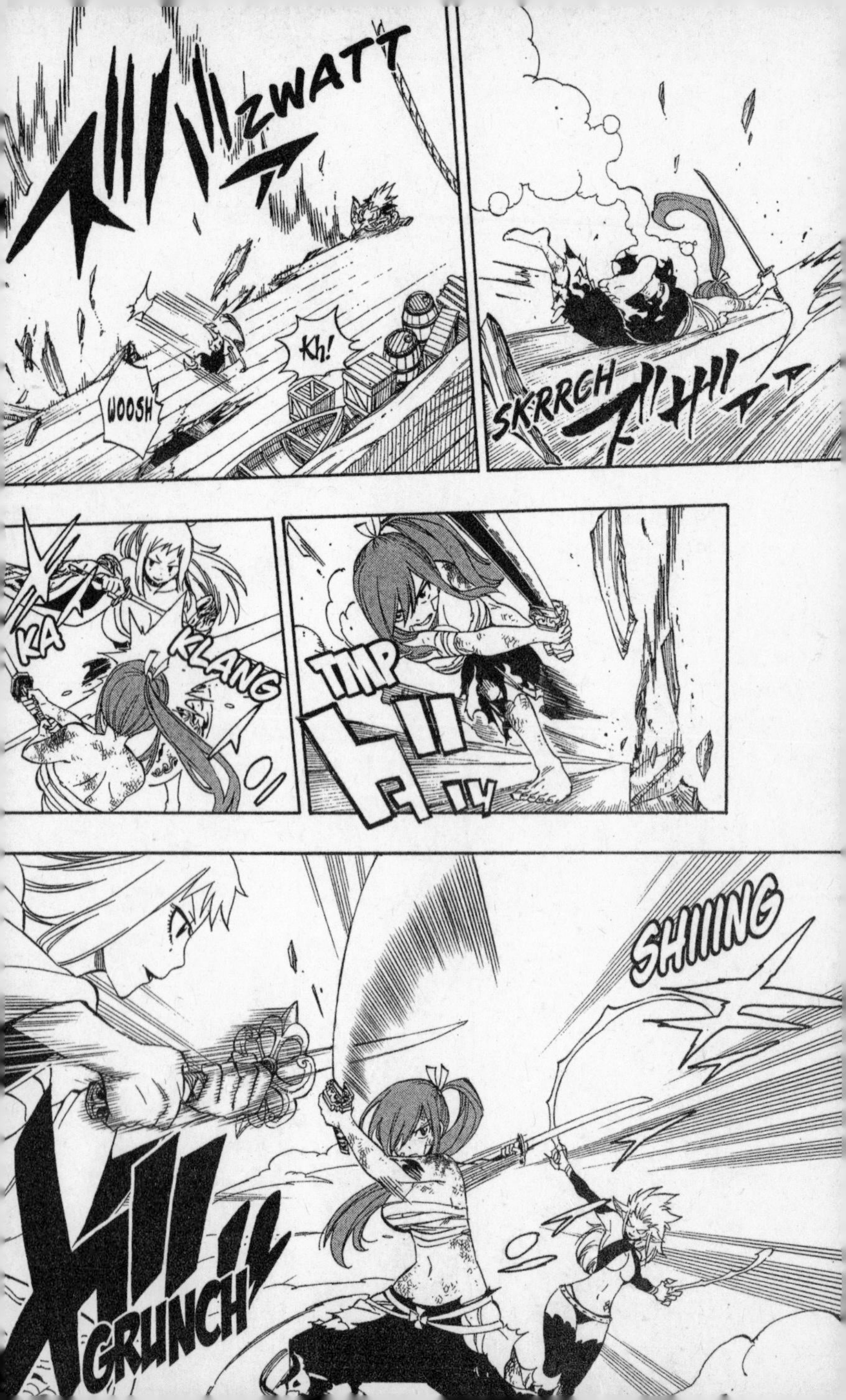
SKRRCH
ZWATT
Kh!
WOOSH
TMP
KA
KLANG
SHIIING
GRUNCH

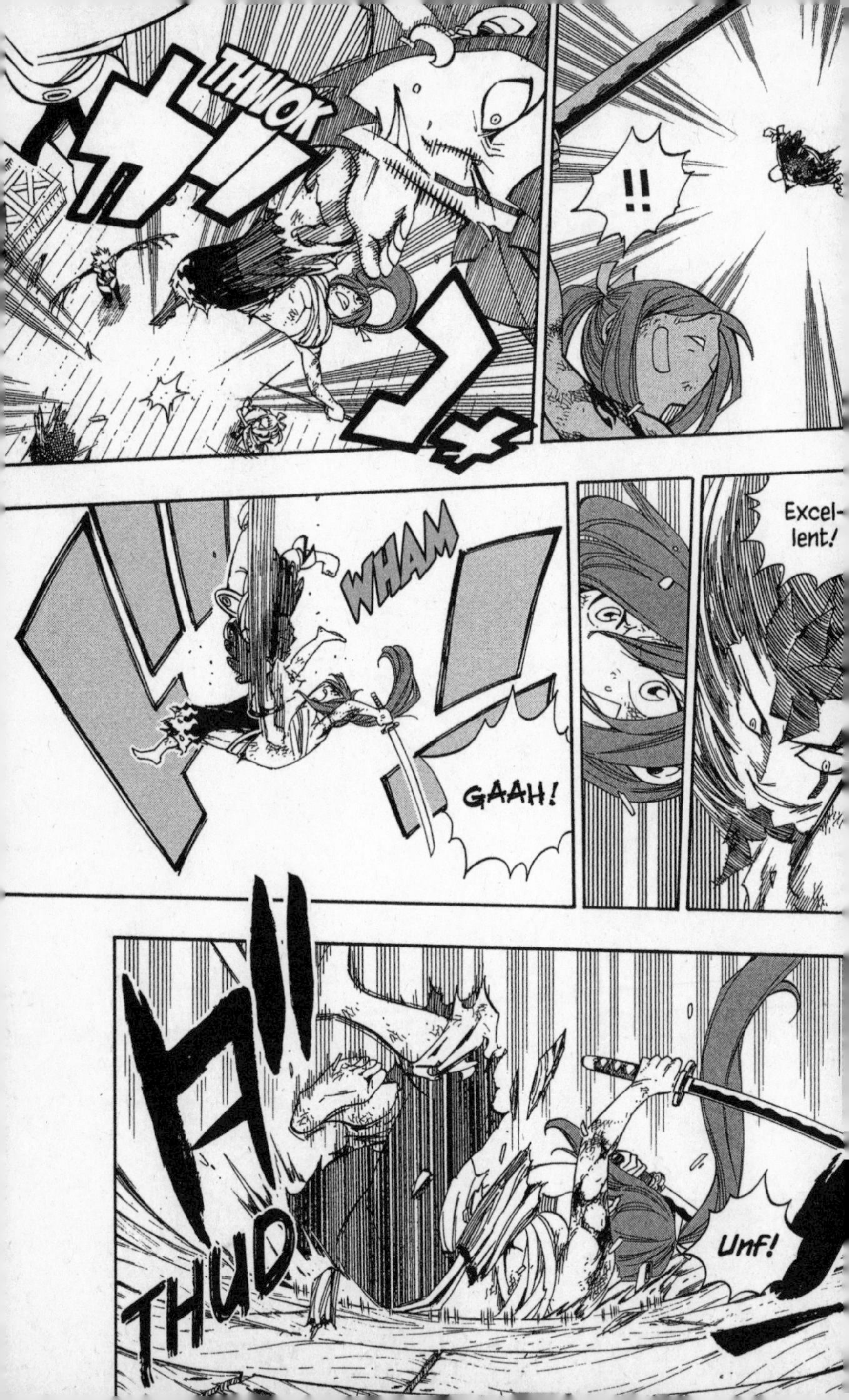
!!
THWOK
Excel-
lent!
WHAM
GAAH!
Unf!
THUD

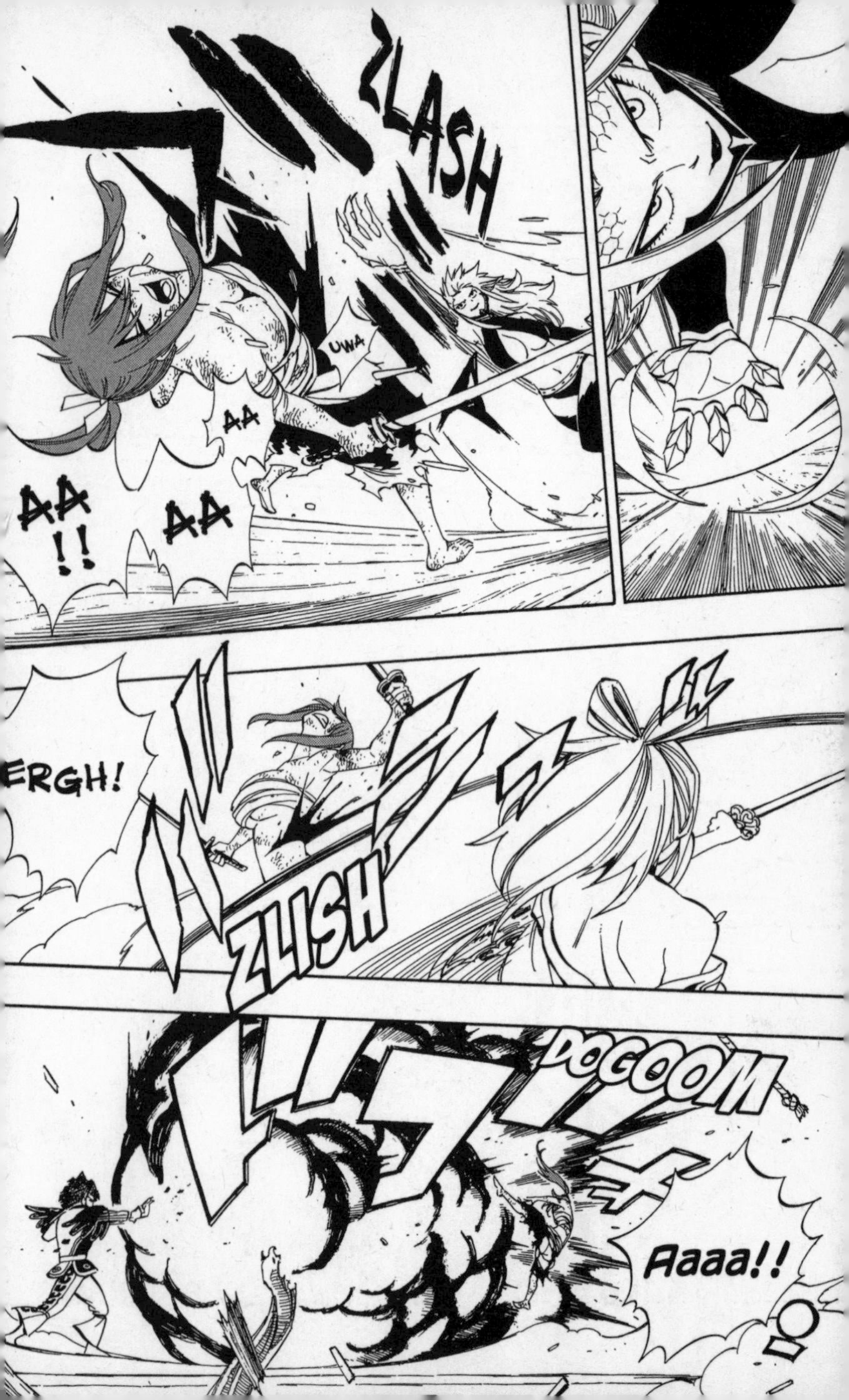
ZLASH
UWA
AA
AA
AA !!
ERGH!
ZLISH
DOGOOM
Aaaa!!

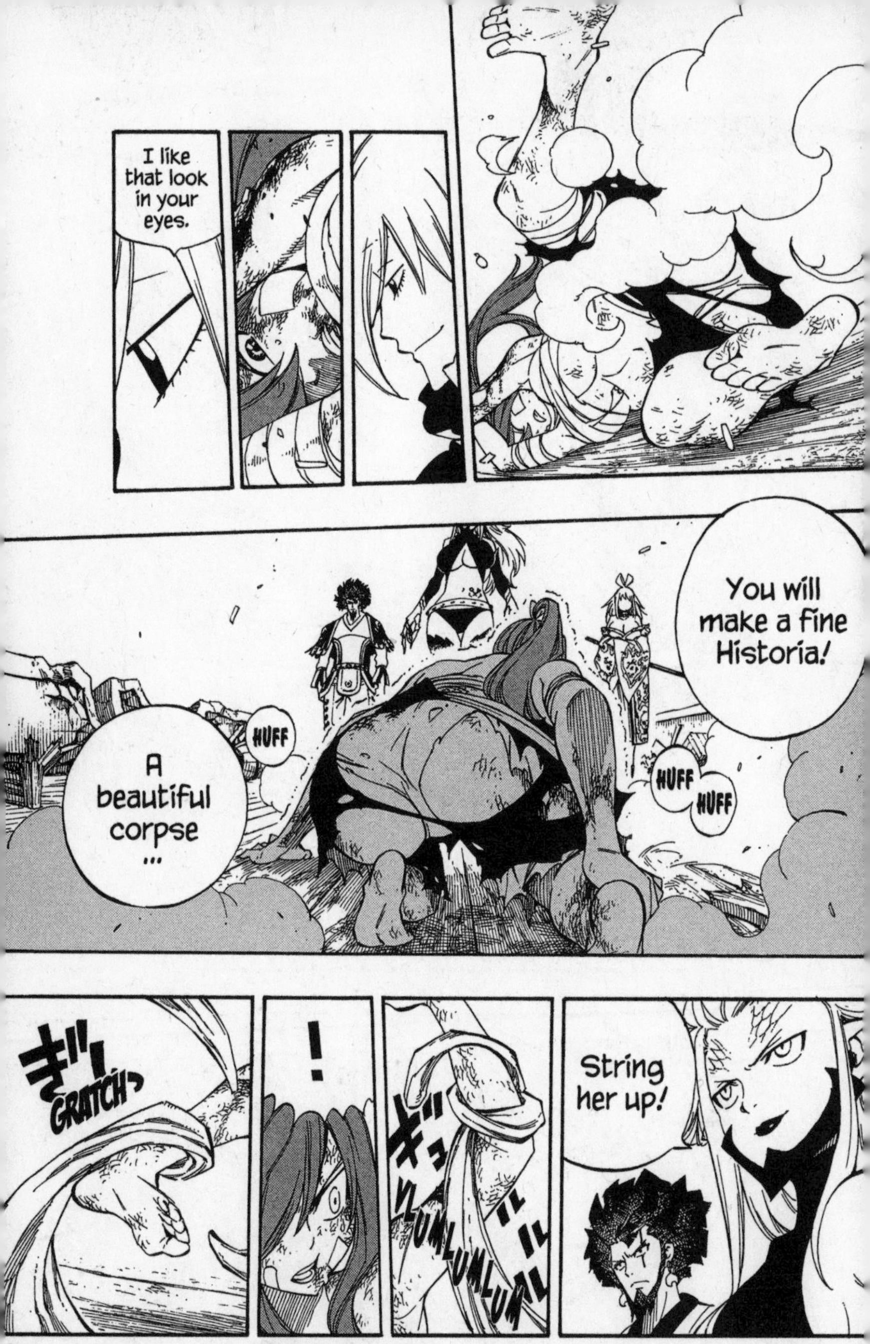
I like that look in your eyes.
You will make a fine Historia!
HUFF
HUFF
HUFF
A beautiful corpse ...
String her up!
VLUMLUMLUM
!
GRATCH

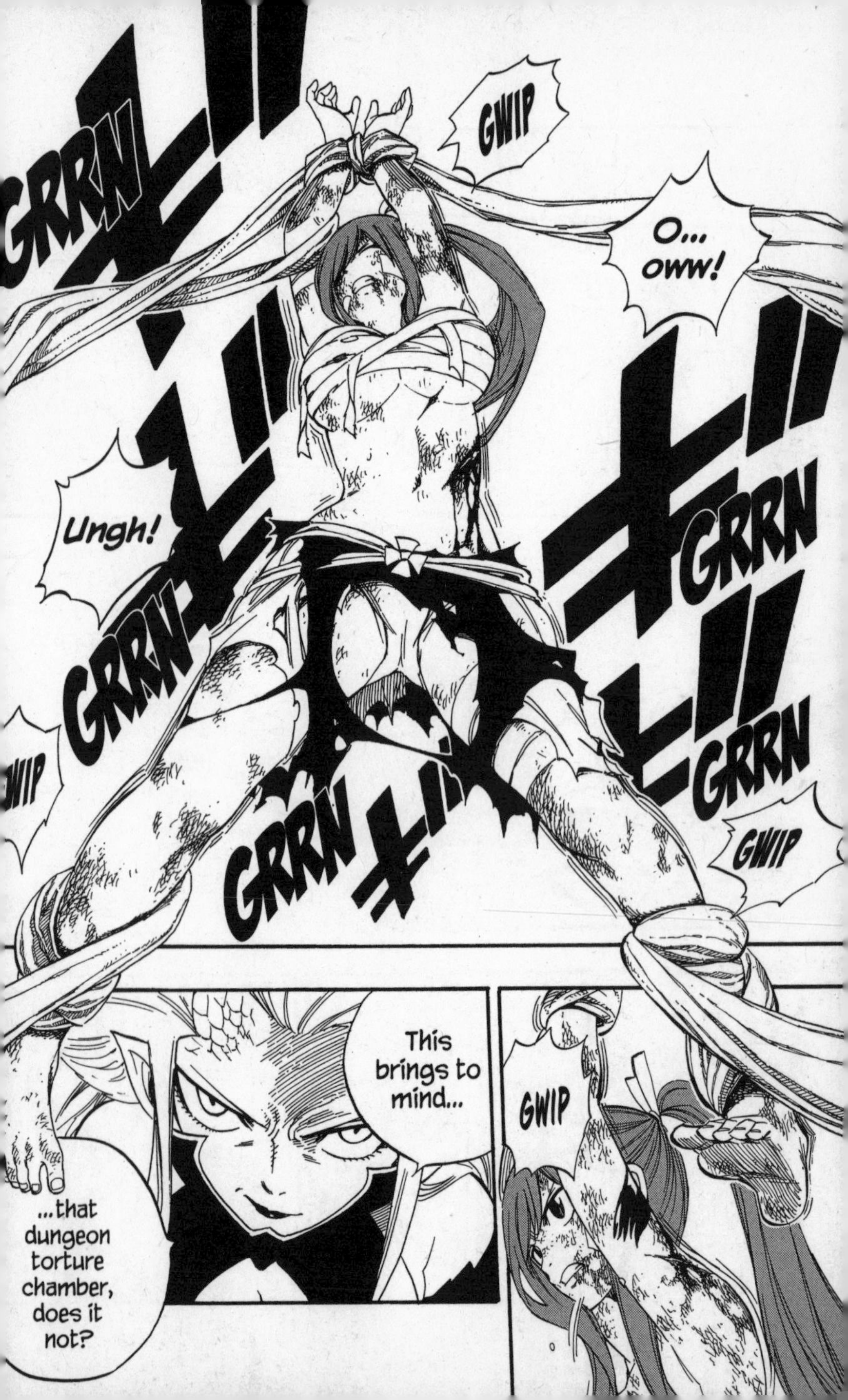

O... oww!
GWIP
GRRN!!
GRRN!!
GRRN
GRRN!!
GRRN
Ungh!
GRRN!!
GWIP
GRRN!!
WIP
GWIP
This brings to mind...
...that dungeon torture chamber, does it not?

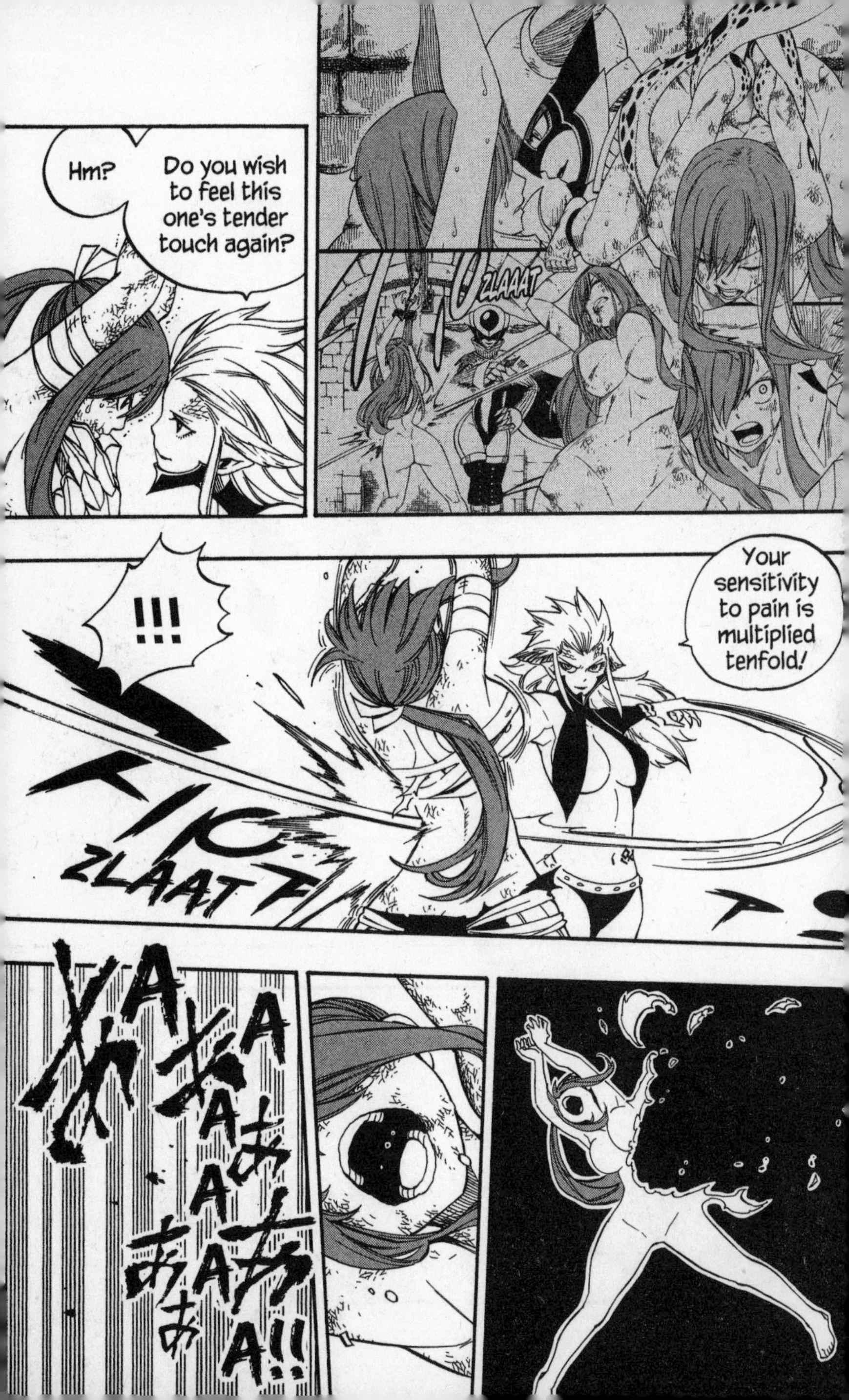

ZLAAAT
Hm?
Do you wish to feel this one's tender touch again?
Your sensitivity to pain is multiplied tenfold!
!!!
ZLAAAT
YAAAAAAA!!

Kyôka-han has unsavory appetites.
You should give your opponents a quick death.
Heh heh heh... Shall this one raise your pain sensitivity even higher?
SPLURT
GRIMP
Agh...
Or raise your pleasure sensitivity instead?
GWISH
Mm...
Does this bring back memories, Erza?
...
Yes...
I think that's enough of this reunion party.
All three of you once stood against me as very challenging enemies.
PLIP
PLIP
But...

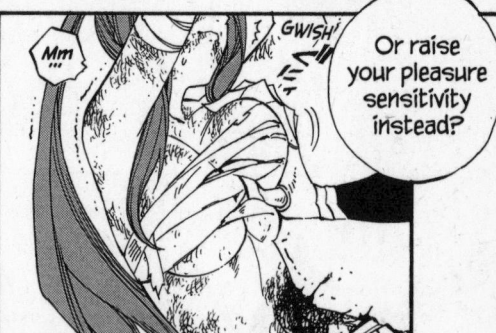

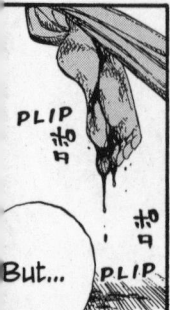

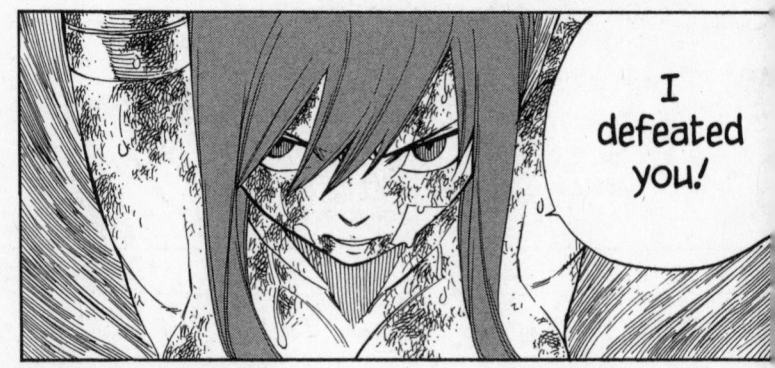

I defeated you!

ZWAT
ZWAT

Silence !!!!

!!

What?

ZLASH

...!!

...!!

ZWAT ZWAT ZWAT ZWAT

SLO

ZWA

ZLAT

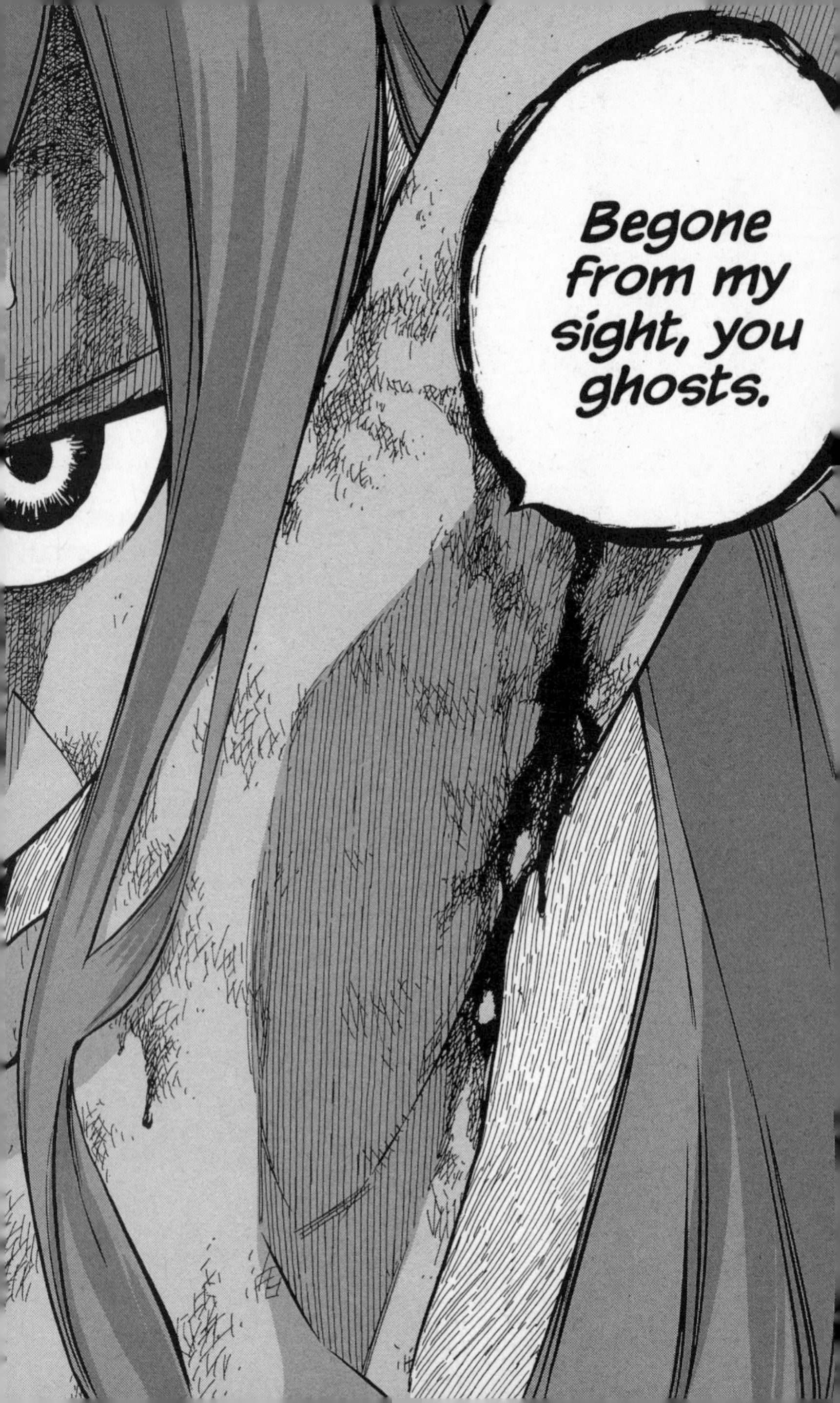
Begone from my sight, you ghosts.

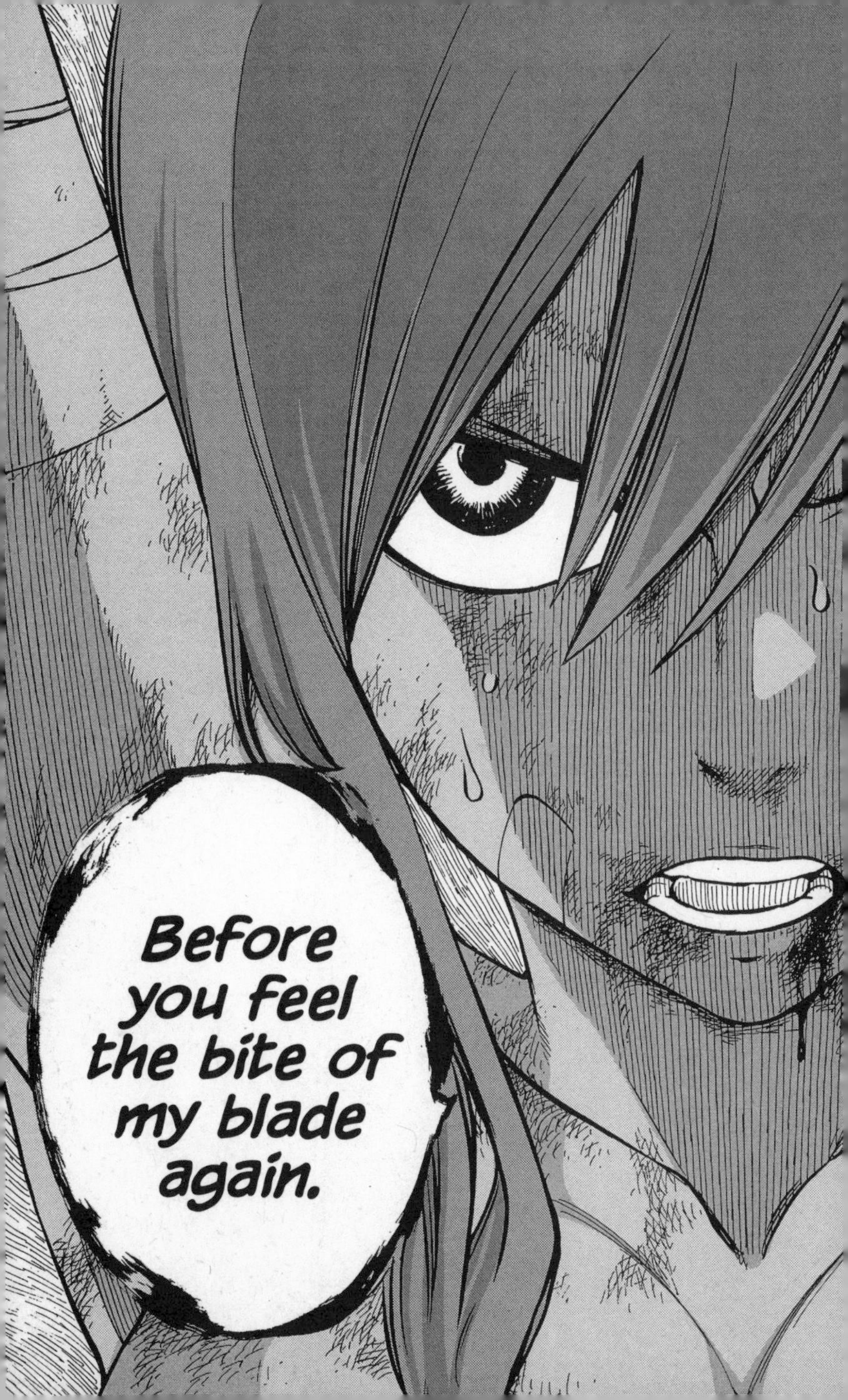
Before you feel the bite of my blade again.

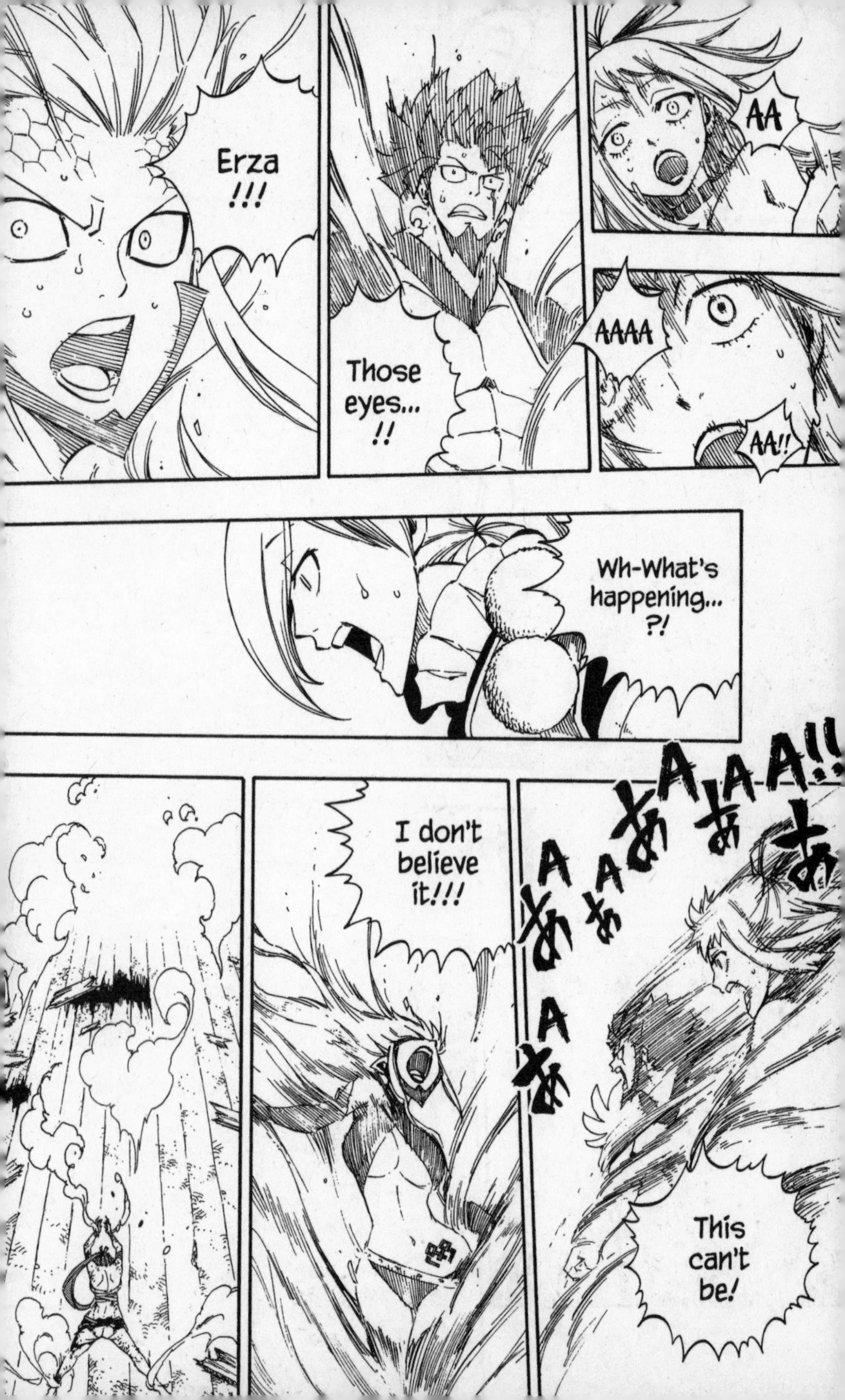
AA
AAAA
AA!!
Those eyes... !!
Erza !!!
Wh-What's happening... ?!
AAAAAA!!
ああああああ
This can't be!
I don't believe it!!!

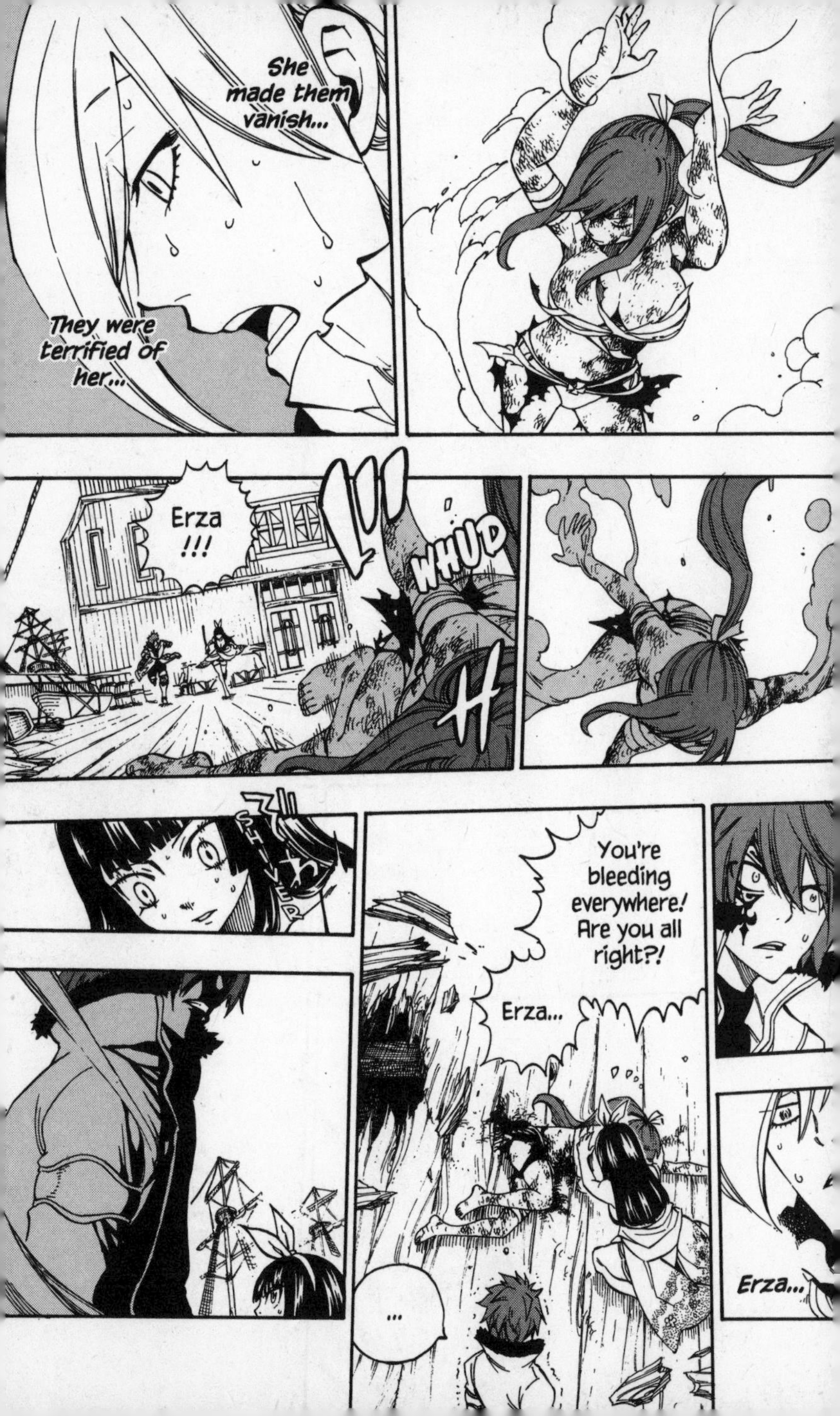
She made them vanish...
They were terrified of her...
WHUD
Erza !!!
Erza...
You're bleeding everywhere! Are you all right?!
Erza...
...
SHIVER

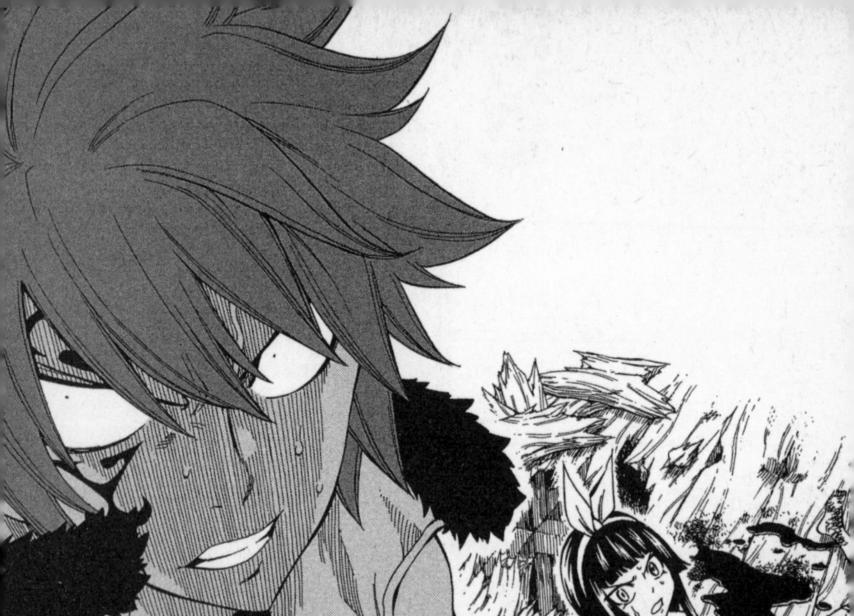

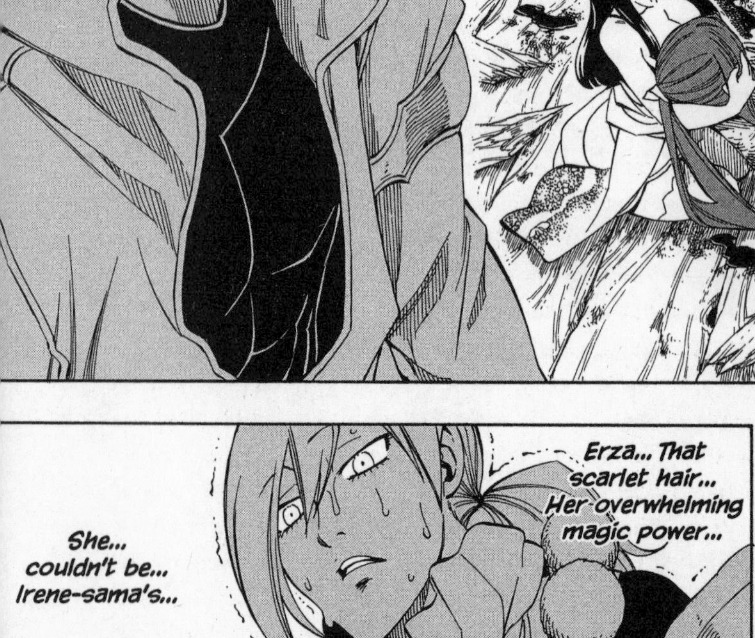
Erza... That scarlet hair... Her overwhelming magic power...
She... couldn't be... Irene-sama's...

TO BE CONTINUED

Afterword

Âge Seal, vanishing out of sight, Historia of the Dead... They're all types of cheating magic, aren't they? For the enemies this time, the Spriggan 12, I decided that they were all going to use "cheating" magic. Each one is something any author could come up with, but since they'd destroy the framework of the story, authors generally choose not to use them.

Historia in particular is a setup that I've been holding back for a long time. I personally **do** like the "...but he should be dead!" plot twists, but the story has consistently reinforced a system where people who die, cannot come back to life. That's why I was really torn about whether or not I'll use this magic. Ultimately, I decided to convince myself that it's not like I'm **really** bringing dead people back to life, so it's okay. The death of Simon and Ur are very emotional scenes, and I didn't want to undermine them with somebody's magic. I tried my best to handle those scenes with care.

For me, "nobody who dies comes back to life" is an internal rule that's as absolute as like, a Fairy Code. There are some characters that might make people say, "Hey! He's supposed to be dead, what's he doin' there?!" In those cases, I'll ask you to use the convenient excuse that they never actually died. If someone is confirmed as dead within the context of the story, I have written it with full intent that they will never actually be alive again. But there are a lot of other characters who, within my own mind, have never been confirmed as dead, so please just let it be and ignore the gray areas, thank you very much!

This is neither here nor there, but Jacob is based on an actor that I like a whole lot. I tried not to make him too much like the actor, so I doubt many people noticed. Because of that, I had planned to have more for him to do. He ended up being a pretty unfortunate character though, because he was in the wrong place at the wrong time—right when Natsu woke up!

Here, I found it for you!

FAIRY TAIL

フェアリーテイル

56

THE COVERRR!!!

HIRO 真島ヒロ MASHIMA

FROM HIRO MASHIMA

In Japan, the flap where a dust-cover folds over inside the book—in other words, where the "message from the author" is usually found in a manga—is called Cover 2 (C2) in the parlance of Japanese publishing.

The main book cover is Cover 1 (C1); the fold over from the back is Cover 3 (C3); and finally, the back cover is Cover 4 (C4). For C3 of the Japanese release, I used to draw alternating pictures of Lucy and Erza, but later other characters started creeping in there.

If you have the Japanese versions and check the C3 on each, you'll find some pretty unexpected characters in there. By the way, I decided that they're always going to be female characters. Probably!

Original Jacket Design: Hisao Ogawa

Translation Notes:

Japanese is a difficult language for many readers and translation is often more art than science. For your edification and reading pleasure, here are notes on some of the places where we could have gone in a different direction with our translation of the work, or where a Japanese cultural reference is used.

Page 21, First Sky Arrow, Second Sky Arrow

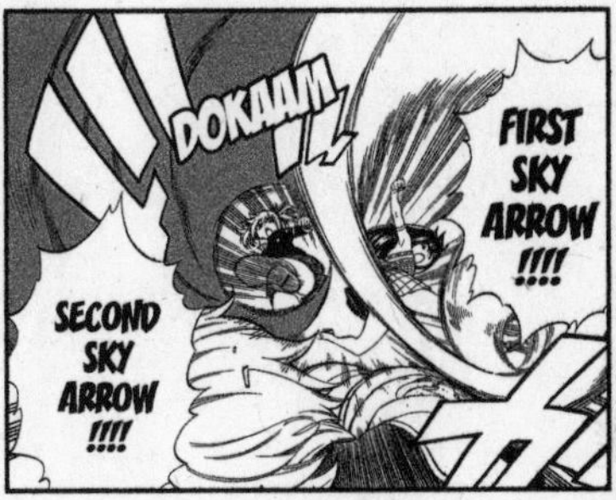
DOKAAM
FIRST SKY ARROW !!!!
SECOND SKY ARROW !!!!

The Japanese names were *haya* and *otoya*. There aren't widely known names for types of fletching in English, so it is instead translated to "first sky arrow" and "second sky arrow" since *ha* and *oto* are "one" and "two" in an old method of counting in Japanese (based off of a fortune-telling system). It is still used sometimes when one has used all of the other numbers and letters for bullets. But actually, *haya* and *otoya* refer to the bends in the feathers of the arrow's fletching that causes the arrow to spin. A *haya*-fletched arrow spins clockwise, and an *otoya*-fletched arrow spins counterclockwise.

Page 34, Chronos

Chronos is the god or personification of time in ancient Greek philosophy and literature. Chronos is often confused with or associated with the Titan from Greek mythology as well—in which he is named Cronus, who is the father of Zeus.

Page 58, Ama no Murakumo no Tsurugi

This is a sword out of the *Kojiki*, which tells the story of the creation myth and other myths of the Shinto religion of Japan. One of the more famous myths tells of a feud between the Goddess of Light, Amaterasu, and her brother Susanoo. Due to the feud, Amaterasu flees into a cave, shrouding the world in darkness. Eventually, she is coaxed out, and when she returns, Susanoo is banished from Heaven. But as a gesture of reconciliation, Susanoo gives Amaterasu a sword called *Ama no Murakumo no Tsurugi*. It was later renamed *Kusanagi no Tsurugi* and appeared in Japanese epics such as *The Tale of the Heike*.

Page 171, Rosen Krone

This attack name is German for "Crown of Roses."

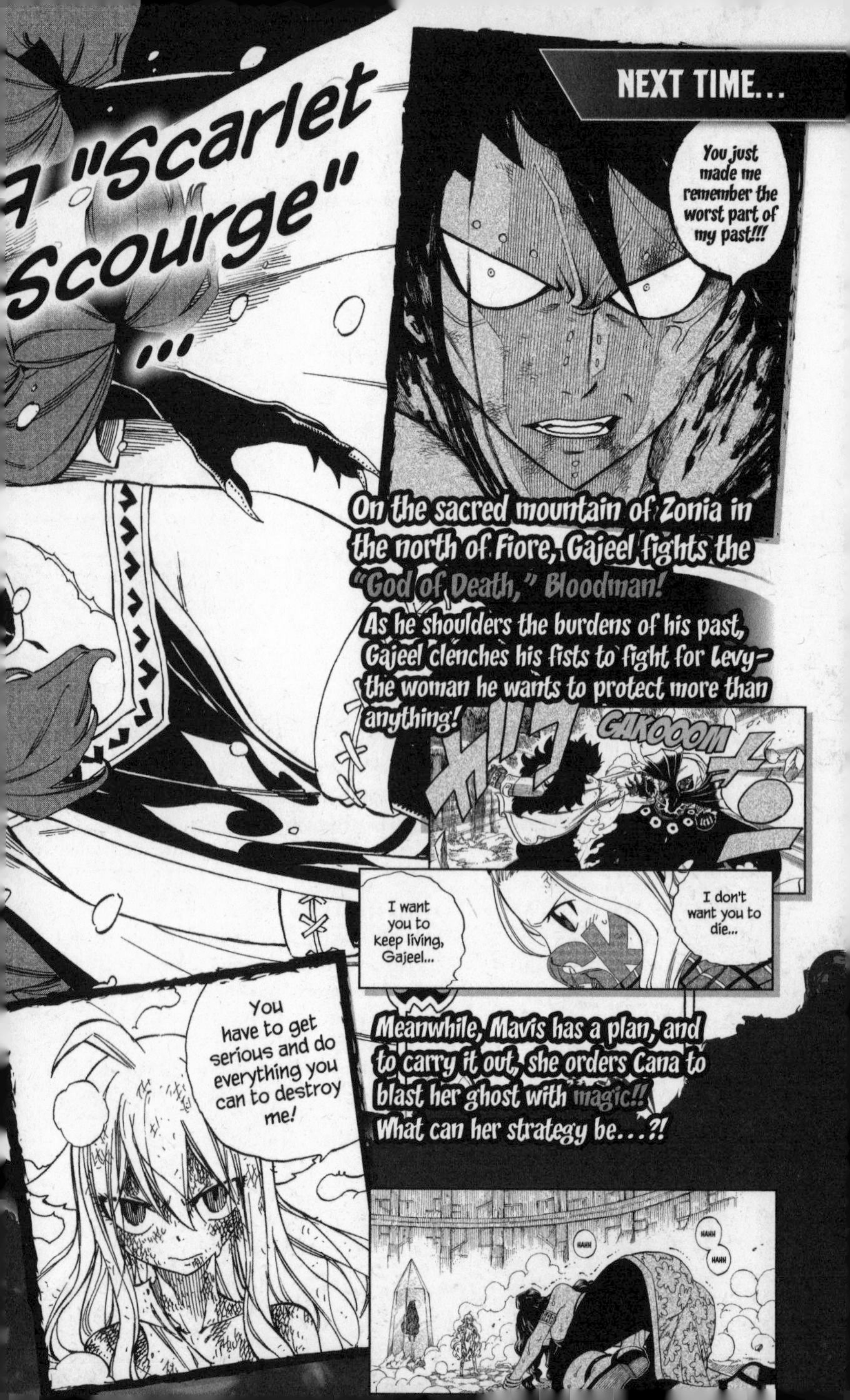
NEXT TIME...
You just made me remember the worst part of my past!!!
7 "Scarlet Scourge" ...
On the sacred mountain of Zonia in the north of Fiore, Gajeel fights the "God of Death," Bloodman!
As he shoulders the burdens of his past, Gajeel clenches his fists to fight for Levy- the woman he wants to protect more than anything!
GAKOOOM
I don't want you to die...
I want you to keep living, Gajeel...
Meanwhile, Mavis has a plan, and to carry it out, she orders Cana to blast her ghost with magic!! What can her strategy be...?!
You have to get serious and do everything you can to destroy me!
HAHH
HAHH

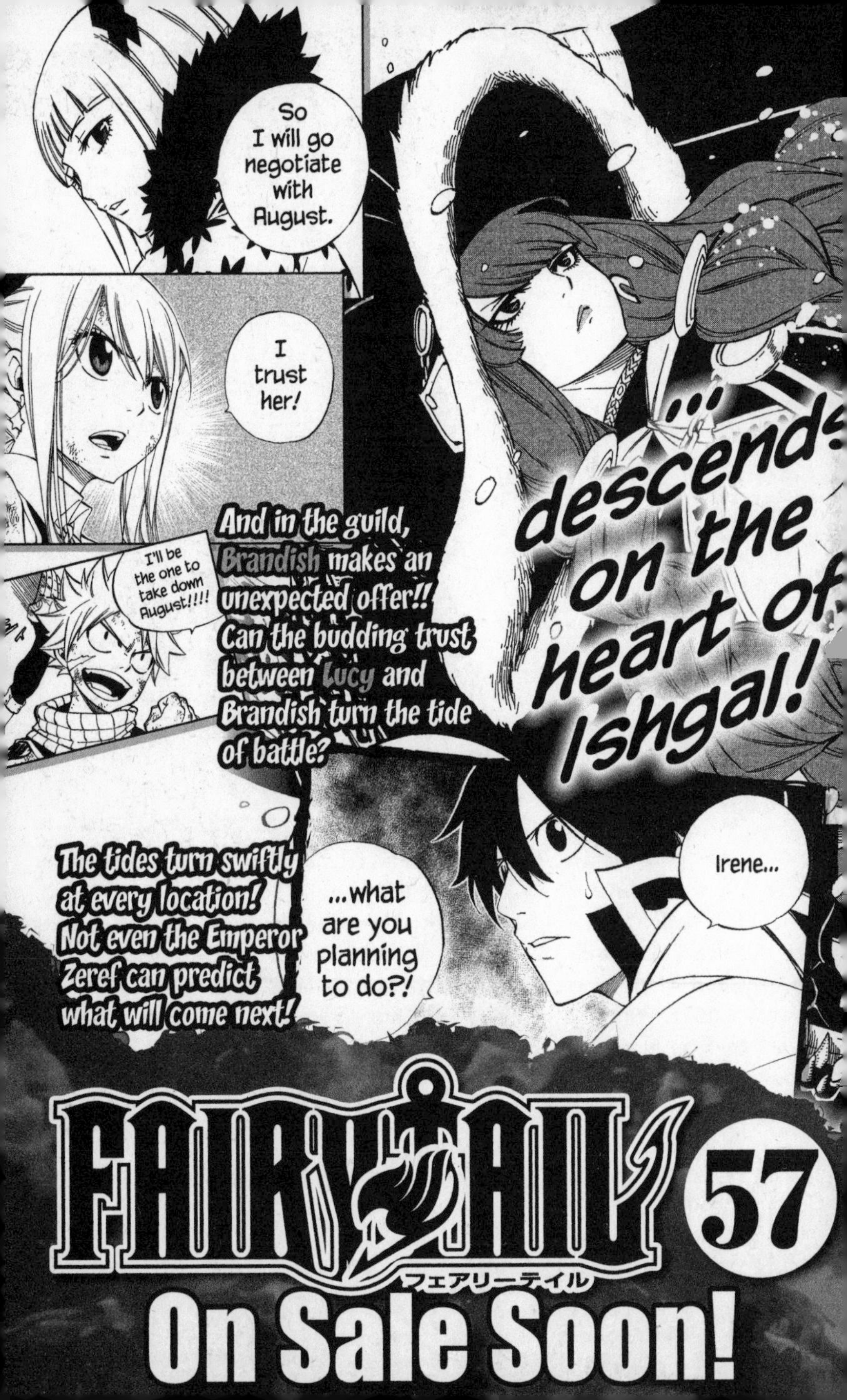

...descends on the heart of Ishgal!
So I will go negotiate with August.
I trust her!
I'll be the one to take down August!!!!
And in the guild, Brandish makes an unexpected offer!! Can the budding trust between Lucy and Brandish turn the tide of battle?
Irene...
...what are you planning to do?!
The tides turn swiftly at every location! Not even the Emperor Zeref can predict what will come next!
FAIRY TAIL 57
フェアリーテイル
On Sale Soon!

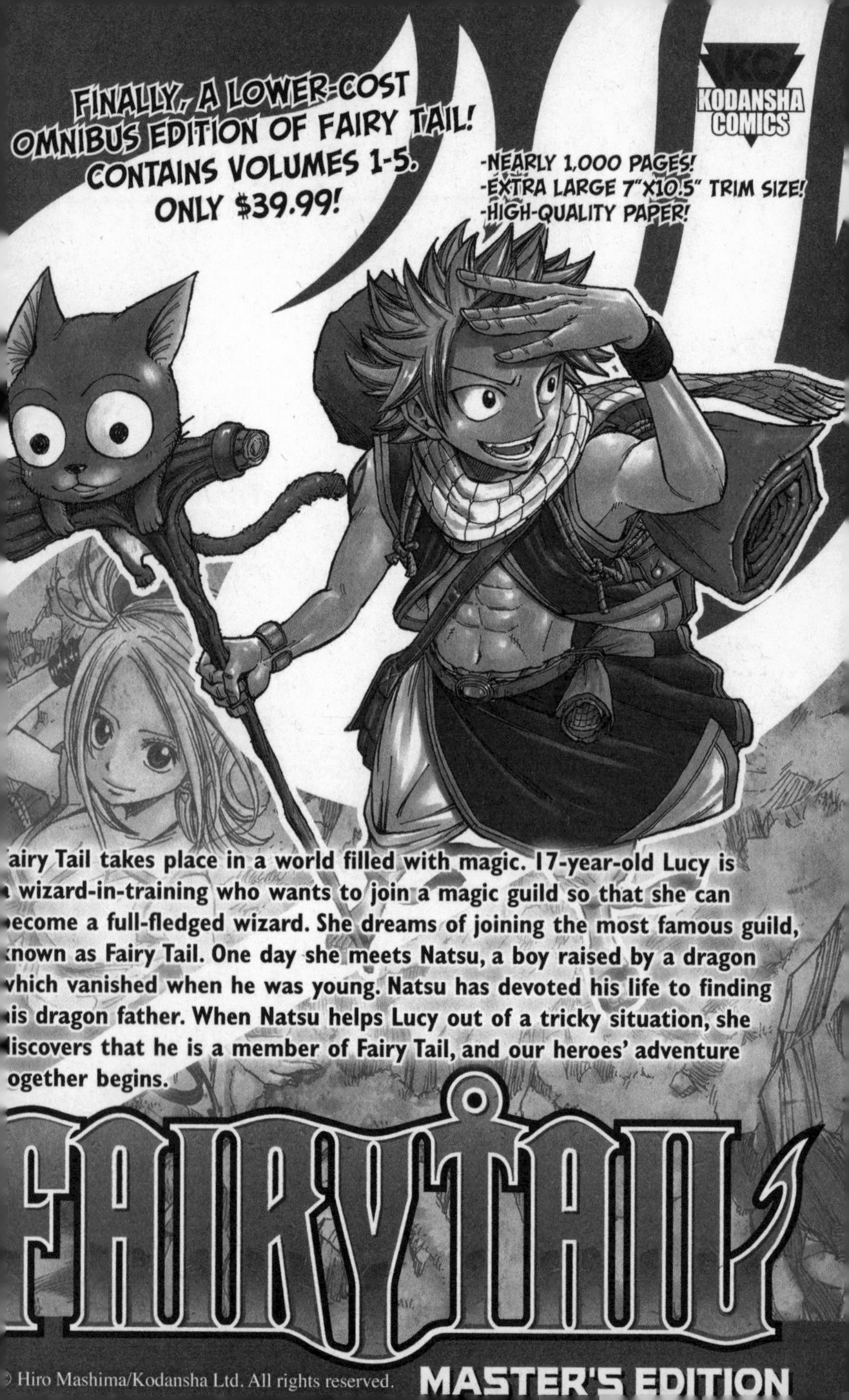
FINALLY, A LOWER-COST OMNIBUS EDITION OF FAIRY TAIL! CONTAINS VOLUMES 1-5. ONLY $39.99!
KODANSHA COMICS
-NEARLY 1,000 PAGES!
-EXTRA LARGE 7"X10.5" TRIM SIZE!
-HIGH-QUALITY PAPER!
airy Tail takes place in a world filled with magic. 17-year-old Lucy is
wizard-in-training who wants to join a magic guild so that she can
ecome a full-fledged wizard. She dreams of joining the most famous guild,
nown as Fairy Tail. One day she meets Natsu, a boy raised by a dragon
vhich vanished when he was young. Natsu has devoted his life to finding
is dragon father. When Natsu helps Lucy out of a tricky situation, she
iscovers that he is a member of Fairy Tail, and our heroes' adventure
ogether begins.
FAIRY TAIL
© Hiro Mashima/Kodansha Ltd. All rights reserved.
MASTER'S EDITION

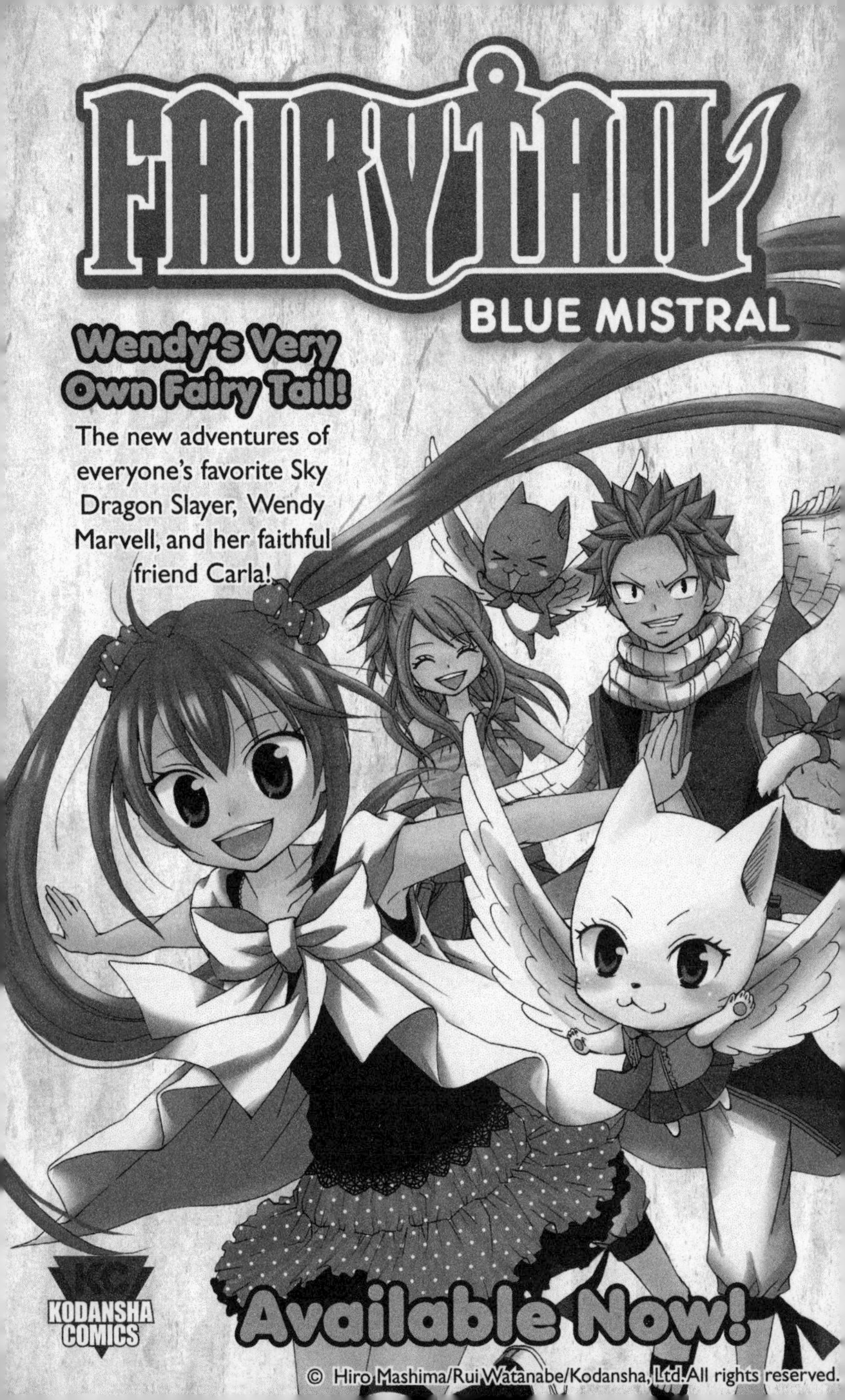
FAIRY TAIL
BLUE MISTRAL
Wendy's Very Own Fairy Tail!
The new adventures of everyone's favorite Sky Dragon Slayer, Wendy Marvell, and her faithful friend Carla!
KODANSHA COMICS
Available Now!
© Hiro Mashima/Rui Watanabe/Kodansha, Ltd. All rights reserved.

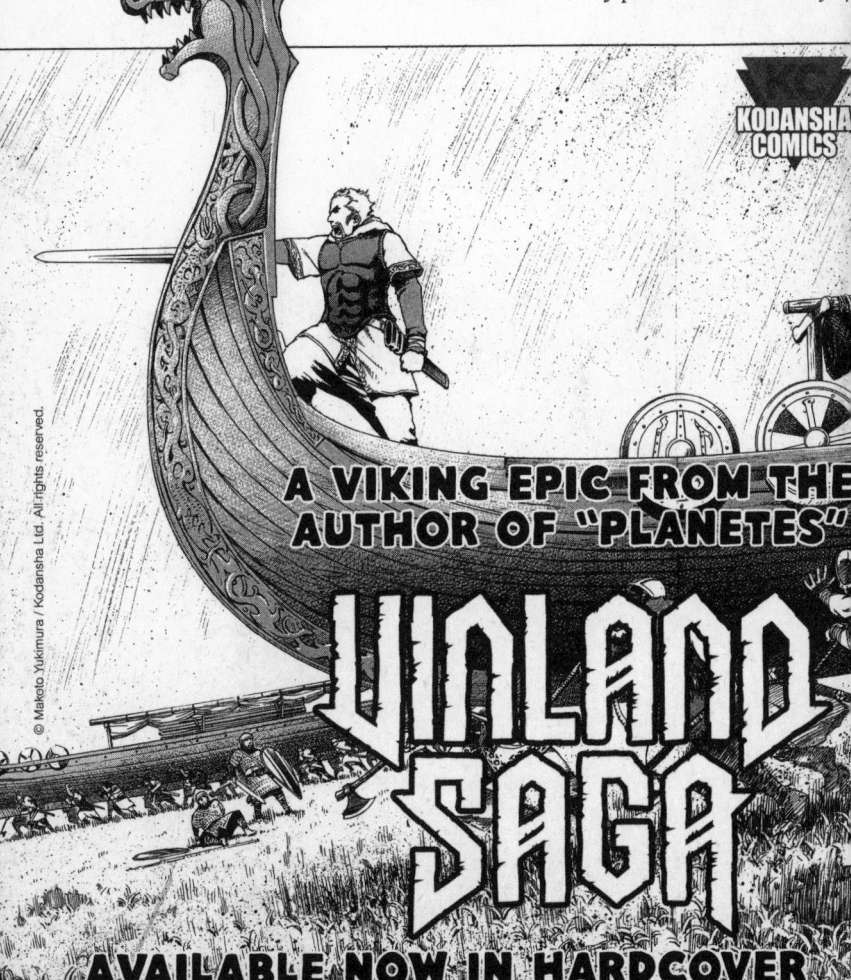

Praise for the anime:

"The show provides a pleasant window on the highs and lows of young love with two young people who are first timers at the real thing."

-The Fandom Post

"Always it is smarter, more poetic, more touching, just plain better than you think it is going to be."

-Anime News Network

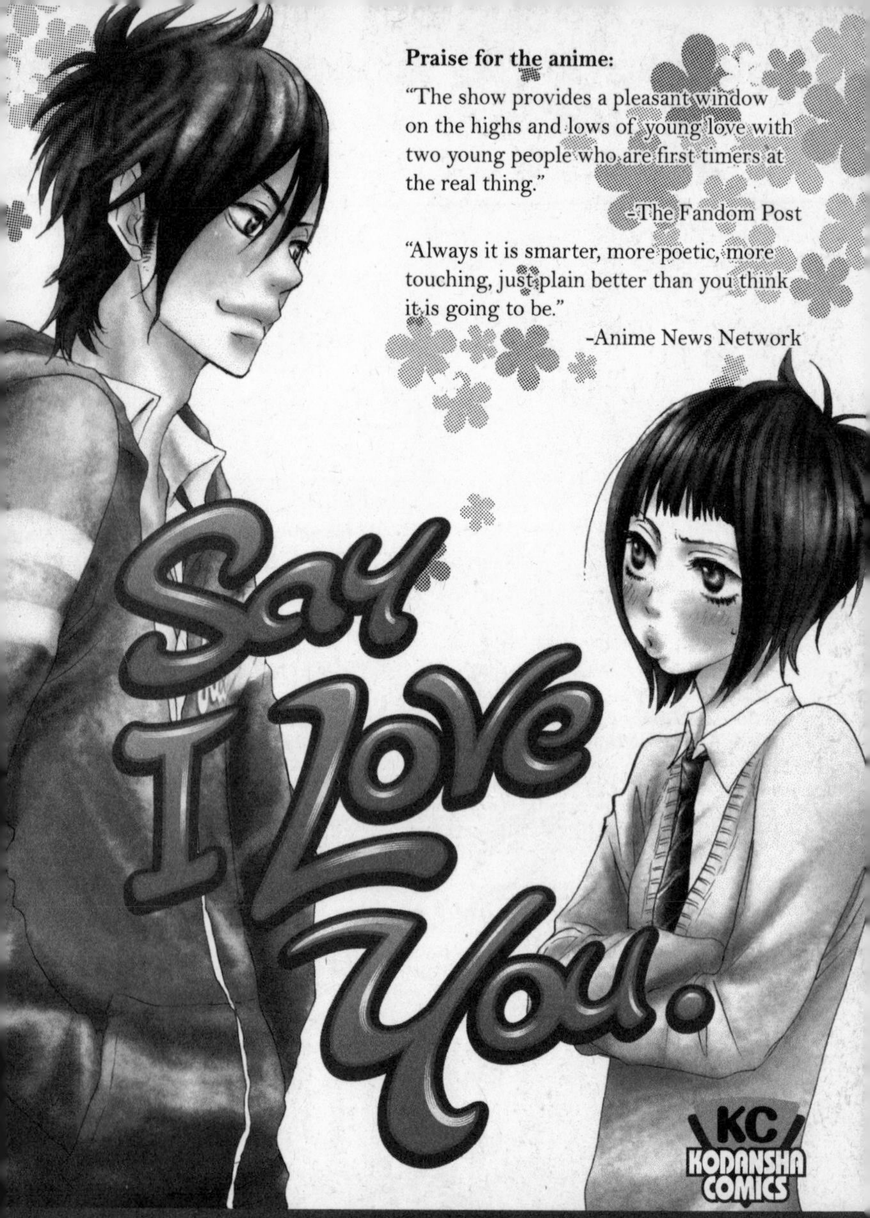
Say I Love You.
KC
KODANSHA COMICS

Mei Tachibana has no friends — and says she doesn't need them!

But everything changes when she accidentally roundhouse kicks the most popular boy in school! However, Yamato Kurosawa isn't angry in the slightest— in fact, he thinks his ordinary life could use an unusual girl like Mei. But winning Mei's trust will be a tough task. How long will she refuse to say, "I love you"?

DEVIL SURVIVOR デビルサバイバー

AFTER DEMONS BREAK THROUGH INTO THE HUMAN WORLD, TOKYO MUST BE QUARANTINED. WITHOUT POWER AND STUCK IN A SUPERNATURAL WARZONE, 17-YEAR-OLD KAZUYA HAS ONLY ONE HOPE: HE MUST USE THE *"COMP,"* A DEVICE CREATED BY HIS COUSIN NAOYA CAPABLE OF SUMMONING AND SUBDUING DEMONS, TO DEFEAT THE INVADERS AND TAKE BACK THE CITY.

KODANSHA COMICS

BASED ON THE POPULAR VIDEO GAME FRANCHISE BY ATLUS!

My Little Monster

OPPOSITES ATTRACT...MAYBE?

Haru Yoshida is feared as an unstable and violent "monster."
Mizutani Shizuku is a grade-obsessed student with no friends.
ate brings these two together to form the most unlikely pair. Haru
rmly believes he's in love with Mizutani and she firmly believes
e's insane.

KC
**KODANSHA
COMICS**

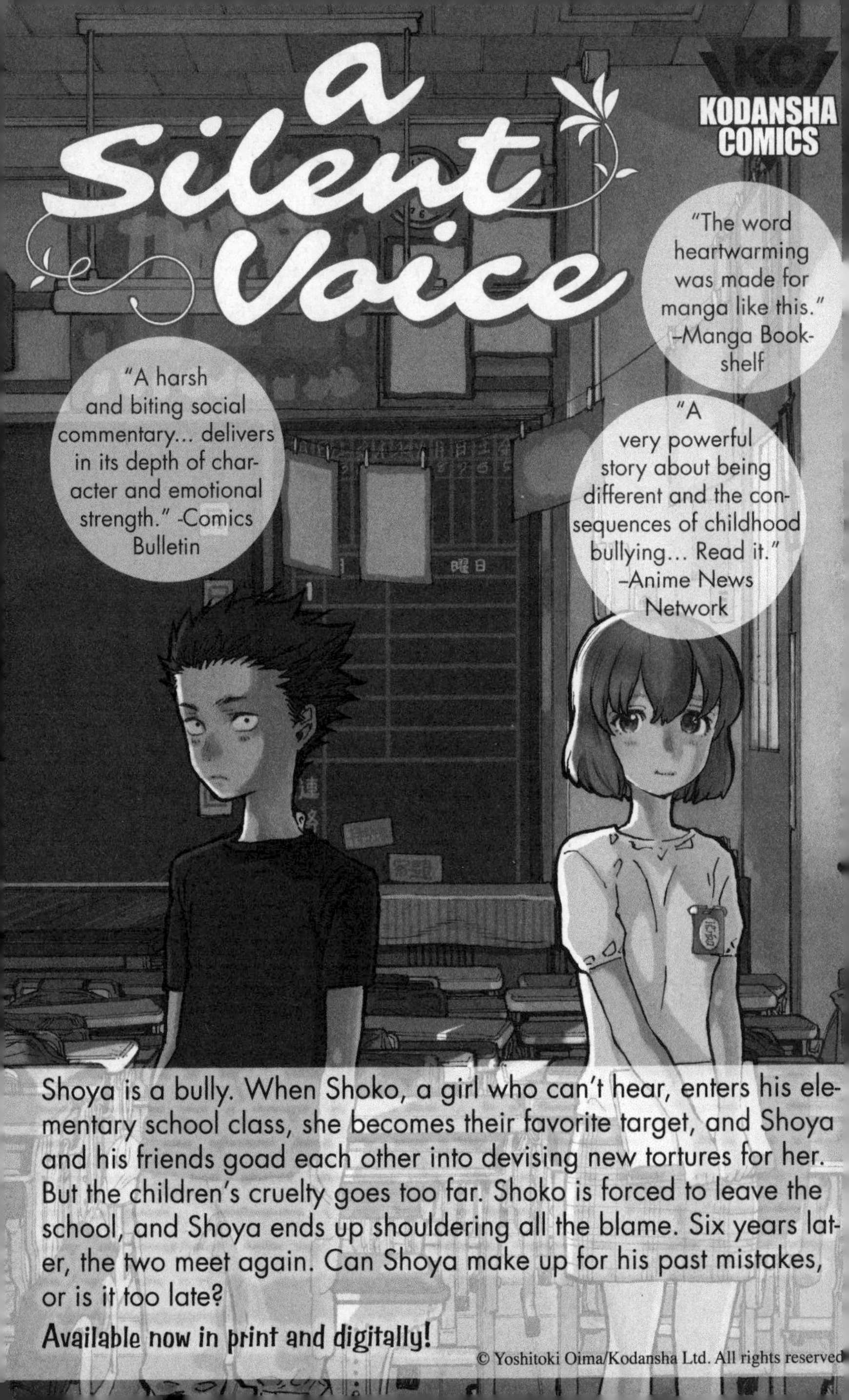
a Silent Voice
KODANSHA COMICS
"The word heartwarming was made for manga like this." –Manga Bookshelf
"A harsh and biting social commentary... delivers in its depth of character and emotional strength." -Comics Bulletin
"A very powerful story about being different and the consequences of childhood bullying... Read it." –Anime News Network
Shoya is a bully. When Shoko, a girl who can't hear, enters his elementary school class, she becomes their favorite target, and Shoya and his friends goad each other into devising new tortures for her. But the children's cruelty goes too far. Shoko is forced to leave the school, and Shoya ends up shouldering all the blame. Six years later, the two meet again. Can Shoya make up for his past mistakes, or is it too late?
Available now in print and digitally!
© Yoshitoki Oima/Kodansha Ltd. All rights reserved

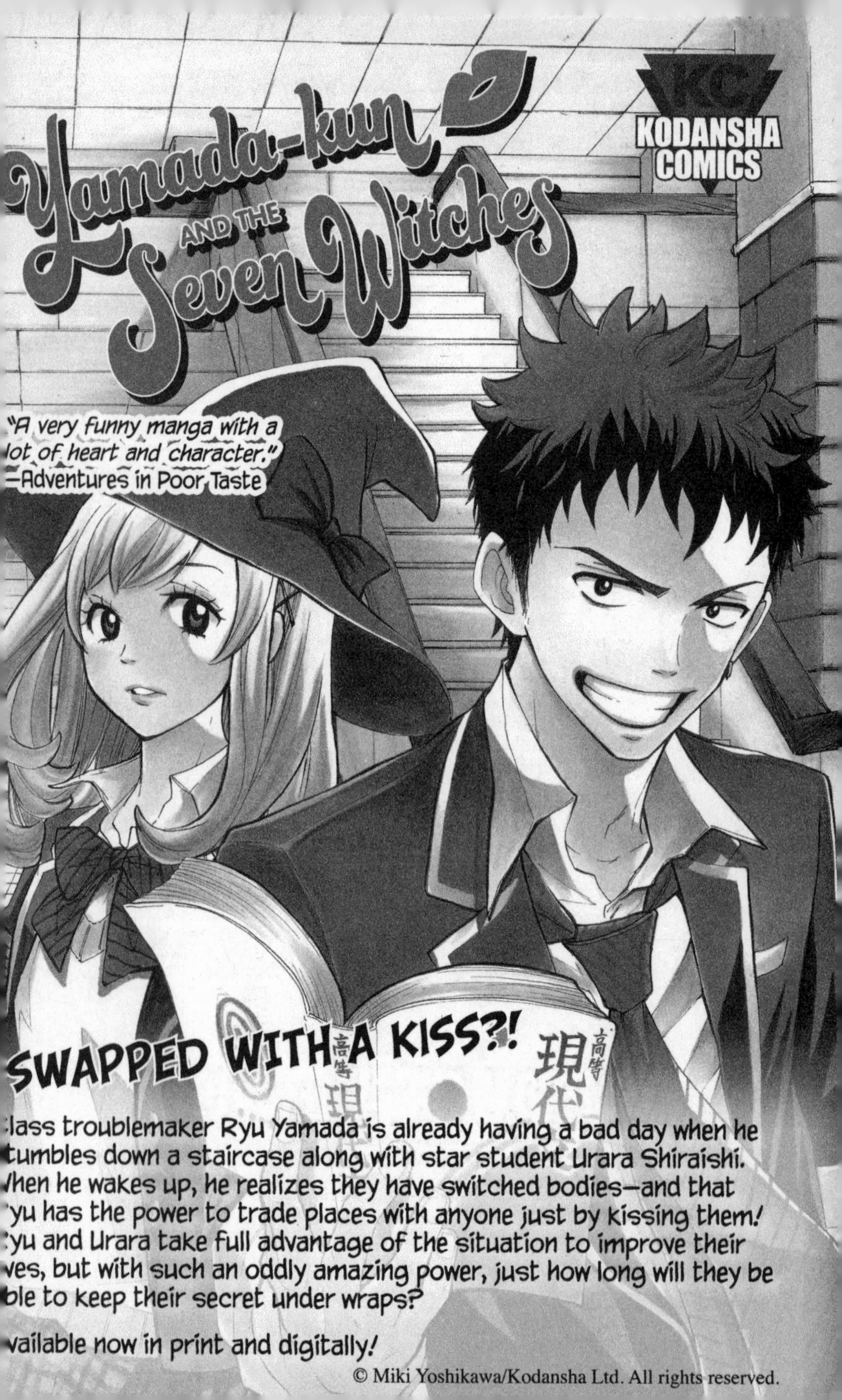
Yamada-kun AND THE Seven Witches
KC
KODANSHA COMICS
"A very funny manga with a
lot of heart and character."
—Adventures in Poor Taste
SWAPPED WITH A KISS?!
高等
現代
lass troublemaker Ryu Yamada is already having a bad day when he
tumbles down a staircase along with star student Urara Shiraishi.
Vhen he wakes up, he realizes they have switched bodies—and that
yu has the power to trade places with anyone just by kissing them!
yu and Urara take full advantage of the situation to improve their
ves, but with such an oddly amazing power, just how long will they be
ble to keep their secret under wraps?
vailable now in print and digitally!
© Miki Yoshikawa/Kodansha Ltd. All rights reserved.

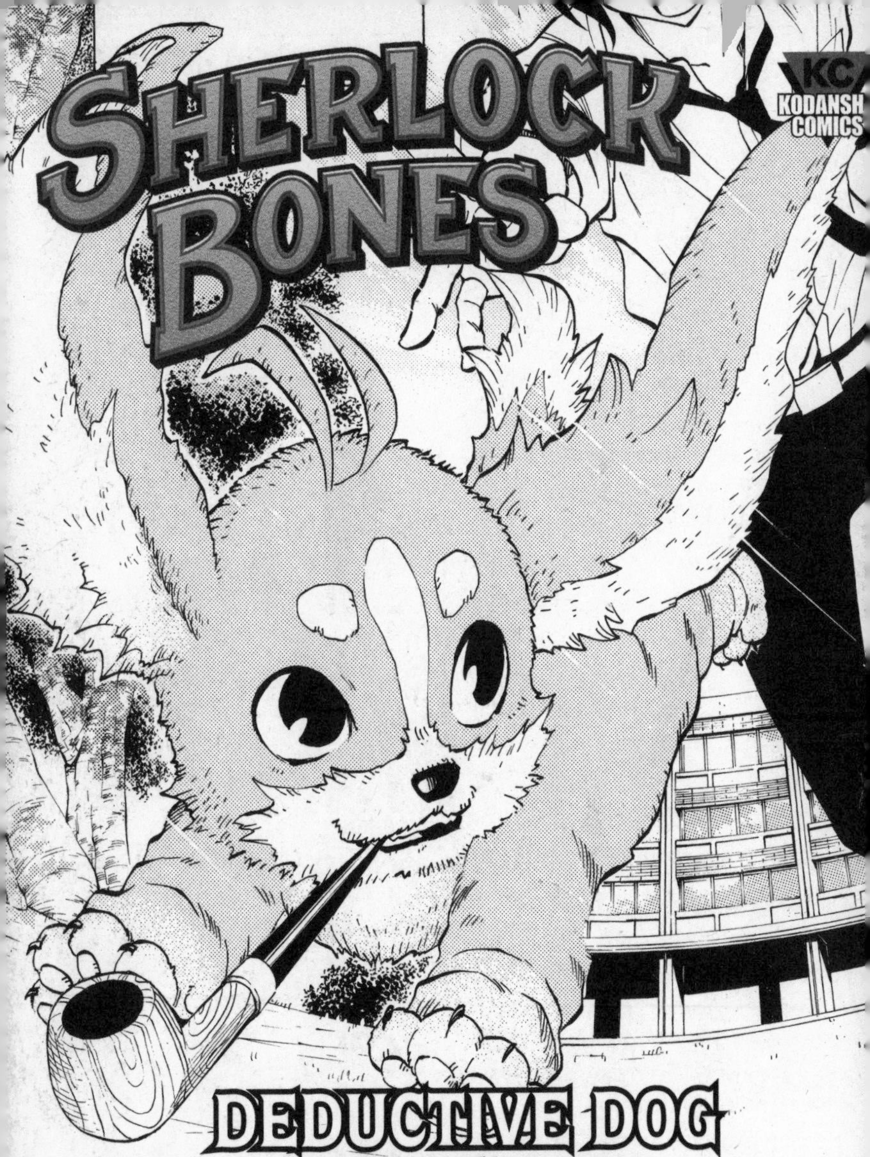
SHERLOCK BONES
KC
KODANSH
COMICS

DEDUCTIVE DOG DETECTIVE

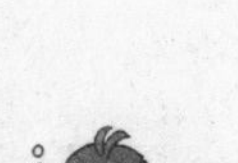

When Takeru adopts a new pet, he's in for a surprise—the dog is none other than the reincarnation of Sherlock Holmes. With no one else able to communicate with Holmes, Takeru is roped into becoming Sherdog's assistant, John Watson. Using his sleuthing skills, Holmes uncovers clues to solve the trickiest crimes.

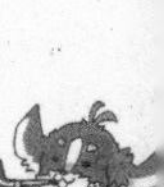

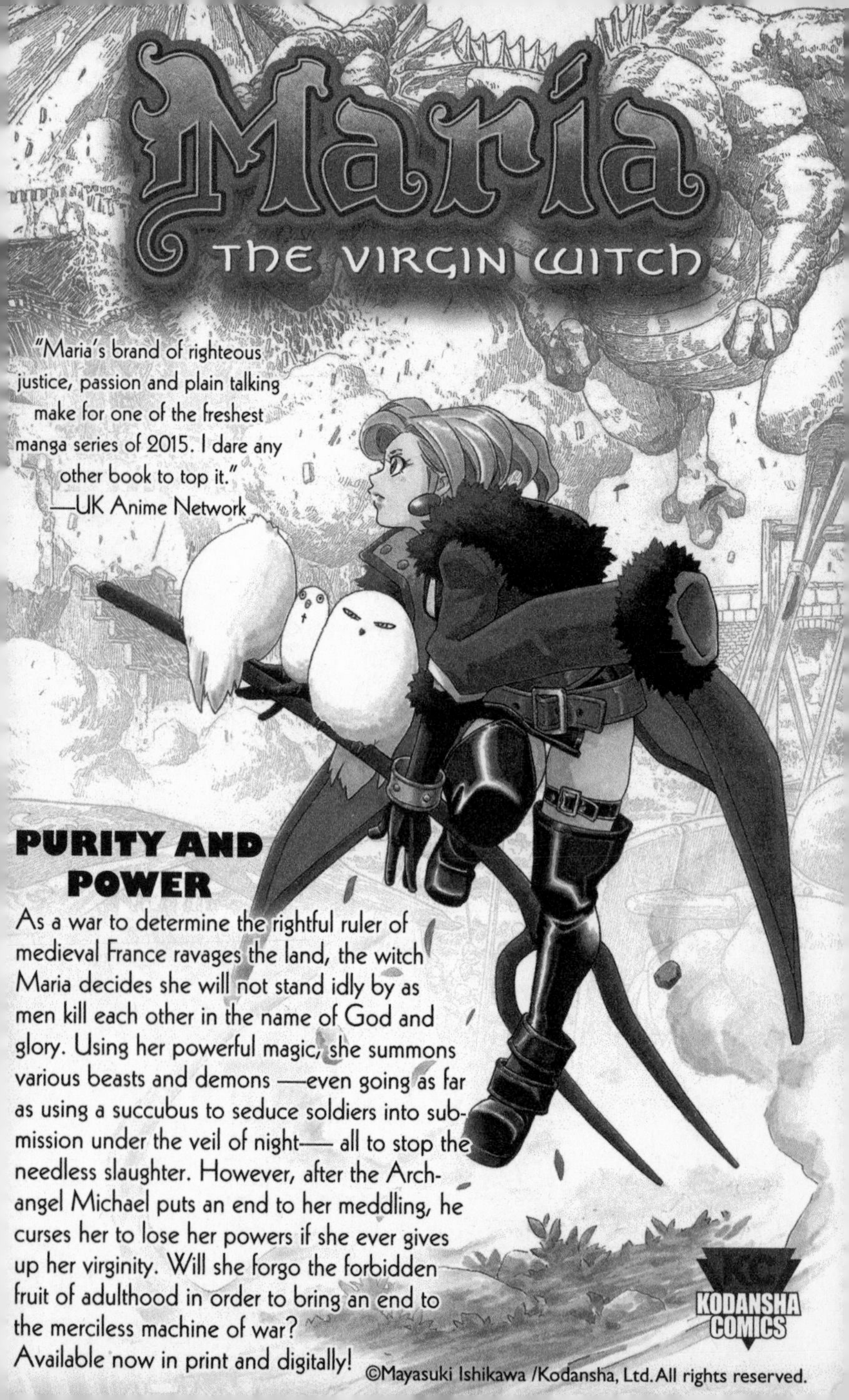
Maria
THE VIRGIN WITCH
"Maria's brand of righteous justice, passion and plain talking make for one of the freshest manga series of 2015. I dare any other book to top it."
—UK Anime Network
PURITY AND POWER
As a war to determine the rightful ruler of medieval France ravages the land, the witch Maria decides she will not stand idly by as men kill each other in the name of God and glory. Using her powerful magic, she summons various beasts and demons —even going as far as using a succubus to seduce soldiers into submission under the veil of night— all to stop the needless slaughter. However, after the Archangel Michael puts an end to her meddling, he curses her to lose her powers if she ever gives up her virginity. Will she forgo the forbidden fruit of adulthood in order to bring an end to the merciless machine of war?
Available now in print and digitally!
KODANSHA COMICS
©Mayasuki Ishikawa /Kodansha, Ltd. All rights reserved.

Fairy Tail volume 56 is a work of fiction. Names, characters, places, and incident are the products of the author's imagination or are used fictitiously. Any resemblance to actual events, locales, or persons, living or dead, is entirely coincidental.

A Kodansha Comics Trade Paperback Original.

Published in the United States by Kodansha Comics, an imprint of Kodansha USA Publishing, LLC, New York.

Publication rights for this English edition arranged through Kodansha Ltd., Tokyo.

First published in Japan in 2016 by Kodansha Ltd., Tokyo
ISBN 978-1-63236-290-2

Printed in the United States of America.

www.kodanshacomics.com

9 8 7 6 5 4 3 2 1

Translation: William Flanagan
Lettering: AndWorld Design
Editing: Haruko Hashimoto
Kodansha Comics edition cover design by Phil Balsman

TOMARE!

止まれ

[STOP!]

You're going the wrong way!

Manga is a completely different type of reading experience.

To start at the beginning, go to the end!

hat's right! Authentic manga is read the traditional Japanese way—
om right to left, exactly the opposite of how American books are
ead. It's easy to follow: Just go to the other end of the book and read
ach page—and each panel—from right side to left side, starting at
e top right. Now you're experiencing manga as it was meant to be!